St. Louis Community College

Library

5801 Wilson Avenue
St. Louis, Missouri 63110

FOREST PARK LIBRARY

MODERN

AMERICAN

WOMEN

POETS

—BY—

Jean Gould

DODD, MEAD & COMPANY
NEW YORK

*In memory of
three modern poets
taken from us too soon:
Jean Garrigue (1912–1970)
Elizabeth Bishop (1911–1979)
and
Muriel Rukeyser (1913–1980)*

Published by Dodd, Mead & Company, Inc.
79 Madison Avenue, New York, N.Y. 10016
Distributed in Canada by
McClelland and Stewart Limited, Toronto
Manufactured in the United States of America
Designed by Trish Parcell
First Edition

Library of Congress Cataloging in Publication Data

Gould, Jean, 1909–
  Modern American women poets.

  Includes index.
  1. Women poets, American—20th century—Biography.
  2. American poetry—Women authors—History and criticism.
  3. American poetry—20th century—History and criticism.
  I. Title.
PS151.G63   1984   811'.5'09 [B]   84-10346
ISBN 0-396-08443-5

CONTENTS

Foreword

Early and Current Creators of Contemporary Poetry

When this work was started nearly ten years ago, it was intended to be a single volume collection of biographical studies, dealing with the lives of women whose literary achievement was outstanding in the development of modern poetry. However, as I delved deeper and deeper in my research, I discovered so many important figures whose lives fascinated me that I decided to write a second book dealing with selected poets among American women writing poetry in the second half of the twentieth century. I subtitled the first, "pioneers" of modern poetry because the women it included were faced with fierce opposition in extending the frontiers of their craft to free verse, exotic imagery, and erotic or personal, secret subject matter (later dubbed "confessional" poetry).

It is inconceivable today to think of Amy Lowell's "Bath" causing such a wave of derisive disdain and disapproval from conservative (mostly male) poets that it split the ranks of the Poetry Society of America into two camps for a time. Yet this poem, which was neither as outrageous as its objectors contended nor as innocuous as its defenders insisted, and the innovative tenets of the Imagist movement as presented in militant terms by Amy in 1916 caused a commotion among poets that has echoed down the decades. It can still be heard rumbling in poetry circles as present-day experimentalists try to discover new forms of self-expression; or, as in the representational renaissance among visual artists, they return to the traditional forms of a more distant past, such as the sonnet, the ballad, and the verse drama.

One point that must be made clear at the outset is that this book is not a survey, nor a critical analysis of modern and contemporary poetry except as it relates to the lives of the poets I have chosen to examine. The choice is purely personal: the poets included are women whose work I not only admire but consider a contribution to the entire canon of modern and contemporary poetry. The arrangement here is chronological only in the light of each poet's emergence into the mainstream. Finally, I have chosen only women as my subjects because I have felt for a long time that the poetry written by women has been unfairly considered in all areas of recognition. From publication of single poems in little magazines or top literary journals to solo volumes and anthologies, the ratio of published poetry is three to one in favor of poetry written by men. If this seems an exaggeration, one has only to glance down the list of names in any anthology that includes the work of both sexes to discover that the majority of authors are male.

When *American Women Poets* appeared in 1980, it was reviewed by Charles Guenther in the St. Louis *Post Dispatch* along with another book, entitled *Lives of the Modern Poets;* the latter book, a collection of essays discussing nine poets, not one of whom was a woman. In giving the title, Guenther added, "(yes, *'the'*)," and remarked that the author, William R. Pritchard, was "continuing the tradition of exiling women from the domain of poetry." He went on to say that such disregard for women poets has driven them to celebrate themselves, and that it justified my collection of life studies of women poets only, as the title clearly states. Since there was no indication of the sex of the "modern poets" in the title of Pritchard's book, the reader would expect to find at least one accomplished woman among their number—such figures as Emily Dickinson, Marianne Moore, Muriel Rukeyser, or Elizabeth Bishop and Denise Levertov, all of whom are included in my selections; because, as Guenther observes, "their work has had a profound influence on much poetry written today." Perhaps Pritchard still thinks of these women as "poetesses," a term that should be obsolete by now, but it still crops up occasionally.

The women's movement has sought to erase the feminine ending in the terminology of all the arts: women who create sculpture now wish to be called sculptors (instead of sculptresses), just as those who paint are painters. No one would dream of saying writeress or novelistess; and "poetess," with its added implication that women are lightweight versifiers, is equally unnecessary and more demeaning. The point is that gender should not make any difference in referring to the author, or in judging a work of art or its creator. The work alone should receive consideration, regardless of the sex of its author. Yet in anthologies and collections the majority of poets selected are male.

The same discrimination is found in the dispensation of awards and honors. Edna St. Vincent Millay was the first of her sex to win the coveted Pulitzer Prize for poetry in the second year of its establishment, 1923; but in the fifty years that followed only a dozen women have won this annual award. In 1950, Gwendolyn Brooks, the first black poet to win it—regardless of sex—was the sixth woman to be so honored, and only seven more have won that prize since. All the rest (except in 1946, when no award was given) have been men. By count, the number of women chosen as recipients is less than one-third of the total, and the figure holds true in other fields of writing. I have limited the discussion to poetry here because it is the medium I have been working with for nearly ten years.

During that decade, numerous "little" magazines have come out, as well as chapbook anthologies containing the current poetry of both sexes equally presented. One of these, *Poets On:*, published twice a year and edited by a woman, Ruth Daigon, actually gave women a slight edge in its summer 1982 issue, *Distances,* when twenty-one of the forty poets included were women. These small presses, now numbering in the hundreds, though many include all categories of creative writing, have become a real force in the circulation of modern poetry. Collectively they have led to publication of an enormous anthology, whose founding editors included Anaïs Nin, Buckminster Fuller, Joyce Carol Oates, Daniel Halpern, Nona Balakian, Ralph Ellison, Rhoda Schwartz, and other noted writers interested in offering "new work from authors with a vision of what is honest and important." Banding together in the early 1970s, they organized the Pushcart Press, publishing *The Pushcart Prize I: Best of the Small Presses.* The undertaking, though risky, was so rewarding that the editors decided to produce a series of such volumes, each year inviting more editors of small presses to submit manuscripts of the best they had published during that period. By the time *Pushcart Prize III* came out, *Kirkus Reviews* commented, "In a publishing scene fast backing off from quality and lapping up the flashy and no-account, Pushcart's annual anthology of the previous year's best work from the small presses can no longer be complacently accepted as a showcase of 'alternative' literary endeavor; we have to see it responsibly, as mainstream." Pushcart's fourth anthology contained sixty-one

selections from fifty-three presses, most cf both authors and
editors new to the series; four thousand nominations were received from one hundred editors. As usual, the majority of the
selections are poems: thirty-two poems as compared to eighteen short fictions and eleven essays. At least fourteen of the
poets are women, and among the editors of poetry nominees
were a number of notable poets of both sexes: Maxine Kumin,
Carolyn Forché, Grace Schulman, John Ashberry, Robert Bly,
and Hayden Carruth. Among honorary editors: Lisel Mueller,
Carol Muske, Ntozake Shange, Allen Ginsberg, and Erica Jong,
to name only a few. Anne Tyler in *The New York Times Book
Review* wrote: "The Pushcart Prize is a distinguished annual literary event." And *Publishers Weekly* asserted: "This marvelous
anthology belongs on the shelves of all who are concerned with
good writing and literature."

Some anthologies are devoted entirely to the work of women:
Black Sister, a chronological collection of poetry by black women
from the seventeenth century to the present reveals a wealth of
"straight" poetry written by women of their race never before
gathered in one volume. The editor, Erlene Stetson, has performed a real service in filling in the enormous gap between
Phyliss Wheatley and Gwendolyn Brooks, who, with her contemporaries, as the reader will see, launched the movement for
modern poetry by black women. Several publishing houses run
by and for publication by women have also come into being.
One such firm is Alice James Books, a cooperative venture
located in Cambridge. Specializing in poetry written by women,
it has established a reputation for producing quality books by
well-known poets, and is among the more successful of small
presses started by a group of women intent on bringing out
their own collections.

Another is the Saturday Press, which grew out of a competition for publication of poems by women over forty years of age
who had received some recognition in magazines, but had never
published a volume. So much material came in that the editors

decided to publish an anthology of the outstanding poems received, besides those of the prizewinner, Chita Orth, whose award was publication of her first full-length volume, *The Music of What Happens.* The unique and attractively designed anthology, the first to celebrate works by women poets over forty years old, appropriately entitled *Saturday's Women,* published in 1982, was deemed by Maxine Kumin, then consultant in poetry to the Library of Congress, "Impressive in its breadth. . . . A storehouse of necessary poems written by women and addressed to the world." Poet Charlotte Mandel, initiator of the project and editor of the anthology, whose work has appeared sporadically in little magazines over the years, enjoyed the further gratification of having her first volume, *A Disc of Clear Water,* deservedly published by Saturday Press. Carol Muske, one of the strongest among younger poets, commented on this volume, "Charlotte Mandel is an observer . . . an ordinary woman in touch with the extraordinary realities of everyday life."

While it is necessary, as Kumin said, for these poems to be given an audience, it is more important that recognition come to women on an equal footing with men. I do not believe that poetry written by men is three times as good as that by women. I am the author of six full-length biographies of American poets—three of women and three of men. The three women are Emily Dickinson, Amy Lowell, and Edna St. Vincent Millay; the men are Herman Melville, Paul Laurence Dunbar, and Robert Frost. The equal division of the sexes in my subjects was accidental: I happened to be interested in the work of these six poets. Yet in my research for the present project, I discovered that most editors, men or women, show a marked preference for the poetry of men in selections for anthologies, magazines, and recordings, because traditionally men have been so favored for generations. It is a sad commentary on the literary segment of our society that women must resort to segregation in order to insure public acceptance of their art. The small publishing houses and journals are helping to equalize the outlets for the works of women with that of men, but until the element of sexism is eliminated, women who write either poetry or prose will continue to struggle for recognition to a greater degree than men.

It is for this reason that I have limited my collection of life studies to poets who happen to be women. No doubt there are readers who will disagree with my choices, and those who will ask why I did not include certain poets. The answer is, as initially stated, that this book is purely personal in the selection of subjects; but I hope that by concentrating on women I will have lessened the constant striving for recognition of gifted poets among the many women creating works of equal caliber with that of their male colleagues.

Acknowledgments

F or most of the biographical material in this book, I am indebted to the poets themselves, three of whom have died
since the work was begun seven years ago. Muriel Rukeyser,
the subject of the opening chapter, was a long-standing friend,
who, as always, was generous with the time and interest she
gave me in relating the salient events of her many, varied experiences; her death, in February 1980, cut off a final interview. Similarly, Elizabeth Bishop, whom I had met but not
known well, was stricken with a cerebral hemorrhage in 1979—
her death marking the end of our meetings. And finally, Isabella Gardner, a close friend who died unexpectedly in 1981,

was unstinting in sharing with me the memories of her own life and work, and in so doing recalled incidents and anecdotes of earlier poets she had known—the "pioneers of modern poetry" who comprised the first group of figures in my biographical studies of women poets. For the photograph of Gardner reproduced here thanks are due sculptor Blanche Dombek who took the picture when both were at the MacDowell Colony.

In addition, poets Jane Mayhall, Arthur Gregor, Aileen Ward, Stanley Kunitz, Nancy Sullivan, and several others were most helpful in furnishing details in the life and multifaceted personality of Jean Garrigue, whom I had known only slightly when her untimely death occurred in 1972, five years before this work was begun; members of her family—her sister, pianist Marjorie Garrigue Smith, and her niece, Jorrie Smith Davis, also gave me assistance. Composer Ann McMillan related colorful anecdotes and notes in connection with Anne Sexton, and generously gave me a cassette of a Sexton poetry reading made when McMillan was music director at radio station WBAI. Photographer Nancy Crampton contributed the photograph of Anne Sexton reproduced here. I am indebted to poet Howard Moss, who provided a copy of *World Literature Today,* containing much material in the featured section, "Homage to Elizabeth Bishop." Allen Hughes, music critic of *The New York Times,* furnished background notes on Conrad Susa's opera-setting of Anne Sexton's "Transformations" (of classic fairy tales) and was instrumental in my gaining attendance at a performance of the opera in New York.

I wish to repeat my thanks here to writer, critic, and editor Paul Kresh, and to painter Penrod Scofield for information concerning the recorded readings made by most of the poets discussed in this extended work. Mr. Kresh, as editor of the Spoken Arts series, *A Treasury of 100 Modern American Poets Reading Their Poems,* gave me an account of tracking down and working with a hundred poets, a number of whom are included here. Also editor of the later (1979) Spoken Arts series,

Acknowledgments

Twenty-five American Jewish Poets Reading Their Poems, Kresh told me of Muriel Rukeyser's participation despite her ill-health, to the extent that she is the only one of the twenty-five who has a whole side of a disc devoted to her poetry. Penrod Scofield, who had illustrated four of her "Akiba" poems when they appeared in the *American Judaism Reader* (1967, edited by Paul Kresh), was consulting with Rukeyser on a prose-poem text she had agreed to write for a book comprising Scofield's drawings and watercolors of "street people" in New York City—a project she did not live to realize.

The late Lesley Frost (Ballantine), who died in 1983, gave me much information about the early modern poets and the little-known promotion of women poets that her father initiated at his publishers' as well as through fellowships at Breadloaf Mountain Conferences and those from the Academy of American Poets. Marianne Moore, Babette Deutsch, May Swenson, Ruth Whitman, to name only a few, were among those who benefitted from the various programs organized by Robert Frost, though in this instance, I learned from Lesley, he kept his participation in the background.

My gratitude goes to all the poets who cooperated with me in this project, sending me copies of their latest published volumes, arranging interviews by telephone or letter if not in person. Special thanks go to Gwendolyn Brooks for her cordial cooperation and encouragement in the completion of these biographical studies. May Swenson, Denise Levertov, Maxine Kumin, Jean Burden, Freya Manfred, Carol Muske, Marge Piercy, Audre Lorde, Grace Schulman, Carolyn Stoloff, Ruth Whitman, Harriet Zinnes were all helpful in contributing their works and ideas on poetry today, as well as biographical data.

The New York Public Library, as always, gave me ready assistance in locating material now out of print, chronologies, and periodical reviews concerning various poets. The same service was offered by the staff at the Avery Hopwood Room at the University of Michigan, the Ward Canaday Center of the Carl-

Acknowledgments

son Library at the University of Toledo, and the Alderman Library at the University of Virginia, as well as the Sweet Briar College Library, both of which I consulted during residencies at the Virginia Center for the Creative Arts, Mt. San Angelo, Sweet Briar, Virginia, where the major portion of this book was written.

I wish to thank Director William Smart, Assistant Director Stephen Humphrey, and the entire staff at the Virginia Center for providing ideal conditions in which to write, and to express my appreciation for fellowships there in the fall of 1981 and the spring of 1983. I am equally grateful to Director Christopher Barnes and the MacDowell Colony for the residency I received in the spring of 1982.

Muriel Rukeyser

When Muriel Rukeyser was twenty-one, she came of age in more than years: she had her first volume of poetry published. Moreover, this signal event occurred in the depths of the Great Depression, 1935, hardly a promising year for publication of poetry. Like most poets, Muriel had to run the gauntlet of rejection slips, revisions, multiple mailings of manuscripts before she had accumulated enough acceptances to warrant a published volume. To add to her trials, during her early years of creativity, before her college education could be completed, her family's fortunes like so many others had been sharply reversed by the onslaught of the Depression. From wealth

I

the Rukeysers were reduced to a state of near poverty, altering the pattern of the poet's outer life completely.

She had been born at a moment in history when World War I still seemed a minor military skirmish in Europe. New York City on December 15, 1914, when Muriel Rukeyser first saw the light of day in Manhattan's Upper West Side (in "the shadow of Grant's tomb and near the haunt of the famous gangster, Gyp-the-Blood," as she liked to point out), was a bustling, burgeoning metropolis. Businesses and beer parlors were thriving; the 1913 art show in the Armory had "revolutionized" American concepts of art; and lights around Broadway and Forty-second Street were fast building the area into the "Great White Way." Muriel's parents both felt an enormous excitement about the city, stemming in large measure from their love of the theatre. Her father, Lawrence Rukeyser, had been named for the actor, Lawrence Barrett, a leading Shakespearean star of the day. (Muriel's paternal grandparents, who came from Germany and finally settled in Milwaukee, Wisconsin, had obviously been theatre buffs.)

Lawrence Rukeyser elected to leave his native city, where his parents had made a fortune and reared a family of boys. After earning a degree as a construction engineer, he came to New York to make his own fortune. Here he met Muriel's mother, Myra Lyons, who had been born and bred in Yonkers, then a small rural village, quite apart from New York City. The Lyons family, said to be direct descendants of the first-century Hebrew sage, Rabbi Akiba, had come to America from Rumania, bringing with them the gypsy lore of that country as well as the religious legends of their illustrious ancestor. Myra Lyons was well versed in the Bible and Emerson, and Muriel remembers as a child hearing her mother read from the Old Testament, or the poetry of Emerson, or recounting the legends of Rabbi Akiba. (When asked whether she believed that the famed scholar and religious leader was really her ancestor, she confided with a slow smile and a touch of nostalgia, "I don't know whether it's true or not, but I've always thought it was a nice thing to tell a little girl." She might have added "like me," since not every little girl would have had the same reaction—a poet's response to a genealogical fact that would bore many children.)

After their marriage, Myra and Lawrence Rukeyser settled in the Upper West Side apartment where Muriel and her sister—the only children the Rukeysers had—were born. Mr. Rukeyser started a construction firm which prospered and was the principal force in building up the whole area now known as Riverdale. In the "boom" years following World War I, the Rukeysers became wealthy to the point of finding themselves in the "millionaire" category, although Muriel was not particularly aware of their wealth during her childhood and adolescence.

From the time she was a small child, Muriel wrote poetry, which seemed to be a natural mode of expression for her. Sometimes it took the form of runes, repeated rhymes that made a melody; sometimes it was a wild flight of fantasy that made her mother smile, but wonder with slight apprehension at her small daughter's outlandish imagination. Muriel was a curious mixture of the mundane and the mercurial. Physically strong and sturdy, she was an extremely sensitive child, who had the capacity to identify with the suffering of others. The story of a pink rabbit caught in a hunter's trap sent her scurrying under the table in tears, inconsolable. The irony of suffering in the midst of a supposedly happy world struck her early in life. Much later, in a poem called, "Effort at Speech Between Two People," she recorded the incident that took place at her third birthday party when she accidentally burned her finger on one of the candles of the cake glowing in her honor. Crying with pain, she was "told to be happy." ("Happy Birthday!" the children and grown-ups must have shouted. Never mind the pain of your throbbing finger. So it would be with the world in general, she was to discover. How much anguish in the midst of celebration people everywhere overlooked!)

The Rukeysers were interested in the Ethical Culture movement as the only viable religion in a society rapidly becoming industrialized. Based largely on Emersonian philosophy, the religion of humanism appealed to Muriel's mother especially, and when the primary school was opened in connection with the Ethical Culture Center at Central Park West and Sixty-fourth Street, she decided to send her children there. Muriel attended for all eight years of her primary education, thoroughly absorbing the seeds of social consciousness and social justice which were to attain full growth and flower in her poetry. As her father's construction firm prospered, the family moved to the Riverdale area; and the Fieldston School of secondary education founded by the Ethical Culture movement, soon to become known for its excellence as a progressive school in the liberal arts, opened in 1927, in time for Muriel to complete her last two years of high school and graduate with honors.

She had applied to Vassar and passed the entrance examinations without any difficulty, and for two years, in spite of the stock market crash of 1929, her father could afford to send her to college. As president of the Colonial Concrete Company, he received a high salary in addition to his stock; but as the Depression set in, deepening in 1931 and 1932, and the vice-president of the company, Generosa Pope, was found guilty of a notorious deal involving false housing loans, Mr. Rukeyser pulled out of the company and declared bankruptcy. The comfortable cushion of wealth was suddenly replaced by the bare board of frugality, and the trial of struggling to make ends meet merely in order to survive as a creative artist began for the Rukeysers' talented daughter. Muriel had to leave Vassar at the end of her sophomore year, and she struck out on her own. She would get a job, she would find some kind of work, perhaps in a publishing house, on the staff of a magazine, or in the theatre. She was ready for adventure in the world outside academia.

During the previous years, beginning in high school, she had been writing poetry and knowing the thrill of seeing it in print.

Her first acceptance came from the *Herald Tribune*, published in the Sunday Book Section, no small achievement for a beginner. Then followed acceptance from the most coveted of literary publications in the 1920s and 1930s—*Poetry: A Magazine of Verse,* whose innovative editor, Harriet Monroe, actually offered to pay for poems worthy of acceptance. The *New Republic, The Nation,* and the experimental *Little Review,* whose pages often held controversial poems, had welcomed her to the roster of new, promising young poets. She was a poet of no uncertain opinions, and no hesitation in giving voice to her outraged feelings at the injustices of the Depression, or expanding on the glories of love. Her parents were terrified by what she wrote and was paid for. To them their daughter's ideas seemed wild, schooled though they were in ethical culture and strong belief in social justice. To her mother particularly, steeped in Emerson's poetry, Muriel's free verse seemed chaotic. She would have preferred to see more sonnets and the regular rhythms of metered lines appear in printed poems by her brilliant daughter.

For her part, Muriel understood her mother's mixed feelings, but did not let them hamper her in pursuing her chosen career as she saw fit. However, it was not easy to find a job in 1931. No magazine staff or publishing house was in need of personnel. In fact, they were besieged by applicants who already had college degrees, and so were considered more qualified than Muriel. She had been active in the theatre workshop at Vassar; her voice was low and musical with an emotional intensity that had the power to move her listeners, especially when she read her poems. (It was the kind of voice one expects a poet to have, but is often disappointed to find the reverse.) Like her parents, she was fascinated by the theatre, and when she left home, she headed for Greenwich Village in New York, where new little theatre groups were always starting up, Depression or no Depression.

She found an apartment—actually one small room—on the corner of West Twelfth Street, at (West) Fourth. The rent was a pittance, and she had saved just enough money to carry her for a few months. She soon made a connection with the Theatre Union, a left-wing group producing plays of social consciousness in the 14th Street Theatre, where the old Civic Repertory Theatre had performed under the direction of Eva LeGallienne. Eleanor Fitzgerald, famous as the efficient secretary of the Provincetown Players, was associated with Theatre Union. Muriel was welcomed into the troupe, which was set up on a cooperative basis. She was extremely attractive, with a kind of gypsy beauty about her: large gray-blue eyes and olive skin, a generous mouth, and white, even teeth; her face, set off by a mop of unruly dark hair, suggested the fiery spirit of a Carmen. All this—renegade and reformer—combined in the poet who was Muriel Rukeyser, soon to become well known in the literary world.

Working in the Theatre Union was rewarding in many ways, but not financially. Profits were practically nonexistent, and the young poet-apprentice soon found herself running out of funds. She did not want to go to her parents, who were hard-pressed, and most of her friends were in the same fix as she. Someone in the company—perhaps it was Mary Heaton Vorse, one of the prime initiators of the Provincetown Players (whose fishing shack at the end of a dock she owned became the original Wharf Theatre in the seacoast artists' colony in 1915) and also an early labor newspaper writer and dramatist—sent Muriel to the office of the League for Mutual Aid. Formed in 1932 by a group of citizens who were deeply disturbed by the lack of legislative action on the part of the Hoover administration to alleviate the suffering caused by the economic Depression, the league offered long-term loans of limited amounts to tide people over a crucial period. Usually it was two hundred dollars to be paid back as the recipient could afford it, and if people could add to the general fund when they got on their feet, they did so. The league also helped applicants find jobs whenever possible so that they could repay the loans, which in turn went to other needy, qualified applicants, many of whom were highly educated, capable workers, some of whom, like Muriel, were creative artists. Others were skilled scientists already seeking refuge from the flaming holocaust rapidly threatening to engulf Germany.

One of the unsung heroines of the dark days of the Depression was the executive secretary of the league, Adelaide Schulkind (Frank), who proved to be a guardian (or avenging) angel and guiding force in launching Muriel Rukeyser on her professional career. Well known as a social worker and young firebrand of pre-World War I days and the twenties, raised by a mother who was a follower of Emma Goldman, Adelaide Schulkind was a supreme individualist, defender of democracy, and devoted lover of the arts, poetry in particular; she took to Muriel at once. She processed the application for a loan, saw that it came through, and scouted contacts for jobs the girl might fill. (When Adelaide went into action she could be both formidable and irresistible. It was said of her that she had a voice like a nutmeg grater, harsh and commanding, but she also had a warm heart that mellowed her tone. Some of the male writers Adelaide was instrumental in aiding were James Baldwin, Murray Kempton, and Jerre Mangione.)

Reminiscing about her in 1976, the poet said, "Adelaide was wonderful to me. After the loan ran out, I was still in a fix, threatened with eviction from the little place on Twelfth Street, and she paid the rent. Then she found jobs for me—all kinds of jobs. When one was over, she would find another." One of the most important of these, because of its far-reaching influence, was with George Marshall, brother-in-law of Lenore Marshall, another noted poet then starting her career. George and his wife, Betty, became close friends of Muriel's, and through them, she and Lenore became lifelong friends. (After the latter's death, Rukeyser completed a foreword to a volume of the Marshall letters and memorabilia.) In every spare minute Muriel had she wrote poetry, and Adelaide, who was convinced of the high caliber of the girl's conventional and experimental verses alike, encouraged her, as she encouraged all young poets of any promise, to continue to send out work. Among the other writers this remarkable woman sponsored was one of the first black women to deal with the particular problems of her race during the Depression—Pauli Murray, who wrote a kind of epic, or series of connected verses that, while heavily freighted with "message," attracted the attention of Stephen Vincent Benet, who gave her valuable advice. For various reasons, Pauli Murray chose to go into the law, becoming a noted woman attorney; but if she had continued her efforts, she might have become a well-known poet. Her novel, *Proud Shoes,* published in the fifties, has the touch of the poet in its autobiographical story of her family. When she retired from practice, she had her volume of verse published (1970), but by then the work was dated and hardly altered from its initial, obvious, propagandistic approach. She merits mention here as a predecessor of poets like Gwendolyn Brooks, Alice Walker, or Nikki Giovanni. Her novel was reissued in 1977, and her poems have been included in recent anthologies of black poets.

Muriel, on the other hand, benefitted greatly from the advice of seasoned poets like Benet and Horace Gregory. The latter helped her "tremendously" she recalled in citing the various influences on her development as a poet. She went to him on her own because she admired his work as both critic and poet, and he was more than generous in giving both time and thought to the sheaf of poems she hoped to see published as a volume. Stephen Vincent Benet in his way was also helpful, though at the time she was not exactly grateful to him. She had entered her poems in the competition for the Young Poets publication award offered by Yale University Press, and in 1934 it was a "toss-up" between her and James Agee, according to Benet, who was an editor at the Press. He advised her to withdraw her manuscript and submit it the following year, when she would have a greater body of work and more polish to her style, which was provocative, but not fully realized. Muriel, impatient and eager for a first volume, found his advice hard to follow; but she did.

In the meantime, she completed another project she had been working on, a biography of Willard Gibbs, a wise and liberal scientist, whose writing had fascinated her while she was still at the Fieldston School. A distant relative of Emily Dickinson, he was an authority on the science of Transformation, a subject that appealed to Muriel. She had already been promised publication by a small press, and so it was that her initial appearance as a published author was in prose; and in 1935, when she had turned twenty-one, she became a published, professional poet.

As Benet had predicted, the manuscript she submitted to the jury at Yale University Press, after further composing, polishing, and revision, won the Young Poet's publication award hands down. *Theory of Flight,* the title she had chosen for her cherished volume, brought the name of Muriel Rukeyser a rightful place among the foremost of a new generation of poets championing the "new poetry" concerned with the proletariat. Never before had the problems of the masses been set to the music of poetry by so many writers of verse; and these young, strong, free-flowing, outspoken lines of Muriel's had a compelling quality that sprang from her own genuine convictions and led her readers on whether or not they agreed with her ideas of social justice or approved her fluid lines of prose poetry. Poems like "Praise of the Committee (Bureau of Mines procedure)" showing the lack of human sympathy; or "The Disease," which begins with an expository line of dialogue, "This is a lung disease. Silicate dust makes it," might turn away some of her readers; but strung in between the poems of social consciousness in free verse would be a sonnet, and those who had been ready to condemn her as a hopeless radical would concede that she was a poet, after all, and read on. Her images were graphic; the line that follows the above, for example, continues: "You'd say a snowstorm had struck the fellow's lungs," giving an instant picture of the destructive disease that attacks miners.

Whatever controversy she might arouse, Muriel felt she was

finally launched as a poet, a career she would not desert. The following year George and Betty Marshall took her to Europe with them. They sailed on July 19, 1936—Muriel's first voyage—and went to England. The Marshalls went on to Finland from there, but Muriel decided to go to Spain. The previous summer, after her book came out, she and Mary Heaton Vorse had gone to Yaddo, the colony for creative artists at Saratoga Springs, New York. Muriel was involved in writing poems for a second volume and had not expected to join in the social life that went into full swing when the racing season opened at the famous Saratoga tracks in August, and prominent families in town invited the artists from Yaddo to their parties. It may have been at one of these that Muriel met the Duchess of Medina-Sodona and Armada of Spain, who had invited the poet to visit her country. The political conflict there was simmering but had not yet boiled over, and a young editor who had published some of Rukeyser's poems in one of the little magazines had asked her if she would cover the counter-Olympics organized by workers' sports clubs to be held in Madrid in 1936 in protest against the official Olympics scheduled to take place under the Hitler regime in Berlin.

Muriel had admitted to him, "At this point, I don't know a football from a bomb," but he had convinced her that she could review the sports events of those Olympics as well as anyone. So in 1936, instead of going to Finland with the Marshalls, she headed for Spain. Her knowledge of sports was never called upon, but she learned about bombs immediately: the terrible bombing of Madrid was at its explosive height when she arrived at the Spanish border. The counter-Olympics never took place. It was characteristic of Muriel Rukeyser that she somehow became involved with the cause of the underprivileged. She joined the Loyalists in the complicated struggle for power that was to put Spain on the wrack and keep the voice of the people repressed under Franco's dictatorship for almost forty years. There is not enough space in this study to relate Rukeyser's fantastic adventures in Spain during 1936–1937. At one moment, because of her connection with the Duchess, she was in the high places of government; but more than once she was nearly captured by the secret police and narrowly escaped death.

Returning to the United States in 1938, Muriel immediately became embroiled in the great controversy of her own country at that time: the explosive question of American intervention against the Nazis in Europe. The Rukeysers, being of German-Jewish descent, had watched with horror the macabre events in Germany from 1933 with the rise of Hitler and the burning of the Reichstag to the "Anschluss" of Austria in 1938, when it seemed clear to a great many people that the rest of the world could no longer ignore or in any way condone the holocaust that was consuming Europe. Many organizations, both Jewish and non-Jewish, were calling for intervention, trying to persuade Roosevelt not to hesitate further.

A principal center for action was at the University of California in Berkeley, where the eminent novelist, Thomas Mann, with his family, who had had to flee Germany in peril of their lives, had accepted a post on the faculty.

Mann's oldest child—his son Klaus—a writer and novelist living in the shadow of his father's fame in the literary world, had tried unsuccessfully to establish a name for himself as a novelist, but was attaining something of a reputation as an essayist, critic, and lecturer, and was trying to launch a magazine which would help to persuade the thinking public of the urgent need to stamp out the disease of Naziism before it conquered the world. He and his sister, Erica (next to him in age among the six Mann children), had written a book called *Escape to Life*, telling of the means they devised to get out of Germany including the offer by his close friend, W. H. Auden, to enter into a convenience marriage with Erica, which would provide the protection of British citizenship, partial immunity from the stringent emmigration laws for Jews under the Hitler regime. (Thomas Mann had been invited to join the faculty at Berkeley and had been granted a visa, but his family had not been allowed to go with him.) Klaus had chosen the name *Decision* for the proposed magazine, and, using the book as a basis, he gave a series of lectures across the country to promote monthly publication. When not on tour, he divided his time between Berkeley with his parents, and New York City, where he lived in a small hotel at 119 East Fortieth Street.

Muriel had been invited to give a series of readings at Berkeley and, whether she had met Klaus Mann in New York before she left for Berkeley or not, she soon became friends with him and the Mann family. True to her usual pattern, and because she herself was a strong interventionist although she hated war, she consented at once when Klaus asked her to join the staff working to formulate and establish his magazine. He was at this time an attractive young man, trim in appearance, with softly waving sandy hair, kindly brown eyes, a short neat nose, and, when he relaxed, a charming smile that won his audiences. He was terribly in earnest about his project and touchy about the dubious prospect of its success, but his own enthusiasm imbued others, and those who worked with him found him amiable and pleasant.*

He and Muriel got along famously. When he introduced her to his parents, they took to her as if she were a newfound daughter. In fact, Frau Mann hinted several times that she hoped Muriel would soon be their daughter (by marriage), and her famous husband was no less approving. Usually reserved and rather remote with young people, Thomas Mann was cordial and even jovial when Muriel was around.

However, both she and his son regarded their relationship as purely platonic. They were friends and colleagues—nothing more. When Muriel Rukeyser espoused a cause she was in a sense married, for she took it so to heart that she would work day and night for its success. She was fond of Klaus Mann, and

---

*By an odd coincidence, this biographer was a member of the group of volunteers who strove to assist Klaus Mann in his efforts.

they worked well together, but there was no sexual attraction on either side. Muriel was well aware that his male friends like Auden, Spender, and the young German novelist, Stefan Zweig (who had gone to South America), meant more to Klaus than any girl, which was perfectly acceptable to her. If they had been in love they probably would not have been such an efficient team.

Besides, she had her share of love affairs and suitors. Her warm, passionate nature and the sensuous beauty of her face inspired the adoration of many men despite her rather stocky figure, which early gave her trouble. "I've always had a weight problem," she said in 1976. And curiously enough, when she was working hard or under pressure, she put on a few extra pounds. She was writing poetry in addition to everything else during the time in Berkeley, as a matter of course. Poetry was an essential part of her life expression, as basic as breath; and her prose books she regarded as "footnotes of the poems." More than a dozen books of poetry have come from her prolific pen since 1935, and half that many of prose, besides several children's books, and translations, including a volume of selected poems of Octavio Paz. *A Turning Wind,* published in 1939 while she was still in Berkeley, brought much critical acclaim to Muriel and increased the Manns' admiration for her talent, and their hopes to gain her as a daughter-in-law.

The first issue of *Decision* came out in February, 1940, with articles by dozens of well-known contributors, color plates, and paper of the finest stock. In an opening editorial, Klaus outlined the purpose of the magazine, and his famous father wrote a short piece, followed by articles from Auden, Stefan Zweig, and authors of like caliber. Letters of congratulation poured in; but obviously such a high level could not continue without capital, advertising, and a wide circulation, none of which *Decision* had. The magazine lasted about a year, but even if it had acquired any of these, publication would probably have ceased with the attack on Pearl Harbor in December of 1941.

That year, Muriel Rukeyser's volume entitled, *Soul and Body of John Brown,* was published, for which she was the recipient of an award from the National Institute of Arts and Letters in 1942. She and Klaus Mann took divergent paths, though both lived in New York most of the time. Muriel's biography of Willard Gibbs was reissued by Doubleday in 1942, and she received a grant from the Guggenheim Foundation in 1943, which enabled her to write a new volume of poetry, *Beast in View,* published in 1944. During the war years and after, she often went out with a number of men she liked, but only one she really loved. When she found she was pregnant, she wanted to marry him, but he already had a wife and could not get a divorce.

It was not like Muriel Rukeyser to hesitate for long in making a decision. If she considered abortion, she early discarded the idea. She was in her thirties; if she was going to have a child—and she had wanted one for some time—it had better be soon or she would be too old. She had longed to have this man's child, though she did not say so. When her son was born in 1947, the story that went the rounds of the literary world was that Muriel Rukeyser did not know who his father was, nor care: she had wanted to have a baby, and she did. That she was twenty-five years ahead of her time can be seen by the varying remarks and repercussions then and now. Many people, including—or perhaps, especially—her family, were shocked. Her parents could not understand what possessed her. They had grown used to her radical ideas and strange poetry, but this was too much to accept. Her father was ready to disown her (and indeed, as she said in 1976, "We were disinherited," for her father had regained his fortune as the country emerged from the Depression). The possibility that much of her attitude was sheer bravado seemed not to occur to them or to many outside her intimate circle. A well-known publisher-editor said recently, "I think it was a courageous, imaginative thing to do." If the event had occurred today, her behavior would not have needed championing or an affected air of devil-may-care toward the question of the father. An indication of the general change is Nikki Giovanni's calm statement in regard to her seven-year-old son. "I had a baby at twenty-five because I wanted to have a baby. I did not get married because I did not want to get married and I could afford not to get married," she is quoted by a reporter in a feature story in *People* magazine.

It would be many years before Muriel Rukeyser felt free to reveal the full situation surrounding her son's birth, or her true feelings about it. In the meantime, she had to care for her child, earn a living for him. She had chosen a poetic name, Laurie* that could suit either sex; but as soon as he was old enough he changed that. He was quick, bright, good-looking, all boy, and he wanted to be "Bill," his formal name changed to William, and Muriel consented. She gloried in his ability to learn, to know his own mind at an early age.

The year after he was born, a volume of her poems, *The Green Wave,* appeared, and the following year, another book of poetry, *Orpheus,* and a prose "footnote": *The Life of Poetry,* which went into several printings. She wrote film scripts, radio and television scripts—all her extra writing helped to make ends meet. Sad, and then tragic news came from and about Klaus Mann. Although the Hitler regime had been demolished in Germany, he was depressed about the terms of the peace, the threat of another dictatorship, the future of the entire world with the advent of the atom bomb. Word came that Stefan Zweig had committed suicide in South America. No publishers were interested in the novels of Klaus Mann, only those of his father. And one day when he was in California, he slashed his wrists; his family found him bleeding and got him to a hospital in time to save his life. He promised he would not be so "foolish" again. But six months later, in a Paris hotel room, he shot himself to death. Many of his friends (including this biographer) received the shocking news by way of a complimentary copy of the

---

*Perhaps a reference to her father's name.

magazine *Tomorrow,* in which he had written the lead article on the subject, "Andre Gide and the Future of the World." A covering letter said that "the late" Klaus Mann had left a list containing the names of people to whom a copy of the magazine should be sent. (Recently it was learned that he deliberately planned this method of letting friends know of his suicidal intentions only after the deed was done.)

Muriel received word from his family immediately; and she had the impression that his mother, heartbroken, somehow felt that if Klaus had married the poet he would not have taken his life. "It wasn't so, of course, but how could I tell her?" Muriel asked rhetorically in 1976. She continued, "The great irony is that Klaus is now being recognized in his own country, hailed as the hero of the thirties, the anti-Hitler youth. Two of his novels have been published and are best sellers. Two volumes of his letters are out, and another is coming soon." She was both triumphant and sad. "It took thirty years, almost a generation and a half."*

In those thirty years, Muriel's son had grown up. She espoused the cause of peace and free speech wherever it was threatened in the world. As ardently as she had worked for intervention in the European war, once it was over, she spent as much effort working with organizations trying to prevent future wars. Along with a great many others, she was alarmed by the wholesale destruction of Hiroshima and Nagasaki, and it was like her to join the most active of groups—the War Resisters League. She became a member of International P.E.N., specifically interested in the committee trying to free writers in prison. Liberal causes and poetry travelled side by side in Muriel's mind. Money, except as a commodity, never concerned her.

"All the Rukeysers are connected with money except us," she said, referring to Bill and herself. It was only natural that her

---

*When she heard I had some of his letters she urged me to contact his sister, Elisabeth Mann Borgese, who would tell the name of the publishing house in West Germany that was eager to bring out all of Klaus's letters.

son absorb her attitude as he grew up. Muriel's *Selected Poems* appeared in 1951; then there was a gap until the volume, *One Life,* in 1957, except for a book for children in 1955, *Come Back, Paul.* She became a faculty member at Sarah Lawrence College, not exactly a teacher, but as a reader and adviser in poetry, a connection that lasted nearly ten years, till 1967. Bill did not inherit his mother's gift for poetry, but he could appreciate it in her, and his quick, inquiring mind responded to the lively conversation that went on around him from the time he was a small boy. Muriel's friends were always quoting him. (May Swenson, whom Muriel came to know in the fifties, was fond of passing along his sayings.) As he grew older, Bill showed a practicality, a journalistic approach to writing. He knew the value of money, but did not value it for the sake of acquiring wealth. He had no desire to enter the field of banking, brokerage, stocks and bonds, or even editing a magazine like *Fortune,* as one of his cousins did. He and Muriel often laughed at the family's proclivity for careers connected with money, which neither of them shared. It took a prank of Bill's to make the family circle recognize his existence, though the cousin mentioned above had the same name, first and last. Bill was in England (on a shoe-string, with a group of students staying at youth hostels) and, going to the club of his cousin at Cambridge, asked for William Rukeyser.

"Who is calling?" asked the clerk coldly.

"William Rukeyser," Bill said, undaunted.

The cousin was not amused, but Muriel and Bill told the story gleefully. Yet in a volume entitled *Waterlily Fire (Poems, 1935–1962),* the stock market report was used with skill in one of the early poems to denote with savage irony the difference between the life of the worker and the profit sheet: Right in the middle of a poem called "The Dam," depicting the workers' struggle in strong imagery, two rows of figures from a stock sheet appear—a Union Carbide listing. No poet except one with a background like Muriel's would have thought of using such a device; the fact that she selected the poem for a 1938 volume is significant of the value she placed on it. For contrast, she placed "Homage to Literature," a lyric poem, on the next page.

The title poem, "Waterlily Fire," intriguing in itself, refers to the flash fire which flared up in the Museum of Modern Art that year, severely damaging (nearly obliterating) one of Monet's finest waterlily paintings. Muriel Rukeyser's poems, intensely personal, are often in first person singular, and in this one she describes her reaction at the sight of the flames on approaching the museum; and she brings a friend, Eileen Bowser, associate film director of the museum, into this poem, assessing the damage a fire does to art. The theme of the startling title poem is also meant to draw an oblique parallel to the flare-up of trouble then beginning in Southeast Asia, threatening to destroy the culture of a gentle people, the Vietnamese.

Rukeyser's reputation as a poet had brought her an honorary doctoral degree in literature from Rutgers University in 1961, an honor well justified by the books that kept coming from this prolific poet. By 1965, the United States was deeply involved in the war in Vietnam, an undeclared war, into which young men were being drafted without any knowledge of the basic reasons or goals to justify American entry. Muriel's son, imbued with his mother's ideals of world peace, was undoubtedly one of the early "flower children" opposed to the war in Vietnam, for when he received a call from a draft board unexpectedly, he went to Canada. His mother agreed with his refusal to fight in a war both opposed, but she was naturally worried about his welfare.

Whether it was due to anxiety over the fate of her son, or overwork with the various organizations for peace in addition to her creative productivity, or a combination of all three, this sturdy poet suffered a slight stroke in 1968, a blow to her unceasing activity. The most serious effect was partial paralysis of her vocal chords. She had to give up her post at Sarah Lawrence, her readings, and lectures. No amount of treatment seemed

to help restore her speech. And, psychologically, the speech difficulty, stubbornly resistant at first, and then demanding months
and months of speech therapy, affected her creative urge for a
time; but finally, almost miraculously one day, she could pro-
nounce words clearly and distinctly again. She was delighted to
be able to accept an invitation to take part in a radio program:
Paul Kresh, writer, critic, director, and public relations man in
various media, wanted Muriel Rukeyser to be one of eighteen
poets whose works were to be aired on his radio series, *Adventures in Judaism*. She had already begun a series of poems based
on the legends of Rabbi Akiba she had learned from her mother,
and which Paul had commissioned her to write for the magazine, *American Judaism,* of which he was editor. Kresh was so
enthusiastic about them that at his suggestion they were published in the magazine, *American Judaism,* before she read them
on the radio program. Once again, as her strength returned, she
resumed her active life.

As the war in Vietnam dragged on, more and more people
joined in the call for peace and Muriel was among those in the
forefront. And when the clamor for peace was finally heeded,
the fight for amnesty began. The quest to secure, for Bill and
thousands of boys like him, freedom to return home without
fear of penalty for having the courage to hold to their convictions, was an endless, frustrating task. Civil Liberties Union
lawyers took on the case, and the poet continued to support by
word and deed not only the goal of amnesty but all liberal causes.
In the course of a march on Washington, led by Maurine Sin-
gleton (senator from Washington State after the death of her
husband), Muriel and several others were arrested for civil dis-
obedience (lying down on the floor of the Senate). She spent a
night or two in prison, enough to show her the hell that political prisoners must be suffering. The experience caused her to
double her efforts on the writers-in-prison committee of International P.E.N., and in 1975, as president of the organization,
she went to South Korea, to Westgate Prison outside of Seoul,

where Kim Chi Ha, the celebrated young Korean poet who was in solitary, was condemned to die for writing dissident poetry. He had been on the brink of execution earlier; had received a pardon, but was arrested and condemned again. Muriel Rukeyser was there to plead for his life, to stand vigil.

As always, the experience (which was successful in staying the execution order, although the condemned Korean poet is still in prison) became the subject of poetry, culminating in a series of dramatic, poignant poems which provided the title and the second half of the next Rukeyser volume, published in 1976, *The Gates*. The significance is threefold: gates of the body, of the spirit, and of the prison, before which an American woman poet stood all day in the rain to protest the solitary confinement of a Southeast-Asian male poet, the drama unfolding like a three-act play. The drama opens with stage directions: "Scaffolding," setting the scene of Kim Chi Ha's heroic struggle. "He has been on this cycle before : condemned to death, the sentence changed to life imprisonment, and then a pardon from his President during a time . . . of terror. The poet has written his stinging work—like Burns or Brecht. . . . An American woman is sent to make an appeal for the poet's life. She speaks to Cabinet ministers, the Cardinal, university people, writers, the poet's family and his infant son." It is this child who is the focal point of the story told in stanzas, though one does not realize it at first. "Among the days, / among the nights of the poet in solitary,/ a strong infant is just beginning to run./ I go up the stepping-stones / to where the young wife of the poet/ stands holding the infant in her arms./ She weeps, she weeps." The verses that follow describe the vigil, silently standing all day in the rain, finally being allowed to stand in front of the cell. In number VII, Muriel mentions standing at the grave of her ancestor Akiba ("The holy poem, he said to me,/ The Song of Songs . . ."), and likens and links it to this moment, standing at the Korean poet's solitary cell. In the next two verses she speaks of the "grief woman," wife of the poet, whose gratitude to Muriel was so great that she gave her a magnificent hand-made "scarlet coverlet/ thick-sown with all the flowers"—the courage shown by that young wife, with her "strong infant just beginning to run." The description brings the climax of the narrative suddenly, as suddenly as the memory of her own son's infancy flooded over Muriel at the sight of the Korean baby boy.

Both XI and XII in the series are startlingly revealing: These two stanzas tell the true story of her son's birth, the bizarre circumstances surrounding his conception through her relationship with a man she truly loved, whose name she knew well, but could never name because he was married and not able to get a divorce—most significantly because his wife was pregnant with a son born just three weeks before the poet's, a fact he failed to tell Muriel until the birth took place. Feeling bereft, torn in two, Rukeyser was strong enough to withstand the blow; objectively viewing her own amazing baby boy, she celebrated and grieved at the strange course Fate had led her to accept. Now, on her mission to Korea to save the life of a fellow poet, she could see the tragic element in the timing of events as the universal wind turned the world around and around.

In the opening lines of stanza XIII she again speaks of the imprisoned poet's son, calling him "a crucified child." The whole story of her emotional struggle at a crucial point in her life is unveiled in this portion of a contemporary epic poem. And when she read it aloud to a packed audience of young people, Muriel Rukeyser received a standing ovation. The young among her devoted readers, also showed by appreciative laughter their approval of a couplet in a lighter vein:

> *I'd rather be Muriel*
> *Than be dead and be Ariel.**

---

* Another favorite was "St. Roach," a satiric, sympathetic poem on the household enemy, the roach, with its implication of wholesale killing of "the enemy" in war.

In view of the course of events, the above couplet is almost prophetic. After her return from Korea, and the stay of execution for Kim Chi Ha, word came from the Civil Liberties Union lawyers that a technical error in the draft papers for a small group of boys served with them at the same time as Bill Rukeyser made the notices illegal. Because of this technicality the lawyers were able to secure return to the United States of the entire group, free of penalty or imprisonment. Bill, in the meantime, had married in Canada, and it was a happy day indeed when he and his wife came to settle in Berkeley where Bill had a job in radio newscasting from the University of California station, a career he had developed from his college days. Moreover, the young couple had a baby boy whom Muriel had never seen, so there was a jubilant reunion in Berkeley. (Bill's career advanced rapidly, and he is presently a network newscaster on TV as well as radio, working in Sacramento. Some people have assumed that Louis Rukeyser, of the "Wall Street Week in Review" program, is Muriel's son. For the record, he is a cousin, son of Merrill Rukeyser, one of the many members of the family connected with the world of finance.)

The Gates was published in the fall of 1976, well received by both the public and critics; it almost seemed that the Rukeyser problems were solved. But in late February of 1977, suddenly, without warning, Muriel suffered a second stroke. After five anxious days, her friends learned that there was no paralysis, but she was very weak, and would be under care of a nurse. She went to live with Monica McCall, her agent, and for weeks led a very quiet life, slowly recovering. In May the happy news came from the Academy of American Poets that she had won the coveted Copernicus Award, which carried with it a prize of ten thousand dollars. It was given to her for "her lifetime achievement as a poet and her contribution to poetry as a cultural force."

The judges, all poets themselves—Galway Kinnell, William Meredith, and Josephine Miles (the last-named a close friend as well) said of Muriel Rukeyser: "From her first book *Theory of Flight,* published when she was twenty-one, through her recent collection *The Gates* (the title poem finds her characteristically outside the prison of the South Korean poet Kim Chi Ha), the work of Muriel Rukeyser has been committed to ideas of freedom. Throughout her life she has been sensitive to encroachments on the freedom of individuals or peoples. She has responded in actions of which poetry was only the highest form. She has taken the risks of life and poetry with equal generosity and success." Coming as it did at a time of trial and need, the award was doubly gratifying. And soon afterward, word arrived that Rukeyser was also the recipient of the Shelley Memorial Award (spring of 1977). It carries a cash prize of fifteen hundred dollars, given in recognition of a poet's entire work. Noncompetitive, the award is made with consideration to the poet's need and is administered by the Poetry Society of America. In her personal life there was cause for rejoicing in the news from California that Bill and his wife were expecting a second child. Muriel was able to go to California for the event. and when she returned, she began to lead a more normal life, if limited in the light of her former activity.

The honors and emblems of fullscale recognition continued to be shown her. Paul Kresh, editing a new project of *The Spoken Arts,* "A Treasury of American Jewish Poets Reading Their Poems," asked her to be one of the principals. Of the twenty-five poets included, Muriel Rukeyser is the only one who has the whole side of a disc devoted to her work. Among the poems she read was her notable, "On Being a Jew in the Twentieth Century." She consented to be in a film portraying her entire career through readings and reminiscences. It was one-third of a production, "Three Women," along with the painter Alice Neel and the dancer-choreographer, Anna Sokolov, which was shown at the New York Film Festival, and later on public television. The script called for many scenes of the poet walking along the streets of New York, showing the seamy side of the city; there were many close-ups of her face as she recalled the significance of certain events in her career, and though she smiled her slow smile in some of them, the sadness of the ages is in her eyes. The making of such a film must have demanded both time and energy on her part, as well as on the part of the producers, and she had not much of either. She was still far from strong, and she was trying to put together major selections from her volumes over the years along with her latest works which were to comprise *The Collected Poems of Muriel Rukeyser*, a full-bodied book of 588 pages, finally published in 1979. Hailed in *The New York Times* (February 11, 1979) by the poet and critic Anne Stevenson as "an occasion for rejoicing," this splendid volume gives the reader a rich, retrospective view of Rukeyser one rarely sees during the lifetime of a poet.

In her assessment, Stevenson cites the variety of creative gifts revealed from the first in *Theory of Flight* (1935) to *The Gates* in 1976, and deems Rukeyser "one of those poets American literature would seem impoverished without." The reviewer adds that "like William Carlos Williams, she has been an indestructible force for the good of poets and poetry for decades." Granted that this poet's free-flowing, quasi-prose lines have a tendency to run on, as in the long narrative, "Tree of Rivers," the stories are never boring. A passage from "All the Way Through the Forest" in "Tree of Rivers" is quoted and held up as "part of a central tradition in American writing," beside Melville, Whitman, and Crane. "But, like Melville's, Miss Rukeyser's realism is really a bridge to an intensely visionary state of awareness. . . . The threshold of the miraculous and the mystical is never far away. . . . Beneath her passion for social justice and her empathy with all sufferers lie deeper apprehensions of what existence and its paradoxes can lead to." The review states further: "It is inevitable that Miss Rukeyser will be compared with Whitman; indeed, 'Leaves of Grass' must have shown her part of the way. Among modern poets she is the equal of Pablo Neruda, and like him, committed to a vision of humanity that acknowledges pain, but leaves little room for despair. She is also patently a feminine poet—feminist but not bitchy."

The reviewer points out that the collection is star-studded with love poems, and that for all her political zeal, Muriel Rukeyser is as passionate in her personal loves as she is compassionate toward the masses. Sometimes she is pleading, as in the early lines, "Oh, grow to know me. I am not happy. I will be open"; and "Speak to me. Take my hand," which runs like a refrain through "Effort at Speech Between Two People," and in the succeeding "Sonnet," concerned with communication between two lovers. At other times, still intent on verbal interplay, as in "Song, The Brain-Coral," she abandons herself to the joy of physical love, letting it lead her into the ultimate mystical core of feeling kinship with all humankind. The poem concludes:

> *We change in images, color, visions, and change;*
> *I bring you, speak you now a changeless stone,*
> *the strange brain-coral,*
>
> *thrown white on beaches beside the peacock Stream.*
> *Lie still, love, while the many physical worlds stream*
> *passionate by,*
>
> *in dreams of the exterior, intricate rainbow world,*
> *dreaming the still white intricate stone of the world,*
> *—bring you brain-coral,*
> *a world's white seeming.*

From such lines, the reader, like the *Times* reviewer, cannot help realizing that, for all her political, sociological activism, Rukeyser's poetry "remains the poetry of the heart."

Other evaluations were no less enthusiastic about *The Collected Poems*. *MS* magazine, carried an article-review, "Muriel Rukeyser, at 65, Still Ahead of Her Time." At receptions and banquets she was the noted guest of honor. The book had appeared in January (1979), and as late as October, 1979, she was honored at the annual banquet of the New York Quarterly Poetry Day Awards for her "outstanding contribution to contemporary poetry." Gratifying as this was, she could not enjoy it because poor health continued to plague her. She was in the hospital several times after her partial recovery from the second stroke. Her legs failed, and she had to learn to walk again, shakily, with the aid of a three-pronged metal tubular cane. Indeed, it was a strain on her to attend these functions, but when she could, she made the effort to be present. And all the time, in spite of her weakened condition, she continued to write, making notes for her memoirs; she took an interest in the work of her colleagues and was open to suggestion for new works.

One of the most interesting projects was a collaboration with the painter Penrod Scofield, who had illustrated four of her "Akiba" poems when they appeared in the *American Judaism Reader* in 1967—a collection of the best poems, essays, and short stories that the magazine had published. Scofield had been working for several years on a series of drawings and watercolors depicting New York's "bag-ladies," those rag-tag, down-at-the-heel, overweight figures, laden with bulging bags of every description, that one sees scrounging among the wastebaskets of the city.

Muriel, with her sympathy for lost souls, had often observed "bag-ladies," but never at close range, and she was fascinated by the portfolio that Penrod brought to her with the idea that she supply a text for a book comprising his drawings and watercolors with appropriate lines by her to complement them. Weak as she was, she began work at once on a series of poems and prose poems to go with his visual art. In her usual zeal, she sought to see the bag-ladies in action for herself; she found them pathetic yet somehow sturdy creatures in their intent search amid squalor for objects they might use. So this poet would continue to be the people's Muse to the end; while the project was still in its formulative stage, Muriel Rukeyser died—almost symbolically on Lincoln's birthday—February 12, 1980. *The New York Times* in its obituary the following day quoted from Thomas Lask's review of her *Collected Poems:* "Poetry was never an artifice to Muriel Rukeyser, never a decoration on life. The woman and the poet were one. She was always committed." That wholehearted commitment shines like a beacon through her poetry.

A memorial tribute "in celebration of her life" was held under the joint auspices of the P.E.N. American Center and the Poetry Society of America on March 19 in the McGraw-Hill auditorium. In the packed hall, those who had loved both the poetry and the woman, heard Muriel Rukeyser's work read by poets Denise Levertov, Jane Cooper, Stanley Kunitz, and Grace Schulman. Writers Grace Paley, Ted Solataroff, and Robert Payne spoke of their close association with Muriel. One of the most moving memoirs was Mr. Payne's account of his last dinner with her. As Denise Levertov had mentioned, Muriel would never say good-bye at the end of phone calls or personal (social) visits. She did not like good-byes. The night she had dinner with her long-standing friend Bob Payne, she was in a wheelchair. She said very little, almost nothing during the meal with him and Monica McCall, her agent, with whom she had been living while struggling to recover from her multiple illnesses. Several times she seemed about to speak, but only smiled. Then, on the way home, as Payne was pushing her in the wheelchair, she suddenly began to say, in her musical voice, looking at the trees in Central Park, "Good-bye, good-bye, good-bye." In his words, "It was like the cry of a bird."

Excerpts from two films made with Muriel narrating highlights of her career brought her back to life for the audience of friends, who experienced another touching moment in the final frame, a close-up of Muriel, holding her infant grandchild. Music on the program varied from Charles Ives's, "The Pond," written on the death of his father, to "His Eye is on the Sparrow," in a stirring rendition by a singer and jazz combo, representing Muriel's love of jazz and the spiritual. The service ended with an eloquent yet informal eulogy by Rabbi Balfour Brickner, who read appropriate lines from the poem, "On Being a

Jew in America in the Twentieth Century"; then, bidding everyone to rise, he recited the traditional Hebrew Kaddish.

In keeping with Rukeyser's universal appeal, the church of St. John the Divine devoted one of its three "Poetry Walls" to her. Poems are posted on the wall for a certain length of time—three months, accessible for readings to the general public. A later memorial was held at Sarah Lawrence College, where Muriel had taught for many years. A year earlier the college had programed a Rukeyser symposium, an entire day devoted to her work and to the creative process. She was present throughout, but collapsed onstage at the end. Of all the women in the world of modern poetry, Rukeyser's voice rings out with startling clarity as the voice of humanity.

Denise Levertov

Like Muriel Rukeyser, Denise Levertov is a poet of definite political and social consciousness; and like Muriel, she has been an activist for peace, for justice, and for freedom of expression; yet she, too, is first and foremost a poet. From the time they met, in 1961, these two were sisters in spirit.

"But I don't want to be known as a 'poet of Protest,' " Levertov said during an interview in October 1980. She was referring to the phrase *The New York Times* had applied to Rukeyser in the caption of the obituary at the time of the latter's death the previous February. "Poet of protest is a *label*," Levertov went on, becoming more vehement. "A foolish label. The applying of labels reveals a mental poverty on the part of the applier."

A vivacious, attractive woman in her late fifties, Denise Levertov, who came to the United States when she was twenty-five years old, in 1948, still speaks with a British accent, a crispness of expression that marks her birthplace. Brought up in London, she was born on October 24, 1923, in the village of Ilford, Essex, a London suburb. Her mother's background was Welsh: Beatrice Adelaide Spooner-Jones was the daughter of the noted Welsh mystic of Mold, Angel Jones. It was through her mother that Denise acquired a lasting love of nature and the ability to read aloud skillfully, with the clarity and dramatic feeling that have distinguished her poetry readings from the start. Her mother was her only real teacher. Except for half a year at a boarding school attended by her sister, Olga, nine years older than she, both girls were educated at home by their mother, a schooling augmented by vague, diversive religious training from their father.

Paul Levertoff was a Russian Jew, a descendant of the famous Hebrew scholar and one of the founders of the Chassidic sect, Rabbi Schneour Zalmon. Young Paul was sent to study at Konigsberg, where he became a convert to Christianity. His family was shocked, but could not dissuade him, and he finally settled in England to join the Anglican priesthood. He was an ardent advocate of the unification of Judaism and Christianity. He translated Zohar, wrote a life of St. Paul in Hebrew, and filled his house with German theologians, Jewish booksellers, Russian priests from Paris, and Viennese opera singers. In such polyglot surroundings, it is small wonder that his younger daughter Denise has stated that her religion might be called "tentative syncretism." It was merely part of the scholarly, cosmopolitan atmosphere in which she grew up.

Her formal education, like her sister's under their mother's tutelage, ended when she was about thirteen. With a houseful of books and an excellent library nearby, neither girl had ever lacked reading matter to their tastes; and from her earliest years,

Denise preferred poetry above other literature. At the early age of five, she decided to be a poet and wrote her first poems. By the time she was thirteen, her sister was grown up and often guided her in the arts. Although Denise was allowed to go about London by herself from the age of twelve, when she visited museums and galleries, Olga introduced her to modern painting as well as modern poetry, particularly the Impressionists. Olga's chief interest was drama, and as a member of the London Group Company, she aroused the poet's interest in theatre and the emerging art of ballet. Denise was so taken by the latter that during her early teens she tried to become a ballet dancer. After poetry, it was a toss-up between ballet and painting. In her later teens, she thought she might become a painter. At home she had plenty of time and the necessary solitude for writing poetry; and as she has said, she "always knew she wanted to be a *poet,* no matter what."

So strong was her feeling that at the tender age of twelve she had the "temerity" to send several of her poems to T. S. Eliot, though she had not shown them to anyone, even her sister, who was usually the first to see her efforts. Despite the difference in age, the sisters were very close. As a small girl of seven, Denise looked up to her sixteen-year-old sister, stared with wonder at Olga's maturing body when they went to bed in their shared room, and Olga undressed slowly, warming herself by the gas fire. A few years later they shared their thoughts and dreams and hopes in their shared bedroom or on long walks over the Essex ploughlands (which Denise called "murple," a mixed shade of mauve and brown they both loved); and the budding poet let her sister see the verses she was constantly writing, asking for helpful criticism rather than approval. The poems sent to Eliot, however, were mailed on impulse, before she had a chance to think of revisions suggested by Olga or anyone else.

She had forgotten all about her rash appeal to Eliot when, months later, she received a two-page typewritten letter from him, offering her "excellent advice." It seemed a miracle, and for years she treasured his letter, and only lost track of it during a move from one apartment to another after she came to the United States. His letter gave her renewed impetus for making poems and sending them out, and she received further encouragement when she met the critic, Herbert Read, who took great interest in the sixteen-year-old girl brimming with talent. At about this time, war was beginning in Europe, and Denise Levertov, along with many other young Londoners, was "evacuated" to Buckinghamshire. Though it was an inland county, they could hear the guns booming ominously in the distance. Because she was acutely aware of the war in spite of the peaceful surroundings, she wrote lines about it while working as a "land girl" on an Essex farm. Two stanzas written just before or during the tense time of Dunkirk she called "Listening to Distant Guns," and they became her first published poem, which appeared in *Poetry Quarterly* about 1940. From then on, her work was accepted by *Poetry London,* as well as the *Quarterly,* and other little magazines like *Outposts* and *Voices.* After Charles Wrey Gardiner became editor of the *Quarterly,* her reputation as a promising young poet grew, winning for her the interest of well-known critics. Kenneth Rexroth recalled, "In no time at all Herbert Read, Tambi Mutti, Charles Wrey Gardiner, and incidentally myself, were all in excited correspondence about her. She was the baby of the new Romanticism. Her poetry had about it a wistful *Schwarmerei* unlike anything in English except perhaps Matthew Arnold's "Dover Beach." It could be compared to the earliest poems of Rilke or some of the more melancholy songs of Brahms." High praise for a novice from an established poet.

During these years Denise was in nurse's training by day to aid in the war effort, and to help rehabilitate wounded war veterans as they returned from Europe. By night she wrote poetry; any spare time she had was spent in perfecting the lines and mailing out poems. One of the editors who had accepted her work suggested that she submit a book-length manuscript to a fellow editor at the Sylvan Press, a house that published new poets. All excited at the prospect, she took his advice, only to find that the Sylvan Press was folding. She was so naïve she had not known it was customary to enclose a self-addressed stamped envelope for the return of one's manuscript, and received a request to pick it up at the Sylvan office. The day she did so she had an appointment with the matron at St. Luke's Hospital in London, where she had applied for a job though she had not finished her nurse's training. A successful interview won her the job right away.

Elated by her accomplishment, on one of her sudden impulses, she walked into the offices of the Cresset Press, which she had spotted on the corner of Fitzroy Square as she went for her interview. In her eagerness, she inadvertently entered through the stockroom and a packer allowed her to take the lift up to the editorial offices. Clutching her manuscript, she approached Irene Calverley, one of the executives, with determination, and offered her manuscript. The lady, though she took the package and opened it, began politely but firmly informing the "crude girl"—as Levertov later described herself—that this was no way to set about dealing with a publisher. Midway, however, something made her stop—perhaps it was the downhearted look on the young poet's face—and after glancing at a few poems, she told Denise to leave the manuscript, her address, and phone number. A few days later, Calverley called with the incredible news that John Hayward had read the manuscript and was accepting it for book publication. Ecstatic, nearly overcome by astonishment, Levertov has written, "I remember going into a church somewhere in Soho to kneel in awe because my destiny, which I had always known as a certain but vague form on the horizon, was beginning to *happen.*"

It was a whole year, however, before she was to hold her first volume, *Double Image,* in her hands. During that time Denise Levertov had made good at her job, and had been sent to the British Hospital in Paris just as the book came out, late in 1946, when the war was over. Many of the poems, like "Christmas

1944" dealt with the anxious days of the turning point in the war. There were signs of the holiday around, she had written: "Bright cards above the fire bring no friends near,/ fire cannot keep the cold from seeping in. . . . Who can be happy while the wind recounts/ its long sagas of sorrow? Though we are safe/ in a flickering circle of winter festival/ we dare not laugh; or if we laugh, we lie,/ hearing hatred crackle in the coal,/ the voice of treason, the voice of love."

Later critical comment on this initial volume observed that much of the verse now "seems artificial and painfully formal in meters and rhymes"; but one thing was certain: the young poet possessed a strong social consciousness and already showed indications of the militant pacifist she was to become. Her actions right then displayed a spirit of dissent: she was fired from the hospital in Paris for refusing to form part of a guard of honor in an unveiling ceremony. She would not honor any war heroes! It was spring (1947), so she decided to go off on a hitchhiking trip around France with a friend. At the end of the summer, their money just about gone, they went to Switzerland to look for work. It was a move that changed her whole life.

As usual, they stayed at youth hostels while job-hunting, and at one of these in Geneva, she met a young American beginning his career as a writer—Mitchell Goodman. The attraction must have been immediate and mutual, for she wrote, "We got married soon afterwards." She was pregnant when they came to the United States in 1948, and a son, their only child, Nikolai Gregory, was born in 1949. Life from then on had a kind of kaleidoscopic pattern, with rapidly shifting scenes, so that the poet had no time to think of preparing another book, though she was constantly writing poems that reflected the different places she and Mitch lived. In 1950–1951, they were back in Europe on the G.I. Bill. For the next few years they moved around to various apartments in New York City during the winter, and spent the summers in New England. (Eventually they bought an old farmhouse in rural Maine.) During 1957–

1958, they lived in Mexico. By then Denise Levertov was listed as an American citizen, having been granted her final papers in 1955. "I never thought of myself as an 'immigrant,' " she said in 1980 with amusement, displaying a copy of *An American Mosaic* she had just received, in which her life was included among those immigrants who became famous. In most anthologies and encyclopedias of authors, Denise Levertov is designated, "American poet."

At about the time she became a citizen, in the mid-fifties, while living in New York City, a sketchy housekeeper who spent more time writing poetry than tidying up every day, Denise received an unexpected letter from Weldon Kees, a name she had heard often in the literary world: He stated that he'd read and liked her work and was interested in publishing a volume of it in a series he and a printer friend were planning. Utterly delighted, Denise set about compiling a manuscript at once, and sent it off to Kees. He replied just as promptly that he was most pleased with it. There were poems that had been published in *Origin* and the *Black Mountain Review* through one of her first American friendships, that with Robert Creeley of the Black Mountain School of writers. Some were in the 1949 anthology, *New British Poets,* compiled by Kenneth Rexroth, who continued to promote her work after she came to the United States. She looked forward to the new book eagerly. But before it went into production, the shocking news came of Kees's sudden death in a leap from the Golden Gate Bridge.

No word of future publication followed until nearly a year later, when she received a letter from a "Larry Ferling," who was actually Lawrence Ferlinghetti; he informed her that her manuscript had come to his desk after Kees died and he wanted to publish her poems in a series he was starting—the *City Lights* books. Shortly after this, Jonathan Williams wrote to her saying that he also would like to do a book. Two offers so close together seemed almost an embarrassment of riches. She wondered if she had enough poems to fill two separate books, though they would be slim. Since the Kees-Ferlinghetti bid had come first, she gave it first choice in her selections from all the poems she managed to pile up; to Williams went the "rejects" and some of her latest verses, written during the months between offers. In a mood she calls "compulsive anxiety" when she is writing articles or working systematically to make a deadline, she threw the two books into shape with a kind of joyful, carefree frenzy, letting the job take precedence over all else.

One of the poems in the second manuscript, "The Dogwood," (from *Overland to the Islands*, not published till 1958) gives a clear picture of the happy but harassed poet-wife-mother and her haphazard housekeeping: "The sink is full of dishes. Oh well./ Ten o'clock, there's no/ hot water./ The kitchen floor is unswept, the broom/ has been shedding straws. Oh well." Two short stanzas then depict her household: "The cat is sleeping, Nikolai is sleeping,/ Mitch is sleeping, early to bed,/ aspirin for a cold. Oh well./ No school tomorrow, someone for lunch,/ 4 dollars left from the 10—how did that go?/ Mostly on food. Oh well." Then, to take her mind off the dreary chores, the poet almost decides to hear some chamber music, but instead begins to recall bits of beauty glimpsed that day: ". . . some huge soft deep/ blackly gazing purple/ and red (and pale)/ anemones. Does that/ take my mind off the dishes?/ And dogwood besides./ Oh well. Early to bed, and I'll get up/ early and put/ a shine on everything and write/ a letter to Duncan later that will shine too/ with moonshine. Can I make it? Oh well."

Thus the poet, coping with her household and her profession. She and Mitch both were busy with writing projects; they lived mainly on travel articles that Mitch turned out for various magazines. As for Nikolai, the poet later wrote, "Although I think it was a good thing for me that I was not sent to school, we never considered educating Nik at home for a variety of reasons." During his high school years their son attended the Putney School in Vermont, and at his graduation in the late 1960s, Denise was invited to be one of the principal speakers.

Her remarks, sparked with humor, were filled with concern for the future in the face of increasing warfare, the senseless struggle in Vietnam. Her words, and the poems she read made a lasting impression on students, faculty, and trustees alike. In the last stanza of the poem quoted above, "Duncan" refers to Robert Duncan, one of the few poets she knew well during the first years in the United States. In fact, through Mitch's Greenwich Village companions, she became acquainted with more painters than poets, especially the Jane Street Gallery painters. Albert Kresch, for whom she wrote a poem, was a close friend. It was Duncan, however, to whom she showed all her poems in typescript; but after the two slim volumes were published, he pointed out to her that she "should not have let either book be so loosely, thoughtlessly thrown together." Much later (1979), she said in the "Author's Note" to her *Collected Earlier Poems*, ". . . and for the first time I realized that a book of separate poems can in itself be a composition, and that to *compose* a book is preferable to randomly gathering one." She was grateful for Duncan's criticism.

The greatest kindness came from Kenneth Rexroth, whose efforts on her behalf were unfailing. She was quite sure it was he who told Kees and then Ferlinghetti, as well as Jonathan Williams, about her. "Most certainly it was he who persistently brought me to James Laughlin's attention, and so—once James Laughlin felt I had a voice of my own—to the happiness and honor of becoming in 1959 a New Directions author," she wrote in a tribute to both men. Laughlin soon became a "dear friend" to Denise and Mitch. As consistent as Rexroth had been in praising her work, Levertov had met him only a few times and had not maintained much correspondence with him since 1948 when he was compiling the anthology of new British poets. In 1957, when her first American volume, *Here and Now,* was published, Rexroth wrote: "Denise Levertov is incomparably the best poet of what is getting to be known as the new avant-garde. The *Schwarmerei* and lassitude are gone. Their place is taken by a kind of animal grace of the word, a pulse like the footfalls of a cat, or the wingbeats of a gull."

Richard Howard called it "a very little book which is a kind of progress report on her affair with the American language of poetry." He felt that she had made herself "not merely an agent but an origin of that language, a means by which poetry obtains access to reality." Reading the poetry of Wallace Stevens and William Carlos Williams, conversations with Robert Duncan, Robert Creeley, and other Black Mountain College poets increased her mastery of the American idiom; and by the time her third volume came out—the first of many to be published by New Directions Press—she was regarded as a bona fide American poet, but one who kept intact her identity of self. The critic Thomas Parkinson wrote of *With Eyes at the Back of Our Heads* (the title the poet finally chose for this important book): "[It has] a special tone of indolence and isolation. . . . The author celebrates the world around her from a carapace of self from which she reaches but never quite destroys." M. L. Rosenthal said in an article some years later that he had welcomed the book for "some vivid simple, impressionistic poems which show her able to catch the essential details of sensuous experiences and to relate them so as to organize a world of insight and of emotional response with great economy and objectivity."

The title poem won the Bess Hokin Prize from *Poetry* in 1959, and other awards followed. In 1962, Denise received a Guggenheim Foundation Fellowship, coincidently with the publication of Mitch's first novel, *The End of It;* she recorded with wry humor, "We bought a washing machine, a dryer, a dishwasher, and a new vacuum cleaner; they have made a great difference in my life." With household duties eased, the poet found she not only had more time for writing poetry, but could take on part-time assignments to improve their financial situation. In 1961, and again from 1963 to 1965, Levertov was poetry editor of the *Nation;* she and her husband both began teaching college (part-time), a demanding yet rewarding task, as they both discovered new facets in their own creativity from questions raised by the students. They both held visiting lecturer posts at various colleges, and from 1964 to 1966 Denise was associate scholar at the Radcliffe Institute for Independent Studies in Boston.

Those years brought tragedy and turmoil as well as professional achievement. In 1964, her sister Olga suffered an untimely, painful death at the age of fifty, after wearing down her body and soul in frenetic service to the cause of human rights. From the "Olga Poems" that Denise wrote directly after her sister's death, one is able to trace the downward path that Olga's life took from the time she began trying "to shout the world to its senses,/ . . . to browbeat the poor into joy's/ socialist republic," as Denise put it in the second of the series. There are glimpses of the early days in Ilford when Olga had been the young poet's guide and heroine. Then for a number of years the sisters were estranged, when Olga was "picking/ those endless arguments, pressing on/ to manipulate lives to disaster . . . To change,/ to change the course of the river!"

After their reunion through Olga's final illness, Denise, gazing at the dying figure on the hospital bed, sees that Olga's hatreds have burned out ". . . as your disasters bred of love/ burned out." In a significant image, the poem continues, "while pain and drugs/ quarreled like sisters in you—." Her sister "lay afloat on a sea of love and pain"; "all history/ burned out. down/ to the sick bone, save for/ that kind candle." The series ended with a sort of eulogy to Olga's eyes that were "the brown gold of pebbles under water"; the eyes she kept remembering: "Even when we were estranged/ and my own eyes smarted in pain and anger at the thought of you./ . . . anywhere where the light/ reaches down through shallows to gold gravel. Olga's/ brown eyes." Dated, "May-August, 1964," these poems were followed two years later by "A Note to Olga (1966)," depicting the scene of a demonstration against the war in Vietnam: The poet, shuffling along with the others on the Times Square sidewalk, a cardboard sign, "Stop the War," slung round her neck, suddenly heard her sister's voice (though she knew Olga wasn't there); it rang out behind her when they began to sing "We Shall Overcome," and with the last word, it came again hoarsely, from somewhere at the front of the line, just as "the paddy-wagon gapes," and a "limp, ardent form" that seemed to be Olga was lifted off the dark snow and shoved in. Olga must have undergone more than such humiliation proudly in her zeal to save the world.

From the early sixties, when she and Muriel Rukeyser had formed a fast-ripening friendship, Denise had developed her sense of social consciousness, though never to the extent of touching the fanatic fringe as her sister had. She was, however, passionately opposed to the war in Vietnam; and in 1965, the same year she received a medal from the American Institute of Arts and Letters, she was one of the founders, with Muriel and many of their fellow poets, of the Writers and Artists Protest against the War in Vietnam. Her husband, Mitch, was as deeply involved as Denise, and he, as well as her sister came into her poems and prose poems dealing with the resistance and the prominent activists she admired—A. J. Muste, Father Berrigan, deCourcy Squire, Jennie Orvino, Judy Collins, Dr. Benjamin Spock, to name only a few. Richard Howard, writing in the fall issue of *Tri-Quarterly,* 1966, said of Levertov's work: "Her poems of sexual fulfillment and protest represent her most successful attempts to find images that will ritualize experience, in this way reconciling mysticism and reality, spirit and flesh: the longing for ritual . . . is the subject of all her later poems." The "Olga Poems" first appeared in *The Sorrow Dance,* (1967), a volume devoted in large measure to the sufferings of the victims of war and reprisals against those who tried to resist it. Many of the poems sought to arouse those who showed no concern or even awareness of the cruel struggle in Southeast Asia. It was inevitable that her crusade should affect her poetry, and all of her subsequent volumes until the war ended contained poetry that some critics considered "preachy." Others found it strong and compelling. But no matter what the critics felt, Denise Levertov had to write poetry that expressed her personal, emotional response, viewed with as much objectivity as she could summon, to the crucial and trying events of her life and times.

In 1968, an entry in her *Notebook* dated, "Puerto Rico, Feb. 23," stated, "Mitch has been indicted." He was arrested along with Dr. Spock and three others for conspiring to oppose the draft. While they were awaiting trial, friends of theirs wrote to Denise expressing sympathy in words like "my heart aches for you," which only aroused the poet's fury: Much as she appreciated her friends' concern, she was exasperated by the lack of understanding such words showed. The arrests, however upsetting and discomforting, brought a kind of satisfaction in fulfilling the need to confront the warmakers with their crimes and to arouse the bystanders to action. Mitch and the others were "spokesmen" for many who supported their aims: to stop the draft, to end the war. Their conviction was reversed on appeal, the cases against Goodman and Dr. Spock ordered to be retried. Their experience went into a long poem, "Prologue: An Interim," part of the section "To Stay Alive," and was linked to the celebrated cases of deCourcy Squire, the eighteen-year-old girl who risked death by fasting in order to be released from jail to speak her mind against war; Alice Hertz and Norman Morrison, who took their lives because they had no lawyers to defend them. These are "the great savage saints of outrage."

Within another year Levertov herself had skirmishes with the police and the courts. While a visiting lecturer at Berkeley, California, in 1969, she took part in demonstrations held by students in the People's Park. When they tried to clear the park of illegally thrown garbage, making a "green space" for themselves during the week-long program of protest, and in a day's frenzy of community work and fellowship had succeeded in cleaning that area and digging a garden plot in another place, "law and order" took over with a cordon of police ringing the park. With clubs and tear gas they were guarding the bulldozers that had moved in during the night; a fence "twice a man's height" was already being put up. The tears of frustrated students "fell on cement," and those who in anger tangled with the police in their efforts to stop construction were brutally beaten back. . . . "The War/ comes home to us."

So wrote the poet. She had pitched in beside her students with her usual zest, laughing and singing despite the rough, dirty work, exulting with them, though dog-tired, when the job was completed. But now she was aghast, outraged, at police brutality. All her emotional fury went into her poetry, into a long open-ended *Notebook* from which she drew in narrating the incredibly cruel experience of that particular day: a note at the back of the volume, *To Stay Alive,* published in 1971, reads, "*Thursday, May 15th*—the day in 1969 when James Rector was killed, Alan Blanchard, an artist, blinded, and many people wounded by police buckshot fire while protesting the destruction of the People's Park." In this volume she also included, in a poem about Chuck Matthei, the young revolutionary folksinger, some lines from an earlier poem, "A Man," written of Mitch when he was in jail, awaiting retrial. Chuck found in it a message for all prisoners, and recited or sang the lines in his "journeyings" to jails across the country, giving support to other activists.

This poem-within-a-poem and other new sections of the *Notebook* gave rise to the suggestion by Mitch and Hayden Carruth that she include more earlier poems clearly related to these by their common theme. So in preparing *To Stay Alive* for the press, she decided to reissue the "Olga Poems," placing them at the beginning of the volume. In an explanatory preface she wrote: "The personal response that moves from the identification of my lost sister, as a worker for human rights, with the pacifists 'going limp' as they are dragged to the paddywagon in Times Square in 1966, to the understanding by 1970 that 'there

comes a time when only anger/is love,'* is one shared by many
of us who have come bit by bit to the knowledge that opposition to war, whose foul air we have breathed so long that by
now we are almost choked forever by it, cannot be separated
from opposition to the whole system of insane greed, of racism
and imperialism, of which war is only the inevitable expression." She hoped that readers would understand that the reissue of earlier poems was necessary if the whole fabric of her
work was to be evaluated not as "mere 'confessional' autobiography," but as a "record of one person's inner/outer experience
in America during the sixties and the beginning of the seventies."

Before the sixties were over, Denise Levertov, like Muriel
Rukeyser, was jailed by the Justice Department for her part in
the demonstrations. These two poets strove valiantly for peace,
and in their efforts became close friends. Both were in the delegation of women headed by Jane Harte (wife of the then senator from Michigan) that went to Hanoi to investigate the war
in Vietnam for themselves and to bring back a report which
they hoped would influence Congress to end the war. Nearly
all of section four in *The Freeing of the Dust* is devoted to poems
of the Vietnam experience, beginning with "Weeping Woman,"
a poem of deep pathos, depicting a sorrow-filled mother with
her child, both victims of the war; her right arm is gone and
the baby has been burnt by napalm bombs. Perhaps the most
telling of this group is "In Thai Binh (Peace) Province (For
Muriel and Jane)"—a tribute to her sisters in the resistance
movement and to the valiant Vietnamese who bore their suffering with such quiet stoicism. Both poets expressed their feelings in strong, though different lines of free verse. In contrast
to Rukeyser's flowing lyric often runelike repetition, Levertov
wrote with an economy of words, which in its own way pointed
up the starkness of the war. In "Enquiry," a poem addressed to

*A line from " 'I Thirst,' " one of the new poems in the *Notebook*.

the pilots who dropped the bombs, she asks if they know who is watching them and answers: "She is not old,/ she whose eyes/ know you./ She will outlast you./ She saw/ her five young children/ writhe and die;/ in that hour/ she began to watch you,/ she whose eyes are open forever."

When the delegation returned, through Jane Harte they requested a hearing in the Senate, but it was not granted, and in protest the women delayed a session of that congress body by lying down on the floor by the doorway, blocking entrance to the senate chambers. Refusing to move on orders from the guards, the entire delegation was hauled off by the police and spent a night in jail before appearing before the Justice Department. Thrust all together into an airless cell, "hand in hand, blinded, retching," as Denise wrote of an earlier jailing, but "taking a kind of joy in bodily anguish," because it "meant knowing the grim odds they were up against." They took comfort in each other's company. Muriel's presence, her quiet humor as she viewed their plight with a philosophic eye, struck Denise more than ever as a source of strength; the tie between them increased.

In *The Freeing of the Dust,* copyrighted under the name Denise Levertov Goodman, there is a whole section—number six—devoted to poems concerning her divorce from Mitch. The titles themselves form a record: "The Woman"; "Cross Purposes"; "Living for Two"; "Living Alone (I)"; "Living Alone (II)"; "Living Alone (III)"; "Cloud Poems—for Mitch"; "Don't you Hear the Whistle Blowing?"; "Divorcing"; "Strange Song"; "Grief"; and finally, "Libation." A feeling of regret, if not outright grief, dominates the entire group. As late as September, 1969, she had written, "Love Poem *for Mitch,*" a strange, brief lyric like a portent of the irreparable breakup soon to come. The title of a poem written the same month, "3 a.m., September 1, 1969—for Kenneth Rexroth," indicates sleepless nights; but the mood is calm, a description of the predawn landscape. The lines are from one professional to another: she and Rexroth, with

William Carlos Williams, had been compiling an anthology of contemporary poetry to be published by Penguin. She did not let her marriage problem halt her professionally.

From the time she started teaching as a visiting lecturer at various colleges, she entered into the work of students with lively interest, offering encouragement and constructive criticism, occasionally giving a reading of her own work. Students could bring their friends on these occasions, and the girl friend of one young hopeful at the then City College of New York in the early sixties still remembers the excitement of those events. By the end of the decade, the poet so deeply involved in the peace movement and her personal problems took time to write portraits of her students at the Massachusetts Institute of Technology. She called the series, "A New Year's Garland for My Students/MIT: 1969–70"; the fifth one, "Ernie," a vivid picture of a young guitar-playing poet, closes with the significant lines: "What can I say, Ernie?—/ Younger than my son, you are/ nevertheless my old friend/ whom I trust."

Besides her busy schedule of teaching, lecturing, and working in the resistance movement, Denise Levertov finds time to write occasional reviews of her colleagues' work, articles, criticism, and translations which she attacks with "compulsive anxiety" to make the deadlines. A collection of these essays and lectures was published in 1973 under the title, *The Poet in the World*. Certainly few poets, except possibly her friend Muriel, could be more involved in public welfare generally, in addition to world peace. She fought racism equally as much as she opposed the arms race. And she stood her ground even when her audience deserted her, as they did at Goucher College, Maryland, an incident she embodied in a poem, "The Day the Audience Walked Out on Me and Why." She was speaking at a memorial for the Kent State students who had been fatally shot during an anti-war protest rally; two of her own poems (mentioned in this poem) had been read—all well and good, she said, but a mockery unless the gathering also remembered the black students who had been shot at Orangeburg, and she cited other blacks who had died in the cause of peace. By the time she finished, the chapel was empty, save for one man who said she had "desecrated a holy place." A strong concluding stanza shows her total commitment to society.

It was typical of Denise Levertov's warm, enthusiastic nature that she went to great lengths to promote the work of a sister poet, Hilda Morley, whose gift she felt had not received proper recognition. By a coincidence of birth, these two poets had certain similarities of background and cosmopolitan upbringing, yet their poetry could not be more dissimilar in mood and content. In contrast to Denise, Hilda is a lyric poet, whose lines are reminiscent of H.D., a poet she admired and met early in her career.

Born in New York City of German-Jewish parents, Hilda attended the "progressive" Walden School until her high school years when her mother, who was an ardent Zionist, took her to Israel to live. There the girl studied Hebrew and became proficient in that classical language, a skill that eventually changed the course of her life. Like Denise, Hilda had loved poetry and began writing verse as a small child. From Israel she went to England to attend the University of London. Although shy, she summoned up the courage to call H.D., and to her surprise, the Imagist poet invited her to tea.

"Maybe it was because we both had the name Hilda given us," Morley said in 1981. "And because I was an American, and told her how much I revered her poetry." At any rate, H.D. showed much interest in the young girl's work, and offered to introduce her to T. S. Eliot, but the offer was turned down, for shyness overcame the student-poet. She grew panicky at the thought of meeting Eliot or any of the great names H.D. suggested. After two years at the University of London, she returned to the United States and finished her college education at Wellesley. While still in college she met and married the painter Gene Morley. Both were young, struggling, and hypersensitive, and they soon separated. However, it was under this married name that Hilda began sending out an occasional poem, and the first accepted credited Hilda Morley as author. She retained the name, although she could have used a more famous one, that of her second husband, the well-known composer, Stefan Wolpe. The two met when Wolpe, who had just immigrated from Israel, needed someone to translate Hebrew lyrics of his songs into English, and Wellesley College suggested Hilda Morley. The composer, twenty years older than she, was struck by her youthful beauty as well as her skill in translating from the Hebrew; Hilda on her part was carried away by reverent admiration for the man and his music. Wolpe, like her, was separated from his spouse, and when both had won their divorces, they were married.

During the 1950s they joined the Black Mountain School of creative artists, then in its heyday under the guidance of Charles Olson, Robert Duncan, and Robert Creeley. Wolpe was on the staff, teaching as well as composing, and Morley practised her skill as poet in the shadow of her husband's career. He urged her to send out more of her poems, but she rarely did, preferring to wait until she was sure of her skill. Robert Creeley has recalled that she was "like some extraordinary English milkmaid, walking along through Black Mountain as on some summer day." Toward the end of the decade she came into contact with Denise Levertov, first through the latter's poetry, and then after a reading by Denise, when they met and discovered their mutual love of making poems. A close friendship followed; with Denise as a prod, Hilda sent out a few poems, but they were usually rejected, which left the poet so dejected that she would not send more. Levertov, however, was convinced that a poet who could write such a phrase as "burning with travail" in describing Keats when he was "striving for the ultimate accuracy" was worthy of publication. So were poems like "Truro, January 1964" written "for Denise Levertov," an impressionistic description of the snowy scene outside the window where the poet sits writing, and, behind her, the room rising into her consciousness: "a movement/ of breathing/ inhalation/ of warmth/ a wideness/ resurgent toward me." The sensuous appeal of accepted elements and objects is uppermost in Morley's poems.

However, she was sending them out less and less, due largely to her husband's illness: Wolpe had developed Parkinson's disease, which became more distressing over the years, and Hilda devoted herself to making life as easy for him as possible. So it was Denise Levertov who systematically sent out Hilda Morley's work. "I used to include two addresses for the return stamped envelope. If a poem was rejected, it was to be returned to me; if accepted, Hilda was to be notified; that way she would never know how many rejects there were for every acceptance." But the ratio gradually equalized, and one day, after Morley's poems had appeared in *Black Mountain Review, The Nation, New Directions, The American Poetry Review, The Hudson Review,* and publications of like quality, Denise decided it was time for a manuscript of book length to be compiled. She helped her friend to make selections, offered key suggestions in the matter of presentation, and finally, with the aid of a grant from the National Endowment for the Arts, a volume entitled, *A Blessing Outside Us,* from the last poem in the book, appeared under the imprint of Pourboire press, a small, quality house.

More than that could hardly be expected from one poet to another, but Levertov was not satisfied until she had launched her friend's book in full sway. Wolpe had died after the long struggle with Parkinson's, and Hilda was still under the pall of his passing, too drained to promote her own book. One of the deeply poignant poems, "For Stefan 26 Months Later" reveals the extent of her sorrow in the wish "only/ to see you sitting with me/ at a table & a red-and-white/ tablecloth between us,/nothing more." So it was Denise who brought the little volume to the attention of Hayden Carruth, poetry editor at *Harper's,* who was astonished at the caliber of Morley's poems. He had met her, and knew vaguely that she wrote, but he had no idea that hers was "an absolutely sure lyrical voice," as he phrased it in a review in *Harper's* magazine. "*A Blessing Outside Us* is published by a very small, subsidized press. But it is worth searching for. It is a splendid book." With such praise as this, and an excellent review by Rosellen Brown in the *American Book Review*, Morley's first volume was a complete sellout, and orders for more copies kept coming.

"It would never have happened without Denise's help," Hilda said in 1981. As for Levertov, she is continuing to promote her friend's work, and that of any poet whom she feels is worthy of recognition. In 1983, Hilda Morley received a Guggenheim Fellowship, and was the featured poet in a leading literary journal.

Like many modern poets, Levertov has had her share of detractors. There are those who call her lines "Shredded prose." She has been labelled a feminist William Carlos Williams; and she freely admits the influence of Williams in her work. But her own voice rings clear also. It often has been publicly recognized by her peers. As winner of the 1975 Lenore Marshall Poetry Prize, she was accurately portrayed by Hayden Carruth, who said: "For twenty-five years Denise Levertov has been one of our most prominent poets. . . . Today she is a woman at the crest of her maturity, acute in perceptions, wise in responses, and an artist, moreover, whose technique has kept pace with her personal development." His esteem was justified by her next volume, *Life in the Forest,* published in 1978. A year later, when Levertov's *Collected Earlier Poems, 1940–1960* appeared, her publishers through the years pointed out that "readers have the opportunity at last of following Ms. Levertov's remarkable poetic development from its very beginnings." One of these early poems, "Illustrious Ancestors," calling up the memory of her two grandfathers, the "Rav" (Rabbi) of Russia and the Mystic of Mold (a tailor by trade), seems to epitomize the aims and achievements of this poet. From the devout Rav who declined to learn the language of birds, but listened well as he prayed "to the bench and the floor," and the Mystic of Mold whose meditations were sewn into coats and britches, she drew inspiration and formula for creation of poems: "I would like to make,/ . . . poems direct as what the birds said,/ hard as a floor, sound as a bench,/ mysterious as the silence when the tailor/ would pause with his needle in the air."

Her later poems are proof that she has realized her desire to emulate her ancestors. At the ceremonies of the American Academy of Arts and Letters in June of 1980, Denise Levertov was honored as a newly elected member of the institute; and in October she was one of the delegates to a World Peace Parliament held in Bulgaria. She told this interviewer shortly after her return, "There were three thousand people taking part—people from all over the world." Her eyes shone. "It was very exciting." She went on to tell of a writers conference held the week after the parliament, during which two hundred fifty writers in all fields—poetry, fiction, nonfiction, "but no journalists!"— drew up a statement against war and the preparation for war. One had the feeling that the parliament or the writers conference would soon be a poem, as all her experiences became. This is her life: "To make/ of song a chalice,/ of Time,/ a communion wine."*

*The closing lines from no.V of a series, "Entr'acte," in her volume *To Stay Alive*.

Elizabeth Bishop

I t has been said by Babette Deutsch and others writing literary criticism that Elizabeth Bishop may be considered one
of Marianne Moore's literary descendants, which may have been
accurate in the 1940s and 1950s, but by the mid-1970s it was
not an overstatement to say that Elizabeth Bishop rightfully assumed the mantle of Marianne Moore. Although she herself died
unexpectedly only seven years after Moore, Elizabeth Bishop is
still the star of late twentieth century American poets of her sex,
whose light is one of the brightest among poets, regardless of
sex.

Her rise to this shining eminence was not meteoric, by any

measure. Her early childhood, which might have been idyllic, was marked by the traumas of tragic events. She was born in Worcester, Massachusetts on February 8, 1911, of a family on her father's side well known in prosperous middle class society for the construction firm started by her grandfather—J. W. Bishop & Sons—responsible for such imposing municipal edifices as the Boston Public Library and the Museum of Fine Arts. J. W. had originally come from Canada's Prince Edward Island, but on his marriage to a girl from a pioneer New England family, the Fosters, had settled and "made good" in Worcester. Elizabeth's father, Thomas Bishop, as the oldest son, had joined the firm after completing his education. He was evidently a gentle, good-looking, thoughtful man with literary leanings, who was thirty-seven before he married.

His wife, ten years younger than he, was a Canadian girl, Gertrude Bulmer, the middle one of three daughters in a country household of Nova Scotia's picturesque Acadian landscape. Elizabeth's mother, a frail beauty, was apparently dependent emotionally (as well as financially) on her husband, particularly after Elizabeth's birth, which occurred two and a half years following their marriage. The future poet was only eight months old when her father died suddenly. The shock was too great for her mother to bear, bringing on a nervous collapse and eventual insanity from which there was no recovery. Elizabeth was virtually an orphan at eight months, although she saw her mother several times in the next few years.

At first, Gertrude Bulmer Bishop had gone home to the tiny hamlet of Great Village, Nova Scotia, carrying her infant child. "Then she had gone away again, alone, and left the child. Then she had come home. Then she had gone away again, with her sister; and now she was home again. . . ." So Elizabeth Bishop gave the background to a superbly wrought, heartrending story, "In The Village," written long after her mother's final attempt to regain sanity had failed disastrously. By that time Elizabeth was nearly four years old, and considered her grandparents' simple country house as home. The Bulmers had come from a New York State family of early settlers who had been given land grants in Nova Scotia at the time of the American Revolution. Her grandfather was a small farmer, quiet, good-natured and kind. Her grandmother, no less kind, was the daughter of a seafaring master mariner, William Hutchinson, part owner of a sailing vessel that had gone down during a storm, the fury of which cost the lives of captain and crew. Three of Elizabeth's Hutchinson uncles were Baptist missionaries in India; and another, George, ran away to sea at the age of fourteen, and later became a painter (portrayed in her poem, "Large Bad Picture"). Her own love of the sea, of travel, and adventure obviously came from the Hutchinson family.

Her mother, when she had gone away the second time ("with her sister"), had been taken by her concerned sister Grace (Elizabeth's older aunt) to McLean's sanitarium, outside Boston, where a year's stay under supposedly expert care had brought no improvement. So in the summer of 1916, Gertrude Bishop had come home to stay, the goods from her well-to-do household in Worcester preceding her. It was hoped that the familiar surroundings of her childhood and youth in the peaceful village would restore her. And, significantly, at the opening of the autobiographical narrative—more of a prose poem than a short story—she had decided to "come out of black"—the first step toward casting off grief, and was being fitted by the village dressmaker for a bright purple dress, while her mother, two sisters, and small Elizabeth stood watching. From outside came the clang-*clang* of the blacksmith's hammer and anvil, to Elizabeth a beautiful sound, "a pure angelic note."

Suddenly, in the midst of the fateful fitting, her mother, who had been fretting about the brightness of the color of the material (sent by her mother-in-law), without warning, gave a fearful scream, the frail, frantic scream of a madwoman. Terrified, subconsciously sensing crisis, her small daughter "vanished" instantly, finding refuge in the blacksmith's shop, "where things

hang up in the shadows and shadows hang up in the things";
where Nate, the strong sweaty blacksmith, pumps his bellows
and sings; and the "attendant horse" stamps his foot and nods
his head "as if agreeing to a peace treaty. . . ." While her
grandmother and her mother, between her "older" and "younger"
aunt, sit on the back porch sipping red raspberry vinegar to calm
themselves, the young Elizabeth Bishop found infinite comfort
in the elemental surroundings of the blacksmith's shop. The descriptions of the horse and the big Newfoundland dog, the
shoeing process and the drivers who watch, standing at ease,
gossiping, chewing (or spitting) tobacco, or a matchstick, are
testimony to the observant eye of the poet in the four-year-old
Elizabeth Bishop.

There were momentary signs of improvement in her mother
during that uneasy summer, and the scream they were all ap-
prehensively expecting did not occur again. Through the daily
routine, as the child takes the family cow to pasture every
morning, the reader gathers salient details of the village and its
inhabitants, their friendliness and simple, peaceful existence. But
toward fall, a fire in a neighbor's barn, which destroys in a fierce
red blaze the newly harvested hay, also destroys the remaining
fragment of sanity in the deranged mother, and she is taken away
soon afterward. Her bedroom is empty; her mourning clothes
hang in the closet—the purple dress was never finished. Every
week a parcel packed with fruit, cake, perhaps a jar of preserves
or a box of chocolates is mailed to an address the child keeps
hidden from sight under her arm as she takes the package to
the post office. Only the kindly old clerk knows where it goes.
He says, "Your grandmother is very faithful." The daily life of
the village continues, but it is never the same. The scream,
though faint, still pierces the peaceful atmosphere and will echo
down the years forever. To balance it comes the *clang!* of the
blacksmith's shop: "It is the elements speaking; earth, air, fire,
water. . . . Oh, beautiful sound, strike again!" ends the story.

The actual facts of Gertrude Bishop's final breakdown in 1916

are so close to the events of the story that the latter is undoubtedly a faithful, and poetic presentation. The poet's mother had
lost her American citizenship when her husband died, and so
she could not return to McLeans in Boston, but had to go instead to a mental institution in Dartmouth, Nova Scotia. The
Bishops in Worcester made every effort to secure permission
for her return, but were unsuccessful. She was kept in the Canadian hospital, insane, for the rest of her life. Though she did
not die until 1934, Elizabeth never saw her again. The tragedy
was accepted sorrowfully but fatalistically by the family in Great
Village, and their little granddaughter absorbed their views.

"Sestina," a touching, profound poem, recalls a scene that illustrates the attitude with the perception of the poet as both
child and adult; in six stanzas of six lines each, followed by a
three-line coda, Bishop has created a universe of the inner and
outer worlds in the days after her mother was taken away.*

> *September rain falls on the house.*
> *In the failing light, the old grandmother*
> *sits in the kitchen with the child*
> *beside the Little Marvel Stove,*
> *reading the jokes from the almanac,*
> *laughing and talking to hide her tears.*
>
> *She thinks that her equinoctial tears*
> *and the rain that beats on the roof of the house*
> *were both foretold by the almanac,*
> *but only known to a grandmother.*

As the iron kettle starts to sing on the stove, she cuts some bread
and tells the child it's time for tea, but the child sits watching
the kettle's "small hard tears dance like mad"—surely a sublim-
inal reference to her mother—on the stove, equating them with
the rain on the roof. The grandmother hangs up the "clever"
almanac by its string on a hook over the stove, where, "bird-

---

*First published in *The New Yorker,* 1953.

like," it hovers half open above the child, above the grandmother and her teacup brimming with "dark brown tears"; she
shivers and puts more wood in the stove.

> It was to be, *says the Marvel Stove.*
> I know what I know, *says the almanac.*
> *With crayons the child draws a rigid house*
> *and a winding pathway. Then the child*
> *puts in a man with buttons like tears*
> *and shows it proudly to the grandmother.*
>
> *But secretly, while the grandmother*
> *busies herself about the stove,*
> *the little moons fall down like tears*
> *from between the pages of the almanac*
> *into the flower bed the child*
> *has carefully placed in the front of the house.*
>
> Time to plant tears, *says the almanac.*
> *The grandmother sings to the marvellous stove*
> *and the child draws another inscrutable house.*

The masterful craftsmanship of this poem came about after
years of creative effort, but the perception and feeling had to
be present from the beginning. Elizabeth Bishop lived with her
Bulmer grandparents a few more years and spent her summers
with them for a number of years. "Manners (For a Child of
1918)," written around the same time as the above poem, epitomizes the feeling she had for her grandfather, as well as his
gentle, genial character. (A devout Baptist, he was a deacon in
the church, and she once recalled that he used to slide a spicy
white peppermint into her palm when she put her offering in
the collection plate he was handing around.)

> *My grandfather said to me*
> *as we sat on the wagon seat,*
> *"Be sure to remember to always*
> *speak to everyone you meet."*

Elizabeth Bishop

> *We met a stranger on foot.*
> *My grandfather's whip tapped his hat.*
> *"Good day, sir. Good day. A fine day."*
> *And I said it and bowed where I sat.*

> .   .   .   .

> *When automobiles went by,*
> *The dust hid people's faces,*
> *But we shouted "Good day! Good day!*
> *Fine day!" at the top of our voices.*

> *When we came to Hustler Hill,*
> *he said that the mare was tired,*
> *so we all got down and walked,*
> *as our good manners required.*

Although she attended the small country school in Great Village (where children in the primer class were provided with bottles of water and rags to wipe their slates), Elizabeth Bishop's early education was interrupted by illness from the beginning: she suffered from severe bronchial colds with a tendency toward asthma and had to be kept home from school frequently. Whether it was due to the harsh winters of Nova Scotia, the stringent life—there was no electricity, no plumbing, no "central heating" in the Bulmers' farmhouse—or simply that her Bishop grandparents thought she would have more "advantages" living with them, the future poet was sent to live with her paternal grandparents in the fall of 1918.

The abrupt change was cataclysmic. Gone was the simple, quiet life of Great Village, the peaceful home and family affection she had known (virtually) since birth; and in its place was a bustling, noisy city, an alien, complex household. Her Bishop relatives were not unkind, but they were as bewildered as she by the effects of this enormous disparity on an unusually sensitive, intuitive child. Her bronchitis grew woefully worse and she suffered actual asthmatic attacks (now known to be brought on by psychological causes); eczema, and signs of St. Vitus' dance appeared. The unpremeditated change in this particular child's life was like "a fall from innocence"* to her; it was unforgettable and, perhaps, unforgivable.

The Bishops finally sought the help of her mother's sister, Elizabeth's Aunt Maud (the "younger aunt" of the story), who was married, but had no children. She was glad to provide a home for her niece in their childless household in Boston, and her very presence provided a link for Elizabeth to her lost life in Nova Scotia. The little girl's health slowly improved, but for the next nine years she never was able to go to school for a full term. The long winter months were spent in bed, reading, devouring books far beyond the grasp of an eight-year-old. Her passionate love for music as well as books began during those solitary months, for she was able to take piano lessons and to spend part of her day practising. Ill, and without playmates for the usual pastimes, she began to write poetry.

By the time she was twelve, she was strong enough to spend two months at the Nautical Camp for girls, in Wellfleet, Cape Cod. As the name suggests, sailing was emphasized, and, perhaps because of her Hutchinson ancestry, Elizabeth quickly acquired the skill of handling a skiff, a favorite sport for the rest of her life. From then on, her summers were divided between Nova Scotia and the camp; and when she was sixteen she was sent to boarding school at Walnut Hill, Natick, Massachusetts, where, as at camp, she made a few friends. However, in the main, her childhood and adolescence were lonely. Despite the fond devotion of her aunts—her "older aunt" also lived in Boston—Elizabeth Bishop, because of shyness and her chronic afflictions, led a solitary life. And, in contrast to Louise Bogan, who turned to books to escape her parents, Elizabeth Bishop discovered in books a more companionable world to compensate for the lack of parents.

She had a preference for books of poetry. Whitman was her

*From Anne Stevenson's *Elizabeth Bishop* (See Bibliography), p. 34

favorite at fifteen, and when, at sixteen, she received a copy of Gerard Manley Hopkins's poems, she was so carried away that she learned most of the volume by heart. An English teacher at boarding school led her to Shakespeare and the Romantic poets, lent her books, and urged her to write. But it was at Vassar College, which she entered in 1930, that Elizabeth finally found among both students and faculty members kindred spirits with whom her intelligence and keen insight was not only appreciated, but encouraged; and she suddenly began to flourish, physically as well as intellectually. Henry MacCracken was still president, and the liberalism, "creative gaiety" and awareness of social issues that had prevailed during Edna Millay's years at the college had, if anything, increased with the onslaught of the Depression, which assumed serious proportions in 1930. Little more than a dozen years had passed since Millay graduated, and the effects of her escapades among succeeding classes had not yet subsided; and it is likely that Bishop attended one of the readings that its celebrated alumna gave at Vassar in the early thirties.

Although Elizabeth Bishop began to shed her shyness in her freshman year, she was selective in her choice of companions and, similarly, was attractive to people who were her peers in perception and wit. One of these was Mary McCarthy, who was in the class ahead of hers. The latter, who later caricatured some of their circle in her novel, *The Group,* (omitting Elizabeth out of esteem) was quick to recognize the younger girl's gifts, and they became lifelong friends. A bond between them may have been that both had known exceptional grandmothers from early childhood. (Mary, who came from Seattle, Washington, was to immortalize her Jewish grandmother in her "Memories of a Catholic Girlhood," published in the *New Yorker,* the magazine that has been the outlet for so many of Bishop's poems.) *

---

*Three years after graduating from Vassar, Mary McCarthy married Edmund Wilson, (his second wife), who insisted that she write the above stories for *The New Yorker.*

At one point during Elizabeth's sophomore year, she and Mary banded together with a few rebels to protest against the editorial policies of the *Vassar Review* by starting a strictly "modern" literary publication. After a few issues, they were invited to join the older magazine, and a merger followed. However, the conflict between the "intellectuals" and the average run of Vassar girls continued as it always had. A page of caricatures appeared in an issue after the merger depicting Elizabeth Bishop with two of her friends above the legend, "The Higher Type." This sort of ridicule arose no doubt from the poet's natural reserve, which probably seemed to many of her college-mates a lofty self-esteem, but was in reality a leftover shyness from her years of seclusion and sickness.

In general, she was approachable and had many close friends among her classmates. One of them proposed a walking trip in the summer of 1932. As she grew stronger, Elizabeth was eager to prove (to herself as well as others) that she could lead a normal, even strenuous life; and she suggested that they tour Newfoundland on foot. Since it was then a wild, relatively untraveled region, the venture required the utmost temerity, but they surmounted the obstacles and returned triumphant—an exhilarating experience for the poet, who from then on was an addictive traveller, active in hiking, sailing, swimming, and fishing. Like many victims of asthma—the most notable, Theodore Roosevelt—she probably found that the more outdoor exercise she had, the healthier she became.

Her poetry during the last two years at Vassar became more polished in style, mimicking the seventeenth century metaphysical poets, clever, even satiric; or sometimes macabre, mysterious, and dream-haunted, revealing the influence of Rimbaud and the nightmarish narratives of Poe. But while she perfected her style, Elizabeth Bishop protected her emotions, allowing only brief glimpses of sorrow or sympathy to come through. A sonnet entitled "Some Dreams They Forgot" begins darkly, "The dead birds fell, but no one had seen them fly,/ or could guess from where. . . ." and ends in a series of queries, the questing uncertainty of subconscious and conscious life. She also wrote a quantity of brilliant, parable-like short stories at Vassar, one of which, "In Prison," was published in the *Partisan Review* for March, 1938, four years after her graduation.

She was editor of the college yearbook in her senior year, one of the outstanding students receiving her A.B. degree in literature. That year, 1934, strangely joined by fate, two events occurred: she received word that her mother died in the sanitarium and, almost at the same time, she met Marianne Moore. Although she had hardly remembered her mother except for the scream—and certainly in this instance death was a blessing—it represented a loss. And when Elizabeth Bishop met Marianne Moore, who was more than twice her age, it can perhaps be said that a soul mother replaced the blood mother she had never known. Not that Marianne Moore was in any way maternal— she would be the last to adopt a maternal air—but, aside from being a lifelong friend, she was someone that the younger poet could look up to as a guiding star or even a (very earthy) guardian angel.* The year following her graduation, Elizabeth lived by herself in a "garret" in Greenwich Village, and she must often have exchanged visits with the older poet, frequently making the trip to the Moores' Myrtle Avenue apartment in Brooklyn. The angel image is subtly suggested in the explicit expression of her affectionate admiration, "Invitation to Miss Marianne Moore," a gaily designed birthday tribute:

From Brooklyn, over the Brooklyn Bridge, on this fine morning,
    please come flying.
In a cloud of fiery pale chemicals,
    Please come flying,
to the rapid rolling of thousands of small blue drums

*The concept has basis in the attitude of other poets: Louise Bogan called M. M. "the saint of American poetry" in voting for the H. Monroe Poetry award, 1944. (Letter to Morton Zabel)

descending out of the mackerel sky
over the glittering grandstand of harbor-water,
   please come flying. . . .

Written some time later and patterned after a more serious poem by Pablo Neruda, with whom Elizabeth Bishop became friends in 1943, this delightful paeon of praise for Marianne Moore is a definitive example of Bishop's gift for combining whimsical imagination with a brilliant display of technique. The panegyric goes on offering gems of poetic fancy, as, for example, "For whom the grim museums will behave/ like courteous male bower-birds;/ for whom the agreeable lions lie in wait/ on the steps of the Public Library,/ eager to rise and follow through the doors; up into the reading rooms. . . ." The reprise of succeeding stanzas echoes the "invitation" to "come flying over the Brooklyn Bridge on this fine morning," achieving a rhythmic harmony that is rare in modern poetry, and signalizes the rapport between the two poets.

Keeping her forty-dollar-a-month Greenwich Village apartment, Bishop began her travels in 1935 with her first trip abroad. She lived mainly in Paris, but spent most of that summer in Brittany, staying in an isolated farmhouse by herself, but she apparently had little time to be lonely for she was reading Rimbaud in French with intense excitement, and there is ample evidence of the effect of his poetry in her work. The winter was spent in Paris with a friend. Here surrealism was at its height among the artists, and there is little doubt that Elizabeth Bishop felt its influence, or rather, recognized in the surrealists her own tendency to interrelate the mundane with the dream world. "A Miracle for Breakfast," set on a hotel balcony overlooking the Seine, as she and her friend wait for the dawn, for "coffee and the charitable crumb," and the "beautiful villa" that bursts upon her vision with the rising sun, correlates the real with the imaginary, ending on an ironic note. Even more pronounced is "Jerónimo's House," a later charming octavial poem in which each

of the eight (and eight-line) stanzas is filled with cogent details
that create the "fairy palace" of the peasant—and which could
easily stand for the poet's own flimsy "shelter from the hurricane." The charm lies in both form and theme:

> My house, my fairy
>   palace, is
> of perishable
>   clapboards with
> three rooms in all,
>   my gray wasps' nest
> of chewed-up paper
>   glued with spit.
>
> My home, my love-nest,
>   is endowed
> with a veranda
>   of wooden lace,
> adorned with ferns
>   planted in sponges,
> and the front room
>   with red and green

> left-over Christmas
>   decorations
> looped from the corners
>   to the middle
> above my little
>   center table
> of woven wicker
>   painted blue,
>
> .   .   .   .
>
> and on the table
>   one fried fish,
> spattered with burning
>   scarlet sauce
> a little dish
>   of hominy grits
> and four pink tissue-
>   paper roses.

Besides Paris, the poet visited England, North Africa, and
Spain before returning to New York in 1936. She spent part
of the winter on the west coast of Florida. A friend invited her
to go on a fishing trip to Key West, and she was so taken by
the town as it was then—sparsely populated, with long stretches
of sandy shore bleached by the brilliant sun, uncluttered by
tourist places—that she made up her mind to settle there later.
That summer she travelled in Ireland, then stayed in Paris again
for six months, from there making journeys to Provence and
Italy.

Returning to New York in 1939, she made plans to live in
Key West at least during the winters. (Like D. H. Lawrence,
part of Elizabeth Bishop's search for a sunny climate stemmed

from her susceptibility to colds and respiratory problems.) She had the foresight, however, to keep her Village garret in New York, and for the next nine years, although most of her time was spent in Key West, Elizabeth had a stopping-place when she came north in the summer, which she usually spent in Nova Scotia (in Cape Breton, not Great Village); sometimes on the way up, she stayed in the mountains of North Carolina. Small wonder that her first volume of poetry, which won the Houghton Mifflin Poetry Award (and included publication) in 1946 was entitled, *North and South*.

Whenever she was in New York, Elizabeth saw her friend Marianne Moore frequently. As might be expected, Bishop began to experiment with syllabic stanzas, and in some instances, the disciple exceeded her mentor. The seemingly simple stanza pattern of "Roosters" is actually most demanding, but so skillfully wrought that the lines smoothly slide into one stanza from another to form cohesive sentences: "In the morning/ a low light is floating/ in the backyard, and gilding/ from underneath/ the broccoli, leaf by leaf;/ how could the night have come to grief?/ gilding the tiny/ floating swallow's belly/ and lines of pink cloud in the sky,/ the day's preamble/ like wandering lines in marble. . . ." This sort of enjambment leads the reader on without straining the attention; and the success of her first volume—which no doubt was most gratifying to her mentor—was due in large measure to the ease and clarity of style which makes the poetry of a profound thinker like Elizabeth Bishop distinctive among American poets.

Except for the interchange between Moore and herself, Bishop's friends were not instrumental in shaping her work. In Key West, through the painter Loren MacIver, she met and became close friends with the philosopher John Dewey. (The poem, "A Cold Spring" is dedicated to his daughter Jane.) Ernest Hemingway's second wife, Pauline, was another good friend. While in New York in 1942, she met the woman who was to become her closest friend, the one with whom she eventually shared her life, Brazilian born Lota Costellat de Macedo Soares. Whether at the suggestion of her new friend, or on her own impulse, Elizabeth spent nine months of the following year (1943) in Mexico where she met Pablo Neruda. The meeting, purely by chance, led to another friendship with a colleague, and through him, Bishop continued her study of Spanish, taking lessons from a Spanish refugee friend of his, a rewarding experience.

Following the recognition brought by her first volume, she was generally accepted as a noteworthy poet, and began to become acquainted with more of her peers, but only a few proved to be close friends. One of these was the late Robert Lowell, whom she met through Randall Jarrell. Lowell remained an interested and inspirational friend until his sudden death in 1977. Perhaps at his urging she applied for and received a Guggenheim Fellowship in 1947, and in 1949 was consultant in poetry at the Library of Congress. She moved to Washington, though she did not care for life in the nation's capital. It was at this time that Ezra Pound was caged in St. Elizabeth's Hospital, a victim of his own fanaticism, perversely brilliant and stubborn. Like a number of poets, including Robert Frost, Bishop often visited the paradoxical Pound, and out of her treks to the sanitarium came her stunning tour de force, "Visits to St. Elizabeths," a parable-like poem, employing the ancient Hebrew (and later nursery rhyme) form* in telling the story of the Exodus from the House of Bondage in Egypt:

"This is the house of Bedlam," it begins. And the second stanza adds to and repeats the first: "This is the man/ that lies in the house of Bedlam." The third adds a descriptive adjective: "This is the time/ of the tragic man/ that lies in the house of Bedlam." She gives a sympathetic yet analytic picture of Pound and some of his fellow inmates, including the "weeping Jew" who goes up and down the corridors dancing and shedding tears:

---

*"This-is-the-house-that-Jack-built"—taken from the Haggadah, the book of ceremonies read on the Seder night of Passover, relating the story of the Exodus.

This is a Jew in a newspaper hat
that dances weeping down the ward
over the creaking sea of board
beyond the sailor
winding his watch
that tells the time
of the cruel man
that lies in the house of Bedlam.

Each time the characters are mentioned, especially "the man," a different word describes him, enlarging his story. After "tragic," Ezra Pound is the "talkative" man, the "honored," the "old, brave," the "cranky"; and, a masterly touch, in the verse above which introduces the Jew, he is the "cruel man/ that lies in the house of Bedlam." Pound is also "busy" and "tedious"; not until the next to the last passage is he designated "the poet"; and in the finale he is in a combined state, "the wretched man/ that lies in the house of Bedlam." The work is signed, "November, 1950." Here is power in poetry.

Shortly after completing the poem, her consultant post terminated and, having received several awards, including the first Lucy Martin Donnelly Fellowship from Bryn Mawr (through Marianne Moore), and that of the American Academy of Arts and Letters, plus word of a Shelley Memorial Award in the offing, Elizabeth planned a long journey around South America, through the straits of Magellan. Her friend Lota, who had returned to Brazil, had been urging her to come to Rio de Janeiro, where she and other friends of the poet lived. She decided to make Rio her first stop, but it was also her last at that time: She was given the fruit of the cashew at a gathering and ate it unknowingly; she was instantly seized by the violent allergies she had suffered in childhood. It was months before she recovered, and by then she had fallen in love with Brazil, her friends, especially Lota, who took tender care of her; for the next fifteen years, the two shared an apartment in Rio and a handsome modern house in the hills of nearby Petrópolis. The latter became something of a literary center for visiting artists in all fields, from Aldous Huxley to Robert Frost and his daughter Lesley (when the good gray poet was literary ambassador to South America.)

Bishop's second volume, *Poems: North and South—A Cold Spring* came out in 1955 and received the Pulitzer Prize for poetry in 1956, along with the *Partisan Review* Fellowship and the Amy Lowell Travelling Fellowship. During this time she translated a Brazilian classic, *The Diary of Helena Morley*—the self-told story of an early adolescent in a remote mining town, which probably recalled Elizabeth's childhood in Nova Scotia. (She translated other prose pieces from the Brazilian and had hoped to bring out a book of them.)

Travel kept luring her to see new sights, of ancient civilizations. She and her friend took a trip down the Amazon and to the "interior" of Brazil. A high point was a journey with Aldous Huxley to Mato Grosso in 1961 to see the Indian tribes. More fellowships came her way. In 1964, on receipt of such from the Academy of American Poets, the summer was spent in Europe again, mostly in England and Italy. It is not surprising that her third volume, which appeared in 1965, should be entitled, *Questions of Travel,* and appropriately begins with her "Arrival at Santos" (in 1952) which was the beginning of her life in Brazil. "Here is a coast; here is a harbor," the first poem opens. "Here, after a meager diet of horizon, is some scenery." But it is meager scenery, and the initial question of travel is indefinite: "Oh, tourist,/ is this how this country is going to answer you/ and your immodest demands for a different world,/ and a better life, and complete comprehension/ of both at last. . . . ?" The title poem asks more cogent questions: "Is it right to be watching strangers in a play/ in this strangest of theatres?/ What childishness is it that while there's a breath of life/ in our bodies, we are determined to rush/ to see the sun the other way around?/ The tiniest green hummingbird in the world?/ . . . Oh, must we dream our dreams/ and have them, too?" Then doubt vanishes: "But surely it would have been a pity/ not to have seen the trees along this road,/ really exaggerated in their beauty/ . . . Not to have had to stop for gas and heard/ the sad, two-noted, wooden tune/ of disparate wooden clogs/ carelessly clacking over/ a grease-stained filling-station floor." Herein lies a clue to Elizabeth Bishop's insatiable thirst for travel, her humanity in selecting the sights she wishes to immortalize, the sounds to remember.

Rarely does the reader find a reference to great cathedrals, well-known works of art, or even (as in Louise Bogan) a Roman fountain in Bishop's entire canon. If she mentions a church, it is like the one in the above poem, directly after the lines quoted. Continuing the thought, she observes: "A pity not to have heard/ the other, less primitive music of the fat brown bird/who sings above the broken gasoline pump/ in a bamboo church of Jesuit baroque: three towers, five silver crosses." For all of these glimpses of beauty amid homely sights, the last stanza still questions travel: *"Continent, city, country, society:/ the choice is never wide and never free./ And here, or there . . . No. Should we have stayed at home,/ wherever that may be?"* The poem that follows is called "Squatter's Children," and on the surface is a delightful picture of two peasant children playing in the mud, trying to dig holes and build a house out of the hard clay soil. They are pitted against the trials of earth and sky, ominous with storm clouds. They laugh at thunder, a yellow puppy dances around. The "Mother's voice, ugly as sin,/ keeps calling to them to come in." The poet speaks: "Children, the threshold of the storm/ has slid beneath your muddy shoes;/ wet and beguiled, you stand among/ the mansions you may choose/ out of a bigger house than yours,/ whose lawfulness endures./ Its soggy documents retain/ your rights in rooms of falling rain." So the smallest "specklike girl and boy" near a "specklike house" are related to the universe. A monologue, "Manuelzinho," evidently the name of the tenant-farmer of her friend Lota, shows the relationship between the classes of society in Latin America as they existed until the 1960s. It is both anthropological and intensely personal. Manuelzinho, who is perhaps the father of the children in the previous poem, is presented as "half squatter, half tenant (no rent)—/ a sort of inheritance," is a source of extreme exasperation and love to the speaker. A vegetable gardener, he is incorrigibly hapless with his crops. In his garden, cabbage and carnations, lettuce and sweet alyssum grow side by side, invariably destroyed by umbrella ants or a spell of incessant rain. He is wily, deals in petty dishonesty, muddles his bookkeeping. He starves himself, his horse, and his family, yet spends his last penny on a hired bus, at the death of his father, to drive the delighted mourners to the funeral. His hat is holey, yet holy; he paints it different colors: gold, and when the gold wears off, green. (The speaker called him "Klorophyll Kid," a quip that made her visitors laugh, for which she apologizes.) The last six lines round out the portrait of both speaker and subject:

> *You helpless, foolish man,*
> *I love you all I can,*
> *I think. Or do I?*
> *I take off my hat, unpainted*
> *and figurative, to you.*
> *Again I promise to try.*

Elsewhere in the Brazilian-laid scenes Bishop describes the lavish and varied foliage of the country in January, not only for the sake of descriptive beauty, but to sympathize with the Indian women—"those maddening little women"—who kept retreating before the plunder of the first Portuguese explorers. "Brazil, January 1, 1502," is a poem that must be read in full to be appreciated. For sheer, lilting rhythm, "Song for the Rainy Season" is a prime example of precise phrasing, evoking the "dim age of water":

> *Hidden, oh hidden*
> *in the high fog*
> *the house we live in,*

> *beneath the magnetic rock,*
> *rain-, rainbow-ridden,*
> *where blood-black*
> *bromelias, lichens,*
> *owls, and the lint*
> *of the waterfalls cling,*
> *familiar, unbidden.*

In the article, "Brazil in the Poetry of Elizabeth Bishop," Candace Slater of Dartmouth College observed: "Having spent almost twenty years in the states of Rio de Janeiro and later Minas Gerais, Elizabeth Bishop is the only major contemporary American poet with a deep firsthand knowledge of Brazil." One has only to read these poems with a Brazilian setting to realize that not only the knowledge but the feeling runs very deep in the poet from the North. The move to Minas Gerais—Ouro Preto—came in 1967, when Bishop restored an old colonial house (built in 1690) which she had bought in 1965. While it was being renovated during 1966, she taught two terms at the University of Washington in Seattle, her first teaching post.

In 1969, a collected volume, *The Complete Poems,* was published and received the National Book Award. Among the lyrics gathered together here is a series of "Songs for a Colored Singer," written and published first in the *Partisan Review* in 1944. According to the poet herself, they were conceived with Billie Holiday in mind. ("I put in a couple of big words just because she sang big words well—'conspiring root' for instance," she said when asked if she had composed the poems to tunes. "I was hoping somebody would compose tunes for *them.*") Songs I and II deal with the man–woman relationship; Song I practically sings without notation, a blues ballad:

> *A washing hangs upon the line,*
> *but it's not mine.*
> *None of the things that I can see*
> *belong to me.*

Elizabeth Bishop

The neighbors got a radio with an aerial;
  we got a little portable.
They got a lot of closet space;
  we got a suitcase.

Her man, LeRoy, has money, but most of it goes for drink.
She sings: "I sit and look at our backyard/ and find it very hard./
What have we got for all his dollars and cents?/—A pile of bottles by the fence." Still, he is faithful and kind, so she will settle
for her meager lot. But when he strays with "other friends" she
says it's time to call a halt. An independent woman, she is going
to "take the bus/ and find someone monogamous." This semi-
comedic tone is altered in the third and fourth songs to express
feelings of concern and sorrow as the subjects change to mother-
and-child, and the welfare and future of an oppressed people.
Song III, composed in the shadow of World War II, is a sombre
"Lullaby"—a word repeated at the start of each stanza. "Adult
and child/ sink to their rest" is followed by: "At sea the big ship
sinks and dies,/ lead in its breast./ Lullaby./ Let nations rage,/
let nations fall./ The shadow of the crib makes an enormous cage/
upon the wall." The blending of tenderness, sorrow, and
toughness toward the stupidity and cruelty of war creates the
effect of a dirge while remaining a lullaby as well.

Song IV is surrealist in its evocation of an ancient grief with
runelike rhythms and strong beat, like an African drum. She asks
what is shining in the leaves "like tears when somebody grieves,/
shining, shining in the leaves?/ Is it dew or is it tears,/ dew or
tears,/ hanging there for years and years/ like a heavy dew of
tears?/ Then that dew begins to fall,/ roll down and fall./ Maybe
it's not tears at all./ See it, see it roll and fall." The poet suggests that the falling dew is a heavy rain of black seeds, and the
sixth stanza carries the image forward: "all the shining seeds take
root,/ conspiring root,/ and what curious flower or fruit/ will
grow from that conspiring root?" The sources of Bishop's prophetic vision are twofold: "Strange Fruit" was one of Billie

Holiday's biggest successes; and it was the song that inspired the title for Lilian Smith's best-selling novel, *Strange Fruit,* published in 1944, the same year that Bishop's "Songs for a Colored Singer" appeared in *Partisan Review.* (An interesting parallel written a generation later is *For Colored Girls Who Have Considered Suicide When the Rainbow is Enuf,* by American-born Ntozake Shange (originally Paulette Williams), produced on Broadway in 1976, and one of the "long-runs" for three seasons. Shange's poetry has been called "mordantly witty, unpredictable, and disciplined." The amazing similarity in point of view, although the technique of the two poets differs widely, is testimony to Bishop's insight and empathy for humanity in general, the oppressed in particular.)

Thus far no composer has set "Songs for a Colored Singer," but Elliott Carter has combined six of Bishop's poems under the title, "A Mirror on which to Dwell," presented by the Speculum Musicae in 1976. His choices were "Anaphora," "Argument," "Sandpiper," "Insomnia," "View of the Capital from the Library of Congress," and "O Breath." The score of the fourth song ("Insomnia") is inscribed by the composer, "for Elizabeth Bishop—a poet on which to dwell." The works were performed again on December 28 of the same year at the Modern Language Association convention in New York when a session was devoted to Bishop's poetry.

From 1970 on, when she was offered a teaching post during the fall term, Elizabeth Bishop taught at Harvard University part of every year. The other months, until 1974, were spent at Ouro Preto, combined, as always, with her travels. (In 1972, she visited Ecuador, the Galápagos Islands, and Peru. Her beloved friend Lota was not well, having suffered a cancerous condition for several years, and Elizabeth wanted to be with her as much as possible. The same year, 1972, an *Anthology of Contemporary Brazilian Poetry,* which she had co-edited with Emanuel Brasil, was published by Wesleyan University Press. (Earlier she had been given the Order of Rio Brannco by the Brazilian government.) When her friend Lota succumbed to the dread disease, she left Brazil. The household at Ouro Preto was no more. And aside from her personal reasons, Brazil under the present political regime is no longer the country she loved so much in the early fifties that she could not leave. She made no secret of her displeasure with the present government.

After teaching at Harvard and the University of Washington again, she took a long trip to the Scandinavian countries, and finally moved to the Boston waterfront to make her home in 1974. Awards kept coming her way, culminating in the *Books Abroad/* Neustadt International Prize for literature awarded by an international jury of writers convened at the University in Norman, Oklahoma, where she received the prize on April 9, 1976, in impressive public ceremonies, including a double presentation by Marie-Claie Blais of Canada and John Ashberry, her distinguished colleague. Papers were given by internationally representative figures, from Octavio Paz of Mexico City to Penelope Mortimer of London, and Howard Moss of New York. (Paz made the definitive statement, "The poetry of Elizabeth Bishop has the lightness of a game and the gravity of a decision.")

Geography III, Bishop's latest volume, received universal acclaim from the critics, and one expected that this poet would go on producing the kind of poetry Howard Moss cited as "ageless" as long as her observant eye, her amazing flashes of insight, her controlled emotion and imagination continue to be aware of the marvels of life: its amusing, beautiful, homely, and human facets, closely interrelated with the world of nature and animal life. Her friends found her considerate, amusing, and gently ironic in her humor, an extremely civilized and lively person. (Elizabeth Bishop was a beautiful child judging from her photographs, whose features, especially the large dreamy eyes, give evidence of the above qualities at an early age; and in later years she was a beautiful woman, despite the traces of time and sorrow one saw in her face.) Her voice in her poetry readings had the New England rasp reminiscent of Robert Frost's matter-of-fact yet somehow mystical tone, rising from the otherworldly outlook of a poet. One has the feeling, as the novelist Celia Bertin pointed out, that "her main concern is the secret and mysterious chemistry which induces her to feel and to care for, to observe and to react to all that happens around her! . . . Her mixed impressions are always strong, and can be very painful." She is "closely akin to the fine artisan who faces the concrete job of making a masterpiece out of good materials and skillful work." Carrying the analogy even farther, Howard Moss wrote, "Starting with 'The Map,' we are in the hands of an artist so secure in the knowledge of what makes and doesn't make a poem that a whole generation of poets—and remarkably different ones—has learned to know what a poem is through her practice. . . . There is no need to revise them for future editions, the way Auden revised and Marianne Moore revised and Robert Lowell revised. Nothing need be added, nothing taken away. They constitute a body of work in which the innovative and the traditional are bound into a single way of looking." He concludes, "From a poet's point of view, these poems are the ones of all her contemporaries that seem to me most to reward rereading."

The "Poet Laureate" herself, in accepting the Neustadt Prize, commented on the fact that her poem "Sandpiper" had been selected for printing on the program: "Yes," she reflected, "all my life I have lived and behaved very much like that sandpiper—just running along the edges of different countries and continents, looking for something." Unlike the sandpiper, however, Elizabeth Bishop turned the morsels she found into immutable art. She died suddenly, unexpectedly, of a cerebral hemorrhage, in October, 1979.

May Swenson

It has been said that some people are born disillusioned—in the best sense of the word—and May Swenson might be considered one of the few. The eldest child in a brood of ten children whose Swedish parents had left the faith of their fathers to become ardent Mormons, May, born in 1913, on the twenty-eighth day of the month for which she was named, in Logan, Utah, was indoctrinated into Mormonism at the age of eight; but five years later, when at thirteen, she was teaching Sunday school, she began to regard the fundamentalism of Bible stories as fables or myths. Her viewpoint would have shocked her parents, particularly her father, whose heart and soul was bound up in his religion.

Daniel Arthur Swenson had come to the United States from his native Sweden as a young seeker of the religious truth he found in all he had heard about Mormonism. He worked his way across country, on the railroad, as a cowhand, till he reached the Mormon Center in Utah. A hard worker of high intelligence, he educated himself, took a Bachelor's degree in agriculture and then a Master's in mechanical engineering and wood building. At the age of twenty-one, he was "called" on a mission, sent back to Sweden to spread the word of Mormonism. During his years there he converted and fell in love with a very young girl, Margaret Elizabeth Helborg, but they could not be married until she had been formally indoctrinated into the Mormon church in Utah, in the beautiful Temple or Tabernacle in Salt Lake City. The couple settled in the little town of Logan, and immediately began to beget and raise a large family. One of the cardinal precepts of their chosen religion was the reproduction of the human race, no matter what social changes were wrought by the mechanization of the means of livelihood, or the possibility of a future population explosion. Procreation was—and is—a prime precept, one with which the future poet could not agree, perhaps because as the oldest she had to help most with the babies as they came along, but more because from early childhood she was a thinker, interested in books. Many years later, she related that she had always liked to observe and think things out for herself. "Your own perceptions and senses come first," she said. "Then perhaps you can look at others'."

She expressed little of her feelings to her parents. They were strict in a way, but quiet, never quarreled audibly—or inwardly, as far as May could see—since they were of one accord in their beliefs and actions. With their Scandinavian heritage they were hardworking, thrifty, always occupied with useful and spiritual pursuits. Her father's woodworking skill enabled him to design and build much of the furniture in their house. As the children became of school age, they all were given household duties to perform and they worked together as a family.

They all went to church and to Sunday school as a matter of course. And all but May and her youngest brother, Paul, who became a journalist and publishes a magazine in Utah, accepted the Mormon precepts without question. However, she kept her own counsel, out of respect and love for her parents, as well as sheer common sense, of which May Swenson has full measure; it told her that open rebellion would only bring sorrowful rebuke from her parents and concerned alarm for the safety of her soul in the "hereafter." (Two evenings a week her mother went to sit with the church circle that prayed for the conversion of the souls of her ancestors who died without benefit of Mormonism.)

Her childhood, moreover, was not overburdened with religious rigour; like most children with an ounce of imagination, and May had more than enough to balance her common sense, she was able to create her own fantasy world, particularly in outdoor pastimes during the long golden days of summer. Her poem, "The Centaur," in the early volume, *A Cage of Spines,* is one of the delights of Swenson readers in its description of her make-believe and real world. "The summer that I was ten" begins the first of twenty three-line stanzas and one final four-line revealing a little tomboy's solitary joy of living-playing. She is "the centaur": we learn in the first six stanzas how the transformation takes place as she goes each day to choose a fresh horse from her stable, "which was a willow grove/ down by the old canal./ I'd go on my two bare feet." But when, with her brother's jackknife, she had cut and peeled a willow wand and "cinched her brother's belt around the thick knob of her horse's head"; she would "trot along in the lovely dust," her head and her neck were hers, "yet they were shaped like a horse." Drawing a graphic picture, she shows a horse who "shied and skittered and reared, . . . pawed at the ground and quivered," an accurate, action-filled picture: "I was the horse and the rider," she proclaims, "and the leather I slapped to his rump/ spanked my own behind."

After several more striking strophes, the girl-centaur suddenly becomes two separate creatures as they drew up to the porch of the Swensons' house. Reality returns, but not entirely. "I tethered him to a paling./ Dismounting, I smoothed my skirt/ and entered the dusky hall./ My feet on the clean linoleum/ left ghostly toes in the hall." The last three stanzas form a masterly rendition of parent-child relationship and the merging of two worlds through the medium of a mature poet:

> Where have you been? *said my mother.*
> Been riding, *I said from the sink,*
> *and filled me a glass of water.*
>
> What's that in your pocket? *she said.*
> Just my knife. *It weighted my pocket*
> *and stretched my dress awry.*
>
> Go tie back your hair, *said my mother,*
> *and* Why is your mouth all green?
> Rob Roy, he pulled me some clover
> as we crossed the field, *I told her.*

Here is an encapsulated account of May Swenson's childhood in a small western town. Although her parents' partiality for Mormonism had some influence on her early life, it did not smother her capacity for "thinking things out," as in her querying poem, "The Universe," ("What/ is it about,/ the universe/ the universe about us stretching out?") which is set in a visual pattern suggesting a puzzle and a puzzled mind seeking an answer. (One must read the poem to figure out the full significance of the pattern; for example, the key words "think" and "about" and "universe" are repeated in the same place—"think" at the end of six consecutive lines—to form half-hidden columns vertically within the horizontal lines.) Perhaps this makes too much of a game of poetry, but in this, and the poem, "God," which follows it in a different pattern, the device is so skillfully done that it is an integral part of the inner meaning of the metaphysical poems in the volume, *To Mix With Time*. Such mental creativity, sometimes profound, sometimes merely dextrous, was the result of Swenson's Swedish-American-Mormon upbringing.

Her father's reverence for religion was exceeded only by his respect for education; and May, working summers to help pay for tuition in addition to scholarships she received, attended Utah State Agricultural College (now a state university), graduating at the age of twenty-one, with a B.A. degree in English. She worked on the *Deseret* and on the Logan *Herald* newspapers as a regular reporter for three years. She kept abreast of all that was going on in the literary world, and realized that the East was the center of artistic activity, and that New York was the publishing center of the country. When she heard that a cousin of hers was going East to Jacob's Pillow for the summer in 1937, and would like to have May accompany her, she made up her mind to leave Logan and live in New York City, but again, she said nothing to her parents. Her plan would depend on her ability to find a job in New York. If there was none to be had, she would be coming home anyway, so there was no need to make an issue of the matter. Yet she had the feeling that she would not be going back to Logan. The lure of New York was too strong: She had read about the American Place Gallery, made famous by Georgia O'Keeffe and the artists in all fields photographed by Steiglitz, who ran the gallery; e.e. cummings, whose poetry May admired, and Marianne Moore, one of May's early idols, who was to become her friend. So after Jacob's Pillow, she headed for New York.

Her first job, which she got "through *The New York Times*," was as an "amanuensis to an author"; it sounded grand to a budding poet-journalist. After one interview she got the job, which paid more than her post on the Logan *Herald*. She wrote her family that she had found a well-paying job and thought she would stay in New York for a while. They offered no objection; May was over twenty-one; she had been more or less on her own ever since she started working. She soon discovered that *The New York Times* ad had neglected entirely to mention that her employer was a *would-be* author, who expected more than secretarial assistance from an amanuensis. In fact, he seemed more interested in seducing May, a round-faced young blond with a pert, retroussé nose and sharp blue eyes that should have warned him the daily chase around the davenport was futile. If May was astonished at this interpretation of her title, she was no less equal to meeting the situation with resolution.

In relating the story, her wry humor came to the fore. "I had doubted the Word of my religion," she said, "but believed implicitly every word of *The New York Times.*" When she saw that the would-be author was hardly discouraged, and that she was expected to welcome instead of ward off his clumsy advances, she left him and tried another, a *published* author this time. However, although her second employer took some interest in perfecting his manuscripts, he was almost as eager for sex as her first. She finally "left the field," as she said, and became an office secretary-typist, at which she "made out better."

All this time she was writing poetry, sending out her poems with persistent regularity and, finally, had two poems accepted by the then *Saturday Review of Literature.* It was her big breakthrough, bringing her name to the attention of the quality publishing houses. By 1952, as a result of her appearance in such periodicals as *Poetry, The Nation, Hudson Review, Partisan Review,* and *Contact,* she was on the staff at New Directions Press, working from nine until 3:00 P.M., hours which gave her time for her own writing, but still were too confining for the number of hours she needed to accumulate enough poems to make up a volume. Then one day a letter came in the mail informing her that she, May Swenson, had been selected by the Rockefeller Foundation to receive a grant of two thousand dollars. With the confidence she felt from the unexpected award, she applied and received a residence period at Yaddo. New Directions, which had included May Swenson in their *Poets of Today* series with a small collection entitled, *Another Animal: Poems,* in 1949, gave her a leave of absence so she could complete a volume to be published individually. After her residence at Yaddo was over, she received a fellowship to the MacDowell Colony, where she spent the summer.

At about this time she met a young woman who seemed ideally suited to be her roommate: Pearl Schwartz was a hearty, down-to-earth person with a good sense of humor and a deep appreciation of the arts. She and May were a congenial pair at once, and while May was at the MacDowell Colony Pearl visited her, staying at a nearby inn. She met the artists in residence with whom May had become friends and everyone agreed that she was a fine foil for the poet's makeup, physically and emotionally. Pearl's brunette coloring, her olive skin and dark curly hair, her snapping dark eyes and ready laughter bespoke a warm, outgoing nature in contrast to May's blond, Nordic physical features and reserved, inward searching psyche. They complemented each other and understood each other's needs and desires.

Soon after the MacDowell residency ended, the two found a place in Greenwich Village which had the advantage of a balcony at the back overlooking the garden of St. John's church, which ran the length of the block between the two streets (Eleventh and Perry), a hidden oasis that became the subject of a poem, one of Swenson's early works suggesting its substance by the diagonal, wall-like structure of its stanzas. Titled simply, "The Garden at St. John's," this is no mere description of an unexpected beauty spot in the half-sordid, half-splendid city, but a keen combination of skepticism and compassion that is the hallmark of May Swenson's religion in poetry. It begins, "Behind the wall of St. John's in the city"; but it is as much, if not more concerned with the rector's wife, holding her new-and-first-born baby in her arms "like a basket of tenderest fruit" than the sheltered garden in which she walks, accompanied by a frisky, little white dog. The reader is aware of the poet on the balcony looking down on the scene and interpreting the thoughts of the novice mother, who "thinks as she fondles,"

> *the nape of the infant its sweat is like dew*
> *like dew and its hair is as soft as soft*
> *as down as the down in the wingpits of angels.* . . .

After an interlude depicting the little dog as he "scoots in the paths of the garden's meander/ behind the wall of St. John's in the city," the poet takes up the interpretive meditation again: "She walks where the wrinkling tinkling fountain/ laps at the granite head of a monk"; and continues:

> *A miracle surely the young wife thinks*
> *from such a hard husband a tender child*
> *and thinks of his black sleeves on the hymnbook*
> *inside the wall of St. John's in the city*
> *the Ah of his stiff mouth intoning Amen*
> *while the organ prolongs its harmonious snore.*

(The "hard husband" was the late Father Graf, an eminent clergyman in the Episcopal hierarchy; but as administrator of the church property, which included the row of brownstones on Perry Street where the poet and her friend lived, he was as hard a man of business as any landlord. Privately the girls called him Father "Graft.") The final stanza states the more obvious contrast: "A miracle surely this child and this garden/ Of succulent green in the broil of the city," and brings in the sound from "under the wall of St. John's in the city" with accurate imagery, through the mind of her subject,

> *the rectal rush and belch of the subway*
> *roiling the corrugate bowels of the city*
> *and sees in the sky the surgical gleam*
> *of an airplane stitching its way to the West*
> *above the wall of St. John's in the city*
> *ripping its way through the denim air.*

The above conclusions of "the garden at St. John's," (seen from behind, inside, below, and above the wall) are significant whether they represent the rector's young wife or the poet's projected feelings about her surroundings. Landlord relations aside, May and Pearl enjoyed their apartment, and at a little ceremony witnessed by a few friends, during which they exchanged Indian silver fidelity rings (worn on the third finger), they pledged a lasting alliance and set up a smooth-running household, which in due course included a cat, who in turn was included in a poem.*

Weather permitting, many a poem was conceived and created on that balcony-porch, and many a friend enjoyed the view of the garden from that vantage point. At parties, it was indispensable for an overflow of guests, or if someone had to be revived with a little fresh air, winter or summer. It was not long before the household at 23 Perry Street was well known for its genial atmosphere, its lively talk, literary and otherwise, and the general charm of the place. Like many brownstone apartments, it had old-fashioned fireplaces in both the ample living room and bedroom. On the mantle in the latter was a pipe rack holding four small white clay pipes, which May and her friend smoked when they wished to cut down on cigarettes. Somehow those small neat white pipes personified the bachelor air of the well-organized menage. Both roommates were meticulous in their housekeeping, down to the budgeting of incomes. Pearl kept a daily log of the marketing expenses, setting down in a hardcover lined notebook the cost of each item in the daily list of their individual tastes. " 'Swen' likes more fruit than I do," she said once, "and I eat more eggs."—a remark which might have triggered one of May's *Riddling Poems*, "At Breakfast," again an amazingly accurate view of her subject in depicting both the physical and metaphysical aspects of the egg, without naming it once.

Pearl worked in an office and was studying for a college degree at night, so May had the place to herself for her poetry writing after her hours at New Directions until dinnertime, and several evenings a week. (Meals were cooked together or alter-

*"Cat and the Weather," a feline first experience with snowfall; succinct, quiet humor; amazing power of observation of animal behavior mark the piece.

nately by one or the other; occasionally there would be a guest or two, usually on weekends.) In spite of their busy schedule, the two found time not only to entertain but to help their friends in various ways; but let anyone take advantage of their concern, as one writer did by making more and more demands on their time, and the friendship was severed abruptly, with a finality that left no room for reconciliation. There were those who criticized the action, but May was adamant. When the demands of a friendship interfered with her writing schedule it was not possible to continue the relationship. (Subsequently her expedience proved just, for others had a similar experience with the same writer.)

The second big breakthrough for the poet from Utah came in 1954, when she was "discovered" by Scribner's through the good offices of [the late] John Hall Wheelock, who had been commissioned by the publishing house (with whom he kept his connection, though he had retired from editorship some years before) to uncover new and promising talent. Swenson was informed that Scribner's would like to publish a volume of her poetry as soon as she had one prepared which met the approval of the editorial board. Years later, toward the end of the sixties, Wheelock said, "May was the first of the six young poets I discovered for Scribner's—and she was the best."

It was a cause for celebration, and a fine celebration there was at 23 Perry Street. Poets and writers in all fields, painters, composers, all the people May had made friends with at the various colonies, and more she had met through them showed up for the event. To one early arrival, Pearl confided, "Howard Moss is coming!" her inflection implying another possible breakthrough for May: Moss had been poetry editor of *The New Yorker* for a number of years at that point, and was the target then already of every poet aiming for publication in the magazine. He arrived at the party along with John Hall Wheelock, who, though nearing seventy, looked like a man in his early fifties; he regarded May as his prodigy, his gaze resting on her occasionally with pride and satisfaction. His tall, lean figure could be seen moving among the guests, as he conversed with the ease, graciousness and good humor that had won Sara Teasdale's heart more than thirty years before.

Those two innovators of electronic music, Otto Luening and Vladimir Ussachevsky, were on hand to toast the poet and her future success. Luening had set May's poem, "Night Wind," to his experimental music, turning into an extended, weird whistling sound the cadence of the poet's lines. As the crowd increased, the decibel of high talk and laughter rose in direct ratio. The noted artist, Beaufort Delaney, then just about to leave for Paris where he gained recognition for his striking abstract expressionism, added to the level of happy din as he beat out rhythms on a bongo drum he had brought along. A ring of admiring listeners stood around him, either clapping hands in time or, if they held glasses of wine, stamping their feet to the beat. Several clamored to try out their skill and begged Beaufort to show them the correct way to handle the drum.

The occasion was memorable in many ways. It marked the beginning of May Swenson's association with Scribner's and Wheelock, who proved her friend and adviser as he had to so many young poets. And soon after the party, May received her first acceptance from *The New Yorker* for one of her poetic riddles which she called, "By Morning," a delicate description of a snowfall with a philosophic finale containing a biblical reference tinged with Swensonian skepticism. Some of the images are particularly telling:

> *Streets will be   fields*
> *cars be   fumbling sheep*
>
> *A deep bright harvest will be seeded*
> *in a night*
>
> *By morning we'll be   children*
> *feeding on manna*
>
> *a new loaf on every doorsill*

As sophisticated as *The New Yorker* is, the editors felt that the title was too subtle. It was preceded by the explanatory word, "Snow," when the poem appeared in the magazine. May was distressed; she had protested the addition to no avail, and since she did not want to jeopardize this or future publication, she let it stand. But when she prepared her second book, *A Cage of Spines,* she restored the original brief, enigmatic, two-word title, and placed this second in a section called, "Riddling Poems," which led off with "At Breakfast." As things turned out, Scribner's did not want to publish this volume, though Wheelock assured her they were still interested and would probably take the next. It was a disappointment, but May found another publisher.

In the summer of 1957, she received a Robert Frost Fellowship to the Breadloaf Conference at Middlebury, Vermont, where she met William Rainey, editor at Holt & Rinehart (Winston had not yet been added to the company), Robert Frost's publishers. As a "fellow," May was entitled to a reading by "the great man," as she put it. He gave an informal lecture to all the participants at the beginning of the conference, followed by informal discussion. Afterward May went up to him with her portfolio, which he took, telling her to come back the next morning and meet him there at Treman Hall. She showed up on time, in fear and trembling for his verdict. As she approached the table where he was sitting, on the top of which lay her manuscript, he stood up, reaching for the portfolio. Handing it back to her, he said, "It *reeks* of poetry!" and walked away without further comment, or giving her a chance to thank him or question him, leaving her nonplussed, utterly bewildered as to whether he was condemning or complimenting her work.

If she had known Frost better, she probably would have realized that his verdict contained both approval and disapproval. Frost was too keen a craftsman himself not to recognize poetry when he saw it, but hers was not the kind he cottoned to. He was famous for his remark that he would "as soon play tennis with the net down" as write poetry without meter, whether it was iambic pentameter, tetrameter, or hexameter; and though he himself took liberties with form, seeing how far he could go and still stay within the guidelines—he called it "riding easy in harness"—only made the game more interesting. In her poetry, May Swenson plays a different game—one of shapes, startling images, and mystery in her metaphors. The philosophic content, though not foremost, is always present, sometimes as an afterthought or an ironic twist, as in "Southbound on the Freeway," when a "tourist from Orbitville, parked in the air," observes that "the creatures of this star/ are made of metal and glass." After nine two-line stanzas the Orbitvillian asks: "Those soft shapes,/ shadowy inside/ the hard bodies—are they/ their guts or their brains?" Whether Frost agreed with her technique or not, he obviously realized that this was an original poet, for Holt published *A Cage of Spines* in 1958. William Rainey became her editor there and could have had something to do with the decision to publish, but it is quite likely that the Board asked Frost's opinion, and that he gave his recommendation without ever mentioning it, just as he had in the case of Babette Deutsch. May should have made the connection but she did not, and his remark remained a conundrum to her for almost twenty years. She kept it to herself all that time and only in 1976, when she was a counsellor at Breadloaf, did she have the courage and the confidence to tell the anecdote to the aspiring poets. And a little later, in September, talking with someone who suggested the above, did she realize, with relief, that Frost's succinct critique was not scathing or entirely negative.

A Cage of Spines, moreover, received such good notices that Scribner's decided the time had come to fulfill its promise of publication. Swenson's third volume, *To Mix With Time,* was the first to appear under the imprint of that house and was followed by at least half a dozen more. As the title implies, in the collection which came out in 1963, this poet, like many of her colleagues, is concerned with the passage of time, the inevitability of death;* but her outlook is objective, even optimistic. The title itself is contained in a poem that exemplifies Swenson's wit and calm approach to age, to the usually terrifying aging process. "How To Be Old," written in straight stanza form, is one of the poems of a group Swenson made during a journey through France, Italy, and Spain while on an Amy Lowell Travelling Scholarship, which she received in 1961.

"It is easy to be young," this poem starts. "(Everybody is/ at first.) It is not easy/ to be old. It takes time./ Youth is given; age is achieved./ One must work a magic to mix with time/ in order to become old." In the second stanza the poet likens youth to a doll that is given but must be put away in a closet, to be played with "only on holidays." She gives the formula for preserving the doll, adoring it, remembering it in the dark on ordinary days, "and every day congratulate one's aging face in the mirror." The closing stanza summarizes the results of the prescribed "magic":

> *In time one will be very old.*
> *In time, one's life will be accomplished.*
> *And in time, in time, the doll—*
> *like new, though ancient—may be found.*

The scholarship, intended for one person, was not large, but Pearl, who had never seen Europe, was longing to go, and with the savings she and May had managed to put away, they decided to make the funds do for two. New Directions, where May was still on the same schedule, gave her a leave as they had before, and Pearl took off from her job. Though both were in their forties, they planned to stay in youth hostels whenever possible, hire a car so they could drive wherever they pleased, and provided themselves with sleeping bags, so they could sleep

* Swenson's father died in 1963 at the age of eighty-three, though he was still alive when the volume appeared.

on the ground if necessary or the weather permitted. It was a frugal but fruitful safarilike grand tour, yielding all the poems in section two of *To Mix With Time*. And though the subjects might be old as the hills they travelled—one poem, "Instead of the Camargue," where they "hoped to find wild bulls and flamingos," narrates the experiences of a motor trip through Cezanne and Van Gogh country—the treatment was brand-new. Elizabeth Bishop wrote of Swenson's unique style, "If you have thought that no one could ever again react as originally, and, above all, simply, as though she were the first tourist to see the Pantheon, say, or the Arno*—you should buy and read this book." Robert Lowell was of the opinion that "Miss Swenson's quick-eyed poems should be hung with permanent fresh paint signs." Her technique of designing visual typography is especially effective in "Fountains of Aix," where the reader sees a stream of "water" running diagonally down the page. The word, repeated fifteen times, forming the ends of fifteen lines but separated from the rest of the words in each by a single-spaced gap, gives the impression of a constant flow from fountains placed at intervals down the terraced land.

Back in New York, May returned to her post at New Directions, which always seemed to be open to her when she needed it, but was not binding when funds came her way. In 1959 she had received a Guggenheim Fellowship, and in 1960, an award from the National Institute of Arts and Letters. She had also begun to go on reading tours, which were more of an interruption than an inspiration for her creativity, but they provided a few weeks' income and kept her name before the literary public.

The flexible relationship with New Directions was maintained until 1965 or 1966, when May Swenson became poet in residence at Purdue University, and the leave of absence (which

---

*In Florence, where the exchange rate was high, they stayed at an old hotel; "Above the Arno," the title of a poem written from the vantage point of May's room.

started in 1965 at her departure for Purdue) became permanent. By then, Scribner's was eager to have her name on their roster of regular authors and, in 1966, brought out *Poems to Solve,* a collection of the riddling poems for a younger audience. A year later *Half-Sun, Half-Sleep,* a slim volume of her most recent work, appeared (1967), and in 1970 the controversial *Iconographs* came out. May coined the title word, chose the typography, and designed the cover in black and red, signifying a typewriter ribbon. The controversy arose over the makeup of the book, and the fact that the majority of the poems were set in varying shapes or "graphs" suggesting the image employed in the content (hence May's new-minted word).

Some found this graphic poetry a stunning innovation; to others it seemed stilted on one hand because of the typescript, and on the other too diffuse because of the varying shapes, which were a distraction. For example, "The Lowering,"* a memorial poem concerned with the military funeral honoring Robert Kennedy, a powerful denunciation in ironic terms, decrying the falseness of pomp and ceremony, was first published in *The New Yorker* in straight stanzas. The lines offering a folded flag to members of Kennedy's family instead of the dear one they had lost, and to the "Nation, instead of a leader, to take/ this folded flag" had tremendous impact. But in *Iconographs* the poem appeared in graphic shape, intended to depict folding and burial of the flag, thereby heightening the drama. However, some of the power was lost in the figured presentation since the reader was occupied with puzzling out the shape. When asked during an interview† why she changed the framework of this poem, and indeed, devised so many typographical tricks, she answered slowly, as if trying to puzzle it out for herself: "I can't tell you why exactly. I guess it was instinctive. About halfway through the preparation, as I began to type the manuscript, I suddenly felt that this was the way to offer these poems, and I had to do it."

* Arlington Cemetery June 8, 1968.
† September 21, 1976, with the author.

May Swenson

At the back of the book is a rather ambivalent explanation of both title and technique, in which Swenson says in part: "To cause an instant object-to-eye encounter with each poem even before it is read word–after–word. To have simultaneity as well as sequence. To make an existence in space, as well as in time, for the poem. These have been, I suppose, the impulses behind the typed shapes and frames invented for this collection." Then, after an explanation of the derivations of the title (quite obvious to anyone with a rudimentary knowledge of language), she resumes, "I suppose these were my aims. But I come to definition and direction only *afterwards*. . . . I have not meant the poems to depend upon, or depend from, their shapes or their frames; these were thought of only after the whole language structure and behavior was complete in each instance. What the poems say or show, their way of doing it with *language*, is the main thing." (The italicized words are the poet's.) The discussion seesaws between justification and negation of her method in this volume, and the "Note" concludes: "The first instrument to make contact, it seems to me, and the quickest to report it, is the eye. The poems in *Iconographs,* with their profiles, or space patterns, or other graphic emphases, signal that they are to be seen, as well as read and heard, I suppose."

The final phrase indicates the tentative attitude Swenson herself took toward the experimental volume, which was so uneven in its appeal and achievement. The hymnlike lyric, "Black Tuesday," praising the heroic martyrdom of Martin Luther King, with the dedicatory line at the end bearing his name and the date, April 4, 1968, is much more successful than "The Lowering," which follows it on the opposite page. Here one sees at a glance that the poet is holding a flag aloft for the murdered black leader. The title, "Black Tuesday," repeated six times and running vertically alongside the lines, forms the pole. And the lyric beginning, "Blessèd is the man of color/ for his blood is rich with/the nuclear sap of the sun," a series of stanzas set in straight sequence, suggests a flag flung out against the infinite sky. The word "blessèd" is repeated as each aspect of the man of color is brought out; and the whole has the Biblical tone of a Negro spiritual. The visual frame of the flag adds to the tribute paid. Swenson did not seem perturbed that some readers found her technique, though successful in poems like "Black Tuesday," (or the early "Fountains of Aix") often failed, or detracted from the deeper meaning of others. Instead of taking offense, she was interested in the various reactions, negative as well as positive.

One might assume from the examples given so far that May Swenson's poetry is entirely cerebral, but it is balanced by an earthy eroticism that is present in all her descriptions of the bodies of the human and other animals. Breasts and buttocks are noted in her lines with a tactile sense, along with hips and thighs and genitals. Of a lion, his "unused malehood" swaying idly as he paces in his cage; or a young gondolier, his testicles bulging like a limp frog beneath his tight trousers; "big-hipped nature bursts forth . . . / from pelvic heave of mountains/ On swollen-breasted clouds he fattens and feeds"; and "fireflies throw/ love winks/ to their kind/ on the dark." The effect is sensual as well as sexual. Even a poem with the innocuous title, "One Morning in New Hampshire," has its appeal to the senses with sexual overtones: "we are ripe/ as fruits ourselves, enjoyed/ by lips of wind our burnished slopes" and "rapt bumble-eyes of susans are deployed/ as if to suck our honey-hides. Ants nip/ tasting us all over/ with tickling pincers./ We are a landscape to daddy-long-legs/ whose ovoid hub on stilts climbs us like a lover,/ trying our dazzle, our warm sap."

As she became known, May's contact with her colleagues increased, and she found new friends among those whose poetry she admired. One of these was Elizabeth Bishop, as her poem, "Dear Elizabeth" (A Reply to Elizabeth Bishop in Brazil), clearly indicates. It opens, "Yes, I'd like a pair of 'Bicos de Lacre'— meaning beaks of 'lacquer' . . ."; and in the fourth stanza she plans, "on the back porch on Perry St.; here, I'd/ build them a little Brazil./ . . . I can see them as I write—on their perch on my porch." The poem first appeared in *The New Yorker* in 1964, then in the volume, *Half-Sun, Half-Sleep;* but it was not included in *Iconographs,* nor in *New & Selected Things Taking Place,* Swenson's latest collection (1979). At a poetry reading by Elizabeth Bishop and Howard Moss at the YMHA in New York City in 1976, it was Swenson who was asked to introduce Bishop, and in her remarks one heard her high esteem for her colleague and friend.

Shortly before *Iconographs* appeared, May met a young woman of Scandinavian background—Roxana Knudsen, a buxom, blond teacher and author of children's books—and she was so taken with her new friend's well-rounded person, intellectually and physically, that the close ties with Pearl began to weaken. The latter had begun to write poetry, which might have put a strain on their relationship. In any case, those who had always known them together were more than startled when Swenson decided to move from Perry Street to the home Knudsen owned in a seacoast suburb. The news that May and Pearl were separating after so many years caused a great commotion among their long associates in the literary world. No one could understand why the alliance was breaking up. Speculation ran high among their mutual friends. Babette Deutsch, meeting one of these on the Fifth Avenue bus, began discussing the situation. On hearing that Pearl had been writing poetry, she nodded her head sagely. "That could be cause for divorce," she said.

Whether it was or not, the two parted amicably, and May Swenson has lived on the Atlantic seaboard and in Southern California for at least ten years, writing, appearing in poetry readings, observing and enjoying a new kind of life. Several poems in *Iconographs,* such as, "A Trellis for R.," seem to refer to her companion, whose name she soon shortened to "Zana." Roxana had no objection, and "Zana" she has remained.

In the early seventies, May was commissioned by the University of Pittsburgh to translate the poems of Tomas Transtömer, a Swedish contemporary poet. It was a challenge she could not resist. She had spoken Swedish at home until she was six years old and, though she had lost most of it, the effort of translation brought it all back. However, her grammar was "shaky," so she was given an assistant, Leif Sjoberg, with whom she worked for over a year. He would do a "word-for-word" translation, and so would she; and then she would make poems of them. Transtömer later came to the United States, after the University of Pittsburgh published the volume of translations, and the two poets gave readings of them together, in Swedish and English.

For several years, Swenson had not been satisfied with her publishers, and her latest volume, *New and Selected Things Taking Place*, was brought out by Atlantic/ Little, Brown. In 1979, with many honors and awards to her credit, Swenson, still the skeptic, designated her work as "things taking place" rather than poems. Anne Stevenson, an American poet living in England, was of the opinion (in *The New York Times Book Review*) that they took place "in a number of shapes and a few too many tricks" for the critic's taste, but she praised the overall effect of the book for its keen wit, sophistication, and the accuracy of Swenson's descriptive powers in drawing word-pictures of birds and landscapes. She concedes that "there is no doubt that underneath the verbal fireworks lies a sophisticated seriousness" and that Swenson "has a heart but keeps it strictly under the discipline of her brain." Unfortunately Stevenson reviewed the volume along with the superlatively laudatory estimate of Muriel Rukeyser's *Collected Poems,* which detracted from the praise she bestowed on Swenson. Her opening sentence, "It would be difficult to conceive of a greater contrast to the spiritual and moral commitments of Muriel Rukeyser than the clever, skeptical poems of May Swenson," unwarrantedly puts one on guard against mistaking brilliant technique for genuine poetic genius. And though the critic follows her statement with the acknowledgment of Swenson's heartfelt—if controlled—emotions, and goes so far as to admit, with validity, that the poems about May's parents, their lives and deaths, are moving in their objective yet tender view, the reader cannot help feeling that Swenson's art lacks the depth of Rukeyser's.

Another reviewer, in the *Christian Science Monitor,* spoke of Swenson's poems as "sparkling jewels," but perhaps gems that had been polished too highly: the glitter outshone the substance in many instances, he felt. Yet, in spite of occasional objections to her dazzling technique, May Swenson's *New and Selected Things Taking Place* was received with critical enthusiasm and admiration. Stevenson ended her appraisal by linking Swenson to Rukeyser and another of her peers, Elizabeth Bishop; citing the qualities they have in common despite their differences, she observed. "They are all survivors, and they are all wise." The review closed, "It is good to read these collections, in which Ms. Swenson and Ms. Rukeyser, in their different ways, celebrate so much without any trace of sentimental ignorance."

Swenson's volume, her eighth, was nominated for the 1979 National Book Award, and the Academy of American Poets awarded her its 1979 Fellowship of ten thousand dollars for "distinguished poetic achievement." Her career as poet has shown a steady rise in stature, the kind of growth that stems from a directness of purpose marking the dedicated poet. Nowhere is this attitude more clearly illustrated than in the series of seven meditative poems under the title, "October," published first in *The New Yorker* in 1978. Here is the early autumn of the artist's life, her recollections of her father, his skilled hand marred by a scarred nailless thumb that was "nipped by a saw," peeling a pear while her mother boiled the bottles for "putting up." Part of these meditations take place as the poet sits in the barber chair, her "round head a newel poked out of the . . . sheet."

To a stranger, May Swenson's round head, her round Swedish face, her hair worn in a straight cut with a line of bangs across her forehead, makes her seem at first meeting a stolid, even stern person; but her playful wit soon comes to the fore when one talks with her. She will make a comic remark, keeping a straight face, and not until she smiles, when the lines around her eyes crinkle with silent laughter does one realize that she is full of mischievous humor. Life to her is a game, earnestly played, as much of her poetry is a game. And nowhere is this contrast in mood to the meditations of "October" more apparent than in the semisatiric, punning fantasy piece, "The Pure Suit of Happiness," a first-line title, followed by, "/not yet invented. How I long/ to climb into its legs," the poem continues, and goes on to the second of the seven three-line stanzas: "fit into its sleeves, and zip/ it up, pull the hood/ over my head." She gives other features of the sought after suit: "It's/ not too heavy, not too/ light. It's my right./ It has its own weather,/

> *which is youth's breeze,*
> *equilibrated by the ideal*
> *thermostat of maturity,*
>
> *and built in, to begin with,*
> *fluoroscopic goggles of*
> *age. I'd see through*
>
> *everything, yet be happy.*
> *I'd be suited for life. I'd*
> *always look good to myself.*

Contrived? Too clever? Perhaps. However, the poem catches the essence of May Swenson's personality as well as her outlook on life—skeptical, but often playful, gently satiric, imaginative, perceptive, and subtly serious.

Jean Garrigue

When Jean Garrigue was three years old, according to family legend, she ran away at night and was not found til three o'clock in the morning; but it is more likely that this poet, born Jean Garrigus, December 8, 1912, in Evansville, Indiana, simply decided she would take a walk in the moonlight; for when they finally found her in a cemetery some miles from home, she was calmly making her way between the tombstones, looking all around admiringly. And when they asked her, "Why did you come here, Jean?" she answered, "It's so beautiful here," smiling serenely at the flowers and shrubs that grew by the gravesites. She was not at all afraid or even perturbed at being discovered by disapproving, agitated elders.

The story is in a sense symbolic, or prophetic, of Jean Garrigue's life and work. A calm, though complex being, extremely giving of her time, sympathy, and love, she also possessed a quietly determined and independent spirit. The small girl of three who got out of bed to go for a walk late at night unconsciously set the pattern for the emotional, professional, and physical life the future poet was to lead. Like several of her sister poets, she was the lateborn child in her family, having been preceded by a brother and sister almost a generation older than she. Perhaps the age difference itself was responsible for her behavior, causing her to consider herself a grown-up at this early stage. In any case, her exceptional self-possession in a situation that was potentially traumatic, reveals more than the prankishness of a precocious child. She must have been born with the intuitive wisdom of a poet. (The graveyard eventually became the subject of a poem, and the night walks were duplicated many times, frequently with a friend.) The "reckless grandeur" of her poetry (so appropriately phrased by the writer Jane Mayhall in a memorial tribute) must have been present in her psyche from the beginning.

The poet herself once said, "Every line in a poem is an autobiography"—a penetrating observation—and, unlike Marianne Moore, she never sought to hide behind a clever metaphor, or claim that her poetry was not biographical. It was part of her consistent candor that, in reporting the vital statistics of her life for the supplement to *Twentieth Century Authors* (1955), she did so in the first person and explained the origin of her surname. After stating her birthplace, that she was the daughter of Allan Colfax and Gertrude Heath Garrigus, she went on to explain, "It was my grandfather, who, in a burst of stars and stripes, changed the name from Garrigues to Garrigus, rendering vaguely Irish what had been French; and it was my older sister and afterward myself who restored the name to one at least of its proper vowels, thereby causing some confusion. For with a name so French, ought we not therefore to be French?

Dim Huguenot ancestry on one side mixed with Scotch on the other—both families have been—alas!—in this country since the Revolution."

Obviously Jean did not inherit the spirit of patriotism of her grandfather. The gift for writing may have come in part from her father, who in his early youth had written and published short stories. After his marriage he took a steady job as a postal inspector, which left little time for creative work. Jean's mother was musical, and it was this culture that dominated the household in which the poet grew up. For her sister, Marjorie, had inherited their mother's talent to such an extent that she made a career of music. She later became a concert pianist, and all during Jean's childhood "made by her playing a very paradise of sound," in the poet's words. Jean adored this older sister, who was both mentor and guide to her, since the age difference between them, though it precluded contemporary companionship, eliminated sibling rivalry. Jean also looked up to her brother, Ross H. Garrigus, who became a newspaper editor.

As her father was transferred from place to place, most of Jean's childhood was spent in various Indiana towns, both small and large, including Indianapolis, where she went to high school. (She commented, however, that she "never felt the flatland to be her very own home, and was happy only in mountains or cities with ports that lead to the sea.") She was a winsome child, who made friends easily, but as her family moved frequently, she did not have much opportunity to make lasting connections or put down roots in any one community. She early developed a love for reading, and by the time she reached high school had acquired a wide range of literary interests, with poetry in the ascendency.

In a single year, when she was fourteen, she discovered Shelley, then Keats, then the Imagists. Fourteen is an impressionable age, and all of these poets no doubt left their imprint on Jean Garrigue's sensitive psyche, but it was the Imagists, she said, "who made daring to write poetry seem possible, especially H.D." (In the light of the current reevaluation of the Imagist movement, particularly H.D. and her spare, concentrated use of words and cadences, the influence on Garrigue is not surprising. Both had a directness, and dedication to the exactness of words while seeking freedom of form.) Those pristine attempts must have been set down with a sense of venturesome if not fearful apprehension, but luckily an English teacher in that Indianapolis high school, Elizabeth N. Brayton, who was—significantly—after the poet's sister, her main mentor and "rare guide," encouraged her pupil's efforts. She read "what I wrote with that sympathy so necessary for first tender-minded exertion," Garrigue recorded in her 1954 account.

Following graduation from high school, Jean did not go directly to college because she wanted to be in New York City with Marjorie, who had married. Her husband, a prominent radio personality, Fred Smith, of Station WLW, credited with the origin of the famous "March of Time" program, had been transferred to New York, and Jean, eager to see the city, went east to stay with them. From New York he was sent overseas in charge of foreign newscasts, and when they went to Europe, Jean went with them. She spent the next year there before entering college, always writing, writing her impressions in poetry and prose, storing her efforts away for future time. On her return to the "flatland," she enrolled at the University of Chicago from which she graduated in 1937.* The university was then in its heyday (with Robert Hutchins, as the youngest college president heading up a progressive program of learning based on the great books, and with people like Thornton Wilder in the English department); the studies were so stimulating

---

*One of her classmates and close friends in both high school and college was the poet-novelist, Marguerite Young, author of the gigantic book, *Miss McIntosh, My Darling,* which she calls an epic poem. Although Marguerite had been a familiar figure in Garrigue family life, and had gone to school with Jean, they parted ways when they both came to live in New York, due to a basic difference in attitude toward sex, and they rarely saw each other afterward.

that Jean stayed on for some graduate work. She found some "serious employment" editing a weekly newspaper. But the life was too confining and could not satisfy her inner urge to create literature of her own, so in 1940 she came to New York to live on her own.

"It was only then that I felt myself delivered, and in possession of a tongue," she stated flatly in 1954, adding for emphasis, "All dates from that." Even the loss of the trunk-load of the "proverbial journals, notes, poems, and prose—that trail of attempts and explorations the writer must blaze"—which she had sent on ahead of her arrival, could scarcely offset the exciting sensation of living in New York's Greenwich Village, answerable to no one except herself, meeting people of like interests and talent, poets, and writers in all fields. Within a year her work was introduced to the literary world by *Kenyon Review* (1941) in a group of nine young poets, and in 1944 she appeared in New Direction's series of *Five Young American Poets* with a sizeable presentation, "Thirty-Six Poems and a Few Songs." Her work stood out plainly from her colleagues', including that of such talented poets as the witty Eve Merriam, who since has become more known for her satiric theatre pieces.

The freedom and joy of living the kind of life she always wanted to lead come through in Garrigue's first poems. We do not need to be told that she knew the ecstasy of an early love affair if we read the delightful, "Waking, I Always Waked You Awake," which is both title and opening line of a love poem that continues, "As always I fell from the ledge of your arms/ Into the soft sand and silt of sleep/ Permitted by you awake, with your arms firm." The two stanzas in between contain the aura of lovemaking remembered; and the poem ends disarmingly, guileless, yet acutely aware of the impact and power of passion:

> *As waking, always waked in the health of your eyes,*
> *Curled your leaf hair, uncovered your hands,*

Good morning like birds in an innocence
Wild as the Indies we ever first found.

Jean Garrigue had no lack of lovers, no dearth of admirers among both men and women. She was described briefly in *Twentieth Century Authors* as being "five foot two, blue-eyed, with a wiry mop of tawny hair, brown flecked with gold." Such externals give the merest hint of the vitality and sparkle, the glow that came from within. Her deep, violet-blue eyes were always alive with interest, humor (ever close to the brim), or sympathy for the problems of others. One of her early intimates, Jane Mayhall, who as both poet and short story writer, graduated from the Black Mountain School of creative artists and had come to New York at about the same year as Jean, had met the poet a few times, but it was during a party in 1944 that they fell into a fascinating conversation which they continued after the party, walking through the Village all night, talking poetry and books in general. As the first streaks of dawn showed over the rooftops, they felt like—and indeed, were—fast friends from then on.

That was only the first of many nightlong talks, outdoors and in, that Jean enjoyed with Jane and other friends. She was totally alive at every moment, creative in her relationships, but never aggressive; she never pushed anyone, but drew people out, gave them a sense of being. At the various artists' centers or colonies to which she received grants following the 1944 publication of her poems, she was universally liked by the other fellows in residence. One of the first of these was the Cummington (Massachusetts) Art Center, where she met Marianne Moore, who had helped to organize the communal center for dedicated artists. Jean, who, as recently as October 16, 1978 was cited by Helen Vendler (writing in *The New Yorker*), as, "so far Moore's best critic," was quick to see that the senior poet spoke with authority in highly individual, if not mandatory tones. Jean was to write in her critical study: "Of *Observations* one might say:

it is first and last a voice. The voice of sparkling talk and sometimes very lofty talk, glittering with authority." The word "glittering" indicates Garrigue's perceptive powers; and although she
admired Moore, she was too much of an individual herself to
follow or try to imitate the older poet, as many did, with small
success.

Jean was also an innovator, but she used no gimmicks like
Moore's collage of quotations to set forth her equally keen but
less acerbic "observations" on life, in all its forms. She was constantly "developing innovations on the always newly discovered
subject—of being human," Mayhall was to say in her memorial
to the poet. "She knew well the human person, with its power-
drives, its evil beauties, its desecrations and delight. Garrigue
was a radical . . ." (though she abhorred the word) ". . . and
to her very broad acquaintance with the classics . . . to literature, philosophy . . . and plays and history, she brought a zest
and modernity that transformed whatever the substance into the
daily life, and yet into somehow abruptly timeless implications."

One of the poems in her first-published group, "The Stranger,"
has strong Shakespearean overtones. Hamlet could be speaking
the opening lines: "Now upon this piteous year/ I sit in Den-
mark beside the quai"; yet it deals with some experience she
had been through, a lost opportunity for love perhaps, that occurred during the year in Europe, and which was admirably
served by Elizabethan shades of language. The theatre ranked
high among her interests (after poetry and music), and at
Cummington's drama festival she appeared in Auden's verse play,
"The Ascent of F-6," an exciting event in the life of a young
poet. She was also in "The Red and the Black," and in her poetry the art of acting plays a large role. Her use of language was
unique and sometimes startling: In the above poem the
"stranger," elusive, " . . . moved ahead of me/ So tensile and
so dancer made . . ."; and, in the closing lines, ". . . the swan
adorned/ With every wave and eddy/ The honor of his sexual

beauty,/ Create her out of sorrow/ That, never perishing,/ Is a stately thing." Rarely has the fascination of the swan been so graphically described, recalling, in a remote reference, the story of Leda and the swan in Greek mythology.

Garrigue was daring also in her religious references. Her next volume, *The Ego and the Centaur,* published in 1947, contains a description of her tenement "Flat-house" on Jones Street in the Village as it appeared in the sunrise, perhaps on her return from the nightlong walk with her friend or after working during the predawn hours (for she was a known night-bloom, often burning the midnight oil till morning) when she would take a short walk. "I saw the mountains in a rose-fire light," the lines entitled "Poem," begin, and continue, "Upon my ill-housed street, whose old-law flats/ Were stained a blood light, rose-christ light." This and the succeeding stanzas form a sacred celebration of the sun, particularly in the third and sixth stanzas:

> *As if a skiey flame could crucify*
> *Our lives, the prisons of conceptual plight,*
> *I saw, I wept, for we were all burning,*
> *Our faces all, in crucibles of light.*
>
> . . . .
>
> *Vision and illusion, Oh return!*
> *That I with joy and fire and light*
> *In fire and light and delicate joy my life*
> *May live in crucibles like that, and burn.*

To give Christian theology a pagan interpretation in 1947 required a venturesome spirit, and Jean Garrigue possessed the necessary will to challenge limitations by steadfastly asserting her freedom to think and write—and live—as she pleased. The battle against limitations extended to animal life, for, as she said, she "felt close to all furred things, especially the cat—mystic companion—and the lion and the fox, because he will not submit to captivity." And nowhere did she express her feelings more clearly than in the final poem of this volume, "The False Country of the Zoo," which the reader enters as she observes: "We are large with pity, slow and awkward/ In the false country of the zoo." She moves from cage to cage, accurately depicting the oddities that have caused these creatures to be objects of curiosity; her similes show rare imagination. In speaking of the emu, for example, she says, "His body, deep as a table,/ Droops gracelessly downwise,/ His small head shakes like an old woman's eye." The last stanza, like the preceding ones, starts with the line, "In the false country of the zoo" and is followed by, "Grief is well represented there/ By those continents of the odd/ And outmoded, Africa and Australia." She mentions "The bear, wallowing in his anger,/ The humid tiger wading in a pool." And so on, until "The eye, plunged in sensation, closes." And, "Thought seizes the image." The "shrieking jungle . . . blurs." The poem ends poignantly: "The oil from the deer's eye/ That streaks like a tear his cheek/ Seems like a tear, is, is,/ As our love and our pity are, are."

The closeness Jean felt for "all furred things" amounted to a kinship. One summer when she was at Yaddo she went with Jane Mayhall and novelist Marjorie Fisher to a circus in Saratoga Springs. As they were standing in front of the cage that held the tiger, her friends were horrified to see her stretch her hand through the bars; both cried out in alarm, but she said calmly, "He won't hurt me," and proceeded to pat the tiger's head. He did not move, but remained tranquil as Jean stroked his head gently, while the others looked on in amazement. Jean laughed at her friends' fears. She knew her love and concern for animals communicated itself and took in a broad range of extrahuman existence. In listing a few of the "furred things" she felt for, she wrote, "This is not to forget the great, heraldic beasts." She might well have added, many miniscule insects, for they inspired her with poems, giving them equal voice, as in "The Maimed Grasshopper Speaks Up," a moving, perceptive monologue in Garrigue's next volume, *The Monument Rose*, 1953.

With this volume, which begins on a musical note, "The Opera of the Heart: Overture," and continues the theme in "Lightly Like Music Running," a charming love lyric, recognition as a poet of rare quality came from many quarters. Howard Nemerov termed it "romantic in richness and strange and curious elaborateness of detail." He spoke of the balance between "Rhythm and syntax, the wave-motion . . . which makes all one, and most fine. This . . . weaving and stitching is the most neglected part of poetry at present, but attention to it is the mark of mastery, and the gift for it. the melodiousness, which . . . is the final and distinguishing sign of a poet, is something Miss Garrigue wonderfully has." Such praise was indeed gratifying.

Like most poets, Garrigue had to earn a living, and during the early years in New York she held a number of "odd journalistic jobs," which included rewrite work on technical articles for an aviation magazine and "making phrases in regard to toy trains." An occasional book review for *The New Republic*, the *Saturday Review, Kenyon Review,* or *Tomorrow* magazine helped to make ends meet, but she was "broke much of the time." During part of World War II she edited a publication for the USO. Then she received a scholarship to the University of Iowa and taught as a graduate assistant while completing work on her Master's degree. Though her schedule was a full one, she did not forsake poetry. She was up all night long if an idea seized her; she smoked a lot, but never drank while she was writing. "I don't want to lose my clarity," she would say. And when she worked she immersed herself literally: Jane Mayhall, who went to visit her in Iowa, found her with type-sheets or scripts of poems in first or second draft piled on the desk, all over the floor, surrounded by unheeded overflowing ashtrays. Jean would sleep about half an hour, then get up and work, and might or might not get back to bed before morning. Yet she would take time out to talk if Jane felt so inclined. The clutter of papers, books, notebooks, coffee cups stained from the cold dregs, on the table or edge of the desk for days did not seem to bother her in the least. Neatness was not one of her virtues, although she was bodily immaculate, always attractively attired, indicating an intuitive flair for style. The "reckless grandeur" that characterized her poetry was true of her person. Men fell in love with her and she with them. She lived with two or three different men at different times during her life, but never with any one person, man or woman, for more than a year or so. Domesticity was not in her ken, and she wanted no permanent alliances. Domesticity was not in keeping with her life-style.

No one was more open and generous in her loves, as she defined her feeling in the above-mentioned poem: "Lightly like music running, our blood/ In the darling dogdays of early youth,/ We nimbled with vines, ferns were cast over/The limpid lip of the sky . . ." Rarely has a poet caught the aura and the throb cast by young love around the lives of those lucky enough to experience it. She must have been aware of her gift when she wrote that poetry is "a searching for language which takes its rhythm from heartbeat and blood, wind, water, light . . ." Even when love had run its course, as in the poem that follows the above, entitled, "This Day Is Not Like That Day," Garrigue celebrates its beauty: "It was a day of gods—sweet provisions/ From the wine realm! tournaments!/ Castles! our wondering psalms/ Bearing up day to its summits day long!" Unlike Millay, she spared small space to mourning the brevity or loss of love, "now in its dustfall time," but counselled and consoled herself by positive words: "Patience and faith, my heart!/ All urns are gathered in dark/ With leaves that sang in the sun/ Of some rapt mind burning long/ In its visions, which vanished."

It is not surprising that her friend wrote, "Poetry was not for Garrigue a stick to beat the world. And it wasn't a retreat for private mesmerizing. She was a very lawless, anarchic person, always creative and not destructive. . . . The impetus was to overcome barriers, to eliminate conventional borders; and finally, among the dangerously deep levels of self, to transform,

reinterpret, change." Or, as Jean herself said, ". . . by metaphor and rhythm, to equate perception with experience." And
for her each day was a new experience to be sampled and savored, like each love, or personality, or book—of poetry, fiction, history, art, classic or contemporary—that drew her attention. Among poets of the past she preferred Marvell, Donne,
Coleridge, Blake, Keats, and Hopkins. "As for the poetry of my
age," she declared, "it is a medium I explore with as much delight and necessity as the world around me." Among modern
poets she was most influenced by Hart Crane. It was typical of
her to add that she liked "Comets, lightning, and fireworks,"
all vivid vehicles of excitement, edged with danger.

Once she had gained her Master's degree and taught at the
Iowa workshop, Jean Garrigue was seldom without a post in
some university or college, including Smith College and the
University of Pennsylvania. And as her reputation grew, she was
often heard on the poetry circuits around the country. When
she was in the vicinity of Cincinnati, she usually visited her family
(and she always came home for the "big holidays like Christmas"). They were proud of her career, especially her sister. Her
niece, Marjorie's daughter, always called "Jorrie" to distinguish
her from her mother after whom she was named, has related
the anticipation and pleasure of those times when "Aunt Jean"
came from New York.

There was a special bond between these two, born of a love
of books as well as family affection. No matter how strapped
Jean was for money, she always found enough to send presents
to her niece, and it was most often a book. Jean gave Jorrie her
first collection of fairy stories, reading them aloud when she was
there. Once, after listening to tales of trolls, elves, gnomes, and
fairies, the little girl remarked, "But they don't really exist, do
they?" Jean's immediate answer was, "Of *course* they exist!" And
always after that, when she gave her niece a book, whether it
was the tales of Beowulf, or the series of the Greek classics for
children, she would inscribe it to the effect that fantasy crea-

tures "really did exist" (in the pages of books). It was "sort of a game" with them all during Jorrie's growing years.

Jean was to be involved in her niece's life in a way neither could have foreseen. The little apartment on Jones Street, which she kept for many years, whether she was there or not, was the scene, inadvertently, of a momentous meeting for Jorrie when she graduated from high school. The years in between were full ones for Jean, taken up with teaching, writing, and her own momentous meeting with the sterling poet, Stanley Kunitz. They were immediately drawn to each other, not only because of their common interest in poetry and mutual admiration of each other's work, but for the emotional magnetism both experienced on meeting. The two spent an idyllic year together in Italy, which resulted in Jean's next volume, *A Water Walk by Villa d'Este,* published in 1959. Here the themes of love, light, water, and air are commingled in a celebration of the land they were exploring, as in "The Land We Did Not Know" or "A Garland of Trumpets," heralding "That festival day by the sea"; or the exuberant, three-part poem, "For the Fountains and Fountaineers of the Villa d'Este." In Part II, the lines, "Fountains, our volatile kin,/ Coursing as courses the blood,/ For we are more water than earth/ And less of flesh than a flame/ Bedded in air and run by the wind— /Bequeath me, be with me, endow my hunger/ With sweet animal nature," the poet links the elements and all earthly creatures with art, through love's eyes.

Yet when the year was over, happy and inspirational as it had been, Jean made no effort to extend or make the alliance permanent. She may have felt that two poets should not marry, or even try living together longer than a year. Or perhaps she knew that lost ecstasy leaves a bitter aftertaste, and she preferred to have the sweetness remain in memory. That her decision cost her deep moments of sorrow mixed with terror is expressed in "My Frantic Heart," in which she identifies with the sufferer "at every street, these mourning crowds at noon, Numb to their exit," and asks: "How may you and I and they/ Endure enschooled reality?" The poem ends, "The image of your stricken face is they/ And I am crying in the street miles away." Nevertheless, she abided by her decision to live alone.

She had received a Rockefeller grant in 1954 (word of which came while she was travelling in Europe), and later in the 1950s, a Guggenheim Fellowship which, with a term or two of teaching, enabled her to concentrate on creative work and complete the "Villa d'Este" and other poems (including a "Mourning for Dylan Thomas") by 1959. It must have been about then that Jorrie graduated from high school and, as Jean had done twenty years earlier, came to spend some time in New York with her favorite relative. Like others, Jean's niece was struck by the number of books the poet had accumulated over the years. As her friend (and executor) Aileen Ward was to say, the apartment on Jones Street was "overflowing" with them—"books on the shelves, on the floor, in chairs you wanted to sit in, books piled in corners, on the kitchen table, even in the fireplace. The books were overflowing with herself: You would open one and a letter would fall out, or a clipping, a pressed flower, a concert program, a book review, a marketing list, a ticket stub. . . ." There were papers scattered around also, fragments of poems, as always, along with the usual clutter. Jorrie offered to play "housekeeper" for her aunt, and Jean, laughing, was glad to let her.

This niece, who had inherited the musical talent of the maternal side of the family, was a violinist who had hopes of studying and making her mark in the big city. At Christmastime there was no thought of going home for the holiday. Jean decided to give a big party, inviting the poets (and writers in other fields), the painters, composers, and musicians she had come to know through the various artists' colonies. For Jorrie's benefit she asked a number of young musicians she had met through the composers. Among them was a promising violinist, Arthur Davis. He and Jorrie naturally had much in common, but more mutual interest in living a life of musicianship together led to a torrid love affair and marriage a week later, much to the consternation of everyone in the Garrigue family, especially Jean. She was leery of marriage between artists of any sort, creative or performing, and she never dreamed of such an outcome from her chance invitation, much as she wanted her niece to be happy. And unfortunately, her fears were well founded.

Though the pair seemed blissfully wed at first, there were disruptions and dissentions caused by the struggle of their careers soon after their first child was born. Jean felt sympathy and concern for her niece and, typically, she blamed herself for the ill-fated marriage because the couple had met through her. Several times in the last years before her death, she said to her sister Marjorie, "I hope you forgive me for the part I played in Jorrie's marriage." Marjorie knew that Jean would never be a matchmaker intentionally, but it worried the poet, particularly toward the end of her life, when the couple was expecting their fifth child.

Except for family and health worries, and to her last days she overrode the latter, Jean Garrigue's life was continually exciting, stimulating, and artistically rewarding. In 1964, her fifth volume, *Country Without Maps,* published by Macmillan, proved a landmark: it received nomination for the National Book Award in poetry. The book opens with an impressive tribute, "Cortege for Colette," to the French novelist whose works she revered, and who had just died. A book of people rather than places, it also contains, "Amsterdam Letter," which, while capturing the atmosphere of that diverse city, features the "old Frisian lady, . . . affable, amusing and helpful," who taught the poet a few words in dialect Dutch, including "beauty and love." The book closes with "Pays Perdu," a long narrative poem, at once contemplative and terrifying, an account of a rugged climb to a lost hamlet in the mountains of Provence. She and her companion, a woman this time, parched and footsore, came upon a handful of half-roofless huts and two lone fading families who led them to the single stream of piped water to quench their thirst. And, when a sudden shower came, gave the travellers shelter in one of the two houses that were "sound and whole." The poem is a drama of decay and proud survival. This was the "country without maps."

The success of this volume led to awards from the American Academy of Arts and Letters, *The Hudson Review* and *The Virginia Quarterly;* and Jean herself was invited to be a judge for the National Book Awards in poetry, the Brandeis Awards, and to serve on various committees. Her critical study of Marianne Moore, which she wrote for the latter's seventy-fifth birthday, was published in 1965, and Macmillan proposed a volume of new and selected poems, which appeared in 1967. In between, she wrote a novella, *The Animal Hotel* (1966), edited an anthology of translations, and made a professional excursion into prose poetry, which resulted in an unusual book, *Chartres and Prose Poems.* Much of her creative work was done during summer residences at the MacDowell Colony or Yaddo, or at periods when her teaching schedule permitted. Through her residences at Yaddo, she became associated with Skidmore College in nearby Saratoga, at first through poetry readings and visits with friends she made in the town, and then as a faculty member, teaching courses in poetry. It was a fruitful affiliation for both.

The stays at the colony in Saratoga also brought a rewarding alliance with novelist Josephine Herbst besides the other friendships she formed among her colleagues. There was a circle of poets about the same age whose company she enjoyed, exchanging ideas and reading engagements: May Swenson, Muriel Rukeyser, Isabella Gardner, Jane Cooper, Elizabeth Bishop, Stanley Kunitz, Howard Moss, the late Allen Tate, Arthur Gregor, and several more who were close friends. She was to be connected professionally as well as socially with Gregor soon after they met in the early 1950s, when he became editor at Macmillan. He was responsible for her joining that publisher, and was her editor for *Country Without Maps* (1964) and the fine volume of *New and Selected Poems,* published in 1967. They were the best of companions and worked well together, though he admitted that "Jean could be difficult at times." She was stubborn about certain details, but you always knew where she stood: when she was angry, she came right out with it; and when she was pleased or enthusiastic she was equally open and expressive; she generated tremendous excitement, he recalled.

It was Josephine Herbst, however—older than Jean, worldwise, compassionate champion of the underdog—who influenced Garrigue's subject matter more than any of the poets. Herbst, born in Sioux City, Iowa, had become a labor journalist, reporting urban and farm labor strikes for the *New York Post* and *The Nation.* (In 1937, she was in Flint, Michigan, covering the auto workers' strike, following reportage of farm labor strife in Iowa, and in the same year was in Madrid during the historic bombardment; in 1939, she was in South America, writing about revolt and unrest of the paisanos.) Early in her career she had published short stories—the first in *Smart Set,* 1923—and in the forties she returned to fiction, becoming a successful novelist, well known by the time Jean met her.

The two found much to talk about; Jean was a good listener as well as a lively contributor and the stories Josephine could tell fascinated her. They opened up a whole new world for her when, after an especially illuminating all-night talk at Herbst's country house in Pennsylvania, Jean discovered in herself a sense of social consciousness such as she had not felt before. Not that she had ever averted her eyes from poverty, injustice, or injured creatures; they had come into her poetry occasionally, but she was essentially an aesthete. For her poetry "was not a stick to beat the world," as her friend Jane Mayhall wrote. However, with the impetus of Josephine's active protests against the world's inequities, the insanities of war and industrial pollution, the poet herself became involved in various movements to right the wrongs of her time.

One has only to look at the titles in Garrigue's final volume (section four) to realize that a smoldering rage in her had been released: "A Civilization Constantly Worrying About Itself As It Goes on Doing What It Is Worrying About That It Is Doing" (unfortunately an overly long, complex heading for the clear strong statement of the poem itself); "Lead in the Water"; "For Such a Bird He Had No Convenient Cage"; "The War Has Just Begun"; "Resistance Meeting: Boston Common." All of these reflect the influence Herbst had on Garrigue's outlook and self-expression.

The poet spent long periods at the latter's place in Erwina, Pennsylvania, living and writing in a little cottage (formerly the henhouse) on the grounds. Taking along her cat of the moment, for Jean always had a cat (a favorite was "Nemur," the king of the cats), she usually spent the spring months there. Josephine's generous nature made her home a gathering place for friends in the literary and publishing world, a haven from the city where they could relax and read and hold informal "May Festivals" as they came to be called. Led by one Tambi Mutti, a Celanese writer, editor, literary jack-of-all-trades, different groups came out for the whole day at various times. They wrote plays and performed them on the wide terrace at the top of a slope that led down to a brook below, the perfect setting for outdoor theatre. Besides Jean and Josephine, Jane Mayhall and her husband, Leslie Katz, publisher of Eakins Press books, Tambi Mutti and Arthur Gregor, there were any number of literary people like William Phillips of *Partisan Review*, Aaron Ascher, Edith Ventura, Stanley Kunitz, art critic Hilton Kramer, Harvey Swados, biographer Aileen Ward, and a varying number of painters or composers. Guests brought picnic baskets with provisions enough for three days, as the festivals frequently ran on longer than expected—as long, indeed, as their creative minds brought forth fresh scripts for impromptu production. Jean, whose second love was acting ever since the days at Cummington, entered in with a will. It was not without basis that her final volume (published posthumously) was to feature the title poem, lyrical yet analytic, "Studies for an Actress."

The May Festivals at Erwina became an annual event during the late fifties and early sixties, when they ceased after the departure of the brilliant but erratic instigator, Tambi Mutti, who was a victim of alcoholism; he could find no more wealthy women to support his publishing ventures, and so returned to his native India. By then the Vietnam War had cast its pall over the country, and Jean, along with Josephine and many writers in all fields, became involved in the Resistance movement. As always, Herbst threw herself into the struggle, though she was not well; and she never lost faith in the goals for which they were striving, though she did not live to see the peace. The modern ode, "In Memory—Josephine Herbst, 1897–1969," which Jean wrote soon after this dedicated woman's death, crystalizes her credo and the esteem in which the poet held her. It begins: "You believed in a world that has never come/ With or without hope of this one/ And therefore you would say/ 'I believe in what I do not see'/ Insurgently or laughingly/ And walked through parts of your storm/ With angels of the enfranchised one/ That had been truly born,/ . . ."

There was small sign in this poem or in the two memorial poems that follow it, honoring her mother ("Dry Summer"—1965) and her father ("Out of Memory"), both of whom had died a few years before, that Garrigue's own death was not far off. In 1954, listing love and death among the subjects for poetry, she had added, "the odd prospect of one's own"; and in 1969, though she was soon to fall ill with the disease that took her life, the idea of her own death must still have seemed "odd" to her. For there was no falling off of the energy and originality of her language, the vigor with which she attacked the world's evils—and she did not, like Edna Millay, make the fatal mistake of becoming propagandistic, or even, like Muriel Rukeyser, the voice of the people. If she hit upon a truth with one striking blow, she did not continue to hammer. And conversely, her lyrics lost none of their lilt, as in the utterly captivating "Song for 'Buvez Les Vins du Postillon'—Advt.," with the refrain of parting lovers or travellers:

> *O it was lovely at the buvette*
> *In the time of the lilac and cherry*
> *Not to think of the Hôtel du Départ*
> *But be drunk on the wines of the postilion* . . .

And the magnificent rhapsody of "The Grand Canyon," (called a masterpiece by the *Yale Review*) delineates "the terraced massed faces/ of the brute Sublime" as perhaps no painter has ever done. Citing a single passage, to describe this gigantic "maw" in terms of "Aztec pyramidal temples rising in hundreds of steps/ to the summit of the seemed shrine/ curtained, girdled with snakes and necklaces of hearts, wet with sacrificial blood," is to reproduce the awesome sight as no painter's palette or camera's eye.

Whenever she could, Jean spent the summer abroad; and in 1969 she and Arthur Gregor roamed Europe together, going farther afield than Jean had been before, visiting Yugoslavia along the Mediterranean coast. In the old city of Dubrovnik, they attended an opera performance of the famous Galina Vishnevskaya, and after the final curtain call, Jean sat like one transfixed while everyone around them was getting ready to leave. Arthur knew she had been deeply moved, and, suspecting that a poem was already forming in her mind, he waited before nudging her gently back to reality. Out of this experience came the long, analytic "Studies for an Actress" (subtitled, "After having heard Galina Vishnevskaya sing in Dubrovnik")—a poet's soliloquy on the conflict between human life's mortality and the creative urge to render it immortal. "The actress represents ourselves," Mayhall says in discussing the poem. "It is the ability to perform in the situations that arise during one's lifetime that the diva portrayed so admirably in the poet's eyes." Whether one accepts this interpretation or not, the poem remains a profound statement in the rich language of Garrigue's gift for phrasing. "She prays to praise. She prays to be/ Condensed now to one desire/ As if it were very life performing her," the closing lines proclaim in an arresting play on words and the contrasting significance that may be derived from skillful juxtaposition.

The final poem of this volume, the last Garrigue was to prepare for the printer, is, by contrast, a lyrical celebration (rather than an analytic "study") of Keatsian dimension, "Moondial," a modern, multilayered interpretation of the thrall cast by Endymion's fabled mistress. Yet this poem, too, is based upon contrast, or the "heart's counterpoint" to a scorching day in late summer, depicted with a masterful use of alliteration: "Earth ribbed to a near extreme,/ Balding of grasses burnt and white with dust," followed by the "thin harsh and hacksaw whirr/ Of insects that succeed the soft-set song/ Gritting and grinding like the shears of time/ This last of summer lags/ Where cobwebs keep their dusty disrepair." Such is the sere unlikely scene that paradoxically evokes the moonlit memory of a vanished love.

Suddenly the sun-blanched fields are silvered, become moon-drenched forests, as the poet recalls,

> *We walked in moonstuff, lawn and tissue of it,*
> *Past forests chained by it and molded so*
> *That levels of its fountains of dark growth,*
> *Tier upon tier of rich, broad-plated leaves,*
> *Were sculptured by the massy flood*
> *Fey governor of the insubstantial.*
>
> . . . .
>
> *And walked we by the harvests of the light,*
> *By meadows where it lay so heaped we might*
> *Have gone to gather it and toss the stuff*
> *And play it out like spray or tuft*
> *Or dip our hands in it to the wrists.*

The ecstasy reaches a crescendo "Of wildest, most cross-flowing intricacy./ Such wildness asked for ceremony./ We rose and then we danced a formal tread/ . . . We drank the air that drank of moon,/ Deceptions that it practised—or were they/ Intensifyings of the way things were . . . ?" Just as suddenly, "There is a moment on the moondial. It has come." The inevitable dawn brings queries: "Must the moon thin and the light grow dull . . . ? Must the dawn wear the world away/ Of mystifying touch in twining light. . . . And the wings open of day and you perceive/ A slaughter of innocents—/ Some long antennae or a gossamer thigh—Fragments of the ephemeras." We are thrust back into the blistering, sunbaked day when the poet asks: "Must I beg to be washed of the moon dust/ As I soothe the enfevered flowers of fissured earth?" The answer lies in the calm and mystical close:

> *I raise again these moon-splashed fields,*
> *Like half-remembered legends I recount*
> *How apparitions skeined us in a coil*
> *Where wholly given, wholly found,*
> *Our beings' threads were wound.*
> *Secessions, then, by sun!*
> *But not from the One.*

These stanzas, and those in most of Garrigue's work, flow so smoothly, it is hard to believe that she had to spend much time on revision, but in reworking lines she was second to none, save Marianne Moore; and it is possible that Jean picked up the impulse to continue perfecting a poem indefinitely from the senior poet, who was her friend, and in a sense, her mentor from the days of their association at Cummington. (After her fellowship terminated, Jean was connected for a time with the Noonday Press, a small poetry house headed by Moore and the directors of the center.) Garrigue's poetry was definitely her own (with only an occasional echo of Hart Crane); she was as much a "voice" as she deemed Marianne Moore; but she spoke in lyric phrases rather than intellectual exercises, which does not mean that she was any less intellectual than Moore, and she was often more profound, because her emotions ran deep, and her warm embrace of life was wide-reaching. (Marianne herself said: "Music should be directed by the ear; poetry by the imagination. . . . Jean Garrigue must have heard of the Philistines, might have spoken to one. If so, no imprint of any such meeting has been left on her.") There was mutual admiration between the two, different as their expression of individual genius was; and the younger poet was ready to follow the older's work habits from the first. "Jean revised and revised," Arthur Gregor said. "Even after a poem was in print she would revise it." And Moore's obsession with revision was well known. Helen Vendler claims that Moore's famous poem, entitled, "Poetry," beginning, "I, too, dislike it," had been revised beyond all recognition by the time the *Complete Poems* was published. Garrigue did not go to such extremes, but did revise.

Like many poets of their age, she and Arthur adored the senior poet. To celebrate her eightieth birthday, they took her to dinner at the Coach House in Greenwich Village, a favorite spot of hers. By then she was famous for her eccentricities, her tricorne hats and triple-entendre remarks. As they entered the restaurant, a murmur arose around the room. "There's Marianne Moore!" and, "M.M.," "It's M.M.!" The exclamations were quite audible, but Moore seemed not to have heard them. Not flustered or flattered, she was perfectly natural. They had a delightful evening, talking and laughing, toasting each other to long life. None of them could know that in five years both women would be gone. Jean, twenty-five years younger than Marianne Moore, was still in good health.

It was not until three years later, in 1970, that she began to feel the first symptoms of the fatal disease that she struggled in vain to override. In June of that year, Skidmore College, where she had been teaching during the spring semester, conferred upon her an Honorary Degree of Doctor of Letters. In accepting the honor (with "a certain startled gratification"), she said, "I might have written some verse to commemorate this occasion had I not been so occupied in teaching our dear, great Robert Frost and in conversing with my verse-writing students on the mysteries of how to make a line come right, sound clean, and ring true." (She evidently had no more use for "occasional poetry" than Frost himself did.) After a few remarks on the labor of writing poetry, she read five of her published poems, beginning appropriately with, "Last Letter to the Scholar," a profound love poem. She had been working very hard on new poems, besides teaching and starting to compile an anthology of love poems.

The first inkling she had of her illness was the disturbing low fever she began to run every day. Tests for suspected lung cancer did not show anything; she and Arthur Gregor celebrated the medical report with a dinner. Her doctor, however, advised her strongly to give up smoking, and for a time she tried, but she could keep away from cigarettes no more than she could stop working so many hours of the day and night and take the frequent rest her doctor advised. Like Elinor Wylie before her, Jean drove herself to complete the projects she had undertaken: to assemble an anthology of love poetry and compile a new volume of her own. The former was fraught with frustrations of one sort or another, which only led to further delay in completing and composing new verses for her next volume.

She was at the University of California at Riverside when she became seriously ill. Returning to New York in slow stages as soon as she was able—it was then that she visited the Grand Canyon and was inspired to write her monumental poem—she submitted to extensive tests in February, 1972. They revealed that she had been suffering all along from Hodgkins Disease, cancer of the lymph glands. She took a series of radium treatments, which brought slight improvement, but by no means a cure. She continued doggedly to push toward publication of the two projected books. A friend of hers, the painter Nell Blaine, well known for delicate drawings and watercolors of flowers, was illustrating the anthology; she also designed a bookplate for Jean's library, by now a collection of two thousand books, which the poet had decided to give to the Skidmore College Library.

She must have known that she had not long to live, though she showed little outward sign of serious illness, and spoke about it very rarely, even to close friends like Arthur Gregor and Aileen Ward. She had known the latter a number of years, but not well until they were at Yaddo together while Ward was working on her biography of Keats (which won the National Book Award), when they became intimate friends. Aileen, who lived in Boston, stayed at Jean's apartment in Jones Street whenever she was in New York, and Jean stayed with her in Boston frequently, as she did in 1972 after the doctors prescribed chemotherapy treatments. In April, she had planned to go to Providence for a poetry reading by Arthur, and a party afterward, arranged by their friend, poet Nancy Sullivan, who was on the faculty at Rhode Island College. Jean was not feeling well enough to go, and by June she was back in the hospital. It must have been about this time that she asked Aileen to be her executor, and she was also planning to dedicate her new volume to her friend.

In July, Jean was well enough to go with her intimate circle—Aileen, Arthur, Nancy, and her sister Marjorie, and brother-in-law—to spend two weeks at the country home of Jane Mayhall and Leslie Katz, near Saratoga. The visit seemed to do her a lot of good, for in September she began teaching at Rhode Island College in Providence, a post she was offered through Nancy Sullivan. Every few weeks she went into Boston for chemotherapy treatments, always staying with Aileen. But the condition refused to yield, and in December, while she was at Aileen's, the end came suddenly. She never ceased her creativity, or her active interest, or enjoyment of life. Three nights before she died she was playing poker with some of their friends who had come to call on the "patient." Frail as she was, she entered into the spirit of the game with her old vivacity and sense of fun. The next two days she spent poring over the sequence of poems for her new volume, making notes on ideas for future ones. (There are enough fragments and whole verses among her papers for perhaps another posthumous edition of her work.) She wrote out the dedication, set in three separate lines: "To Aileen, my sister Marjorie, and my dear friends," in that order. On the third day she was gone.

Religious and memorial services were held in St. Luke's Episcopal Chapel,* not far from Jean's apartment in Greenwich Village. When *Studies for an Actress* appeared, a memorial reading of the poems, arranged by Arthur Gregor, was given in the Jefferson Market Library in the Village, to an overflow attendance by the many who mourned the loss of an impetuous, warm, imperious, and wholly delightful friend, quite apart from her inestimable value as a lyric poet. Finally, on April 25, 1974, the formal presentation of Garrigue's personal library (including annotated volumes of her own poetry and inscribed works of her contemporaries) was made at the Lucy Scribner Library of Skidmore College, Saratoga Springs, in ceremonies alluded to earlier. Besides the comment of Aileen Ward, who, as Jean's executor, made the presentation of the gift, and Jane Mayhall's address on the subject of Jean Garrigue's poetry, a memorial verse, "Poem (in memory of Jean Garrigue)" by poet and faculty member Laurence Josephs was read. Following the ceremony, Jean's sister, Marjorie, presented a concert that included some of the poet's favorite piano compositions.

Completion and editing of the anthology of love poetry was taken over by Nancy Sullivan, who established the Jean Garrigue Prize at Rhode Island College: a one hundred dollar annual award for the best undergraduate poem. Students everywhere relate to Garrigue's poetry because it is contemporary as well as classic. Richard Eberhart wrote, "In her combination of music and form Jean Garrigue suggests early Milton. She exemplifies his ideal of linked sweetness long drawn out." Her

---

*Now the Church of St. Luke in the Field

poem, "Rain Song," set to music by the noted composer, Louise Talma, is a favorite of concert artists and audiences. But already in her 1947 volume, searching for the significance of V-J Day, she observed, "Our armless men are all our statues now"; and her later poems show strong commitment to the problems of society besides resistance to the scourge of war. She was acutely aware of the total dramatic experience of life, and unafraid to sample its pleasures or challenge its trials. Students at the Radcliffe Institute who read her poetry since her death have asked to learn more about her life.

Those who knew her well agree that she was a creature of the spirit. "The spirit of the poet was a presence in itself," Arthur Gregor said. "There was often more body to that than to the physical body." Yet—and this was the contradiction in her—though she might neglect to give her body the proper food and rest, she never denied herself its pleasures of love and wine or sexual, human passion. The spinster asperity present in much of Marianne Moore is never found in Garrigue's work—and her work represents her life. As she said in the beginning, "Every line a poet writes is autobiographical," and, in an early poem, transposing a line from Hart Crane,* "Permit me candor of an excited world!"

* Crane's line, which relates to Garrigue's attitude toward poetry of the heart, leaves no doubt of her source: "Permit me voyage, Love, into your hands."

Sylvia Plath

S o much has been written about the peculiar talent and tragic fate of Sylvia Plath that it is difficult to evaluate her contribution to modern poetry. Was she a demon endowed with poetic genius, or a genius possessed by a destructive demon, a dybbuklike force roiling within her that ruled her actions?

Her particular dybbuk could have been her father, who died when she was eight years old. And it may or may not have been significant that she was born in the crucial year of the Great Depression, 1932, on October 27, in Boston Memorial Hospital. The emotional climate of the country was one of despondency, bewilderment, and despair, not unmixed with rebellion.

Moreover, her father's reaction to her birth was one of disappointment, because she was a girl. Record has it that he declared that same day, "All I want from life from now on is a son, born two and a half years to the day." And his wife, Aurelia, Sylvia's mother, obligingly delivered that desired son on April 27, 1935.

Her amazing accuracy caused his colleagues on the faculty at Boston University, where he was a biology professor specializing in the behavior of bees, to offer a toast to "the man who gets what he wants when he wants it." Although playfully spoken, such a toast may well be indicative of Sylvia Plath's father as an authoritarian figure, one whose words and wishes were respected, a result of his Prussian background. Otto Plath's parentage was German (though it was from Poland that he emigrated to the United States during his adolescence), a heritage that sets the father on a pinnacle, in supreme power as head of the household. An academic intellectual, he was known for his cool, scientific mind; besides biology, he taught scientific German and was obviously revered in the halls of academe as well as in his home. In 1934, when Sylvia was only two years old, his book, *Bumblebees and Their Ways,* was published to some critical acclaim in scientific circles, and this professional approval undoubtedly had its effect on his family, particularly on his imaginative, impressionable daughter. The sound of bees hums through her poetry like an entomological theme song, with a dissonant sting hovering in the background—the love-hate duality that developed over the years toward the ghost of her father. "The Beekeeper's Daughter," one of the strange garden poems in *The Colossus* (1960) represents the culmination of Plath's conflict of emotions toward the father who deserted her by dying, and has been called "the most overt of all incestuous poems." *

Sylvia's mother, Aurelia Schober Plath, a highly intelligent,

---

* Robert Phillips in "The Dark Funnel: A Reading of Sylvia Plath."

down-to-earth person, came from Austrian parents. The Schobers lived in Winthrop, a seaside suburb of Boston, where the Plaths bought a home when Sylvia was four years old. As a small girl, Sylvia must have enjoyed a happy childhood, surrounded as she was by loving parents and grandparents. An exceptionally bright child, she received attention and approval from her father, despite his dictum for the arrival of a son. Sylvia was, after all, the firstborn; she was a chattering, charming three year old before her brother Warren could speak a word or take his first steps; and consciously or unconsciously, she sought to keep her advantage over her brother, a goal she won handily. It was not so easy, however, to divert her father's devotion to her mother; from her later poems, the feeling of rivalry with her mother, though subconscious at the time, is unmistakable.

Evidently her father was not so involved with science that he could not spend time with his small daughter, in both recreation and education. In the summer the family made good use of the sandy beaches that bordered the seacoast town. Long afterward, when Sylvia wrote her thinly disguised autobiographical novel, *The Bell Jar,* it was the delight of those hours she chose to record, giving her father and herself an additional year of life together. As Esther Greenwood, the anti-heroine, she recalls nostalgically that the happiest time of her life came when she "was about nine and running along the hot white beaches with my father the summer before he died." In reality, her father died just a week after her eighth birthday. His death came after a long and painful illness during which one leg had to be amputated, but in the mind of his imaginative daughter he drowned himself, and in so doing, deserted her.

Whether or not her mother was aware of Sylvia's intense feeling about her father, his death brought about such a radical change in the family life that there was little time for probing. A pragmatist by nature, Aurelia Plath realized that some arrangements would have to be made at once, for her husband had never trusted life insurance salesmen enough to take out a policy naming her as beneficiary, and his protracted illness had no doubt exhausted their savings. As for Sylvia, events occurred so swiftly that it was years before her inner conflict emerged. Her maternal grandparents moved in with the Plaths, and her Grandmother Schober took over the housekeeping while her mother began teaching shorthand and typing in the School for Secretarial Studies at Boston University. Sylvia had been attending public school for two years—entering the first grade at the normal age of six—and now it was her grandmother who greeted her when she came home every afternoon. Her grandfather, about whom there seems to have been an air of "gemütlicheit," worked as a maître d' at the Brookine Country Club, where he lived during the week and came home only on weekends, bringing choice morsels for the family larder—pastries, a round of paté or caviar.

Sylvia thought of him as a good-natured, benevolent, but rather remote relative (as pictured in *The Bell Jar*). She could not get to know him as she did her grandmother, who was always there. Her mother, who had to commute to Boston for her job, often came home tired; and though she did all she could to encourage her gifted daughter, was perhaps overzealous in her desire to see those gifts recognized, and to take her dead husband's place—she never reached Sylvia's heart. The child poet, who began to make poems, accompanied by strong-stroke india ink drawings, as soon as she learned to write, though she was ambivalent toward her mother, truly loved her grandmother.

One of the few poems of tender feeling Plath was ever moved to record was written at the death of her mother's mother. "Point Shirley" in her first collected volume, *Colossus*, is graced by homely details that reveal the place her grandmother held in the family circle and in Sylvia's psyche. "She is dead,/ Whose laundry snapped and froze here, who/ Kept house against/ What the sluttish, rutted sea could do. . . ." In the fourth stanza she compares the desolation of the Point Shirley house to its lived-in state when her grandmother "kept house." In a single, telling detail—"The planked-up windows where she set/ Her wheat loaves/ And apple cakes to cool. . . . A labor of love, and that labor lost"—the poet gives the reader a glimpse of her grandmother's devotion and small Sylvia's response to it. (An earlier line describes the drudgery of that devotion: "She wore her broom straws to the nub.")

Only one poem, "The Disquieting Muses," portrays Plath's mother, directly, and then it is as an inadequate maternal figure at first, trying to comfort her children during the disastrous hurricane of 1938, which hit the town of Winthrop with such terrific force that the twelve windows in Professor Plath's study were smashed to pieces; this is followed by the monstrous mother-love, hungry for reflected glory, pushing her daughter into every field of culture with or without talent, forcing her to become an overachiever. Resentment burns beneath every line. In Sylvia's sick, satiric fantasy it is three weird satanic muses, unwittingly invoked by her mother, who push her around. The key to the complexity of the mother-daughter relationship—indeed, the core of her behavior pattern—may be found in the last lines: "And this is the kingdom you bore me to,/ Mother, mother. But no frown of mine/ Will betray the company I keep."

For outwardly Sylvia was the same sunny, winsome little girl she had always been. Neither her mother, her grandmother, nor her teacher at the Winthrop school she and Warren attended had any indication of Sylvia's intense feeling about her father. Miss Abbie Willard, her teacher at the time Otto Plath died, recalled that both children were well-behaved, bright pupils, Sylvia adopting a protective, big sister attitude toward her brother, who obviously looked up to her. (There is no record of sibling rivalry in Sylvia's history; it might have been healthier for her if there had been.) Both of them were taken out of school when their father died, and soon afterward they came to say good-bye, Sylvia carrying a copy of their father's book for Miss Willard. Their mother was moving the family to the inland town of Wellesley, which had more cultural advantages to offer her children, particularly her gifted daughter. It was at about this time that Sylvia's first poem and drawing appeared in a Boston newspaper, and her mother was convinced she had produced a genuine genius, or at least one of definite potential; and Aurelia was determined to develop that potential to the nth degree.

The move from Winthrop did not cause any trauma for Sylvia as far as her mother could tell, but in the poet's memoir of her childhood, "Ocean 1212-W," (their telephone number), she calls it "the end of a fine, white flying myth," and, significantly, makes no reference to her father's long diabetic siege or his death. In 1944, Sylvia entered Phillips Junior High, where she was a straight "A" student and had poems published in *The Philli-pian;* those issues of the school paper inspired her to write more and, prompted by her mother's proud praise, still more. At graduation, she won Honorable Mention in the National Scholastic Literary Contest, and broke all records by being the first student to gain a sixth letter, plus an achievement certificate from Carnegie Institute. Ostensibly, she was the perfect student and American adolescent—friendly, outgoing, an earnest worker with creative talent that showed great promise. She breezed through Bradford High School with the same ease she had shown in junior high, winning honors and friends—though few were close to her, she was popular with both sexes—joining the editorial staff of the paper, and playing a lead role in the senior class play.

In only two instances did she reveal signs of inner turmoil that were somehow connected with her parents. Haunted by the ghost-image of her father, she was driven by a desire to equal and exceed his perfectionism. She enrolled in a German language course, and though she admitted that she hated it, she tried frantically to master the declensions. Even more frantic was her frenzied, continual pouncing out of "Bumble Boogie" on the piano in the student lounge. The notation of the piece, de-

signed to simulate the buzzing of bumblebees, seemed to symbolize her feeling toward the father who could have taught her
German and all he knew about other winged creatures besides
bees had he lived. (Professor Plath was also an ornithologist.)
At any rate, she banged out the piece with a vengeance, in a
kind of fierce joy on achieving the dissonant sound of buzzing.
(It was called her "piano special" in her senior yearbook.)

As for her mother, Sylvia felt even more ambivalence. She
must have inherited some of Aurelia's practicality—in fact, she
later referred to herself as "a rabid teenage pragmatist"—for she
systematically set about winning both academic and literary goals.
During her high school years she sent forty-five pieces to the
magazine *Seventeen* alone, and though the rejection slips piled
up from there and other sources, she kept on writing and submitting her creative work. She needed her mother's praise and
prodding, but was also irked by it because the gush of words
and affection was almost always accompanied by a reminder that
her mother's meager salary could not provide the college education both of them desperately wanted for Sylvia so her high
marks must be maintained in order to win scholarships. It may
well have been after one such prodding that the girl wrote a
satiric poem, "A Family Reunion," full of malicious humor in
its caricature of her relatives. She published it anonymously in
the school paper, but did not disguise her targets by changing
the names of those jabbed by her poison pen. Her mother was
astounded, hurt to the quick—a reaction Sylvia probably expected. She must have convinced her mother it was only a joke,
but the lines should have given Aurelia Plath an inkling of the
dark spirit that churned beneath her daughter's surface layer of
sweetness and light.

She did win those scholarships necessary to enter Smith College in the fall. One came from the Smith Club in Wellesley,
and the other endowed by Olive Higgins Prouty, novelist and
author of the best-selling *Stella Dallas, Now Voyager* and many
short stories, who became Sylvia's friend and patron. In Au-

gust, 1950, the young writer's first short story, "And Summer Will Not Come Again," was published in *Seventeen,* which had finally accepted her work. At the same time her poem, "Bitter Strawberries," a scathing comment on war, appeared in the *Christian Science Monitor*. It augured well for her college career. And indeed her freshman and sophomore years at Smith continued to bring honors and academic awards.

During these years she wrote poetry on a strict, self-imposed schedule, circling words in the red leather thesaurus that she had appropriated from her father's belongings. She maintained a detailed journal, scrupulously filled a bulging scrapbook, and studied "hard." Her scholastic record remained high; she was elected to class and college offices, became a member of the editorial board of the Smith *Review,* accepted weekend dates at men's colleges, and published short stories and poems in *Seventeen*. In short, she was an above average, all-American college girl, pretty, popular, and successful; she wrote in a letter, however, "For the few outward successes I may seem to have, there are acres of misgivings and self-doubt."

From all accounts, a goodly portion of that self-doubt stemmed from the mixed emotions toward the opposite sex. She was attractive and attracted to men, but reacted like a skittery colt when someone tried to come really close. As she grew conscious of herself as an object of sex, a conflict rose within her life as a poet-intellectual and as a woman, a future wife and mother. Her passion was for poetry, her male models W. H. Auden, Wallace Stevens, and Dylan Thomas. Among the women she admired were Emily Dickinson, Isabella Gardner, Edith Sitwell, Sara Teasdale, and Marianne Moore; she was so well acquainted with Edna St. Vincent Millay and Elinor Wylie that she borrowed—or lifted—an unmistakable image from each of them in her parable poem, "Spinster." Here Plath chose the concepts of two intellectually independent women poets as she spun out the old yarn of the female artist who solves the problem of the need for self-expression separate from the male by retreating from love. The cold clarity of Wylie's "Puritan Sonnet" and "Velvet Shoes" is felt in Plath's lines, "Ice and Rock, each sentiment within border,/ And heart's frosty discipline/ Exact as a snowflake." Stanzas one and four are even more declarative of debt to Millay's poem, "Spring," with its famous image of April as "a babbling idiot strewing flowers." Plath sets her story (stanza one) during an April walk of a girl (presumably the poet herself), accompanied by her latest suitor, when she is suddenly "intolerably struck/ By the birds' irregular babel/ And the leaves' litter." The climax in stanza four is practically an outright steal of Millay's memorable image as Plath declares, "Let idiots/ Reel giddy in bedlam spring," which is followed by the poem's resolution, "She withdrew neatly." The final stanza depicts the impenetrable barricade she sets up around her house, "As no mere insurgent man could hope to break/ With curse, fist, threat/ Or love, either."

As her sexual desires grew, burning beneath the surface but repressed by her intellectual and creative pursuits, her conflict deepened, and she realized that she had been avoiding, or was unaware of a major life-experience. "It's quite amazing how I've gone around for most of my life as in the rarefied atmosphere under a bell jar," she wrote significantly to a friend, revealing the genesis of *The Bell Jar* some ten years before the novel jelled in her mind. Her "latest suitor" in April of 1953 was Gordon Lameyer, a senior at Amherst College, an English major of like-minded literary interests, who was to become her most consistent male friend as well as suitor. Though at first put off by Sylvia's effusiveness—at the time of their first date she was madly in love with the poetry of Dylan Thomas—he soon became used to her enthusiasm, and her bubbling laughter, her ready interest in all he had to say besides her physical charm, made her a desirable companion. He was delighted that like him she was fascinated by James Joyce and could discuss *Ulysses* intelligently, but deferred to his judgment of *Finnegan's Wake*. He could not see any sign of the compulsive striving that marked her academic career. They discovered that both were from Wellesley and their families lived only about a mile apart. He was looking forward to seeing her often after his graduation in June.

One day in May, however, she told him ecstatically that she had won a *Mademoiselle* contest and was to be guest editor of the magazine on a salary, living in New York—all expenses paid—for the month of June. Previously she had been one of the two national winners of the magazine's fiction contest—"($500!)" she wrote in her scrapbook—a fact she had not mentioned to Gordon; she seemed to underplay her achievements when she was with him. Her need to see perfection in men as she had in her father made her tend to idealize Gordon, causing him some embarrassment, but he was disappointed to learn that he would not be seeing her for the whole month of June, especially since he was leaving in mid-July to enter the Naval Reserve O.C.S. program at Newport, Rhode Island.

Of that momentous month of June, Sylvia wrote in her journal-scrapbook: "Fantastic, fabulous, and all other inadequate adjectives go to describe the four gala chaotic weeks I worked as guest managing editor. . . . Living in luxury at the Barbizon, I edited, met celebrities, was feted and feasted by a galaxy of UN delegates, simultaneously interpreting, and artists . . . an almost unbelievable merry-go-round. . . . This Smith Cinderella met idols: Vance Bourjaily, Paul Engle, Elizabeth Bowen." She wrote an article via correspondence with five young male teachers—poets Alistair Reid, Anthony Hecht, Richard Wilbur, George Steiner, and William Burford. She wrote the lead editorial in the breezy style of the world of fashion and posed with the other girls (twenty in all) for a photo in star formation, Sylvia at the top. When the issue finally came out, however, the piece that gave her the most pleasure was a poem on page 358: "Mad Girl's Love-Song, A Villanelle by Sylvia Plath, Smith College, '54," the magazine stated. It was significant not only as her first in a big magazine, but indicative of future events. There is an aura of both Ophelia and Ariel in lines Sylvia noted as "my favorite villanelle." To speak of the stars "waltzing out in blue and red," followed by a galloping and "arbitrary blackness," combined with the theme line to a lover, repeating the make-believe being inside her head, is an intimation of the poet's tendency toward insanity, though the villanelle itself has a devil-may-care charm and lyric rhythm.

The six stanzas should have given a clue to the drastic means she was to take in an attempt to solve her subconscious conflict. The last two stanzas especially give credence to the theory that the ghost of her father must have been haunting her. Yet when she returned from New York at the end of June, her life and mood still seemed on the upsurge. *Harper's* magazine paid one hundred dollars for three poems, which Sylvia considered her first professional earnings. "All in all, I felt upborne on a wave of creative, social and financial success," she wrote later.

For the first two weeks in July she saw Gordon Lameyer, apparently enjoying his company every day; they took trips to the mountains and the ocean, discussed Dylan Thomas's poems and the intricacies of Joyce's *Finnegan's Wake;* they listened to their favorite Beethoven and Brahms on his record player, and not once did he detect any sign of "incipient schizophrenia," as he said. Sylvia did not complain of insomnia at any time or let him glimpse the morbidity she must have begun to feel. After he left on July 13, she no doubt missed his company, judging from the adoring letters she sent him, idealizing his intellectual powers and minimizing her own. With Gordon away, and the excitement of the month in New York a confused memory, she began to brood on the dark events of 1953—the electrocution of the Rosenbergs, the McCarthy witch-hunts made the pressure of the fashion magazine world of her recent triumph seem superficial. As she herself described it later in outlining her autobiographical novel: ". . . the return home to the dead summer world of a suburb of Boston: Here the cracks in her nature which had been held together by the surrounding pressures of New York, widen and gape alarmingly. More and more her warped view of the world around her—her own vacuous domestic life, and that of her neighbors' suddenly seemed unbearable. On August 24, she took an overdose of sleeping pills, crawled under the latticework of the porch of the Plath home, hid herself in a mudhole, hoping to die before her disappearance was noticed.

Either she had not taken enough pills, or her body was strong enough to withstand their effect: two days later, her frantic grandmother heard moans coming from beneath the porch. Sylvia was found, rushed by ambulance to the hospital, revived, and subsequently spent five months in McLean's, an expensive sanitarium, where her bill was paid by Mrs. Prouty. The novelist's generosity was repaid by a mocking caricature in *The Bell Jar,* but in 1953–1954 Sylvia was grateful to her patron as she emerged from the "agony of despair" and began the slow rehabilitation. She underwent shock treatment, which she never forgot; but, through treatment with a skillful analyst, she began to gain insight into her dual personality and was able to return to Smith in February (1954). She threw herself into her academic studies with renewed vigor. Gordon Lameyer, who had been shattered when his mother called him with the shocking news of Sylvia's attempted suicide, had been writing to her all during her hospitalization and stay at McLeans. He was deeply concerned for her health; he had begun to think of Sylvia as his girl and wondered if his ardor had anything to do with her breakdown.

At the time of her return to Smith, he was on destroyer duty as an ensign, but he received a steady stream of letters from Sylvia in response to his own, and he was both happy and relieved to read her enthusiastic accounts of her return to academic life, the strict but joyful regimen of study she set for herself. She was ecstatic over her literature courses, particularly the one in Russian literature with George Gibian. The novels of Tolstoy and Dostoevsky, especially the latter, whose examination of duality provided a much clearer insight into her own conflict than she had been able to find through analysis, though she kept up her sessions on a bimonthly basis for over a year after leaving McClean's. By the time Gordon came home in June of 1954, Sylvia seemed completely cured.

She was in the swing of college social life as well as her scholastic pursuits, mingling with her classmates and close friends at Lawrence House, where she lived, and cultivating visiting lecturers like Elizabeth Drew and novelist Mary Ellen Chase, both of whom took a great interest in her career. The only change in her appearance was her hair, which she had started bleaching; when asked, she explained that she thought the platinum blond color would distract attention from the scar under her left eye, the trace of a deep cut suffered in her suicide attempt. Otherwise she rarely referred to her nightmare experience.

That summer she and Nancy Hunter, one of Sylvia's few intimate friends at Lawrence House, took an apartment with two other Smith girls in Cambridge, where all were enrolled in summer courses at Harvard. Nancy recorded the weird events of those months in her memoir, *A Closer Look at Ariel,* and in her cameralike close-up the poet's blemishes come into full view. In odd ways Sylvia showed herself to be less an Ariel than a narcissistic, grasping, yet insecure schoolgirl. After a joint party the four roommates gave, she marked all the boxes and containers of items she had bought with her initials in big black letters, a hands-off warning to the others. She flaunted her newfound—through analysis—attitude toward sex verbally, but panicked under a violent reaction when put to the test. Although she saw Gordon Lameyer regularly, and they were unofficially engaged by the end of summer, she took advantage of his absence on a two-week Naval cruise to have a fling with a boy she "picked up" on the library steps. Impressed with his intellectual brilliance, she precipitated a sexual encounter with him, which proved a disaster, as it brought on torrential hemorrhaging. Sylvia, fearful for both her health and her reputation, relied totally on Nancy to get her to the hospital under an assumed name, to keep their roommates from learning what the trouble was, and to give her moral support. The whole ugly incident is described almost too graphically in Hunter's account. Miraculously, there were no lingering effects, and Sylvia emerged emotionally unscathed resuming her attachment to Gordon on his return as if nothing had happened.

Back at Smith in the fall, Sylvia dyed her hair a chestnut brown to free herself from the frivolous look of a platinum blond, and buckled down to a strict regimen of work, principally on her honors thesis, a study of Dostoevsky's use of the double. She was also trying to master German again, having started in summer school, which might have been a cause for her wild behavior. Now she determined to wipe off the only "B" she had ever received; but halfway through the semester she learned that she already had more credits than she needed to graduate *summa cum laude,* and she still hated German, the gutteral sound of the language, so in midsemester she dropped it to concentrate on her thesis and poetry writing. She was so involved in her studies that she often had no time to see Gordon on weekends when he came. She sailed through her senior year, winning poetry prizes and influencing professors, seeking a fellowship for graduate study the following year. Both Alfred Kazin and Mary Ellen Chase sponsored her for a Fulbright at Newnham College, Cambridge. Before the year was over, her engagement to Gordon was broken, since he did not care for being at her beck and call; but they remained friends, even taking a European trip together on a platonic basis as late as 1956, two months before she was married to Ted Hughes, the British poet then coming into prominence. At Cambridge her brilliant record continued; her poems appeared in *Variety,* and she was connected with *Granta,* Newnham Publications; she took in little theatre productions, and generally earned a reputation for excellence, or, as one friend wrote, marked capability in all she did. Few could know that she was consciously striving for normality in her life, trying to erase the memory of her suicide attempt with multiple activities that would also serve to hide the fact that the evil double in her still leaned toward self-destruction if she thought someone was deserting or abandoning her.

In April (1956) word came that her grandmother, Aurelia Greenwood Schober, died of cancer, which must have brought a sense of genuine loss rather than a feeling of desertion. By then Sylvia was seeing Ted Hughes, whom she had met toward the end of February at a party in celebration of publication of some poems by Ted and a select literary group, *St. Bartolph's Review*. She had been so impressed with his poems that she found a way to get invited to the party, and the mutual attraction between them was evident at this first meeting. When her grandmother died, on April 29, Sylvia and Ted were practically engaged; Sylvia felt she had finally found a man she could look up to, one who measured up to her father in her eyes and exceeded him in several ways, for Ted was lover as well as a father figure: he was her contemporary, they shared like interests, both were creative, intense personalities, both were physically good-looking. They were married in London on Bloomsday, June 16, 1956, with Sylvia's mother in attendance. When Mrs. Plath realized that her darling daughter was having a serious romance she came hurrying over to England like a protective mother hen, and it was due to her presence perhaps that the pair were married in a private ceremony in June. They wanted to spend the summer together in Spain, and by her mother's standards, as well as society's in the fifties, a young couple still were "living in sin" if they were not married.

The two had an idyllic summer, gloriously happy, and remarkably productive of new poems by both of them. Sylvia's housemates saw a complete change in her manner when she and Ted returned for the fall term. The striving, the frenzied outside activity was gone; she concentrated on her courses and poetry; she was much quieter in expressing her enthusiasms. The reason for her newfound serenity was not mentioned; though she and Ted were together most of the time, it was as an engaged couple. For in her rush to be married. Sylvia had neglected to get the "tutorial permission" required by an old college rule regarding undergraduate fellows who wished to marry. The secret came out when she received a letter, probably from her mother, addressed to "Mrs. Edward Hughes," and the senior resident in charge of her house reminded her that she could lose her Fulbright if the authorities found out.

It was a measure of Sylvia's fearful respect for authority that she was both terrified and outraged; she called on her supervisor of classical studies, Dorothea Krook, with whom she had become friends, and in great agitation asked for advice. It was the only time Mrs. Krook ever saw the rage and resentment that came out in the later poems. She tried to soothe the girl's troubled emotions, agreeing with her on the "idiocy" of old college laws, but advising her to confess to the tutor, I. V. Morris, what she had done; and after some further histrionics, Sylvia took the advice, and was told she had nothing to worry about: she would not be "sent down" and furthermore, she and Ted could live together as man and wife.

Sylvia was as wildly ecstatic with joy as she had been disturbed by angry fear. It is notable that she was not contrite about having broken the rule, though she made it sound as if she had committed a crime; her main concern was for her career, her image in the public eye. This does not mean that her love for Ted was not genuine: it was overpowering, and in the end proved destructive; but in 1956 her love brought the strange, diffuse talents of this brilliant but demented poet into the budding stages of full flower. She and Ted found a tiny flat on Eltisley Avenue, around the corner from Grantchester Meadows, where her supervisor lived. Both Mrs. Krook and I. V. Morris, besides classmates, have commented on Sylvia's glowing happiness, which gave an incandescence to her whole being. Her creativity increased and matured; the second term of 1957 marked Plath's first acceptance by *The New Yorker*, one of her cherished goals.

Among those published in the magazine during 1957, "Watercolor of Grantchester Meadows," a bucolic picture of the neighborhood, lets the reader glimpse her serene happiness in such succinct lines as, "It is a country on a nursery plate." Yet even this poem ends on a faintly sinister note. The "watercolor" is muddied over by the students who "stroll or sit,/ Hands laced, in a moony indolence of love— / Black-gowned, but unaware/ How in such mild air/ The owl shall stoop from his turret, the rat cry out."

The second year at Cambridge was undoubtedly the most tranquil and rewarding of Sylvia Plath's brief life. Her marriage meant a great deal to her, particularly since she had found a mate who could understand and share her aspirations, her love for their chosen art. During this first year of their marriage she and Ted basked in each other's lights. When in March Ted was notified that his work, *The Hawk in the Rain,* had won the New York Poetry Center Award, with publication in America and England, Sylvia rejoiced with him and was proud of the fact that *her* husband had won it. Her immense ego, so well hidden by her outward manner, made her experience all events and emotions, including love, with a terrible possessive intensity, and her actions were all too often predicated on pressure which she erroneously felt was put upon her.

Directly after her Fulbright was successfully terminated, Sylvia was offered an instructorship at Smith. Although she was pleased, she was also scared, not because she feared for her ability to teach, but because she was afraid she would be "diminished" by her former faculty members, treated like a schoolgirl. She and Ted left for the United States in June, and spent the summer at Cape Cod, a present from Sylvia's mother. In September the former prize student was welcomed back to her alma mater, a returning heroine. As it turned out, she proved to be an inspiring teacher; and Ted, after collecting his award, found a teaching post at the University of Massachusetts in nearby Amherst. Both were writing poetry. On the surface it seemed the perfect setup, but before the second semester was over, the two decided that teaching and creativity could not be combined successfully and both gave notice to their respective colleges, much to the dismay of Mary Ellen Chase and other professors at Smith, who felt that Plath owed the college at least a few years on the faculty for past favors. Miss Chase thought her protegé had made a dreadful mistake in getting married, though she knew Sylvia was deliriously happy.

The Hugheses, whether they were aware of this disapproval or not, moved to a small apartment in Boston's Beacon Hill. In Sylvia's words, she and Ted were "living on a shoestring for a year of writing, to see what we could do." She had collected nearly a volume of poetry, which she began sending out in manuscript, but it was rejected regularly. They did manage to eke out a living, and both wrote a great deal. But the most influential factor in the development of Plath's work was Robert Lowell's poetry seminar at Boston University. which she audited along with Anne Sexton and George Starbuck. The introduction to Lowell's "confessional poetry," as it came to be known, served as a release for the locked-in memories of her childhood, of her father's ghost, up till now only half-recognized. She learned to write in syllabics, to mold method to content, to exercise not restraint but control in baring her soul. Lowell described her as "willowy, long-waisted, sharp-elbowed, nervous, giggly, gracious—a brilliant, tense presence, embarrassed by restraint."

Equally important was the Friday cocktail hour at the Ritz bar, when, weekly classes behind them, she and Anne Sexton sipped martinis and savored the exchanged experiences of their attempts at suicide. George Starbuck, who accompanied them must have wearied of hearing the sordid details over and over, which never seemed to tire the girls. As Sexton said, they "talked death and this was life for us." Such a topic could only be destructive in the long run, even though they spoke of their individual triumphs of life in taunting yet defying death. Unlike her companion, Sylvia did not allow the technique of poetry to evaporate in the classroom even while downing martinis. The practical side of her stored up and put to good use the suggestions and comments made by Robert Lowell whenever she shyly showed him some of her lines. At home, she studied his *Life Studies,* and in the poems that were piling up for her first volume, *The Colossus,* she experimented with both metrics and syllabics, with iambic pentameter and hexameter. She applied for a Eugene Saxton grant, established in honor of Edna Millay's beloved editor at *Harper's;* but the trustees, though deeming Plath's poems "above reproach," decided that she had had so many awards "dropped in her lap" that it would be wise for her to teach a little longer. However, the letter was very encouraging and she determined to try again later.

When she and Ted returned from a camping trip the next summer, she was pregnant at last: from the beginning of their marriage she had wanted a child, the experience of birthing a baby. Conversely, the talks with Anne Sexton brought back suicidal tendencies. From September to the end of November (1959) she and Ted were at Yaddo, where Sylvia completed enough poems to make a volume, many of them indicating her preoccupation with death in the midst of life. In "All the Dead Dears," "Full Fathom Five," "Suicide off Egg Rock," "The Ghost's Leavetaking," and the title poem, "The Colossus," she reveals a desire to meet death in midstream and so discover her father. Most unveiling of all is "The Beekeeper's Daughter," with its outspoken last lines: "Father, bridegroom, in this Easter egg/ Under the coronal . . . / The queen bee marries the winter of your year."

In December the Hugheses returned to England to live, and in April, 1960, at about the time Sylvia gave birth to their first child, Frieda Rebecca, the American poet's first volume, dedicated to Ted, with all of the above poems, was accepted by William Heineman, Ltd. for fall publication. Again it seemed a good omen, and events immediately succeeding appeared to bear this out. Sylvia and Ted were both writing and receiving recognition; both were happy with their baby. Sylvia secretly felt an emotional emptiness at not having a being within her body anymore, and it was difficult to care for an infant in a tiny flat. She said nothing of this to Ted except that she wanted to have more children and she hoped they could move to a larger place. She did conceive again, but lost the baby through miscarriage in February 1961; and a month later was rushed to the hospital for an emergency appendectomy. And all the time she was writing, had inveigled the BBC into hiring her for a broadcasting "spot," and edited *American Poetry Now,* a supplement for *The Critical Quarterly.* In June of 1961 she reapplied for and received the Saxton Fellowship, an outright grant of money to cover expenses (listed by the author) for one year while working on a definite project. Plath's project was her novel, *The Bell Jar,* a plan for which had come to her suddenly, while she was negotiating for an American edition of *The Colossus,* later published by Knopf.

"Seized by some fearsome excitement," as she said, she stayed awake all night as the novel she had been wanting to write for nearly ten years unfolded in her mind. The next morning she got up and started to "belt it out." The story concerned "a college girl building up to and experiencing a nervous breakdown," her own story, thinly disguised. It is interesting to note that Sylvia chose her grandmother's maiden name, Greenwood, for her fictionalized surname, and for her first, Esther, the Old Testament queen. Again it was an omen, for she and Ted needed a real home, a strong structure like her grandmother's in Winthrop; and before Sylvia was well into her final draft, the Hugheses had found a place that exceeded their fondest hopes: Court Green, a two-acre property in Devon, comprising an old farmhouse and outbuildings, on rich land. They jumped at the chance to buy it, borrowing from their mothers to make the deal. Sylvia was pregnant again and, at the prospect of their new life, happy again, bursting with energy, with plans.

Significantly, a primary project of hers was to become a keeper of bees, and before the house was furnished, she had made the proper arrangements, and eventually, besides six jars of gleaming honey, she harvested a narrative sequence of six strong, bittersweet poems from the venture. In addition, she was able to rid herself of her father's ghost: she was no longer the bee-keeper's daughter, but the queen, powerful yet pure, casting out all men: "The bees are all women,/ Maids and the long royal lady./ They have got rid of the men,/ The blunt, clumsy stumblers, the boors. . . ." Such deadly triumph would come later when, within the year, her idyllic marriage was smashed to smoldering bits in the heat of her rage at the discovery of her adored husband's adultery.

The time of their move to Court Green, however, brought a brief period of bliss. "Letter in November," like the calm before the storm, is one of the few poems expressing a modicum of contentment. As she shuffled through the fallen red leaves of late autumn, Sylvia, pregnant, egocentric, and possessive as always, proclaims that this is *"my"* property, *"my"* seventy trees," not "our," as one might expect from the apparent closeness of the two poets up to this point of their marriage. The last lines betray a sense of battle ahead, despite the temporary peace of mind and body. "O love, O celibate./ Nobody but me/ Walks the waist-high wet./ The irreplaceable/ Golds bleed and deepen, the mouths of Thermopylae."

Brushing her fear of the future aside, Sylvia pushed ahead with her novel, only taking time off to give birth to a baby boy, Nicholas Farrar on January 17 (1962), and was able to send off a detailed report to the Saxton trustees when it was due early in February. Systematically, she divided her time between housework, the babies, and her writing. Luckily, she found a strong, calm woman to help with the housework; and one of the first rooms to be fixed up was a study for Ted, so he would not be disturbed by the "babes." She took grave pride in his literary successes and rarely spoke of her own, according to Elizabeth Sigmund and her writer husband, who lived in North Devon, closer than any other of their literary friends. When Elizabeth asked Ted if Sylvia "wrote poetry too," he said, "No, she *is* a poet." His high regard seemed equal to hers, their lives closely intertwined.

Six months later, however, the bucolic paradise of Court Green had become emotionally a barren land, though the earth bore fruit, and the beehives gave forth honey. *The Bell Jar* was completed; new poems, written out of fury, at a furious pace were pouring from Sylvia's seared heart: Ted had all but deserted her. He had begun by going up to London frequently, more than was necessary, and evaded—"lied," she was sure—about his reasons. Catastrophe came when she discovered he was having an affair with someone who purported to be a friend. Sylvia's mother came over during the summer, but her efforts to help the situation only seemed to increase the strain. Nor was Ted's family a source of help. Sylvia could not abide them, especially his sister, Olwyn, who had been jealous and disapproving of the poet from the first. During her sole visit there in Yorkshire where the Hughes family lived, Sylvia, after an argument with Olwyn had run out of the house and wandered on the moor until Ted found her and brought her back. The painful incident was the genesis of her poem, "Wuthering Heights."

With the writing of *The Bell Jar,* she exorcised the spectre of suicide, but not the ghost of her father, which, except for the symbolic activity of beekeeping, had been banished to a certain extent by her worshipful love of Ted. And in *Three Women: A Monologue for Three Voices,* a radio play in verse, completed in May, 1962, she asserted her womanhood, three contrasting facets of the female nature. On the surface at least, she must have felt encouragingly close to the return of normality, which made the blow of Ted's adultery all the more crushing. She was equally disturbed by his diminished stature. "He has become a *little* man!" she cried out to Elizabeth Sigmund one night. Grasping her friend's hands, she pleaded, "Help me, help me!" And then frighteningly, "When you give someone your whole heart and

he doesn't want it, you cannot take it back. It's gone forever."
She could not accept a fallen idol.

Things went from bad to worse. After a nasty scene involving a phone call from Ted's lover, when Sylvia, in a fit of violent anger pulled the cords from the wall, Ted left for good. Later he asked her to bring the children to Ireland and spend a month in a friend's house, but it was no reconciliation, for he left a few days after they arrived; she again felt abandoned and enraged. She had begun to realize the link between the death of her father and the death of love, the lifelong love-hate conflict that had been her inner torment through the years. It was at this point that Plath saw clearly the need to break the stranglehold that the ghost of her father—and Ted or any other living man—might have upon her inner self. Her famous, and unjustifiably celebrated poem, "Daddy," is a vicious, vengeful invective hurled against father, husband, and by implication, all men; it was therapeutic for her injured ego and a gratuitous shock treatment for the reader. As poetry, however, it is too much of a mishmash to be successful. It is valid to state bluntly in the first two stanzas of this coldhearted ballad, "You do not do, you do not do/ Any more, black shoe/ In which I have lived like a foot/ For thirty years . . ." which Robert Phillips has called a metaphor of incest; and to continue in stanza two, "Daddy, I have had to kill you./ You died before I had time.— Marble-heavy, a bag full of God . . ." Here again the father has drowned, not died in a sickbed. It is believable to read, "I used to pray to recover you./ Ach, du./" And then to bring out the sorrows of childhood, including her inability to speak German. (Notably she chooses the word, "Ich"—"I"—as the one that sticks in her throat like a barb wire.) But to accuse her father of being a Nazi, berating him for "chuffing her off like a Jew," to identify her suffering with the magnitude of the Holocaust not only reveals her colossal ego but stretches the credibility of the reader, since, as Irving Howe has pointed out, there has been nothing in the poem or in Plath's life experience to warrant the comparison. Extraneous ideas are brought in: "Every woman adores a Fascist." again unwarranted, followed by a reversal to her childhood picture of her father, mild, "but no less a devil" for that—"a black man/ who/ Bit my pretty red heart in two." The narrative continues with her attempted suicide and rescue; her idolization of him, "the man in black with a Meinkampf look."

Then suddenly, following the line, flatly stated, of being "finally through," the metaphor switches to the scene of her broken marriage: "The black telephone's off at the root,/ The voices just can't worm through." The next stanza explains:

> *If I've killed one man, I've killed two—*
> *The vampire who said he was you*
> *And drank my blood for a year,*
> *Seven years, if you want to know.*

Sylvia and Ted were married seven years; and one cannot help wondering if her denunciation of him as "vampire" is not the core of the whole poem. The last stanzas seem contrived in the extreme. Reverting to Daddy again, she speaks of the stake in his "fat black heart," and sticks in another extraneous line, "And the villagers never liked you," a snapshot view developed in the next two lines, followed by the often quoted final words: "Daddy, daddy, you bastard, I'm through."

It was probably not so much her father, for all her wailing, as it was her own ideal of perfectionism that caused her suicidal tendencies. She strove for perfection in all she did, and the fact that Ted's love for her was not perfect, that her idolized husband, her gentle giant had become a *"little"* man, was a blow her ego could not bear: it meant she was not capable of holding his love.

In December (1962), she took her children and went to London for the winter months, intending to return to Court Green by spring. Unfortunately, London was hit by its severest freeze in eons; Sylvia had always suffered from the cold, and the apartment was icy. The one source of comfort was the fact that Yeats had lived here during his London stay: to her it was a miracle, and again a good omen that she had found it for rent, though she had invoked his spirit by consulting his *Complete Poems* as one consults the Bible, and, sighting his words, "Take up your things and come with me," she had gone straight to the house she had often seen with the blue plaque, "Yeats lived here." Overjoyed at finding his place for rent, she had signed a five-year lease. In spite of chills, fever, and caring for the children, she was writing at top speed. *The Bell Jar* was published on January 14 under the name Victoria Lucas; she did not want it to be under her own name for fear of hurting those she had caricatured. When the novel gave promise of being highly successful, she wrote her brother that it must never be published in the United States. All this time she was composing the last poems dealing with death versus life, maintaining a precarious balance between the two. They were contained in the volume she planned to call *Ariel,* after one of the poems describing her own mysterious life-and-death hallucinations. This book would be "for Frieda and Nicholas."

She was going to appear on the BBC program, "The Critics," and give a poetry reading. *Punch* had asked for some articles; she had found a nursery school for Frieda, an "au pair" girl was to arrive soon to care for Nick. Yet she was yearning for Court Green and looked forward to her return in time for spring planting. So she wrote her friend Elizabeth on February 7.

Four days later, early in the morning of February 11th, she took her life by turning on the gas in the oven. Whatever it was that triggered her sudden reversal to suicide remains uncertain. She may have learned that Ted was also planning to return to Court Green with his new love, as he did soon after Sylvia's death. Certain it is that, though Plath's final poems were her strongest, she would not have been so widely discussed or hailed as the bitch goddess of confessional poets if she had not committed suicide and at that particular moment, when she had been abandoned by her husband, was ill—"Fever 103°" is among her more fully realized self-portrait poems—and was able to pour out soul-baring lines at top speed.

Former Lowell disciples, including their mentor, placed her on a pedestal out of all proportion to her worth as poet. If her life story had not been so fascinating, so poignant in its tragic finale, her poetry probably would have been more moderately evaluated. As Irving Howe has pointed out, mere confession does not make great poetry, no matter how pungent or clever fragmentary phrases may be. Plath's poems show passion, passionate hate, but little of love for others, and no true compassion: her references to the suffering of the Jewish people under Hitler are purely for purposes of comparison with her own personal torment, actually an enormous display of self-love, self-pity. Except for the poems about her baby boy "Nick and the Candlestick," "The Night Dances," and "Morning Song," the last showing a disavowal of motherhood as much as tenderness; the poem for her grandmother, "Shirley Point"; and "Mad Girl's Love Song," which is little more than an exercise in villanelle writing, the element of love is lacking in Sylvia Plath's aborted creativity. Deeply as she cared for Ted, giving him "her whole heart" as she said, she wrote no love poems during their courtship or marriage.

After the first flush of acclaim for Plath's peculiar art, literary analysis set in and is still active. The pendulum of assessment has swung all the way from Edward Butscher's hyperbolic hosanna to the "bitch goddess" extolling her as "the first major woman poet in America"—thereby relegating the towering figure of Emily Dickinson to second place if not lower—to Irving Howe's objective judgment that "Sylvia Plath will be regarded as an interesting minor poet whose personal story was poignant." In between these two are the verdicts of Marjorie Perloff and Joyce Carol Oates, praise tempered by serious reservations. Perloff, though conceding that Plath is an important poet, "whose work has influenced the diction, syntax, and imagery of younger writers—especially women"—finds her "imaginative world, despite its power and coherence, essentially a limited one." Oates deems Plath an immature lyric poet who has not the vision to see that she can be part of the living universe and maintain her function as poet. Despite speculation, Plath remains an enigma. As recently as 1982, nearly twenty years after the poet's death, her *Complete Poems,* compiled and edited by her ex-husband, Ted Hughes, won the Pulitzer Prize for poetry—a strange and inexplicable choice. Although the volume itself might be considered contemporary, it is hard to understand why poems that were written nearly a generation ago, and recognized at the time as revolutionary, should be awarded a prize usually given to work created during the previous year. Whatever the reason for the belated bestowal of this honor upon her, Plath remains a figure of questionable quality in the annals of modern American poetry.

Anne Sexton
Maxine Kumin

S ix days after Sylvia Plath's death, in a poem dated February
17, 1963, one of her sisters in poetry and suicide, only
four years older than she and a fellow New Englander who grew
up in the same town, wrote a poem, "Sylvia's Death," an en-
vious eulogy.

The author of course was Anne Sexton; titled simply, "Sylvia's Death," *For Sylvia Plath,* the poem referred to those days
in Boston when they both were "barflys" at the Ritz and mulled
over the subject of death as if it were an old wine to savor along
with their extra dry martinis. The lines recall "the death we said
we both outgrew,/ the one we wore on our skinny breasts,/ . . .

the death we drank to,/ the motives and then the quiet deed
. . ." Later lines admit, "and I know at the news of your death,
/ a terrible taste for it, like salt." Yet Anne Sexton managed to
withstand the terrible desire for death—to cope with "the trial
by existence" as Frost called it—for a full decade and a year longer
than her friend, and in that time to create a more voluminous
and impressive canon by which to judge her genius.

Anne Harvey Sexton was born in Newton, Massachusetts on
November 9, 1928, but she grew up in Wellesley and, like Sylvia, went to school there. According to her own account, she
did not begin to write poetry until 1957 or 1958, when she
was close to thirty years old, so she was no child prodigy like
Plath; but she was obviously highly intelligent and possessed
enough self-confidence to feel that she could make poems if she
chose. "I was watching television," she related, "a program on
the form of the sonnet and I said, 'I can do that.' So I wrote a
poem. It wasn't very good and I didn't offer it for publication."

Anne, unlike Sylvia, had both her parents until she was thirty,
married, and had two daughters of her own, but we catch a
glimpse of the loneliness she felt at the age of puberty in her
poem, a one-sentence piece comprising twenty-three lines and
entitled, "Young." It begins, "A thousand doors ago/ when I
was a lonely kid/ in a big house with four/ garages and it was
summer/ as long as I could remember," and describes herself as
she "lay on the lawn at night . . . the wise stars bending over
me." The house was "white as wax," the light she sees from her
mother's and father's windows imply separate bedrooms, and
the puzzled adolescent lying on the lawn told the stars her
questions and thought that God "really" sees all. In the title poem
of her second volume, "All My Pretty Ones," we learn that her
father was an alcoholic, presumably because of his livelihood as
a high-pressure salesman of wool fabrics and part owner of a
woolen mill, always striving for greater status, living beyond his
means, "in a house you could not afford." As she goes through
his effects, following his death a few months after her mother's

in 1959, we get a picture of upper middle-class life, particularly in the old albums she is leafing through. And a five-year diary that her mother kept for three years "tells all she does not say of your alcoholic tendency."

The speedboat races, the horseshow, their kennel of dogs, the Lincoln Continental mentioned in another poem, all bespeak the smart society surrounding this sharp-sensed poet as she was growing up. She was educated in Wellesley private schools and at Garland Junior College in Boston. In 1948, at the age of twenty, she married Alfred M. Sexton, to whom she would be married for twenty-five years. From the poem, "And One for My Dame," her husband, "blue-eyed as a picture book," was, like her father, a salesman of wool. The penultimate stanza of this poem reads: "And when you drive off, my darling,/ Yes, sir! Yes, sir! It's one for my dame,/ your sample cases branded with my father's name," is a clear indication of the poet's opinion of the salesman's lot, and the hostility she must have felt toward the occupation both as daughter and wife of a salesman. Yet hers was a love marriage involving an elopement, and evidently a happy one during the first years. In spite of the resentment revealed in the last stanza of the above poem, an enjambment of the previous stanza, finalizing the description: "your itinerary open,/ its tolls ticking and greedy,/ its highways built up like new loves, raw and speedy," she found much joy in her marriage to Alfred Sexton at first. The daisies he sent to her every week he was on the road, the "happiness he brought to her kitchen" when he would make charcoal-broiled steaks, his "camp-director" quality, his ability to build things by instinct, all endeared him and the institution of marriage to her.

In those early years, Anne, who was a ravishing brunette beauty with a wide, sensuous mouth and keen, blue-green eyes, followed a career as a fashion model right after college and through 1950–1951. Famous for her wit as well as her facial beauty and shapely figure, she was too intellectually inclined to be content with the vapidity and commercialism of modelling, not to mention the lechery of most agents. Probably the principal reason she left that commercial field, however, was that she became pregnant and within a few years two daughters were born, Linda and Joyce; and at some point a third pregnancy was aborted—a procedure that gave rise to the poignant poem, "The Abortion," with its refrain, "Somebody who should have been born/ is gone." Since she herself had been a third daughter and last-born child—"a mistake" of her parents, as she called it—she may not have wanted to risk a third daughter herself. At six, she, Anne, used to hide in a closet, "all day among shoes,/ away from the glare of the bulb in the ceiling,/ away from the bed and the heavy table/ and the same terrible rose repeating on the walls." When her mother locked her in the bedroom for some misbehavior, she "hid in a closet as one hides in a tree." She felt herself "the unwanted, the mistake/ that Mother used to keep Father/ from his divorce." Eventually, all that remained from the year she was six, "was a small hole in my heart, a deaf spot,/ so that I might hear/ the unsaid more clearly." She would not bring an unwanted child into the world.

The abortion, however, proved such a traumatic experience that it brought on a severe depression which led to attempted suicide, and for the first three years of her second daughter's life, Anne Sexton had to spend her days in a sanitarium.

It was several years before the little girl knew her as Mother. During that time Anne took courses at Boston University, among them Robert Lowell's poetry seminar, and his ideas confirmed the instinctive knowledge of her own gift for poetry writing that she had glimpsed from watching the television program on the sonnet. Like Sylvia Plath, she profited from the freedom of form and content in Lowell's *Life Studies*. She, even more than Plath, became his disciple. And she began by relating her experience in the sanitarium. Her poems were not so much "confessional" as fiercely frank and autobiographical. She evidently did not have to wait long for acceptances and recognition. A year after she started, her poems began to appear in such magazines as *Anti-*

och Review, Harper's, The Hudson Review, Partisan Review, The New Yorker, Saturday Review—all the top literary publications.

In 1960, she gathered these poems together in a starting first volume entitled, *To Bedlam and Part Way Back*. With the opening poem, "You, Doctor Martin," it is largely a record of Sexton's stay at the sanitarium. The enjambment joining the first four and last two of the six stanzas adds to the effect of narration in presenting the daily regimen at an institution for the insane.

> *You, Doctor Martin, walk*
> *from breakfast to madness. Late August,*
> *I speed through the antiseptic tunnel*
> *where the moving dead still talk*
> *of pushing their bones against the thrust*
> *of cure. And I am queen of this summer hotel*
> *or the laughing bee on a stalk*
>
> *of death. We stand in broken*
> *lines and wait while they unlock*
> *the door and count us at the frozen gates*
> *of dinner. The shibboleth is spoken*
> *and we move to gravy in our smock*
> *of smiles. We chew in rows, our plates*
> *scratch and whine like chalk*
>
> *in school. There are no knives*
> *for cutting your throat. I make*
> *moccasins all morning. . . .*

Next comes the session with Dr. Martin, whom she deems "god of our block, prince of all the foxes." Mingled with the events of the daily curative routine—"Noon Walk On The Asylum Lawn"; "Ringing the Bells," ("And this is the way they ring/ the bells in Bedlam . . ."); "Lullaby" (the nightly ritual of the sleeping pills) are poems dealing with memories of the past, presumably called up in these sessions with the psychiatrist—Dr. Martin, the asylum analyst. "Kind Sir: These Woods"

based on a quotation from Thoreau's *Walden,* recalls "an old
game" that children used to play when she was eight and ten,
while her family was at their grandfather's cottage on "The Island, in down Maine." The trick was to turn around once, eyes
shut tight, and you would be lost when you opened them, especially when the fog came in from the ocean; "grandfather's
cottage grew white and strange"; the nursemaid was gone, all
was changed; for a moment that seemed an eternity you were
lost. Thoreau had cited the ancient game and commented, "Not
till we are lost do we begin to find ourselves." Sexton ends the
poem by stating that she has spun around twice with sealed eyes,
and on opening them was afraid to look—"this inward look that
society scorns"—the searching look with the analyst; but she
finds "nothing worse than myself, caught between the grapes
and the thorns."

Other poems reach farther back, to the days she was three or
four, held high on her father's shoulder to see the circus parade, laughing, breathless with excitement. But mostly she remembered the love she felt and "the color of music/ and how
forever/ all the trembling bells" of her father were hers. Going
back farther, she recalled a family legend about her great grandfather, a man of some means who "begat eight genius children
and bought twelve almost new grand pianos," and built seven
"arking houses" that were still standing along the ocean. These
stories and more she must have told the doctor during the course
of her cure or partial cure. The two-stanza poem, "Said The
Poet to the Analyst," begins, "My business is words"; and the
second starts, "Your business is watching my words." She quickly
advanced to the "best ward" of "Bedlam."

Part Two of this first volume deals with the poet's readjust-
ment to her former life after she "checked out for the last time/
on the first of May;/ graduate of the mental cases,/ with my analyst's okay,/ my complete book of rhymes,/ My typewriter and
my suitcases." For a time, only "part way back from Bedlam,"
she stayed at her mother's house in Gloucester, her parents ev-

idently having separated, and gradually came to know her second daughter when the little girls came for occasional weekend visits. Her mother could not forgive Anne for attempting suicide, though she tried to help her daughter with various diversions. For one, she had their portraits painted, first Anne's and then her own, a seven-part poem, "The Double Image," reports ironically. By the time they were completed, cancer had claimed her mother. Anne took care of her and visited her in the nursing home every day until her death, which marks the end of the volume, and "has the cumulative effect of a good novel."

So read the liner notes from the publishers, Houghton Mifflin, who continued to publish all of her books. Her teacher-mentor, Robert Lowell, wrote: "Swift lyrical openness . . . an almost Russian abundance and accuracy. Her poems stick in my mind. I don't see how they can fail to make the great stir they deserve." And they did create a stir that brought immediate success. James Wright called the book "a work of genius. It signifies a moment of major importance to American literature." Sexton received a grant from the Radcliffe Institute for Independent Study (initiating that program) which gave her financial support necessary to prepare a second volume, published in 1962. It was only one of many grants and awards that she, like Sylvia Plath, had bestowed upon her. Even before her first book appeared she held the Robert Frost Fellowship in 1959 at the Breadloaf Writers Conference, where she met her peers and enjoyed an exchange of ideas with them. Yet she always retained the feeling of melancholy and the leaning toward suicide—for all her talk of having outgrown it—evident in this second volume.

All My Pretty Ones, a quotation from *Macbeth*, the cry of lament from Macduff on learning of the deaths of his wife and children, reads like a sequel to the "novel" unfolded in Sexton's first volume. Taking up the story where she left off, she describes her feelings in "The Truth the Dead Know"—"For my mother, born March 1902, died March 1959, and my father born February 1900, died June 1959"—as she walks from church after the second funeral service inside of three months, her father following her mother to the grave. But she does not accompany his coffin to the gravesite beside her mother's. "It is June. I am tired of being brave," the final line of the first stanza states flatly. The title poem follows, in which, as earlier discussed, she "shuffles and disencumbers" her father from the residence he could not afford. The titles of the poems comprising the contents suggest bereavement and contemplation of death: "Lament," "Old Dwarf Heart," "A Curse Against Elegies," and "Ghosts"—the remembrance of things past, when the ghosts were live people, mingled with the search for faith.

With the publication of her second volume, Anne Sexton was an established poet, recognized as outstanding among the younger contemporaries. She began to devote most of her time to writing poems and preparing applications for grants which were successful in providing the necessary funds. In June of 1963, she received a travelling fellowship from the American Academy of Arts and Letters. Shortly before it began, she heard from composer Ann McMillan, whose principal field was electronic music, that the French Radio-Television had commissioned McMillan to select two young poets of importance in the United States to be represented in the Paris International Festival for young artists between the ages of twenty and thirty-five. She had been following Sexton's work since it had first appeared and felt that it was the most representative of the new outspoken modern poetry being offered by young Americans and she contacted the poet at once in regard to making a tape of a reading. There was not much time since it had to be sent to France no later than June 12.

Anne responded immediately with an invitation to Newton, where the Sextons were then living. She had been giving a series of radio broadcasts over station WGBH, Boston's public radio, and they could make the tape at the station studios after an interview in Sexton's home. McMillan's account of the visit, unexpectedly extended, gives a vivid picture of the poet as she was in the early summer of 1963. She had a warm welcome for the composer, who had taken an early plane from New York so they would have plenty of time in the morning to prepare the poems and make the tape. There was no one at home but Anne; her husband was on the road, the little girls were probably at summer camp, though Anne made no mention of them. However, she would soon be starting her travelling fellowship and had had to make some arrangements for them. The house was comfortable but not large, a typical suburban home. In the parlor were a number of old-fashioned china figurines, heirlooms her mother had kept from her grand, and great-grandparents' homes. They looked out of place in the boxy suburban house, but Anne treasured the things that had come from her mother's side of the family, the Grays; she had given Linda, her older daughter, the middle name of Gray.

In back of the house was a small yard, where Anne pointed with pride to a small swimming pool her husband had built for her. She looked very pretty and vivacious as she told about his building the pool, which, though small, was as professional a job as any contractor could have done, she said. She was an inveterate smoker and would interrupt herself to light a fresh cigarette when one burnt down. She noticed she was running low and was delighted when Ann McMillan, who had lived in Paris the last two years, proffered the Gaulois she had brought along. Getting down to the business at hand, they discussed the poems she had chosen for Anne to read—four from both volumes: "Her Kind," "The Double Image," "Ringing the Bells," and "Hutch" from *To Bedlam and Part Way Back*; and from *All My Pretty Ones*, "Old Dwarf Heart," "A Curse Against Elegies," "Ghosts," and "Wallflower." Anne read them through aloud several times; she had a vibrant voice and spoke clearly. McMillan clocked her: only fifteen minutes of the half-hour tape was allotted Sexton; the other fifteen was to be filled by Gregory Corso, a follower of the Allen Ginsberg school of poetry, a sharp contrast to the Robert Lowell school and Anne Sexton's verse. "The Double Image," the poem about Anne and her mother, proved to be too long and had to be deleted, much to McMillan's disappointment.

The two drove into Boston, made the tape without a hitch, after which the composer took the poet to lunch at a select little French restaurant she had learned of through the people at the French Broadcasting System of North America. The food was superb, the wine excellent, and, with their mission accomplished, they relaxed and enjoyed a leisurely lunch, comparing notes on their careers and the struggle common to most creative artists. Sexton was voluble, witty, egotistically concerned with her own problems and inner conflict; but she was also a good listener; she was interested in hearing about Ann McMillan's years in Paris, when, as a music major from Bennington, she had accepted a post on the staff of the French organization, which was a member of the International University of the Air. It grew late as they talked, but they hardly noticed until they realized that the place was empty except for them.

Then Sexton had an idea. "Why don't you come back to Newton with me and spend the night?" She was alone and there was plenty of room. Both felt they were far from talked out, so Ann accepted. At the house, she suggested that they take a swim, a welcome idea on the warm June day. Afterward they lounged by the pool and had a light supper. They drank the strong coffee Anne made and smoked the strong Gaulois cigarettes and talked and talked. Then Anne showed her guest the room she would be sleeping in, remarking rather drily, "That's the room my husband uses whenever he's home." If there was also a note of wistfulness in her voice, it came from the fact that she and her husband had not been using the same bedroom for some years, as she wrote in "I Remember," a nostalgic poem of *All My Pretty Ones:* "what/ I remember best is that/ the door to your room was/ the door to mine." And only a month before, a poem dated "May, 1963," which she called, "Man and Wife," stated flatly at the outset, "We are not lovers./ We do not even know each other." She drew a parallel between their lives and a pair of pigeons, "who came to the suburbs/ by mistake" and can "only hang on,/ their red claws wound like bracelets/ around the same limb." Carrying the figure further, it was finalized by the poignant lines, "Like them/ we neither talk nor clear our throats./ Oh, darling,/ . . . Like them/ we can only hang on."

As she opened the door that was not the one to her room, she said she would be back in a minute with one of her own nightgowns for her impromptu guest to wear, and when they were both ready for bed, they started talking again. It was a warm night and neither one felt sleepy. Noticing that the moon had come up, the poet said suddenly, "Oh, let's go for a walk!" So in their gauzy nightgowns, barefoot, they took a long walk in the moonlight, past the sleeping houses, strolling and talking. At one point Sexton admitted that she still thought about committing suicide, most recently with her "husband's good L. L. Bean knife" (as one of her poems was to phrase it with dark humor), and she wondered if McMillan, who had suffered a nervous breakdown in college and experienced a stay in a sanitarium, including shock treatment, had ever considered suicide; or if not, how she felt about it.

The question was a difficult one to answer, especially since the composer had not been obsessed with the notion of death, self-imposed or preordained. Finally she said she felt that one should not commit suicide because of the effect such a death would have on those who loved the person, family or friends. Her words seemed to give the poet pause, but she merely muttered after a few moments, "You may be right. but I don't know . . ." her voice trailed off. She changed the subject, asking about Gregory Corso and the coming interview.

The next morning after a quick swim and a cup of coffee, Ann McMillan left, promising to send a copy of the Sexton tape and a report of the Corso interview. A week or so later, having kept her word, she received a grateful, lively, and friendly note from the poet at "40 Clearwater Rd, Newton 62, Mass." Sexton had the tape on right then as she was typing her note. She bade McMillan not to worry about the final choice of poems, the deletion of "The Double Image," which could not be helped. She thought the tape sounded "pretty good."

She was thinking of Ann especially as she wrote for, besides listening to the tape, she was wearing the latter's bracelet, which had been inadvertently left in Newton. Asking if she should send it back, she said that she was wearing it to keep it safe, adding, "I like your taste." She was also "smoking Gauloises." The most interesting part of her note, however, came in her comments with regard to McMillan's interview with Corso. She was glad he had proved funny and "such a character." Then: "I bet he had never heard of me . . . why don't the beatnicks have any woman poets? Or I am she? really, I probably am. (not a beatnick but a sicknick!)" she observed with remarkable objectivity. She ended suddenly when she realized that she was leaving in ten days for Quebec—the first stop on the route of her travelling fellowship—and so had to rush the letter off. She signed it with her first name in a backhand scrawl, no more than a series of pinpoint peaks after a round "A."

Such a note hardly sounds as if it came from a potential suicide. Certainly she led an active, productive life, furthering her career as poet, writer of children's books with fellow poet Maxine Kumin, and an occasional article. Maxine, who was perhaps her best friend among the poets who were her contemporaries, had written a number of juveniles to augment the income brought by poetry, and she persuaded Anne to collaborate with her. The Kumins then lived in Newton Heights, a zone away from the Sextons; they had three children, Jane, Judith, and Daniel, not much older than Linda and Joyce Sexton. Maxine, who had been born in Philadelphia in 1925, had graduated from Radcliffe, married Victor Kumin in 1946, only two years before Anne was married. She had come under the influence of

Robert Lowell and had received a Radcliffe Scholarship for Independent Study in 1961, the same year that Anne had been a recipient. The two had a great deal in common and saw each other frequently. Along with her gift for poetry, Maxine had a strong streak of common sense, a down-to-earth quality that more than once may have prevented Anne from going off the deep end.

Their first collaboration, *Eggs of Things*, was published by Putnam this same year, 1963, and sold well enough to evoke a request for a sequel, *More Eggs of Things*, published in 1964, just as the travelling fellowship came to an end, bringing Anne back to Newton. Although her third and most important volume of poetry, *Live or Die*, was not published until 1966, her *Selected Poems*, published in London by Oxford University Press in 1964, was acclaimed by English critics and she was elected to the Royal Society of Literature in London. On her return to Newton, she received a Ford Foundation grant (1964), and she began to write new poems for her next book, which were accepted at once for publication in leading literary magazines before being collected. When she began bringing them together she decided to place them chronologically (1962–1966) "in the order in which they were written with all due apologies for the fact that they read like a fever chart for a bad case of melancholy," she stated in an author's note. Entitled, *Live or Die*, the volume contains her strongest, most carefully structured poems, and brought her wide acclaim, including the Pulitzer Prize for poetry, awarded in 1967, the year she received a Guggenheim Fellowship.

Starting with, "And One for My Dame," already quoted above, dated January 25, 1962, the poems are ambivalent in their attitude toward life, with more emphasis on its trials, frustrations, and pain than its pleasures and personal, sexual joys; but in the final analysis, the will to live wins out. The title itself, "Live," is a positive command to her inner being, to whose recesses the sun had penetrated, revealing cogent reasons for continuing the struggle: "a husband straight as a redwood,/ two daughters, two sea urchins,/ picking roses off my hackles. . . . O dearest three, I make a soft reply." Because of these three and the eight Dalmatian puppies that the Sextons had intended to drown at birth, but did not, the poet concludes: "So I won't hang around in my hospital shift,/ repeating The Black Mass and all of it./ I say *Live, Live* because of the sun,/ the dream, the excitable gift." She dated it, "February the last, 1966."

By then the family had moved to Weston, Massachusetts, 14 Black Oak Road, where they had more space, though their acreage was not "zoned for barns," as the poet said in "Pain For A Daughter," a poignant poem in *Live or Die,* depicting the love and pain that her daughter Linda experienced with horses. Pain both emotional and physical are vividly portrayed in the account of Linda's devotion to her pony suffering from distemper, her mourning the loss of his death by visiting the neighbor's stables, adoring the flashing thoroughbred; and the excruciating physical pain of a smashed, bleeding foot brought on by the thoroughbred's hoof unintentionally standing on it, heavy as a stone building. When Linda came limping home, it was her father, not Anne, who took care of cleansing the wounds while Anne stood in the doorway, unable even to look, but feeling their daughter's pain acutely. When Linda, biting on a towel to hold back sobs, cried out, *"Oh, my God, help me!"* the poet realizes that a child would normally cry "Mama!" but her child-woman, at eleven—almost twelve—calls on God. Self-failure as a mother, unspoken, is only one of the many implications in this perceptive poem, among the strongest in the prize-winning volume. There is another poem about and to Linda, with the telling title, "Little Girl, My String Bean, My Lovely Woman"; and, "A Little Uncomplicated Hymn, *for Joy,*" (her younger daughter), which became quite complex: "I look for uncomplicated hymns/ but love has none," she concludes.

These two tender lyrics indicate a fondness and concern for those close to her that worked to dispel the melancholy and suicidal tendency which kept recurring from time to time. And the book that followed *Live or Die* is a volume of *Love Poems*. Many of the twenty-five included are amazingly free of the bitterness and distortion of much of Sexton's work. The opening poems especially capture the awestruck experience of love's dawning: "The Touch," "The Kiss," "The Breast," and "In Celebration of My Uterus." "Song For A Lady" is a realistic yet sensitive lyric; and "Knee Song" evokes a quivering response to its metaphor, "Being kissed on the back/ of the knee is a moth/ at the windowscreen." However, the poems do not remain dewy-eyed throughout: disillusion arrives with "The Deserted Virgin"; sophistication with, "For My Lover, Returning to His Wife"; and loneliness with, "The Ballad of the Lonely Masturbator" and the series, "Eighteen Days Without You."

Publication of the two volumes brought further honors. The Shelley Memorial Award followed the Pulitzer, and in 1968 she became an honorary member of Phi Beta Kappa, and received an honorary doctorate from Tufts University in 1970. She received offers to lecture and to teach and did both successfully. She held the post of professor of creative writing at Boston University, and later, Cranshaw Professor of Literature at Colgate. Her work was the subject of articles in literary magazines—no less than three in *The Hudson Review*, each one commenting on the power and "raw edge of realism" in her work, the "confessional" element of her themes. Anne herself commented: "It is said that I am part of the so-called confessional school. I prefer to think of myself as an imagist who deals with reality and its hard facts. I write stories about life as I see it. As one critic put it, I am 'metaphor-mad.' I work happily within strict forms that differ poem by poem or in what I call loose poems. Each time I look for the voice of the poem and each time it is a different one. I have been influenced by Rilke, Rimbaud, Kafka and Neruda. My themes deal with life and death, insanity, daughterhood, motherhood, and love. My poems are intensely physical."

Such an objective analysis of one's creative output could come only from an essentially sane mind, and whatever her obsessions with suicide and death, Anne Sexton's mind was brilliant as well, her sanity maintained by a broad sense of humor. Nowhere is the saving grace more evident than in her next book, her *Transformations* of Grimm's fairy tales, published in 1971. Her collaboration with Maxine Kumin on juvenile books—the third, *Joey and the Birthday Present,* also published in 1971— undoubtedly had something to do with these satires of traditional fairy tales. The two poets were very close professionally and in their personal lives, though Kumin's themes emphasized nature and animals, particularly horses, and their relationship to humans, an involvement that probably inspired Linda's devotion to her pony, her admiration for the thoroughbred that mangled her foot. Even after the Kumins moved to a New Hampshire farm, the families remained close. Maxine's books of poetry, which she wrote steadily, along with the books for children, and a novel, drew, like Anne's, from life-experience and won her more praise than any of the juveniles or either of the two novels she wrote. She was cited by Richard Moore as "an accomplished and professional poet of what might be called the Bishop-Lowell-Sexton school." Bishop was more of a friend than a disciple of Lowell's, but Anne Sexton and Maxine Kumin were undoubtedly influenced by his seminar course, and in turn influenced each other, though their subject matter differed considerably. In another year, 1972, Maxine's *Up Country: Poems of New England* was to win the Pulitzer Prize; and both poets rejoiced.

Anne's sense of humor tended toward the absurd, and she gave the tendency full play in her "transformations" of traditional fairy tales. Her retelling of the stories was a mingling of myth, madness, and modernity. The book is dedicated "To Linda/ who reads Hesse/ and drinks clam chowder," a token of affection and a sign that Sexton realized, perhaps with some alarm, that her daughter was practically grown up; and she says, as the narrator or "middle-aged witch" who speaks her mind before each tale: "It is not enough to read Hesse/ and drink clam chowder/ we must have the answers." It was as if she was warning Linda, and all young people approaching adulthood, that life is no fairy tale. The stories of the brothers Grimm, Perrault and Anderson, despite the evil deeds of witches, wolves, wicked stepmothers, and the like, usually end "happily ever after" in marriage; but not so Anne Sexton's. Even Cinderella, "that story," ends ironically, with typical skepticism:

> *Cinderella and the prince*
> *lived, they say, happily ever after,*
> *like two dolls in a museum case*
> *never bothered by diapers or dust,*
> *never arguing over the timing of an egg,*
> *never telling the same story twice,*
> *never getting a middle-aged spread,*
> *their darling smiles pasted on for eternity.*
> *Regular Bobbsey Twins.*
> *That story.*

Earlier, in a hilarious touch: "The prince was getting tired./ He began to feel like a shoe salesman," Sexton leads up to the climactic solution with a graceful, appropriate simile: "But he gave it one last try./ This time Cinderella fit into the shoe/ like a love letter into its envelope."

Other stories contain a sinister as well as a satiric tone: the "wonderful musician," who goes his way playing "fiddle-me-roo" in the wake of the maimed animals he has left behind him is always "saved by his gift/ like many of us—/ little Eichmanns,/ Little mothers—I'd say." Sexton's "Rapunzel" has lesbian flavor: at the outset we read that "A woman/ who loves a woman/ is forever young." Mother Gothel, the witch who holds the beautiful young Rapunzel a prisoner in her tower, and lovingly also holds the virgin with the long yellow hair and young breast close to her old breast: "and thus they played mother-me-do."

But the sexual deviation is mitigated by the ultimate victory of the prince and Rapunzel's love for him, "proving that mother-me-do can be outgrown." Not so with Briar Rose, the poet's "Sleeping Beauty," who wakens from her century-long sleep calling out, "Daddy! Daddy!" and though she married the prince who kissed her on the mouth, Briar Rose was an insomniac, and could not sleep without knockout drops from the court chemist. Once asleep, she would only wake up with a kiss on the mouth, and then she'd call out: "Daddy! Daddy!" Ten lines later: "Daddy?/ That's another kind of prison./ It's not the prince at all,/ but my father/ drunkenly bent over my bed,/ ending the abyss like a shark,/ my father thick upon me/ like some sleeping jellyfish." A not so distant echo of Sylvia Plath's dilemma, it is only one of many instances that reveal in earlier and later poems Anne Sexton's actual experiences with the same situation. And eventually she was to write her own "Daddy" poem.

However, if *Transformations* is hair-raising, even horrifying in its implications, it is also merry and wise. Besides "mother-me-do" and "fiddle-me-roo" there are other felicitous phrases that make this book a delight. Anne's inventiveness is perhaps best illustrated in "The Little Peasant," who turned voyeur as he spied on the miller's wife and the parson. Her version is a delicious tale of food, drink, and philandering: "And thus they ate,/ And thus/ they dingoed-sweet." This perfect epithet for dalliance is featured throughout the story, in the telling of which the poet also takes a swipe at pop art: When the parson is discovered hiding in the cupboard, he stood "rigid for a moment,/ as real as a soup can"; and in the end, "The miller's wife/ smiled to herself. Though never again to dingo-sweet/ her secret was as safe/ as a fly in an outhouse." Snow White, caricatured by such widely separated artists as Walt Disney and Donald Barthelme, comes in for her share of debunking. Until her beauty rivals her stepmother's, she is "no more important/ than a dust mouse under the bed"; and she is "Snow White, the dumb bunny" as she keeps opening the door to said wicked stepmother despite repeated warnings from the dwarfs. A perceptive touch at the end pictures the heroine holding court "and sometimes referring to her mirror/ as women do." Sexton's "Rumpelstiltskin," the dwarf who can spin straw into gold "as good as Fort Knox," represents the doppelgänger in all of us. He turns down a kingdom offered in payment of the queen's debt: "[He] wanted only this—/ a living thing/ to call his own./ And being mortal/ who can blame him?" The poet's version of "Iron Hans" relates directly to her personal struggle: he is a king who has been bewitched into a state of lunacy, but he is cured not "by Thorazine or psychotherapy" but by kindness.

Transformations is perhaps Anne Sexton's most successful book artistically in that, as Christopher Lehmann-Haupt pointed out in his enthusiastic review in *The New York Times,* the subject matter freed her poetry from its former weakness—her "tendency to record raw disasters without curing them with her art. . . . by using the artificial as the raw material . . . and working her way backwards to the immediacy of her personal vision, she draws her readers in more willingly, and thereby makes them more vulnerable to her sudden plunges into personal nightmare." He went on to say that "her technique works" and "the result is a funny, mad, witty, frightening, charming, haunting book." Stanley Kunitz exclaimed: "What a wild, astonishing bloodcurdling book Anne Sexton has written!" and *Publishers Weekly* called it "ribald and rare poetry with a subterranean subtlety."

Eleven poems of the book were dramatized and set to music by the Minneapolis Opera Center to form a provocative, ingenious modern opera. The score by composer Conrad Susa, a combination of classical and popular styles, complemented the text superbly; and music critics in their reviews reinforced the above opinions. Allen Hughes of *The New York Times,* who reviewed the piece in both the Minneapolis and New York productions, said of Sexton's book: "In language that is strikingly simple and direct she has explored psychological implications of the fairy tales that are far removed from childishness and in at least some instances are both illuminating and alarming. Her writing is filled with humorous touches that help to keep the opera lively and amusing on the surface, but . . . it is not difficult to imagine that the opera might well be taking place in a mental hospital." Andrew Porter in *The New Yorker* observed in his estimate of the book that "the charm of *Transformations*— it *is* a charming book, for all the pain it enshrines—lies in the revelation of ingenious, unexpected links between folk mythology and private modern hells. Sexton's use of smart similies is liberal, reckless and eventually tiresome. . . . But the large similes—each tale as a parable of plights that still exist, though wizards and wicked fairies are no more—are deftly handled. The book . . . reads partly as autobiography; . . . it is soon clear that she is not only the witches and cruel mothers but also the variously injured maidens who fill the tales." Between its premiere and the New York production, which was posthumous, the Sexton–Susa opera was performed on a number of university campuses—by the Handel and Haydn Society in Boston, and the Netherlands Opera abroad.

The Book of Folly, published a year later, was dedicated to the poet's younger daughter: "For Joy," with a single telling line, "when she comes to this business of words" and the words forming the poems here are again explicitly autobiographical. We learn in the first poem that it is "the business of words" that keeps the poet awake at night: "all night I am laying/ poems away in a long box. . . . All night dark wings/ flopping in my heart./ Each an ambition bird." An honest admission of every writer's longing for recognition; and although she had received a lion's share of the latter already—in 1972 she was professor of literature at Colgate University, the recipient of three honorary doctorates besides the Pulitzer and other awards—she was far from satisfied with her work or her life. Though she claimed in a poem to "Herr Doktor" that she was "at the ship's prow, . . . no longer the suicide/ with her raft and paddle," the new book was replete with thoughts of death.

For all her bravado, she seems to have been preoccupied with the macabre, which was probably accentuated by her sister's "unnatural death by car, her slim neck snapped like a piece of celery." [An inappropriate, soupy simile] "A one-week bride,/ her dead blue eyes flapping into their solitude/ while I drank with Sweeney and her death lied." Apparently the poet's grief was mixed with guilt because at the time of the accident she was drinking champagne with an Australian tycoon who overwhelmed her with ardor but disgusted her with vulgarity; she called him her "Sweeney" because his courtship brought death though they were far from the scene of her sister's accident. No matter what the subject, blood, murder, and death appear in most of the poems in *The Book of Folly*. Erasmus's text of the same title is a book of nursery rhymes compared to Sexton's. Untermeyer called it "Sexton unlimited . . . wonderfully mad and madly wonderful." But it is more mad than wonderful in many instances: although she revised and revised her work, according to Linda, too often looseness prevails. A wild, driven genius is dashing off lines.

In fact, from this point on, much as she might try, Anne Sexton could not keep her poems from getting out of hand, heading inevitably toward despair and self-destruction. As Andrew Porter wrote in the prelude to his music review, she "became an untidy, self-indulgent poet whose imagery increasingly resembled the uncontrolled—sometimes beautiful—patterns of a kaleidoscope; memories of father, mother, and childhood horrors were fragments of jagged glass in the tube, anguish and madness the confining mirrors within which they were spun." And the title of her next book, *The Death Notebooks,* is in itself an indication of her preoccupation with the random but inevitable harvest of the grim reaper. Sickness was frequently a sign that death was on the way, as in the case of Anne's mother, but more often he gave no warning; her sister could not know the car would crash, nor her father that he would suffer a cerebral hemorrhage while driving on the highway. She often discussed the puzzling onslaught of death with "Max" Kumin, by now her best friend, as the fifth poem in a series called, "The Death Baby," clearly discloses. It opens, "Max and I/ two immoderate sisters,/ two immoderate writers,/ two burdeners,/ made a pact." The two poets vowed: "To beat death down with a stick./ To take over./ To build our death like carpenters." In "those long hushed phone calls," that Anne made every night when Max was laid up with a broken back and could not sleep, they agreed "that when the moment comes/ we'll talk turkey,/ we'll shoot words straight from the hip,/ we'll play it as it lays./ Yes,/ when death comes with its hood/ we won't be polite." The sixth, and final one in the series, "Baby," is a chilling poem which ends, "Someday,/ heavy with cancer or disaster/ I will look up at Max/ and say: It is time./ Hand me the death baby/ and there will be/ that final rocking." One feels both defiance of death and fear.

The defiance and fear was linked to a search for faith. *The Book of Folly* had ended with a series entitled, "The Jesus Papers," Sexton's "transformations" of the Christ, and in answer to those who might call them sacreligious or mockery, she quotes: "God is not mocked except by believers." The *Notebooks* begins with "Gods:"—a fruitless seeking as "Mrs. Sexton went out looking for the gods." She finds "No one" in all the worlds of the sky, the earth, or the learned books; but when she returns discovers them lurking in her own lavatory: "At last!/ she cried out,/ and locked the door." The volume closes with, "O Ye Tongues," a series of ten modern psalms, not entirely successful, for they are neither satiric nor serious, but somewhere in between, and certainly touched with madness.

The search continues in the volume that followed, *The Awful Rowing Toward God*, which, as Fate would have it, was published posthumously. The decision to get a divorce, which the Sextons finally agreed to obtain after "hanging on" for at least twenty of the twenty-five years they were married, undoubtedly had a major effect on Anne's morale. Although she went about it with her usual bravado, writing a series of seventeen poems, "The Divorce Papers," to form a history of the whole relationship from beginning to breakup, the lines are filled with regret and rue, fond memories of the early days and lingering traces of love.

The volume in which the series appeared was entitled, *45 Mercy Street,* and in June of 1974, before *The Awful Rowing* was completely through the production stage, Anne wrote brightly to her agent, "I have actually finished another book, *45 Mercy Street,* but am glad to have time to reform the poems, rewrite and delete." As usual, she consulted friends, principally "Max" Kumin, as to the best of various versions of the poems to be included, sometimes taking her friend's advice, sometimes keeping her own counsel. The title poem, which opens the book, is a mingling of fact and fantasy, a retrospective view of Sexton's life and background, again a search for a solid belief in a past she cannot find, her grandmother's house at 45 Mercy Street; the symbolism is obvious, the recollections poignant. Then follows a section, "Bestiary, U.S.A." including, like Muriel Rukeyser, the ever-present cockroach, loathsome and unloved, and the possible reason for his being. A note of explanation reads, "I look at the strangeness in them and the naturalness they cannot help, in order to find some virtue in the beast in me." The last section, "Eating the Leftovers," discloses, in the aftermath of the divorce, an explicit experience of incest with her father. The poem "Divorce, Thy Name is Woman," begins, "I am divorcing daddy—Dybbuk! Dybbuk!/ I have been doing it daily all my life." The third stanza describes "a long midnight visit/ in a dream that is not a dream," and she has been divorcing her father ever since, even after his death.

It was undoubtedly her divorce from Alfred Sexton that brought her love-hate attitude toward her "Daddy" Warbucks, as she called him in the poem just preceding this one, to a boiling climax. There are echoes of Sylvia Plath's diatribe against the father fixation, a culmination of resentment that resulted in wild outburst. On October 4, she and "Max" Kumin met for lunch, and Anne was telling her sister poet about completing her latest manuscript; as she had said earlier, "part of *45 Mercy Street* is still too personal to publish for some time," but she seemed excited at having another volume almost ready for the press before the current one was released. "Mercy Street" had been the title of a play she had written in 1969, produced by the American Place Theater in New York, a drama of a woman seeking her way out of insanity, the theme that runs through all of Sexton's work side by side with the inevitability of death. The two poets talked about their work, their daughters rapidly growing up, and, as Maxine said, "this mothering business." They must have discussed Anne's divorce. And when they parted, they planned to meet soon again.

Anne drove back to Weston without incident, turned in at her driveway and on into the garage. She let the motor idle, not turning off the ignition. The windows of the car were rolled up, and soon carbon monoxide took over. The motor was still idling when she was found dead some hours later. "It was either suicide or natural causes," the police detective said. Later evidence showed that it must have been suicide. She was forty-five years old, at the height of her career, the recipient of many awards and three honorary degrees, but for all her brilliance— or perhaps because of it—she could not conquer her obsession with death, the fear and the lure of it. Her contribution to modern poetry was considerable in that she added new themes to the subject matter of modern poetry, principally insanity and the fight for recovery. As Thomas Lask of *The New York Times* wrote in his review of her first book: "Its hub has a natural built-in interest: a mental breakdown, pictured with a pitiless eye and clairvoyant sharpness." But in the final analysis, she was not strong enough to maintain mental balance, and after the divorce despair must have taken over.

Her death was of course a terrible shock to Maxine Kumin, the last person to see her alive. "Max," her best friend, who was her mainstay during the trying days of the divorce, had hoped that Anne had weathered the inner storm brought on by the

breakup. In a poem addressed to her "dear friend," Kumin expresses her deep sorrow with restraint and objectivity. She begins by describing the joyful bark and excited tail wagging of
her pet dog, as he recognizes Anne's blue jacket, which Maxine
is wearing. To him it is a sign that her friend (and his) is somewhere near and will appear at any moment. His response only
makes her grief more poignant, but in a sense Anne is there
and always will be. Many of Kumin's poems refer to Sexton.

In the years since the latter's death, Maxine Kumin has not
only survived, but advanced professionally and artistically. Although one critic wrote: "I just wish she'd quit writing about
her damn *horse*," Philip Booth, in his critique of *The Retrieval
System*, published in 1978, speaks of the maturity of her poems
as "the uniquely lovely maturity of a woman who has never
forgotten the girlhood she has long since outgrown." His long
article in *The American Poetry Review* contains a glowing analysis of the poetry—"prime Maxine Kumin." He quotes her lines
liberally and claims that one of her strengths "has always been
the way in which the implied narratives combine a Frostian delight in metaphor with Marianne Moore's insistence on being
a 'literalist of the imagination.'" Kumin has served as Consultant in Poetry at the Library of Congress (1976–1980), and in
1980 received an award from the Academy of Arts and Letters.
In 1983, her *Collected Poems* appeared to great acclaim, marking twenty years of her career as an accomplished poet.

Gwendolyn Brooks

B y her own testimony, Gwendolyn Brooks would have been a native of Chicago, Illinois, but she was taken to her grandmother's house in Topeka, Kansas, to be born. The day was June 7, 1917, a date that might well be termed the advent of modern poets among women of her race. There had been noted black women who were poets before her time, and there were any number who wrote and began publishing concurrently with her, but she is the first to win real recognition in the annals of twentieth century poetry.

One notable woman about to gain a place of distinction around the turn of the century was the poet Alice Ruth Moore, who became the wife of Paul Laurence Dunbar in 1898. At the time of their meeting she was in fact more established than he. He sought her advice in gaining a wider audience, and she obliged, since her name was better known to the general press. She soon perceived, however, that Dunbar's was the greater gift; and after they were married, whether prompted by practical considerations, or because she did not want to compete with her husband, she turned to other fields of writing, mostly in education, since she had been a schoolteacher. The fact that they were divorced in 1904 had nothing to do with their respective careers. Although she only wrote poetry sporadically and continued to use her creative ability as an educator, penning a newspaper column under the name Alice Dunbar-Nelson after her second marriage, her poems merited inclusion in Countee Cullen's *Caroling Dusk,* published in 1927.

Alice Dunbar-Nelson died in 1933, just as Gwendolyn Brooks, at the age of sixteen, began submitting poems to the Chicago *Defender,* the leading Negro paper, but her love and marked penchant for poetry began more than ten years earlier. Like Paul Dunbar, "Gwen" (as she was most often called when she reached her twenties) started putting rhymes together at seven. Her parents, David Anderson and Keziah Wims Brooks, were duly impressed with her unusual ability and, in her words, "expressed confidence that she would be a writer." Their confidence was justified when at thirteen their daughter had her first poem, "Eventide," accepted and published by a well-known juvenile magazine, *American Childhood.*

Blessed with loving parents who encouraged her, and with the close companionship of her brother, Raymond Melvin, a boy who was both merry and industrious, only a year and four months younger than she, Gwendolyn Brooks led a singularly happy home life as she grew up. Her descriptions of holidays as she recalled them in her personal account, *Report from Part One,* portray the harmony that held sway most of the time in the Brooks's household. The glowing details of the Christmas celebrations alone are enough to evoke the envy of many readers, young or old, black or white.

In telling the story of the Brooks's Christmases, the poet commented on the fact that it did not trouble her as a small girl or while she was growing up to see a white Santa in department stores and picture books or, in the Nativity scenes, a white baby Jesus, surrounded by white people except for That One of the three Wise men" whose role was "ever slurred, ever understated." Easter, too, was a high point in the year's holidays, offered and accepted as white. A person of great capacity for the enjoyment of life, Brooks would not realize until many years later that there was no holiday to celebrate black history and heritage. She expressed the thought in an eloquent poem, "Elegy in a Rainbow":

> *When I was a little girl*
> *Christmas was exquisite.*
> *I didn't touch it.*
> *I didn't look at it too closely.*
> *To do that to do that*
> *might nullify the shine.*
>
> *Thus with a Love*
> *that has to have a Home*
> *like the Black Nation,*
> *like the Black Nation*
> *defining its own Roof*
> *that no one else can see.*

Besides her parents and brother, Gwendolyn Brooks's close family circle included a number of lively aunts and uncles on her mother's side who took an active interest in their niece and nephew. One reason for this was that Keziah (named by her father after Job's youngest daughter) was the only one of the five Wims sisters who had children of her own. Aunt Eppie (Wims) Small, who lived on a farm in the celery-growing countryside near Kalamazoo with her husband, Joe (who worked for the wealthy Upjohn pharmaceutical family, adopted three children and was foster-mother to others for a time. One of the latter was Marc Crawford, years later, journalist, editor, novelist, and friend and colleague of Gwen's for several years before they discovered the "family connection." Aunt Gertie, married to Uncle Paul Robinson, who had a "snap" fifty-dollar-a-week job at City Hall, was the wealthiest and the gaiest of Gwen's aunts. She loved to dance and taught Gwen to dance, to do the "Charleston," a jazz step the poet has never forgotten. Aunt Ella, Gwen's third aunt, was poor compared to Aunt Gertie, and, like the other two, she was childless. She and her husband, Ernest Myler, who worked for the WPA, lived in a room heaped with possessions. Uncle Ernest, as the poet remembered him, was a jolly fellow who laughed a lot as he played cards and argued politics with her father.

She was fond of all her aunts and uncles, but it was Aunt Beulah who was "the Queen" of the Wims family. Aunt Beulah, who had a gift for sewing, began to teach her skill when she was a young girl, rising steadily till she became head of the sewing department at Booker T. Washington High School, but did not stop there. She attended the University of Chicago in the summers until she had earned a college degree, for which she was "mightily revered and adored" by her sister Keziah, who had taught in the primary grades following two years of training in "normal school" before her marriage. Aunt Beulah chose not to marry, and so was able to make life easier for her parents, to shower her nieces and nephews with treats and presents (there were two Wims brothers who married and had children—Uncle Tommy and Uncle Willie—but they were not as close to the Brookses as the sisters were.) Aunt Beulah had style, in the best sense of the word. She fashioned and made most of her own clothes and she knew how to wear them. She made so many dresses for small Gwen that the Brookses did not have to buy clothes for their little girl until she was well into primary school. Ironically, the fine clothes provided by her

Aunt Beulah proved to be a mixed blessing to Gwendolyn Brooks.

School itself proved to be a mixed blessing: in spite of the joys of crayon, chalk, and watercolors, of story-time and books, and learning to read; one of the earliest "world truths" the poet had to learn was that no matter how smart a little girl might be at her lessons she had to be "BRIGHT" of skin if she was to be a social success. She always considered the rich, warm brown (as it was then called) beautiful. Some dusky-skinned girls were "accepted" because their fathers were doctors or lawyers, or their mothers schoolteachers. Her mother, Keziah Wims, had been a schoolteacher in Topeka, Kansas, but when she became Mrs. David Brooks and bore him two children almost at once, she gave it up, as was proper in those days. So Gwen did not mention her mother's career. Her father was a janitor who worked for the McKinley Music Publishing Company, and there was no reason to mention his job. The girls who were truly rich were accepted in part because they wore better clothes than the other dark-skinned girls; but among the "lesser blacks," with whom she should have had some chance, her Aunt Beulah's elegantly tailored, dainty dresses only put her doubly "beyond the pale." Since Gwen had "neither brass or sass," did not fight on the playground, was no good at sports (she could not even play jacks!), those who might have taken her in called her "an ol' stuck-up heifer" and let her know they wanted "nothin' to do with no rich people's spiled chirren." As for the boys, the light ones looked through her if she happened to come within their vision, and those of her own deep shade of skin tagged her "Ol' Black Gal."

Home was a refuge, a haven that healed wounded feelings and allowed her to forget the snubs and slurs of outrageous schoolmates. Her slim, quick-stepping, "Duty-Loving," careful mother always had a warm welcome for her children when they came from school. She often sang as she played the piano— "Brighten the cor-nerr where you are!" a favorite song of hers, and one that seems to have epitomized her way of life. She made cocoa and fudge for the children and luscious desserts like prune whip and apricot pie; she drew neat pictures for the children and helped them with their homework. When her daughter was only four or five, she taught her to recite "with expression" so that the little girl would do well in the Sunday school programs at the Carter Temple Church down the block from the Brooks's house at 4332 Champlain Avenue, the house the poet loved and lived in from the time she was four until her marriage.

The meaning of that home with its enveloping warmth came as much from the presence of her father as her mother. His kind eyes, his songs in deep baritone vibrations, his taut telling of stories and narrative poems gave an extra magic to tall tales that held his children spellbound. To add to his artistic talent, he had great practical ability. He could fix anything that went wrong around the house. He could paint it, inside and out. He could spread the American flag "in wide loud magic" across the front of the house every Fourth of July and Decoration Day. And how he would chuckle at his children's admiration! "No one ever had, no one ever will have, a chuckle exactly like my father's," the poet wrote in her *Report*. "It was gentle, it was warmly happy, it was heavyish, but not hard. It was secure, and seemed to us an assistant to the Power that registered with his children." Part of that sense of quiet power his children felt came from his self-taught knowledge of medicine, his ability to cure their colds, to heal bruises and badly skinned knees, and, above all, his compassionate, cheerful "bedside manner." He had longed to be a doctor, but had got no farther than working his way through one year at Fisk University, when he had to relinquish his dream in order to support his mother and the younger children after his father died.

The poet never knew more than "wisps of her father's story." She was certain from those fragments that he and his family had known hardship, hunger, and cruel poverty that brought sickness and death to four of his siblings. His father was a runaway slave and later a tenant farmer persecuted by landowners. No "beggar" was ever turned away from their table or allowed to leave without provisions for the road. The wonder of it was that in the clutches of misfortune her father was sustained by some deep force that made him kind and cheerful, "with that quiet, appealing cheerfulness; hard-working, apprising, with that special practical wisdom." It was almost impossible to discover the source of his strength, but, in a burst of poetic prose his daughter wrote: "I think that his in-life, before he came to know Keziah and Gwendolyn and Raymond and cages nice and belts all tidy and snug, was of cineramic proportions, was suffused with wild organ music deep-center." The "almost musical" harmony of home came from him and from his wife.

Her mother of course was responsible for their smooth-running household. She contributed many of the pleasures and most of her time, to the peacefulness of home. However, the one discordant note that occasionally disrupted the harmony came from Keziah's concern for the family's financial security. Her husband's meager salary of twenty-five dollars a week (thirty-five for overtime) was inadequate to meet their needs. She didn't see why he couldn't leave McKinley's and get a better-paying job with less work; but the poet's father would not be moved. He was loyal to McKinley's and content to stay there, even if it meant skimping a little, as it did during the Depression when the Brook's diet frequently featured beans because the firm itself was hard up and could pay only half his salary. Their dispute over the family income disturbed both Gwendolyn and Raymond as they were growing up because, as she said, "Children often dread, more than anything else, dissension in the house." She and her brother would have gladly put up with a beany diet every day if they did not have to listen to parental arguments.

Fortunately, Keziah Wims Brooks was too intelligent a person to become a nag, and in near-normal times kept her complaints to herself. She was always supportive of her daughter's gift for poetry, and as it developed she relieved her of some of the chores, as she claimed in a "Document" she prepared for the poet's *Report,* so the girl could devote more time to writing. (Brooks presents the data with the amused comment that they hold an unconscious portrait of her mother rather than herself.) When, at about the age of thirteen Gwen was provided with a big old desk given to her father by McKinley's— a desk with many cubbyholes, long drawers below, and a glass-protected shelf for books on top—she placed a copy of Paul Laurence Dunbar on that shelf for constant inspiration; and her mother announced: "*You* are going to be the *lady* Paul Laurence Dunbar!" It was almost an edict. And Gwen had no doubt that she would be—indeed, *was* a poet—and her mother's prediction only underlined her ambitions. She still keeps a copy of *The Complete Paul Laurence Dunbar* in her bedroom.

As she turned into her teens, she spent many hours at her desk. She had discovered *Writers Digest,* and the fact that there were "oodles" of writers in the same boat as she, struggling with words, scrimping for postage money, hoping the poems sent out would be snapped up by some magazine, only to have them returned with rejection slips more frequently than accepted, brought both inspiration and comfort; she realized that she was not alone in the hours she spent reading, writing, perfecting, dreaming. And she had plenty of time to spend, since she was no more popular in school at fourteen than she had been at seven. She went to few parties and when she did, she rarely enjoyed them. The silly "kissing games" only embarrassed her; few letters came her way at "post office," though she might wear a fine party dress made by Aunt Beulah and her hair was all straightened (by the "hot comb") except for the slightly curled ends. The main trouble was, as the boys told her frankly, that she was DARK.

Besides, she was not "fast," like the other girls. Thanks to Aunt Gertie, she could dance and was a whiz at the Charleston, but there was not much dancing at those parties. And rather than the kissing games, Gwen preferred playing checkers with her parents or her brother Raymond at home in the evening. Raymond had early shown talent in art. He was always drawing or painting, and his good-natured smile won him many friends at school. Though they were so close in age, he looked up to his sister as being older and wiser. If he lost at checkers he gave a cheerful shrug and challenged her to another game. There was little sibling rivalry between them. They listened to favorite radio programs together, went to the neighborhood movie house once a week, and teased each other without malice.

Eventually the adolescent party phase was over, and Gwendolyn Brooks gained a reputation as "a girl who wrote." Following her initial appearance in *The Defender*, she produced "over seventy-five of these confident items," as she said, which were printed in the newspaper's variety column called "Lights and Shadows." By the time she graduated from Chicago's Englewood High, Gwen knew that she would go on writing poetry as long she lived, that it would be her calling, for it did call to her with a strong inner voice. Eventually, too, she did have "talking dates" with some of the boys at school: the nice president of the NAACP Youth Council, or with the serious male students at Wilson Junior College, from which she graduated in 1936. She never "had boy friends," like Ida Debroe, or stylish Rebecca Dorsey, or "bright" Rose Hurd. Her first actual lover was her husband, whom she met soon after graduation.

Both were twenty-one years old. Henry Lowington Blakely was a "fella who wrote," and had been told he might find a "girl who wrote" at the NAACP Youth Council. He was eager to meet her, and one evening in 1938 she saw, standing in the doorway of the YWCA Council room, a serious-looking, dignified young man. She said excitedly to painter Margaret Taylor Goss who was sitting next to her, "There is the man I am going to marry." In her words, "Margaret yelled, 'Hey, boy, this girl wants to meet you.' That is how I met my husband." They were married a year later, on September 17, 1939.

The wedding took place in the living room of the Brooks's home on Champlain, a home she found difficult to bid good-bye. After the flush of excitement, the flowers, the beautiful high wedding cake, the presents, and warm wishes of friends following the "Oh, Promise Me" and solemn ceremony, the skimpy two-room honeymoon apartment in the big, barren Tyson building seemed bleak for a time. But before too long it became home, because, in spite of the cramped dreariness, there was fun in small happenings; there was much good talk at the breakfast table or before they went to bed, talk about their writing, their reading, mutual reading; there was company, for both had friends in the intellectual community of the NAACP. Like most young couples, especially struggling writers, they were poor, but they had the joys of the mind as well as body. Wherever they lived—in a kitchenette; a garage apartment, where their son, who was born thirteen months after they were married, (Henry Jr., October 10, 1940) caught bronchitis from the dampness; in other sleazy little places; and finally in a small house of their own—they were happy.

At the outset of her *Report,* with characteristic directness, Gwendolyn Brooks states: "My husband and I were married for thirty years. We were very poor, underwent strains, but chiefly had a deal of fun, sharing our growth. . . . Everyone felt the marriage was not only successful, but a model for other marriages. We were separated in December of 1969. We understood that our separation was best for the involved. (That won't be enough for the reader, but it is enough for me.)" She goes on to explain that the separation did not mean failure of their marriage after thirty years, but simply a final stage in the relationship of a man and a woman, which, as sometimes *"properly"* occurs, is a dignified separation. That theirs was amicable there can be no doubt from the way Brooks writes about her husband, and from her account of events that occurred in those thirty years. They were never divorced and resumed their marriage in the fall of 1973. Today, years later, it continues.

One of the most important influences in shaping their poetry

writing was the advent of wealthy, socially-prominent, and poetry-loving Inez Cunningham Stark in "the very *buckle* of the
Black Belt." The day in June of 1941 that the lady announced
to the select circle of friends having tea in her "Gold Coast"
home that she was going to form a class in poetry writing among
black (then known as "Negro") poets, her friends stared at her
horrified, "as if she had pulled a rattler out of her bosom." She
couldn't mean it! The risk was enormous; she would be robbed,
raped, killed, exiled by high society. But she did mean it, and
she had no fear for her life or her reputation in high society
circles.

The "class," held weekly in the South Side Community Art
Center, might well be called a forerunner of today's popular
poetry workshops, and proved to be not only successful in producing high quality publishable poetry from its frequent, faithful, earnest members; but proved to be the primary turning point
in Gwendolyn Brooks's career as a published poet. Through Inez
Stark, who at one point gave fifteen of the aspiring poets a six-
month subscription to *Poetry,* and through the exciting, analyt-
ical discussions that sometimes ended in a surge of mixed feelings, Gwen was inspired to extend her sphere of publication.
In 1944, a *Poetry* acceptance came through the good offices of
Paul Engle, who had sent some of a series she called "A Street
in Bronzeville" to that prestigious monthly. Engle, then a book
reviewer for the *Chicago Tribune,* knew of the work the group
was doing from its tireless leader, who had once been a first
reader on the literary magazine. She was justly proud of her
protegés.

Among the talented members who came faithfully to those
weekly meetings was the well-known sister poet, Margaret
Danner Cunningham, who later became an associate editor of
Poetry; and Margaret Taylor Goss, now director of the Museum of African-American History; and the noted California
painter, John Carlis; poet William Couch; besides Gwen—and—
Henry, the only married couple. A remarkable corps of poten-

tial artists in various fields, all of whom thrived under the friendly yet objective guidance of Inez Stark. She encouraged student-poets to participate in writers' conferences; and when, in 1943, Gwendolyn Brooks won a poetry award at the Midwestern Writers meeting, Emily Morison, editor at Knopf, asked if she had enough poems for a book; the answer was, *"Indeed* I do!" (Brooks writes and talks in italics, underlining her words with warm enthusiasm when so moved.) At Morison's invitation to send them, she rushed home "in high hysteria" to prepare a bulging packet of love poems, war poems, nature, patriotism, and "prejudice" poems—the gamut of poesy. The word that finally came from Miss Morison was that she had liked the "Negro poems." As soon as the poet had enough for a full book of those, she should try Knopf again.

One of Brooks's maxims, which she passed along to her children and to her readers, is the pithy and wise saying, "When handed a lemon, make lemonade." And so she did now: without waiting until she had written a bookful, she culled the nineteen "Negro poems" from the lot and shipped them off to Harper & Brothers as a sample for a volume. Back came a letter of acceptance. Harper would like to publish a volume of poems in the same vein; she should take her time, two years perhaps. Two years! They did not know "G.B.," as she sometimes refers to herself. Forsaking all distractions and diversions, even the Saturday night movies, she wrote, wrote, and wrote, until she had completed eleven off-rhyme sonnets to form a sequence of "The Progress." Finally, she wrote the first of her surefire hits, "The Sundays of Satin-Legs Smith," a fascinating portrait of a dandy from the black belt—a description of his dazzling appearance, his day, his life, his philosophy, his girl. She mailed the manuscript with a "loud heart," and before long, the golden word came: Harper was going to publish *A Street in Bronzeville*. It was Hallelujah time for the South Side Community Writers and Artists. One of theirs had made it!

It was a time for parties: big parties, little private parties, drop-in "open house" parties at Margaret Goss's barn studio. But the best party of all was the Langston Hughes joyous jubilee, when seventy-five people jammed into the corner kitchenette on Sixty-third and Champlain Avenue (the place of Brooks's most lively memories); and in that big, happy bubbling crowd, "Langston was the merriest and most colloquial of them all," she wrote in her *Report from Part One* and quoted him as exclaiming, "*Best* party I've ever been to!" He enjoyed everyone; "he enjoyed all the talk, all the phonograph blues, all the festivity in the crowded air." The report of that celebration, and of a quiet visit when the "noble poet, efficient essayist and adventurous dramatist" dropped in unexpectedly and was happy to share their simple meal of ham hocks, mustard greens, and candied yams, indicates the esteem Gwen Brooks had for the man as well as his poetry, and she pays full tribute to him in her own poetry and prose.

One of a series of free verse portraits reads in part: "Langston Hughes:/ Is merry glory/ Is salutatory./ Yet grips his right of twisting free./ Has a long reach/ strong speech,/ Remedial fears./ Muscular tears. . . . In mud and blood and sudden death—/ In the breath/ Of the holocaust he/ Is helmsman,/ hatchet, headlight. . . ." Equally perceptive was her delineation of Robert Frost: "There is a little lightning in his eyes./ Iron at the mouth./ His brows ride neither too far up nor down./ He is splendid./ With a place to stand. Some glowing in the common blood./ Some specialness within."

Both poets were alive when the above lines were written and the portraits, though accurate, are slightly mannered. The final lines of the Hughes poem contain a vein of contrivance: "See/ one restless in the exotic time! and ever, / Till the air is cured of its fever." ("That is exactly the way Langston felt about himself," noted Brooks.) When Brooks wrote her autobiography *Report from Part One,* however, both fellow poets were gone, and her memoir of Hughes is a more intimate, penetrating study of the man. Here is a prose that soars into a song of praise—a eulogy in the best sense of the word.

"He was an easy man. You could rest in his company. No one possessed a more serious understanding of life's immensities. No one was firmer in recognition of the horrors man imposes upon man, in hardy insistence on reckonings. But when those who knew him remember him the memory inevitably will include laughter of an unusually warm and tender kind. The wise man, he knew, will take some juice out of this one life that is his gift. . . .

"Langston Hughes loved literature. He loved it not fearfully, not with awe. His respect for it was never stiff nor cold. His respect for it was gaily deferential. He considered literature not his private inch, but great acreage. The plantings of others he not only welcomed but busily enriched. He had an affectionate interest in those young writers.

"Mightily did he use the street. He found its multiple heart, its tastes, smells, alarms, formulas, flowers, garbage and convulsions. He brought them all to his table-top. He crushed them to a writing-paste. He himself became the pen. . . ."

Eventually, the packet of "author's copies" arrived, and the poet, taking the top copy of *A Street in Bronzeville* in her hands, turned the pages of the slim volume over and over, touching them with tender, loving fingers. This was her book. A great thrill came when, after a Saturday night movie, she and her husband, who had been told by Paul Engle that his review of the book would appear in the Sunday *Chicago Tribune,* got an early edition and zipped it open to the book section. There, prominently placed, was the review. "For Heaven's sake!" she cried out almost in disbelief. She and Henry stood there and "read the entire review on the midnight street." No word but "ecstasy" could describe their mood as they waited for the bus, she wrote apologetically, addressing students whom she had cautioned against using that weak word. Henry had looked at her "meticulously," saying, "Gwendolyn, tell me *EXACTLY* how you feel at this moment." And "ecstatic" was the way she felt.

Engle's review launched Gwendolyn Brooks's reputation in full sail. Harper was ready to publish her next volume whenever she had enough new poems. Elizabeth Lawrence, her first editor, who became a friend as well, gave her a knowledge of publishing she had never known. Shortly after the book and other reviews besides Engle's appeared in 1945, she received *Mademoiselle*'s Merit Award, and the following year, a grant from the National Institute of Arts and Letters, as well as a Guggenheim Fellowship, which was extended in 1947. By then she had completed the volume that was to catapult her into fame: *Annie Allen,* published by Harper in 1949. As Don L. Lee, writer-in-residence at Howard University, wrote in 1972, "Annie Allen *ran* away with the Pulitzer Prize. . . . Her winning is significant for a number of reasons other than her being the first person of African descent to do so. One unstated fact is obvious; *she was the best poet, black or white, writing in the country at the time.*" If this is overstating the case, it is indicative of the esteem in which Brooks was, and is, held by her colleagues. He grants that it is an "important" book, since it brought Brooks national and international fame. It opened new avenues of financial support like teaching and book reviewing, though she had begun doing the latter in 1948, for the *Chicago Daily News.* It brought a demand for readings.

However, *Annie Allen,* for all its nobility of spirit, is for the most part an intellectualized view of "Negro life in Chicago." One department, "Appendix to the Anniad," a title that requires a knowledge of Virgil to catch the play on words, bears the subtitle, "Leaves from a loose-leaf war diary," and in Part Three becomes a complicated sonnet-ballad: fourteen lines with a three-part alternating rhyme scheme and couplet at the last two lines. Many readers, especially whites, found it inspiring, but to young black poets like Don L. Lee, the lines were devoid of emotion; they left him "dry." Only in poems like "The Children of the Poor," which asks, "What shall I give my children? who are poor/ Who are adjudged the leastwise of the land" does a strong inner Brooksian feeling emerge.

If *Annie Allen* was an enormous milestone in the poet's career because of the Pulitzer Prize, there was another event of equal importance that kept her willingly from becoming more of a public figure at the time: a month before their son, Henry, Jr. was to celebrate his eleventh birthday, Gwen gave birth to their second child, a daughter her pleased parents named, Nora. Gwen, at thirty-four, with a son halfway to adulthood, started mothering a little girl. Her epithet for their daughter was "Nice Nora." And from the photographs, anecdotes, and Nora's own notes, the phrase was apt. She must have been a charming small child, and a "nice," bright girl as she grew up. Obviously, her "big brother" and both her parents adored her, but they did not spoil her, as she herself observed in a newsstory she wrote at the age of ten, and in her essay, "My Family," a few months later.

Two years after she was born, on October 10, 1953, Henry, Jr.'s birthday, the Blakely family moved into their own house at 7428 South Evans Avenue, where they lived "forever after," where the poet and husband still live. Small though the house was, the Blakelys felt it was good to have a place of their own. All they needed now was more time for writing! One of the telling items in Gwen's autobiographical notes follows two-year-old Nora's constant demand, "Tell me a 'tory," or "More COOK-ie!" Here the poet had jotted down, "Mama's attempt to eke out one hour for herself each day." Her husband had gone into the insurance business in order to make the mortgage payments on their house and wrote, mostly fiction, in whatever spare time he could find. Even little Nora, who found herself locked out of her brother's room (which she loved to explore during his school hours) had to have her "Nora-Corner" that was hers alone.

When the "baby" of the family was old enough to go to school, her mother had more hours for poetry writing; now and then a poem appeared in various literary quarterlies, or monthly magazines like *Harper's* or the *Saturday Review, Common Ground,* and *Beloit Poetry Journal.* She was in demand for poetry readings. But the first long out-of-town engagement, exciting as it was, posed the problem of leaving her family. However, it was soon ved by those involved, as ten-year-old Nora's "newsstory" clearly shows in both headline and text. It reads:

"GWENDOLYN BLAKELY   POET   GOES TO   COLORADO
Gwendolyn Blakely, a mother of two children, Henry and Nora, is making an expense-paid trip to COLORADO to give a speech. She is staying there for a week.
     She is very dedicated to her work   poetry so she deserves this trip I feel.
     I'm left   with a strange sort of   nice father. Who is strict but good."

Not the least item in this revealing account of family relationships is Nora's use of her mother's married name, which had not appeared on any of the poet's published work. Brooks herself, although she did not mention the subject of her professional name, said during an interview in 1971, when asked how it was to be a poet and a family woman, "My husband and I were both writing when we got married. But I'd always felt that it was the marriage that should get most of the wife's attention. So I wrote when other things did not call upon me. . . . I gave a lot of attention to my children. I do not regret doing that. My husband and I are separated now. . . . He put up with a great deal. Of course I wasn't traveling so much during our marriage as I am now, but he encouraged me in my writing all along. He was very pleased when any good thing happened to me, though I know that, being a man, he did have problems adjusting to what I was doing. Often we discussed his own literary ambitions. . . ." Here she gave generous praise to Henry Blakely's talent as a potentially successful writer, but went on to say that she had no intention of getting married again, because "marriage is a hard, demanding state. Especially if you're a woman, you have to set yourself aside constantly. I did it during my marriage, but I couldn't again." Later in the discussion she elaborated on her theory:

"I'm not saying I'm down on marriage; it just will not fit in with my life. I like to be alone more than a married woman can be. . . . I want to be able to give my attention to writing, reading, and doing whatever else occurs to me rather than fixing three meals a day and humoring a man. My husband, I believe, would give me credit for *this*—he knew that I always upheld his faith in himself. I wouldn't talk about my own affairs unless he brought them up, and I tried to make sure that things I said would not be taken amiss."

In those years, when the children were growing up, she felt like a lot of married women, as if she were walking on eggs. "In my case, part of it was due to the fact that we both wrote. It's hard on the man's ego to be married to a woman who happens to get some attention before he does. But I must give my husband this—of all men in that position, I believe he behaved better than anybody I could imagine. He really did have a great interest in my succeeding. He was a very good critic, too. He used to criticize my work. 'Criticize' sounds a little harsh; he would read my work and tell me how he thought I could improve it." When the interviewer asked, "Did you take his advice often?" Gwen Brooks answered at once: "Oh, yes." Thus she described her years as poet, wife, and mother.

Her beloved father had died the year before the new book appeared, and the volume opened with a poem, "In Honor of David Anderson Brooks, My Father (July 30, 1883–November 21, 1959)," intensely personal, yet objective in its restrained sorrow and reverence, especially in the first and last stanzas.

> *A dryness is upon the house*
> *My father loved and tended.*

Beyond his firm and sculptured door
His light and lease have ended.

. . . .

He who was Goodness, Gentleness,
And Dignity is free.
Translates to public Love
Old private charity.

As its title indicates, *The Bean Eaters* dealt in large measure with the poor and poverty-stricken among the poet's people. If she or her publishers expected the new work to be hailed by the critics on publication, they were disappointed: a dead silence met its appearance. Word leaked out little by little in the literary world that reviewers found the volume "too social." Finally, after months, Robert Glauber of the *Beloit Poetry Journal* had the courage to speak his mind in a long, glowing review, which set off a series of notices from those who had been too timid or conservative. The readers who most appreciated these new poems were those who could identify with its living pictures. The title poem, inspired by the sight of an old couple bent over their daily ration of beans, is forceful in its simple, stark reality:

They eat beans mostly, this old yellow pair.
Dinner is a casual affair.
Plain chipware on a plain and creaking wood,
Tin flatware.

In the last of the three short verses, they keep "Remembering, with twinklings and twinges,/ As they lean over the beans in their rented back room that is full of beads and receipts and dolls and cloths, tobacco crumbs, vases and fringes." To a certain extent she had made use of those scenes in *A Street in Bronzeville*, particularly in poems like "kitchenette building";

"Sadie and Maud"; "the mother," a powerful poem of ambivalent feelings toward abortion; "the vacant lot"; "southeast corner"; and the aforementioned "The Sundays of Satin Legs Smith." The new book went a step farther in depicting the life of black slum areas.

In Dunbar's era, it was the "dialect poetry" that caught the essence of the "lowly life" found in his lyrics; reluctantly he put by his "straight poetry," as he called it, for the native speech of the southern Negro, then only two decades away from slavery. In the later time of Langston Hughes, it was the language of Harlem, the big city "blacks"—as Brooks points out, he was among the first to use the term—that he encountered in his adventures and travels which best portrayed his race. Since Gwen and Langston were by this time friendly, it was inevitable that his influence made itself felt in her lines. She had received a warm letter from Countee Cullen after *A Street in Bronzeville* came out; he included a cordial invitation to visit him and his wife in their home outside New York. She was proud of that letter, as well as one from James Weldon Johnson, but she never became friends with either, and Langston was her black literary hero. So it was natural that he should be one of the main influences in her poetry. However, Brooks is no mere imitator: her street language and the characters who speak it are the product of her own observation and originality. Titles like "My little 'Bout-Town Gal," "A Bronzeville Mother Loiters in Mississippi; Meanwhile, A Mississippi Mother Burns Bacon," "Old Mary," "Mrs. Small," "Jesse Mitchell's Mother," and "Bronzeville Woman in a Red Hat—Hires Out to Mrs. Miles" are all indicative of the stories they tell of womanhood among poor blacks. They are strong, moving portraits, often splashed with humor, or tinged with bitter irony. But it is "We Real Cool" (The Pool Players. Seven at the Golden Shovel) that became the best known of *The Bean Eaters* because of its powerful impact on its audience, both readers and listeners. Here the vernacular takes over completely:

We real cool. We
Left school. We

Lurk late. We
Strike straight. We

Sing sin. We
Thin gin. We

Jazz June. We
Die soon.

These four two-line stanzas were always the favorite at poetry readings, due partly to the poet's delivery. She gave these stage directions for the last: "The ending WEs in 'We Real Cool' are tiny, wispy, weakly argumentative 'Kilroy is here' announcements. The boys have no accented sense of themselves, yet they are aware of a semidefined personal importance. Say the 'We' softly." After a reading of this poem in February, 1965, a sixteen-year-old boy, Placido Tugo, wrote: "Mrs. Gwendolyn Brooks gave me a good lesson that I hope I will never forget because I was planning to quit school. But now I know that there is no place like school. I would want to tell her how I feel inside of my heart." The poet, touched by the poignancy of his last line wrote to him at once: "Dear Placido, What a happiness to know that words of mine could influence one of the largest decisions you will ever make: to stay in school! For this alone, I am most happy that I could come to read to you. Please maintain your decision. Staying in school is overwhelmingly important—even though sometimes it may seem hard to do. . . . I am very proud of you. BEST wishes!"

Her note is typical of Gwen Brooks's warm reaction to people, regardless of age, color, or creed, who touch her sensibilities. At a Society of Midland Authors banquet in 1959, she had met Bob (Book Beat) Cromie, to whom she presented an award, along with one to Mark Van Doren. As judge, she had voted for both men, and both became her friends, but Cromie and his "witty writer-wife" Alice became "concerned devotees" and delightful companions of both Gwen and Henry. The four shared many informal social pleasures—picnics, parties, plays, out-of-town lectures—spending enjoyable hours together. As if it were a thing of the past now, the poet writes in her *Report,* "In the days when 'mixed friends' were confidently doing this sort of thing, we travelled many an alluring lonesome road." The Cromies extended themselves in other ways. Bob persuaded Gwen to write reviews for the *Chicago Tribune* at the same time she was writing some reviews for the *Sun-Times* and paid her more for them. Before there was a demand for her lecture series, Bob or Alice would get a little "speaking" for her here and there. Through Bob, Henry was able to secure the major insurance contract that kept his infant company going. The Cromies aided scores of artists in various ways.

Besides the Cromies, Brooks cites other whites who befriended or aided her "along the wilder way." Among the most notable was Nelson Algren, columnist and consistent liberal, who secured her first big magazine *assignment,* a feature story in *Black Life.* Before she and Marc Crawford knew of the family connection between them, they used to sit on the floor in Algren's apartment, deep in literary discussion or shoptalk about writing in general. Years later, when she was in a position to do so, Brooks "stimulated" the Chicago Arts Council into recognizing the multiple talents of Algren with a money award; a photograph shows her presenting him with a check for six thousand dollars. Another of her white benefactors was Mike (Mirron) Alexandroff, president of Chicago's Columbia College, who invited her to start a poetry workshop there. He told her to do anything she liked with it. "Run it in a restaurant," he said. "A coffee shop. Do absolutely anything you want with it!" So she did. She experimented and enjoyed the experience of having young minds respond creatively to her stimulating ideas. Space does not permit a detailed description of her methods, but needless to say, they were brimming with vitality. Perhaps it is best epitomized by the exclamation of one of her students at Columbia, Melvin Forkos: *"This* class is like a SHOW!"

During the sixties, Brooks found herself, to her surprise, in demand as a "good teacher"—to her *mirabile dictu*! Elmhurst College in Elmhurst, Illinois; Northeastern Illinois State College; the University of Wisconsin in Madison, where she was Rennebohm Professor of English, all wanted her to grace their faculties, not only in conducting poetry workshops, but teaching freshman English, twentieth century poetry, and the short story. And she continued to go to Columbia once a week in fall, spring, and sometimes in summer, until 1969, when she resolved to quit the halls of academia because she needed more time for her own work, for developing her true identity with her race. But when the City College of New York proposed that she come there for a year as Distinguished Professor of the Arts, it was too good an invitation to turn down. She was in a special program with novelists Joseph Heller and John Hawkes, and she met many fine people, including Audre Lorde, then one of the younger black poets coming to the fore, and Adrienne Rich, then beginning her leading role among the feminist poets. However, the Monday–Tuesday commuting proved too strenuous (she would not leave Chicago even for one year), and a strain on her heart forced her to leave after the first term. In 1971 she gave up teaching for good.

There were other factors besides the heart strain that led to her decision. In 1968 she had been named Poet Laureate for the State of Illinois, succeeding Carl Sandburg, who had recently died. In her wildest dreams as a child she had never imagined she would be Poet Laureate of Illinois. Her mother and her family were pleased and proud. Her new volume, published the same year, titled *In the Mecca,* showed greater social consciousness than any so far, and the beginnings of the influence brought by the black arts movement and the black civil rights struggle. The turning point in her work had come in 1967, at Fisk University, when, quite suddenly, she met New Black. It was spring; she had just completed a lecture and reading tour in South Dakota, where she had been loved and applauded with a standing ovation at the all-white state college. Satisfied but worn-out, she pushed on to give one more "reading" at Fisk. But even as she entered the auditorium, she could feel an amazing electricity and, as she began to read, she realized that her young colleagues at the writers conference were listening with cool respect instead of the doting love she had found in Dakota.

Here, the heroes were young activists like novelist-director John Oliver Killens, editors David Llorens and Hoyt Fuller, playwright Ron Milner, and, most worshipped, LeRoi Jones (later, "Amiri Baraka"), famed for his strong striking plays, and not yet known by his African name. He entered in the middle of her reading, and when she interrupted herself to say, "Ah, here's LeRoi Jones!" the crowd went wild, cheering, clapping, whistling, and stomping. It was an eye-opener to Gwen. For the rest of the conference, she and Margaret Danner—"another old Girl, also Coldly Respected," went around amazed, bewildered, half dazed at the things they saw and heard. The eyes of both seemed to say, "What in the world is going on here?" And later on Gwen discovered that "there is indeed a new black today. He is different from any the world has known. He's a tall-walker. Almost firm. By many of his own *brothers* he is not understood. And he is understood by *no* white. . . ." If this seems an exaggerated statement, she justifies it by asserting, "I cannot say anything other, because nothing other is the truth." And further:

"I—who have 'gone the gamut' from an almost angry rejection of my dark skin by some of my brainwashed brothers and sisters to a surprised queenhood in the new black sun—am qualified to enter at least the kindergarten of new consciousness now. . . . I have hopes for myself." Glimmerings of her new consciousness gleamed from the pages of *In the Mecca*. The dedication itself gives a hint. Her previous *Selected Poems*, published by Harper in 1963, was dedicated to Bob and Alice

Cromie and to the memory of Frank Brown, the "militant" black author of *Trumbull Park;* this book is dedicated, "To the memory of Langston Hughes, and to James Baldwin, LeRoi Jones, and to Mike Alexandroff—educators extraordinare." A ratio of three to one black writers. And, like the young writers she listened to at Fisk University, Brooks began to write *to* as well as *about* her people.

In the Mecca treats of tenants, some two thousand occupying the old Mecca, once a fashionable apartment house, "a splendid palace, later showplace of Chicago," the dilapidated domain of the city's poor blacks. The poet turns the tenants into characters of an epic drama, reminiscent in a way of Elmer Rice's "Street Scene." The long dramatic poem begins like a parable, or, like a Greek play, addressing the audience: "Sit where the light corrupts your face./ Miës Van der Rohe retires from grace./ And the fair fables fall." Then the characters are introduced: " 'S. Smith' is Mrs. Sallie. Mrs. Sallie hies home to Mecca./ hies to marvelous rest; ascends the sick and influential stair." The poet describes her, and goes on to "old St. Julia Jones, who has had prayer/ and who is inside the door of 215. . . . Out of the dusty threshold bursts Hyena, the striking debutante/ A fancier of firsts, and to the tune of hate,/ in all of Mecca to paint her hair sun-gold." And Mrs. Sallie sees Alfred (the scholar, would-be writer); Yvonne, Melodie Mary; Cap and Casey, and others are named along with Mrs. Sallie's eight children. Her youngest, Pepita, is missing. The life stories of all these tenants come out as they are asked if they know what has happened to the little girl.

In the course of relating their histories, a broad variety of personalities is revealed "against a mosaic of daily affairs: some are pathetic, some violent, grim, or mysterious, but all are full of vitality. Even the grimmest has an occasional streak of sunlight," as she said. The end is tragic, but subdued. Pepita has been murdered. "She never went to kindergarten. . . ." 'I touch,' she said once, 'petals of a rose.'/ A silky feeling through me goes.

Her mother will try for roses." In contrast, there is warlike "Way-out Morgan" who is "collecting guns in a tiny fourth-floor room./ . . . He flourishes, ever, on porridge or pat of bean / pudding or wiener soup—fills fearsomely/ on visions of Death-to-the-Hordes-of-the-White-Men!/ . . . Remembering three local-and-legal beatings, he/ Rubs his hands in glee,/ does Wayout Morgan. Remembering his Sisters/ mob-raped in Mississippi, Wayout Morgan/ smacks sweet his lips and adds another gun/ and listens to Blackness stern and blunt and beautiful, / organ-rich blackness telling a terrible story." He predicts that the Day of Debt-pay shall come soon, and exults in his preparations.

If there were those who criticized Brooks for her abrupt change of attitude and technique, there were more who hailed her new volume for its strength and outspoken reality. Her husband, though he was proud of her, disagreed sharply with her newfound race consciousness and black activism, which had brought a marked change in her whole outlook from the time of her awakening at the new black writers conference at Fisk University.

Shortly after her return from that historic meeting, she had been invited to attend a performance of a black musical, "Opportunity, Please, Knock!" staged by Oscar Brown, Jr. with members of the Blackstone Rangers, a tough gang of black youths who, in their zeal for recognition, often did things that caused trouble with police. Gwen took Nora and a friend of her daughter's to the revue, and all three found it a stunner. That such talent could be shown by members of the tough street gang impelled the poet to ask if any of them had a similar ability for writing. And soon she was involved, with aid from Walter Bradford, teen organizer at Wilson Junior College, in conducting a writers workshop among the Rangers. The spirit of these young minds, once it was channelled along constructive, creative lines, was exhilarating, intoxicating. She was swept into the black arts movement with a vigor that carried her to the point of breaking away from her long alliance with Harper &

Row a move her husband viewed with grave misgivings. They had serious discussions on the subject, but never resolved those differences.

Brooks felt strongly that she should be associated with the new black press coming into existence, and though she asserted that their separation had nothing to do with their disparate views, it is odd that her marriage to Henry and to Harper terminated in the same year, 1969. The parting from both was amiable; Harper was to publish one more book, *The World of Gwendolyn Brooks;* but from this time on her volumes of poetry have been published by black firms. *Aloneness, Family Pictures,* her auto-biography *Report from Part One,* and *Beckonings*—all came out under the imprint of Broadside Press, established by the noted poet Dudley Randall, in Detroit, Michigan. As editor-in-chief and a leading contributor, Randall conducted a one-man publishing business with the aid of a skeletal staff of like-minded writers, who, as Gwen would put it, were "tall-walkers," the gut-talkers who did not hesitate to tell the truth about their feelings against the second-class citizenship that was forced upon most blacks in spite of the civil rights programs, the desegregation of schools; these writers expressed their inner emotions with a passion: they wrote as they pleased—white approval be damned. It was "Gwen's Way"—the title, an obvious reference to Proust that was used by George L. Kent in a Preface to her *Report*—to be compassionate as well as passionate in presenting her people's plight. The new ideal, she held, was not to be *"against whites,* but *for* blacks."

Her credo was crystalized in 1971, when she went to see for herself what Africa was like, and in one way felt she had come home, although Nairobi, Kenya, her first stop, was by no means an ethnic paradise for her race. Whites still had commercial power in the big hotel in Nairobi, and some native Africans were wary of her at first; another Afro-American, she sensed they felt, come to investigate and perhaps hope to take over the development of their third world nation. However, it was a pleasure for her

to see the predominance of her race, the grace of their tall figures, the warmth of their greetings, the strong handshake that
symbolized love and support of one another. And when she came
to Dar es Salaam, where she stayed with the Charlie Cobbs,
Americans who had settled in Africa, she learned a little Swa-
hili, and was able to make friends with the "everyday" people.
She gave a reading at a teachers' college, which was "nicely received." On one of their outings, the poet got a glimpse of life
in the African bush, where the friends they visited lived simply
but contentedly in a neat and attractive hut, surrounded by
beautiful, wild rugged country.

By the time she returned to Chicago, Gwen Brooks was more
than ever convinced that there must be black solidarity, a feeling of kinship among all people of African descent. In appearance her hair had become "natural," as she said in 1969, soon
after she began working with the young Ranger writers: No
more fussing with the hot comb, to force her hair into a shape
other than its kinky natural state. Since 1969 she has worn her
hair in a close cut, fitting her head like a neat woolly cap. Commenting on a photo of herself standing beside the plaque at the
Emily Dickinson home in Amherst, she wrote, "I think Emily,
after the first shock at my intrusion, would have approved of
my natural." Below the thatch and her high forehead, Brooks's
eyes are bright, wide open, and strong, yet full of warmth and
understanding. Her nose is broad, her mouth turned down at
the corners in a kind of wry smile at life's conglomerates.

Nowhere are her features and nature more delicately deline-
ated than in a drawing done by her brother Raymond, which
graces the back cover of *Beckonings* in the 1975 edition of this
important volume. But her artist brother did not live to see his
drawing on the cover of his poet-sister's book. He died the year
before it was published. The poem preceding the table of contents, "To the Memory of My Brother (October 19, 1918–January 21, 1974) RAYMOND MELVIN BROOKS," is, like the
one to her father, intensely personal and moving. Yet no greater

contrast in technique can be found than that used in the two poems, illustrating the change in Brooks's method. Instead of the stately metered, rhymed lines of 1959 in the tribute to her father, the memorial to Raymond is in free verse, almost a prose poem, as the first line shows: "He found industriousness an engrossing challenge." She goes on to speak of his love for people, his "affectionate, warm, and cheerful presence, his exuberant charming and involving smile," to which people responded. The second stanza lyrically concerns his art in relation to his life. Though he "made the paper speak and sing," he "was chiefly a painter of days and the daily, with a talent for life color, life pattern: a talent for jeweling use. . . ."

The deep feeling that evoked her low-keyed eulogy undeniably emerges from the lines. The poet and her brother had been empathetic siblings all their lives. Below a photograph of Raymond with three of his children, she makes a point of stating that his son, Raymond, Jr., "was married on African Liberation Day, 1972." The love she had always felt for Raymond was extended in *Beckonings* to include the family of their ancient but revitalized African origin.

Hoyt W. Fuller, essayist, editor of *Black World,* and literary critic, wrote of this volume: "The aching loveliness of these poems is sometimes close to unbearable. Through the magic of Gwendolyn Brooks's words, we hold in our souls' eye a vivid image of our beauty, we glimpse what we might yet be. An incredible woman, this poet: she would urge us into our ultimate, our transcendent humanity, with her love." Though the book begins with heartrending tragedy in a Brooksian ballad, "The Boy Died in My Alley," most of the poems here are on the upbeat. They are asexual love poems, exuding her love for her race in Africa as well as America, and beyond that, for all humanity, and beyond that, for earth's creatures and the lesson to be learned from them. Here is "A Black Wedding Song," lyrical and strong; and the earlier mentioned "Elegy in a Rainbow," subtitled, "Moe Belle's Double Love Song"; and a stirring "preachment" to "Boys.Black.," a call to action: "Call your singing and your bringing,/ your pulse, your ultimate booming in/ the not-so-narrow temples of your Power— /call all that, that is your Poem, AFRIKA./ Although you know/ so little of that long leaplanguid land,/ our tiny union/ is the dwarfmagnificent./ Is the busysimple thing." And in a later stanza she cautions: "Beware/ the easy griefs./ It is too easy to cry 'ATTICA'/ and shock thy street,/ And purse thy mouth,/ and go home to thy 'Gunsmoke.' Boys,/ black boys,/ beware the easy griefs/ that fool and fuel nothing." A moving declaration follows:

> *I tell you*
> *I love You*
> *and I trust You.*
> *Take my Faith.*
> *Make of my Faith an engine.*
> *Make of my Faith*
> *a Black Star. I am Beckoning.*

A more dramatic finale could hardly be found, yet for some reason this coda has been deleted from an updated version of the poem included in Brooks's 1981 volume, *To Disembark*. In *Beckonings*, however, warmth of feeling predominates, and in the poem, "Horses Graze," it reaches a philosophical height with Dickinsonian simplicity and eloquence: Using one-word lines she observes that "Cows graze/ Horses graze/ They/ eat/ eat/ eat." A cogent description follows: "Their graceful heads/ are bowed/ bowed/ bowed/ in majestic oblivion./ They are nobly oblivious/ to your follies,/ your inflation,/ the knocks and nettles of administration./ They/ eat/ eat/ eat." Then comes the body of the poem, written in full sentence, free verse lines:

> *And at the crest of their brute satisfaction,*
> *with wonderful gentleness, in affirmation,*
> *they lift their clean calm eyes and they lie down*
> *and love the world.*

They speak with their companions.
They do not wish that they were otherwhere.
Perhaps they know that creature feet may press
only a few earth inches at a time,
that earth is anywhere earth,
that an eye may see,
wherever it may be,
the Immediate arc, alone, of life, of love.

And again there is a coda, emphasizing the universality of her statement: "In Sweden,/ China,/ Afrika,/ in India or Maine/the animals are sane;/they know and know and know/ there's ground below/ and sky/ up high." A poem for all peoples, of all ages, and for all time, it might well be included in classical anthologies, and collections for young readers as well as adults.

Four years after Raymond's death, the poet experienced another, even deeper sorrow when her mother died in 1978. Keziah Wims Brooks was a remarkable woman in her own right from the glimpses one catches of her in her famous daughter's *Report,* found in the chapter on childhood years. The encouragement she gave her gifted child continued through the growing years and became the delight, the pride she took in the successes and honors that came to Gwendolyn Brooks. She was, the poet wrote in a letter* in 1981, "such a nourishing influence on me *all* of my life" that it took two years before the fact of her death was even "approximately" acceptable.

Not that Keziah was a dependent mother. After David Brooks died, she lived on in the same house by herself until she died, "two weeks into her ninetieth year." She was so energetic and young-looking that people could never believe she was "out of her seventies." At the age of eighty-five she wrote a book and paid for its publication herself at the age of eighty-seven. A determined woman, once that was accomplished, she must have said to herself, "quite deliberately," that it was "now time to

* To this biographer.

stop living," and she began to stop—or so it seemed to her daughter, who moved in with her during the last illness. One day, shortly before her mother died, Gwen remarked that it was "a pleasure to see her looking so peaceful"; and she answered, with a "specific look, a cheerful deliberateness," "I *am Peaceful*." Then she said even more emphatically, "*Thank You*." The phrase was spoken with such feeling, such "warm pertinence," the poet wrote, that the memory of that moment is a timeless treasure, held precious in her mind.

It was as if her mother were expressing a deep gratitude for all the joy the poet had given her through the years, the honor she had brought to the family. Keziah had attended the ceremonies connected with the awards, appointments, and honors that had come to Gwendolyn Brooks in those years; and there have been many. They continued to come after Keziah died, and, knowing that her mother took such pride in the poet's achievements, helped Brooks to accept the inevitable and keep on with her work in the black movement for equality of opportunity and recognition of black artists in all fields on a level with whites.

One of the honors that had pleased her mother the most was the sight of Gwen's portrait painted on the great "Wall of Respect" on Forty-third and Langley, on the side of a tavern (finally torn down). Everyone from Harriet Tubman and Frederick Douglass, Duke Ellington, Paul Laurence Dunbar, and Langston Hughes and Gwendolyn Brooks, to Bessie Smith, Marian Anderson, and Imamu Amiri Baraka* could be found on this remarkable mural, topped by smoke stacks and chimney pots of the poor. There was a great day of celebration when the Wall was completed.

Other memorable events witnessed by her mother were presentations of the poet's first honorary doctorates. Though she now has forty-plus such degrees, the one she received on June

---

*African name taken by LeRoi Jones.

13, 1970 from Northwestern University was pre-eminent. Un-der an impressive photograph Gwen wrote: "Don Lee, Nora, my mother and I were driven to the ceremony in the chauf-fered limousine of Gaylord Freeman, chairman of the board of the First National Bank. (Hmmmm.)" Whatever the "Hmmmm" means, the ceremony meant a great deal to her mother, and Gwen was gratified by that.

Over the intervening period from then to the present, many honors have come to Gwendolyn Brooks, including two Gug-genheim fellowships, awards, a membership in the American Academy Institute of Arts and Letters, the Shelley Award from the Poetry Society of America, to name only a few. She is in constant demand for readings and usually performs to a full house of listeners who give her a standing ovation at the close. However, her primary purpose and all-consuming interest in writing poetry—or prose—is to speak to and about her people, to join with them in lifting their voices. It took great courage to leave an established, "top" publisher like Harper & Row for the nonexistent financial returns of the struggling new firms run by blacks; but she has remained steadfast in her move. The poems contained in *To Disembark,* published by Don Lee's Third World Press in 1982, are in many instances shortened versions of those included in three previous volumes brought out by the dis-banded Broadside Press, and the book is dedicated to Dudley Randall, with "affection and respect." Often abbreviation has made them pithy, more militant. For example, "Boys. Black." has been cropped at the beginning and end; the place-name "Attica" has been changed to "Africa," altering the context; and the beautiful coda has been cut off, presumably to give more urgency to the call to action, but it is less effective without the affirmation of love, trust, and faith, followed by the final, "I am beckoning," which closes the original version.

Whatever the outcome, the point is that Brooks is willing to take a chance on the thing she feels is the right thing to do. And despite setbacks in the progress toward full civil rights for blacks, facing the fact that the movement has become "dim and dainty," as she says in a poem to John Oliver Killens, appealing to such qualities as his strong temperament for a way to solve the problems of this disquieting situation, Gwendolyn Brooks has the power to radiate hope and warmth for what is human. She does so through her way with words, spoken as well as written, rarely sacrificing the lyric quality of her poems for their polemic content.

Adrienne Rich

B y her own admission, at a meeting of the National Council of Teachers of English, Adrienne Rich was born with an unusually large share of "luck," which implied "the unsaid word" *good* in regard to the quality of that luck. Her heritage was rich in more than name or money: she was "born white and middle-class into a house full of books, with a father who encouraged me to read and write." The date was May 16, 1929; the place, Baltimore, Maryland, the city geographically and culturally a midpoint between North and South.

A common saying among natives is that southern women try harder to please the men than do northern. Whether or not this is true, Adrienne Rich has stated that because her father, Dr. Arnold Rich, led his daughter at an early age into the delights of late nineteenth-century literature in his very Victorian, pre-Raphaelite library, she read Tennyson, Keats, Arnold, Blake, Rossetti, Swinburne, Carlyle, and Pater. Soon after she began to read these Victorian greats, she began to write, again under her father's supervision. So it was that for nearly twenty years, the formative years of her life, she "wrote for a particular man," who criticized and praised her and made her feel that she was not only a talented poet, but a "special" individual and his daughter. Presumably her mother concurred, but the doctor obviously dominated Adrienne's intellectual life. This factor neutralized her luck, since the "obverse side" of the situation was that for a long time she wrote principally to please him, or rather, as she said, not to displease him. As his firstborn, the oldest of his three daughters, she was "special" to both her parents, and was expected to set an example for her little sisters. A good student as well as an avid reader, she was both diligent and creative. In her reading she had noticed that countless poems had been written about women by men, and they all seemed to cling to the same image—women who were beautiful but threatened with tragedy, the loss of both youth and beauty. Herrick's advice to Celia—"to make the most of time," to "gather ye rosebuds while ye may"—seems to have been of prime importance where women were concerned in poems written by men from the seventeenth century on, and is still prevalent in both fiction and poetry written by men in the first half of the twentieth century at least.

To a girl like Adrienne Rich, who possessed the creative urge to write at an early age, it was confusing, not to say puzzling, to find no one among all these mythical female figures created by men who, like herself, knew the drudgery of sitting at a desk trying to put words together in such a way that they would express, thoroughly and artistically, the inspired thoughts within her. So she went back to the older women poets in her reading, each possessed of "a peculiar keenness and ambivalence": Sappho, Christina Rossetti, Emily Dickenson, Elinor Wylie, Edna Millay, H.D.; and, among others closer to this period in Rich's life, Marianne Moore. She discovered that the last named was the woman poet most admired by men at the time—"the one who was maidenly, elegant, intellectual, discreet." (W.H. Auden, who in a few years was to choose Adrienne Rich's first volume for the Yale Younger Poets Award, was among the male poets who greatly admired Miss Moore, though she puzzled him at first.) But even as Rich was reading the work of these older sister poets, she realized later, she was looking for the same qualities she had found in the poems written by men. Young, and naively ardent in her faintly formed feminism as an undergraduate student at Radcliffe, she longed to have women poets regarded as the equals of men, and in her mind "to be equal was still confused with sounding the same."

There were other men besides her father who influenced directly or indirectly the literary leanings and aspirations of Adrienne Rich: teachers in high school and college, writers she adored, the literary masters of her school days. Foremost among the male poets were Robert Frost, Dylan Thomas, John Donne, W.H. Auden, Louis MacNiece, Wallace Stevens, W.B. Yeats. Liking their work, she studied them carefully. Her style was first formed by these poets; from them she chiefly gained a knowledge of craft. The path to self-expression she found by herself, slowly, taking a new step with each volume. However, as she said in 1971, "poems are like dreams: in them you put what you don't know you know. Looking back at poems I wrote before I was twenty-one, I'm startled because beneath the conscious craft are glimpses of the split I even then experienced between the girl who wrote poems, who defined herself in writing poems, and the girl who was to define herself by her relationships with men."

There are more than "glimpses" of that split in her subconscious reaction to the world around the undergraduate poet as she sat in her dormitory room at Radcliffe writing these early poems. Too much has been made of the fact that Rich's first volume was marked by "neatly and modestly dressed" poems, as Auden called them, and was so traditional in its formalism that her later work comes as a complete surprise. One has only to read "Storm Warnings" to sense the churning that must have been threatening to destroy, or actively alter, the set of values she had been given by her father and other members of the elder generation in her family. If the poem brings to mind Robert Frost's lines on "inner and outer weather," it is nonetheless Rich's own experience as a sensitive, prescient person among the multitudes "who live in troubled regions." The most personal (in broad terms) of these poems is "Aunt Jennifer's Tigers," in which the poet's latent feminism shows through the lines as clearly as Aunt Jennifer's tigers are woven into the tapestry that the woman of a distant generation is having great difficulty in making. The poet describes her ancestor's fluttery fingers finding the ivory needle hard to pull through the wool because of the massive wedding band holding down her hand. Such symbolism is hardly subtle, but young Adrienne felt she was being "cool and detached." Not until twenty years later, in reexamining the poem, did she realize that her own anger and hostility toward masculine, patriarchal authority was quite apparent, particularly in the last stanza. This final stanza pictures Aunt Jennifer dead, her fearful hands still weighted down by the rings of ordeal her marital life demanded, while the tigers in the tapestry she made continue to prance, eternally proud and fearless.

Some of the undergraduate poems dealt with abstract, philosophic themes, like "The Springboard," which observes that art itself can do no more than hint at things that distressed a poet like Melville, or soothed the frenzy of a composer like Mahler; and "Unsounded," which probes the depths of untried seas of emotion. Here the novice sailor in uncharted seas must proceed faring for himself, unguided or forewarned; each one is a Magellan groping through the tropics of tangled joys and sorrows; such latitudes are shown separately to each person alone.

By her senior year, Adrienne had produced enough poems for a volume and, at the urging of her teachers, she submitted a manuscript entitled *A Change of World* to the committee for the Yale Younger Poets Award, which included publication. She hardly expected to win, although she had already gained a reputation as a bona fide poet among her teachers and classmates. She was also a scholar, foremost of the Phi Beta Kappa candidates who received an A.B. degree in June 1951. At the time of her graduation, she received the amazing news that she had won the Yale Award, chosen for book publication by W.H. Auden, no less! It seemed to her almost "a fluke," but the book was solid proof that she was looked upon as a poet by others besides herself and her family; and the fact that the poet who selected her work—though Auden, in his brief foreword was certainly low-keyed, if not actually condescending in his praise of her poems—was one she regarded as a "master" served as a signal to her that she must continue her career as poet before anything else. She had been having a love affair with a Harvard student; it was beginning to wane, and now she broke it off abruptly. She wanted no entangling alliances to interfere with her career just at this time.

She took the first job she applied for, found an apartment in Cambridge, and lived alone for a time, working, writing, dreaming vaguely of the future. It was good to be on her own, earning her own living, doing exactly as she pleased. All she needed was more time for writing. Along with many another young poet, she applied for a Guggenheim Fellowship and, perhaps because of the Yale Younger Poets Award, received a grant on the first try. She immediately went abroad, spending most of the year 1952–1953 traveling in Europe and England. Full of joyous energy at age twenty-three, she was almost ecstatic at times as she walked around a strange city by herself, exploring, discovering the treasures she had read about or heard about from countless tourists who had been abroad before her;

many of her classmates had gone or been taken to Europe as children, but it was a source of satisfaction to Adrienne Rich that she was there as a result of her own endeavor, her own will and talent. She made friends with people in the countries she visited, especially in Holland. For some reason she felt at home in the Netherlands and began to take an interest in Dutch poetry. The next year she suddenly fell in love with Alfred H. Conrad, an economist who taught at Harvard, seemingly an unlikely choice for a poet, but since love gives little warning of its power to override reason, she "plunged," as she put it, into marriage before the end of 1953. She was only twenty-four, full of energy, and determined to lead the "full" life of a woman, including the mixed blessings of motherhood. She and her husband agreed that marriage must not interfere with her career, and there was nothing to warn her this would not be true. Many of her classmates had married right after graduation, and in the wake of the wave of feminism that swept through the country in World War II and the Korean conflict, these young brides worked to send their husbands through professional school (on the G.I. Bill); that accomplished, the couples retired to the suburbs to raise their families. In the Conrads' case, Alfred was already established in the teaching profession, so Adrienne did not have to find a new job; she could concentrate on her writing. And since her husband taught at Harvard, they "settled" in Cambridge, their permanent address for the next thirteen years. There was no reason why they should not have children if they wished.

Such was the *modus vivendi* of the fifties. The poet kept on with her writing—or trying to write. She became pregnant about a year or so after their marriage; and although both were happy at the thought of having a child, the anticipation of birthing a baby and the changes taking place in the poet's body must have proved a distraction from her intellectual gestation period: by a remarkable coincidence, a boy whom they called David appeared in the same month in 1955 as her new book, *The Dia-*

mond Cutters and Other Poems, published by Harper & Row; yet Rich was already dissatisfied with her latest poems by the time the book came out. They seemed like mere exercises for poems still within her, poems she had not written or had not the courage to write. Her newborn son was a more perfect achievement than her new brainchild, it seemed to her.

Nevertheless, the book won the Ridgely Torrence Memorial Award of the Poetry Society of America, and was generally praised for its "gracefulness," which was gratifying in a way; but when Randall Jarrell, with his flair for flattery, called her "an enchanting poet," who, with her "easy, limpid scansion, close to water, close to air," resembled the beauty of Sleeping Beauty, who seemed to him "a sort of princess in a fairy tale," it was oddly disquieting to the poet herself. She was no princess in a fairy tale, but a real woman, whose second book was as well received as her first. Her reactions puzzled her, as she wrote later: "I had a marriage and a child. If there were doubts, if there were periods of dull depression or active despairing, these could only mean that I was ungrateful, insatiable, perhaps a monster." Whatever the correct term might be, she was a flesh-and-blood woman, who gave birth to a second son, Paul, in 1957, and a third, Jacob Conrad, in 1959, when she was not yet thirty years old. It is notable that all three boys were given biblical names, though there are few references to the Bible in Rich's poetry. And with the birth of her third child, her doubts and fears increased. It was a strange dilemma: to the outside world she appeared to be successful in every way—as poet, wife, and mother. Yet inwardly she was forced to consider herself either "a failed woman and a failed poet, or to try to find some synthesis by which to understand what was happening to her." She was scared.

Perhaps all young mothers felt such nameless anxieties and fears; it was hard to put your finger on any one cause. The feeling that frightened her the most was the "sense of drift," as she said. It was as if she were being pulled along aimlessly by the current called Destiny, powerless to find her former direction. These were the uncharted seas of emotion she had intuitively sensed as she sat writing in her student room ten years before. Now she was losing sight of that girl who went sailing energetically toward her goal. It was as if she was not only drifting, but drugged into insensibility. Perhaps Randall Jarrell had not been too far off course in his reference to Sleeping Beauty. Some years later Rich was to write of herself in a poem about her grandmother, in which the poet contends that a young girl who seems to be asleep is declared dead.

She wrote almost no new poems in the period right after Jacob's birth, which was only natural considering that she had gone through three childbirths in six years; she was worn out, partly from the demands and "discontinuity" of female life—the endless chores of caring for three small children, one an infant; the errands, the "woman's work that is never done" because it is constantly undone by others; but even greater was the female fatigue that comes from suppressed anger and the loss of contact with her inner being, whose cries for attention had to be suppressed. Like Gwendolyn Brooks, she wrote fragments in snatched moments, but in Adrienne's case the little she managed to write was so "unconvincing" to her that she felt angry and frustrated most of the time. The fact that she actually cared a great deal about her husband and children only complicated the situation because it brought a feeling akin to guilt in her relationship toward both her family and her art: she was neglecting both, and seemingly nothing could be done about it.

In trying to analyze her conflict, Rich realized that the element she needed more than time itself was freedom of spirit, freedom to let her imagination have full play in order to fulfill the function of a poet to interpret life as the artist sees it, in a large and objective way; or, as Rich states it, "to transcend and transform experience it has to question, to challenge, to conceive of alternatives, perhaps to the very life you are living at that moment." She was discovering, with a shock of disillusionment, that "to be maternally with small children all day in the old way, to be with a man in the old way of marriage, requires a holding-back, a putting-aside of that imaginative activity, and seems to demand instead a kind of conservatism." She hastened to add, "I want to make it clear that I am *not* saying that in order to write well, or think well, it is necessary to become unavailable to others, or to become a devouring ego. This has been the myth of the masculine artist and thinker, and I repeat, I do not accept it. But to be a female human being trying to fulfill traditional female functions in a traditional way *is* in direct conflict with the subversive function of the imagination." She stressed the importance of the word *traditional:* "There must be ways, and we will be finding out more and more about them, in which the energy of creation and the energy of relation can be united."

In discussing those early years of trying to combine matrimonial motherhood with artistic creativity, Adrienne Rich apparently did not take into account the fact that she had to cope with an all-male household, a much more difficult task than the all-female household in which she grew up. In referring to her three offspring, she consistently uses the word *children* instead of *boys* or *sons*. Whether intentionally or not, she is overlooking the fact that in the "traditional" household until recent decades, and in some instances today, the sons are not expected to assist their mother with household tasks, whereas the daughters, from an early age, are taught to do the dishes, dust, sweep (with vacuum if not broom), and to cook. True, the pattern is changing, but in the time she is discussing—the early fifties and sixties— a woman was criticized for making "sissies" of her sons if she insisted on such tasks, though it was, and still is, perfectly all right for a boy to mow the lawn or "help Dad" wash the car. The mechanization of the kitchen has not made much difference. It is all a hangover from a bygone agrarian era when the individual farmer begat and raised sons to help till and work the land, and woe betide the wife who could not produce sons.

And if she produced only sons, she was equally lost, since there was no one to help her with the "indoor work."* Adrienne's ubiquitous father had a much easier time as head of a female household than his "special" daughter was to experience with her all-male family.

However, the poet who had such a deep inner conflict was hardly a slave to her household in the first year of her marriage, nor was she chained like the upper-middle-class Aunt Jennifer to the delicate but tedious task of tapestry work. And in her address to the National Council of Teachers quoted previously, Rich—though she does state that by the late fifties she was able to write for the first time about experiencing herself as a woman, during which time she wrote, in fragments, the poems that were to bring her the initial fame she won as a feminist poet—neglects to mention the honors that came her way in the years before those poems appeared in her third volume. In 1960 she received the National Institute's Award for poetry, and was the Phi Beta Kappa poet at William and Mary College. The following year she won another Guggenheim Fellowship, and went abroad again, this time to spend the year 1961–1962 in residence with a family in the Netherlands, where she resumed her study of Dutch poetry. And when she came home, she applied for and received a Bollinger Foundation grant for translation of that poetry, a project that could scarcely be further removed from the drudgery of domesticity. Pursuing it to completion, she received the Amy Lowell Traveling Fellowship for 1962–1963, and along with the translations, she also completed those poems she had been writing in fragments at odd hours, sometimes before dawn, after being roused by a restless child. or during a brief hour of refuge in the library, or during the children's nap time provided they all slept.

Realizing that these "fragments and scraps" had a common theme and a consciousness of her female self, particularly a ten-

* Frederick Manfred's novel, *Green Earth*, gives an authentic picture of farmers' family life in Minnesota until well into the 1920s.

part poem she called "Snapshots of a Daughter-in-Law," she decided to collect in a single volume those poems she would not have dared to offer for publication eight years earlier. She had always been taught that poetry should be "universal," in other words, nonfemale; the "snapshots" concern female reactions of fury and passion, but, though the poem was in a longer, looser mode than any she had written before, Adrienne could not bring herself to write them in the first person; she played it safe by using the pronoun *she* and including literary references—everyone from Cicero and Thomas Campion to Diderot, Emily Dickinson, and Simone de Beauvoir was cited in footnotes as authority for various premises. The book, with its appealing title poem, was snapped up for publication by Harper in 1963, and was reissued by W.W. Norton in 1967, and Chatto & Windus in 1970 in London. *Poetry* magazine awarded the title poem its Bess Hokin Prize for 1963, and the book was hailed by critics quick to catch its meaning.

There is no doubt that the series of ten "snapshots" that make up the title poem comprise a portrait of the poet herself, struggling to establish and maintain her identity, not as a poet but as a woman, a person in her own right who is also a poet, with emotions and intellectual reactions equal to but different from those of a male poet. The second in the series, which shows a woman slamming the coffee maker down in fury, hearing inner voices urging her to rebel, depicts a woman on the verge of madness from the repeated minutiae that fill her days, yet she remains silent; instead of "saving herself" by speaking up, she scalds her arm in the hot tap water, or maims herself in other ways; the poem ends with the frightening fact that the only thing that hurts her now is the gray grit invading her eyes every day. However, as the series progresses, the "snapshots" reveal new and different aspects of this daughter-in-law. She is beginning to see the light that photographs her soul. She realizes, after quoting Samuel Johnson, that women's preachments have rarely been praised; that every facet of woman's life has been male-dominated, even Time. Occasionally, primed with alcohol, the male may hail the fair sex: women's minor qualities are over-esteemed with praise that appears gallant; and, their psyche muddled by sweet but vapid verbiage, the women, lulled, listen to their laziness called self-denial, sluttish thought deemed intuitive, every fault forgiven, except the one of stepping out of the shadow of male rule, putting her own above his. For such a crime she is cruelly punished.

In the tenth and final candid shot, we see a glimmer of hope in the subject's eyes. Borrowing an image from Simone de Beauvoir's *Second Sex,* the poet observes that, though woman has taken a long time coming forward, and is harder on herself than history ever was, she is at last beginning to glow in a new light, beautiful as any boy or helicopter (Beauvoir's simile), sailing through the air with great poise, delivering her cargo, perhaps of questionable worth at first, but of much promise, and, most important, her own, definitely her own. Her conclusion, a tentative approach to triumph, reflects the revelations of the late fifties and early sixties—the sit-ins and protest marches in the South, the Bay of Pigs crisis, and the early anti-war movement. The masculine, academic world surrounding Rich's husband at this time seemed to find "expert and fluent answers" to current problems of society, but Adrienne wanted to figure out her own solutions, her own stand as a poet on the matter of militarism versus pacifism and dissent (violent or nonviolent).

Other poems in the same volume, specifically "A Marriage in the Sixties," revealing the difficulties of communication between a married couple whose close relationship is diminishing because of differing opinions, and "The Roofwalker," designated, "for Denise Levertov," a sister poet whose work and ideas Adrienne Rich admired, and with whom she would soon become associated as a "feminist poet," are clear indications of the road Rich was to take from this time forward.

Her next volume, *Necessities of Life,* published in 1966 under the imprint of the house that was to become her permanent publisher, W.W. Norton, contains poems that take up her life chronologically as well as psychologically where *Snapshots of a Daughter-in-Law* left off: she had begun dating her poems in that volume, and continued to do so in this. The title and opening poem bears the date it was written, 1962, and was at first entitled "Thirty-three," her age that year, when it first appeared in *The Paris Review* in 1964. As if she had just been speaking to us, narrating the years of isolation in the relative confines of domesticity, she begins with a description of the way she seems to have reentered the real world—little by little— first a fragment, creating an image that became famous, likening herself to a dark blue thumbtack. Then through varied heats of coping with life's trials, the dot expands, the color changes to fiery red, grilling green. She began to show, to bloom. She was swallowed (like Jonah) by avid reading of biographies revealing the lives of people she idolized. She took on the identity equally of semanticist Wittgenstein, and feminist Mary Wollstonecraft (whom she quoted in earlier poems), of cinematographer Louis Jouvet, of so many diverse personalities that she was "devoured almost to scraps." She was as scabby as a withered bulb tossed in a basement. Unattractive, she let nobody use her but herself; it was like being on a private dole. Or, invoking the Old Testament, more like the Israelites, "kneading bricks in Egypt." The triplet of two-line stanzas are among her most poignant, as she pictures the Israelite slaves resting occasionally by placing one hand on a brick warmed by the sun, touching the ghost of the sky-god with minuscule joy, secretly sounding the basic song of life, the theme so necessary to continued existence.

The next lines begin philosophically. Then, giving a glimpse of the metamorphosis taking place, they continue with unique metaphor. She will dare to exist in the world as two forms, as slippery as an eel and as rock-hard as a cabbage-head.

It was such rare figures of speech as these that brought Rich's fourth volume high critical praise and a nomination for the National Book Award. When had a woman in any poem given herself the androgynous symbol of a slippery eel or the earthy anonymity of a cabbage-head? Such phrases present the reader with the strong-minded feminist Adrienne Rich was fast learning to be. Having reentered the world, she was ready to grapple with its trials and tribulations. The poem "In the Woods" tells of her soul's sudden reentry into her body, and from a distance, the voice of one of her children is heard, saying that they are hiders, hiding from something bad. It is a reference to a chant sung by her son David at play one day, giving her the theme for the first part of the poem. We are all hiding from something bad most of the time, she feels; but the gloom is followed by a dazzling beam of light as, "outrageously," something good finds her. The "helicopter" of her inner being, which usually whirred distantly over her private Arcady—a stagnant pool where she searched for "difficult, ordinary happiness"—unexpectedly pulled *back* into her body, and she found herself whether she was prepared for the reversion or not.

A whole person again, it was well that she was prepared, for in the next year her troubling trials over lack of communication with her husband deepened. "Our words misunderstand us," she observes in "Like This Together," designated, "for A.H.C." In graphic imagery of the shared bed in marriage, Rich depicts the sad state of affairs she and her husband have come to acknowledge, though they are still married. Her beautiful metaphor referring to hyacinths in connection with their struggle for communication is a triumph of the art of making poems. A concluding stanza, reprinted when the poem first appeared in *Poetry,* was wisely omitted from the volume *Necessities of Life,* a deletion that indicates the poet's maturing judgment of her work.

Trial bordering on tragedy occurred in 1964, when Dr. Arnold Rich died, just as Adrienne at age thirty-five was beginning to feel her own identity, free of the ubiquitous presence of her father whose words echoed in her mind over and over, wherever she went: "I know you better than you know your-self." Even when she was abroad, she heard his words in for-eign languages, like a phonograph needle grinding round and round in the same groove: repeating the same words again and again. "That terrible record!" she exclaims in the ambivalent el-egy "After Dark," written shortly after his death. It is interest-ing to compare this strange, memorial poem with Sylvia Plath's famous "Daddy," written only a year earlier (1963), just before the egomaniacal Plath committed suicide. Instead of the crazed outcry—"Daddy, you bastard, I'm through"—we read in Rich's lines a sane, if sorrowful analysis of the love-hate complex so often prevalent in father-daughter relationships. Following rec-ollections of emotional torture, during her fallow years of childbearing when she "stopped singing," she woke one morn-ing and "knew herself his daughter." She realizes that blood is a sacred poison. And that she only wants to stifle what is sti-fling her and her fellow women already. Now that she was re-leased from her father's hold by his death, the poet would give— "oh, something"—not to know their struggles are ended. In a touching passage she recalls that she used to sit in a grave she'd dug for him and bite her tongue for fear it would babble, "Darling." As if in a dream, she pictures them being found there together, embalmed. At the last, his fears, like hers, drift off, and his hand feels steady. Unlike the mad genius of Sylvia Plath, Adrienne Rich's combined pragmatism and poetic gift is able to overcome patriarchal dominance without suicide.

Another sign of Rich's increasing strength and support of feminism is her homage to Emily Dickinson in "I Am in Dan-ger—Sir—," the title taken from a sentence in a letter the re-cluse poet wrote to her "mentor," Thomas Higgenson, who looked upon her at that time as his "partially-cracked poetess." Rich speaks to her precursor directly as she asks at the end of the second of six four-line stanzas: "who are you?" She answers the question with a description of Dickinson's struggle, her ret-icent, yet aggressive quality. She addresses Emily as a woman,

masculine in her sole concentration on the word, the core of
her being, a poetic genius who held spoiled language Perjury,
but chose silent rebellion instead of shouting and fought her
battle quietly, winning it on her own premises. The play on the
final word ("premises") gives evidence of the later poet's aptitude for phrasing, for creating a narrative sense with a single
word.

The year *Necessities* appeared, Adrienne Rich was the Phi Beta
Kappa poet at Harvard just as her husband was leaving the faculty. Alfred Conrad had decided to accept a post offered to him
at City College of New York, and the family moved to New
York City; the change from the academic world of Cambridge
to the multiple levels of life in a metropolitan area like Manhattan marked another turning point in the poet's work. It became increasingly "political," in more than one channel: at first
the organized protest against the war in Vietnam took priority
over any other interest, and as the terrifying conflict intensified,
Adrienne Rich, like Muriel Rukeyser and Denise Levertov, joined
the activists who devoted time and effort to organizing demonstrations, marches, fund-raising drives. The very titles of poems
in her volume, *Leaflets* (1969), besides the title poem, indicate
her involvement with the "peace-niks," as anti-war people were
called in the beginning. "For a Russian Poet," written in August, 1968, a three-part series, particularly "The Demonstration," reveals her sympathy with Soviet dissidents; "Tear-Gas
(Oct. 12, 1969)," reports the tear gassing of demonstrators
protesting the treatment of G.I. prisoners at Fort Dix, New
Jersey. Summing up, she wrote that her politics was in her flesh
and blood, broadening with each resistance act. Referring to
her childhood, she recalls that when she was locked in a closet
at age four she beat the wall bodily, and that sense of protest
is still in her. If not explicit in the title, "Implosions" contains
in a one-line stanza a trenchant truth, that all wars are useless
to those who have died in them.

Perhaps the most explicit of all of Rich's resistance poems, in both title and content, is "The Burning of Paper Instead of Children," based on the daring deed of Father Daniel Berrigan, his brother Philip, and seven others who broke into the Selective Service office in Catonsville, Maryland and burned several hundred draft records, an exploit widely publicized and cheered by anti-war activists. Many poetry readings were given for the benefit of "The Catonsville Nine," who were tried and imprisoned for their act. The poem brings in the devastating use of napalm in Vietnam, a military strategy that brought disapproval if not cries of outrage even from those who tried to defend the war. This poem, though not included in a volume until 1971, was written in 1968, when the peace movement was at its height. However, as Albert Gelpi points out, the poems cited previously, and many more, are not so much propaganda "leaflets," but personal records and reactions to the upheaval of the times in which we live—a poet's response, not a politician's, and so they escaped the fate of being consigned to oblivion, as Edna Millay's interventionist pamphlets were before World War II. Indeed, if anything, Rich's poetry was more widely read than before, simply because it showed the effect of trying to survive in a time of turbulence rather than trying to persuade others to accept her political outlook. That she was risking her literary reputation in suggesting, as she did in "Burning the Papers," that words—books—are useless in trying to dissuade people from the evils of war, she was quite aware; yet she was willing to take that risk in order to clarify language, at least to her own satisfaction.

The result was that she became more in demand than ever as poet and teacher. From 1966 to 1968 she was lecturer at Swarthmore College, and at the same time held the post of adjunct professor of writing in the Graduate School of the Arts at Columbia University. Her *Selected Poems* was published in England in 1967, the year she received an honorary doctorate in literature from Wheaton College, and in 1968, she received the Eunice Tietjens Memorial Prize of *Poetry* magazine. She also began teaching in the SEEK and Open Admissions Programs at City College in New York, a post that brought new personalities, new horizons into her life. It was then that she met Gwendolyn Brooks and other black women poets who were coming into prominence in the literary world. It was unfortunate that Brooks had her heart attack and had to stop teaching after the first term. One has the feeling that these two might have benefitted from a further knowledge of each other's outlook. Brooks was just beginning to swing her allegiances to the black activist movement, but she was not, and is not, a feminist as such; and Rich was beginning to be identified with the women's movement, but was not yet the radical feminist she became after *Leaflets* was published. Two younger black poets on the faculty at the same time, Audre Lorde and Alice Walker, she did come to know and, through them, enlarge her understanding of the problems confronting black women, which were compounded by racism in addition to the patriarchal attitude of most men toward women. Audre Lorde, for her part, was deeply grateful to Adrienne Rich. "She was so good to me when I was starting to teach at City College," Lorde said in an interview in 1981.

Leaflets had begun with a poem Rich wrote in 1965, "Orion," in which the poet has rediscovered a part of herself she thought lost: an imaginary half-brother whom she connected with the constellation Orion. Though rejoined to him, she gazes at him with a "cold and egotistical" eye; she felt she still had to choose between love—womanly, maternal, altruistic—and egotism, the force behind intellectual and artistic creation. Three years later, while she was teaching at City College, she was inspired to write a companion poem, "Planetarium," after a visit to the New York planetarium. There she read the account of Caroline Herschel (1750–1848), who, like her brother with whom she worked, was a superb contributor to the science, discovering eight comets for which she was never given credit, while he became famous. The poem is inscribed, "Thinking of

Caroline Herschel . . . astronomer . . . and others." In it, Rich tells us, the woman in the poem and the woman writing it at last become the same person. She proclaims that she stands firm even though bombarded, and has been standing all her life directly before a battery of flashing signs. She likens herself to an involuted galactic cloud, so deep it took a light wave fifteen years to travel through her; she terms herself an instrument in woman's shape striving to translate her throbbings into images to relieve her body and reconstruct her mind. This poem, so important in Rich's development, is dated 1968, but did not appear in a volume of hers until 1971. During the intervening years, Fate brought a chasm-like change to her outer life.

In 1970, quite unexpectedly, Alfred Conrad died by his own hand. For a woman like Adrienne Rich to lose her husband after seventeen years of marriage—a marriage that managed to survive "only by fierce attention," as she had written in "Like This Together" (1963)—could not have been as devastating a loss as it would have been if she had followed the traditional path of "a female human being in marriage," as she had done in the first years of her marriage, but had rebelled against. She said in 1971, a year after Alfred died, "Today, much poetry by women—and prose for that matter—is charged with anger. I think we need to go through that anger. . . . Both the victimization and the anger experienced by women are real, and have real sources, everywhere in the environment, built into society. They must go on being explored by poets, among others. We can neither deny them, nor can we rest there. They are our birth-pains, and we are bearing ourselves." She went on to speak of the pessimistic poetry written by men today, and says, "I wonder if it isn't the masculine side of what women have experienced, the price of masculine dominance. One thing I am sure of: just as woman is becoming her own midwife, creating herself anew, so man will have to learn to gestate and give birth to his own subjectivity—something he has frequently wanted woman to do for him. We can go on trying to talk to each other, poetry and fiction can show us what the other is going through, but women can no longer be primarily mothers and muses for men: we have our own work cut out for us."

Certainly Adrienne Rich's work was cut out for her: at forty-one she was a widow with three sons to support; and certain it was that she did not intend to rest in her quest for clarification and equalization of the roles played by men and women in the drama of life, of the power wielded by each sex in making love or making political decisions, or in the "common, ordinary acts" of everyday living.

We catch a glimpse of the poet's response to male dominance in making decisions of policy in the prose passage that precedes and inspired her poem, "The Burning of Paper . . ." (discussed previously), and which, in turn, is preceded by a quote from Daniel Berrigan, on trial in Baltimore: "I was in danger of verbalizing my moral impulses out of existence." Then: "My neighbor," Rich relates, "a scientist and art collector, telephones me in a state of violent emotion. He tells me that my son and his, aged eleven and twelve, have on the last day of school burned a mathematics textbook in the backyard. He has forbidden my son to come to his house for a week, and has forbidden his own son to leave the house during that time. 'The burning of a book,' he says, 'arouses terrible sensations in me, memories of Hitler; there are few things that upset me so much as the idea of burning a book.' " Rich does not give the reader her immediate answer to her neighbor, to his arrogance in banishing her son from his house and companionship of his son without consulting her or even asking her opinion. But her poem, published in *The Will to Change*, the year after her husband died, reveals her reactions to her neighbor's edict in a series of flashbacks, from her childhood, when they took away from her the *The Trial of Jeanne D'Arc* because she dreamed of her heroine too often. The section concludes that there are both love and fear in a house, a constant sense of an oppressor that lets her know how much it hurts to burn. Section three quotes a disordered paragraph written by one of Rich's students in the Open Admissions Program and leads to a series of scenes depicting man and woman during and after lovemaking, speaking in disjointed sentences of loneliness, jealousy. They beat the bed angrily, showing no understanding of each other. The poem ends with another prose passage.

The breakup of form prevalent in the sixties is much in evidence here. Another series, "Winter-Spring '68," analyzes the lovers in bed, asking querulously if, when they have sex, are they more remote than the lovers of former times. The lines mark the first appearance of a four-letter word in Rich, and it cheapens rather than enhances the work. By the late sixties the craze for such words was already on the wane, since the novelty soon wore off; by the mid-seventies they were passé; it is unfortunate that she felt it necessary to join the current parade at the time of writing. "Pieces," "Images for Godard," and "Shooting Script (11/69–7/70)" might be called fragments: single, at most triple, lines suggesting a film scene that epitomizes a poem. "Shooting Script" especially seems to be a series of disjointed thoughts whirling in a bewildered brain; but by the end, the last four two-line segments suddenly become a resolution: to use your own roots to raise yourself, and to eat your final meal in your old locality.

The Will to Change, published in 1971, received the Shelley Memorial Award of the Poetry Society of America, and was regarded by the women's movement as a further step toward feminism on the part of the poet. From this time on, she has become increasingly identified as a radical feminist. Her readings at college campuses around the country increased in number, and audiences, particularly at women's colleges, crowded up to get a closer look and a few words with her even after the lecture's question period was over. When she spoke at Sweet Briar in 1973, the students would hardly let her go. William Smart of the English department, who had arranged for her to appear, was taken with her energy and the vitality that seemed to radiate from her as she answered every question at this conservative college. He was further surprised when he took her back to the small hotel in the nearby town where the college often put up visiting lecturers. He thought she must be exhausted and would want to retire at once, but she accepted readily when he suggested a drink in the lounge. Music was playing, and on an impulse, he asked if she would like to dance; she nodded unhesitatingly and proved to be a good dancer, despite her shorter leg. She was light on her feet and showed no self-consciousness of her disability. This was the young woman who, only a few years before, had felt smothered by a traditional marriage, held within its limited boundaries by the demands of domesticity and the myths of motherhood. Now she felt free to accept the offer of the Fanny Hurst Visiting Professor of Creative Literature at Brandeis University, a post she held during 1972–1973 while preparing her next volume for publication.

Diving into the Wreck appeared in 1973, and was hailed by the women's movement as a guideline in poetry to active feminism. Here, spelled out in exact, explicit language using rare images, the poet defines the process by which, through awareness, anger, and exploration, woman can discover and enjoy her own identity, separate, but not separated from her male counterpart by being cast in the secondary role history has given her, dominated by male power and the myth of motherhood. In "The Stranger," preceding the title poem, she offers a definitive statement before divulging the process; she says with straightforward candidness that she is androgynous, a mind alive, never described by language that is dead. She is the lost noun, the verb that survives in the infinitive only; her name is written under the eyelids of the newborn child; minus punctuation this poem ends, and in "Diving into the Wreck," we watch the poet go about her deep-sea project. After reading a book of myths, loading a camera, and checking her knife blade, she dons the necessary gear: an absurd pair of flippers and a heavy, ill-fitting mask—and, all alone, she descends the ladder, rung by rung, that leads down into the depths, where the wreck that man has made of civilization lies waiting to be explored: what she came for—the wreck, not a story or a myth, but the genuine article. The metaphor is maintained throughout. After further description, now she has found the spot; she is there, both a mermaid with dark hair flowing and a merman in armor. Silently they circle about the wreck and dive into the hold. As both maid and man, in her duo-personality she examines the cargo hidden in barrels, half forced apart and left to rot. Finally, either by cowardice or courage—perhaps by both—she finds her way back carrying her knife and camera with, most important, an old book of myths which does not contain their names. The significance of the conclusion is self-evident.

However, it was "The Phenomenology of Anger" that contained the set of principles seized upon by the women's movement as a concrete example of activism expressed in terms of poetry. The primary tactic was not to kill the enemy but to release a rage that resembles his own methods of chemical warfare; the poet speaks of terrible chemicals like acetylene streaming from her body, trained on her true enemy so that she rakes his body down to a thread of existence, and so burns his lie away. She leaves him a new man in a changed world. But then she sees him burn *that* world! Then a diatribe of venom pours out. She declares deep hatred of her enemy, of the mask he wears, causing his eyes to assume a depth they do not have, luring her into the cave of her skull, the scene of bone. She hates his words; they are false, like fake bills sold at revolutionary battlefields. This outburst is tempered by an idyllic vision. How she would have loved to live in a world of women and men happily collaborating with leaves and stalks of green earth, erecting nature cities topped by airy domes, cities filled with huts of entwined grasses, each of its own design, living by coexistence with the nebulae, the bursting universe, the Mind overall. The impossibility of attaining such a world in the near future brings on a bitter confession. Here the poet admits that the only love she has felt in all her life was for children and women. All else that moved her was lust, hatred of self, and pity. These lines, printed in italics, are germane to the feminist cause—the need for action against a male-dominated world; and Adrienne Rich was regarded as one of the chief exponents of change.

Most of the poems in this volume were written after her husband's death, two of them—"For the Dead" and "From a Survivor"—obviously in memory of their life together. In the latter, particularly, she speaks directly to him in reviewing the "ordinary pact" of their marriage. She ruminated on their marriage, observing that they must have thought their special personalities could avoid the failures of the human race. By some stroke of fortune, good or bad, they didn't even know the race had such failures or that he and she would share them. Like so many others, the poet and her husband thought themselves special. The final stanzas of this poem are distinctly autobiographical. She realizes that in another year she and Conrad would have been married for twenty years; he is needlessly dead, since he could have made the leap they talked of, too late; but she made it alone, in a succession of amazing moves, each insuring the next. These lines underscore her resolve to continue the quest for a harmonious relationship between the sexes, recognizing the masculine and feminine impulses shared by both.

Diving into the Wreck was an immediate success with the critics and received the National Book Award. Instead of joyfully accepting the honor, Rich, in true feminist tradition, rejected it as an individual, causing general consternation among the judges. However, after consulting with two other nominees, Audre Lorde and Alice Walker, with whom she wrote a strong statement, she accepted, in the name of all women. Combining their thoughts, they drew up a revolutionary declaration of independence, which read in part:

"We . . . together accept this award in the name of all the women whose voices have gone and still go unheard in a patriarchal world, and in the name of those who, like us, have been tolerated as token women in this culture, often at great cost and in great pain. . . . We symbolically join here in refusing the terms of patriarchal competition and declaring that we will share this prize among us, to be used as best we can for women. . . . We dedicate this occasion to the struggle for self-determination of all women, of every color, identification or derived class . . . the women who will understand what we are doing here and those who will not understand yet; the silent women whose voices have been denied us, the articulate women who have given us strength to do our work."

Part of this work, so far as Rich was concerned, was to destroy the time-honored but false myths of motherhood by writing a history of childbearing and rearing considered by the majority of men in generations past the principal female function, discounting her ability and performance in all other areas. In order to finance the book she was writing on the subject, she had applied for and received an Ingram Merrill Foundation research grant for 1973–1974. At the same time she held the post of professor of English at City College of New York, and began preparing a volume of poetry. In 1975, *Poems, Selected and New, 1950–1974*, was published. It was dedicated: "For Helen, my mother, and For Cynthia, my sister"—two women she could call friends as well as relatives, who had been supportive of her, especially during the dark days after Alfred's death. The poems in this volume spanned almost a quarter of a century, having been drawn from all seven of her earlier books. This one, she says in a foreword, is not so much a summing up or retrospective of her work as a graph of a process still going on.

"As I type these words we are confronted with the naked and unabashed failure of patriarchal politics and patriarchal civilization. To be a woman at this time is to know extraordinary forms of anger, joy, impatience, love, and hope. Poetry, words on paper, are necessary, but not enough; we need to touch the living who share our animal passion for existence, our determination that the sexual myths underlying the human condition can and shall be changed. My friends—above all, my sisters, the women I love—have given me the heat and friction of their lives, along with needed clarity, criticism, tenderness, and the daring of their own examples. Midway in my own life, I know that I have only begun. In contrast," she added, "I have had an unusual male editor: I want to thank John Benedict: caring, painstaking, supportive in practical and intangible ways."

In the same year, 1975, a Norton Critical Edition, *Adrienne Rich's Poetry,* appeared, selected and edited by her friends, Barbara and Albert Gelpi, at Stanford University. One of the most interesting sections of this study, which covers the texts of the poems, the poet on her work, and reviews and criticism, is the transcript of three conversations that took place in the Gelpi's home informally, among the three friends. Together they discuss the overall objective of the women's movement, the effectiveness of violence, or counter-violence, in combating rape, the problems of all women, regardless of class, color or education, or talent, in being accepted on an equal basis with men. In these conversations one senses the earnestness and utter dedication to the liberation not only of women, but of humanity—society as a whole—from the myths of the past. The quest is noble; the cause is just; but the question is whether her poetry suffers from the polemics of the power struggle that continues between the sexes. Although her friend Albert Gelpi felt, as already noted, that her poems (in *Leaflets* or in later volumes) never became propaganda leaflets, Robert Boyers, literary critic and editor-in-chief of *Salmagundi,* takes Rich to task in this critical edition for her tendency to "fall prey to ideological fashions like the will to change, so that, though she is too intelligent ever to mouth petty slogans, she allows herself to be violated by them. They touch her verse with an almost programmic wand." He cites several homily-like stanzas from the "Ghazals"; for example: "If the mind of the teacher is not in love with the mind of the student,/he is simply practising rape, and deserves at best our pity"; and doubts their value as poetry. The one that offends him most is: "I have learned to smell a *conservateur* a mile away:/They carry illustrated catalogues of all that there is to lose." He is appalled "to think that the poet who could write so persuasively" of her father's loss (in "After Dark," which Boyers praises) should be "so snide about having something to lose." He demands to know what the poet can be thinking when she writes of smelling "a *conservateur*," and whether she believes that men who have something to lose are "necessarily blind reactionaries." He hastens to explain that he asks such questions not to suggest that Rich has lost her senses; but "to suggest how charged she has become with the nauseous propaganda of the advance-guard cultural radicals." He laments that she has "fallen in love with such models."

When her book on the myths of motherhood, *Of Woman Born: Motherhood as Experience and Institution,* came out in 1976, there were others who agreed with Boyers that in her zeal for change in the patriarchal order of society, Rich had sacrificed her poetry; but the majority cheered her stand as the champion of women's liberation. Wendy Martin, teacher at Queen's College, innovator of women's studies courses, after citing "From an Old House in America," in which the woman demands of her man, "What will you undertake?" before entering into a marriage pact or any kind of alliance, insisting that he demonstrate a desire to abolish patriarchy if he expects her to fulfill his desire for sexual love, concludes: "As a feminist poet, Rich contributes her radical subjectivity to political process: that is, by analyzing and articulating her experience as a woman in patriarchal culture, by making private perceptions public, she establishes a coherent point of view, a feminist identity and poetic vision which becomes part of the composite reality of a community. Her poetry, then, like all good poetry, changes the way we perceive and experience the world."

Whether critical reaction is favorable or unfavorable, Adrienne Rich continues to pursue her course of "radical" feminism. Plagued by arthritis in the last years, besieged by requests for book reviews and readings, burdened by the pressures of a big city, she moved to Montague, Massachusetts, then to California where she concentrates on her own work, edits a magazine connected with the women's movement, and finds time occasionally to enjoy her private life.

Photo by Morton Sacks

Ruth Whitman

When Ruth Whitman was nineteen years old she eloped with the man who became her first husband—fellow-poet, classics scholar, editor, and literary critic, Cedric Whitman. If she had not run away the marriage would not have taken place, for her background of Chassidic Judaism would not permit her parents, Meyer and Martha Bashein, to give their consent to a marriage outside the faith. Steeped in the religious tradition of her ancestors, but born and brought up in New York City, Ruth, who had lived most of her life in the urban surroundings of her parents' spacious West End Avenue apartment, was a product of American civilization as much as a des-

cendant of pious Hebraic scholars of Eastern Europe. The spirit
of revolt against tradition came naturally, therefore, when she
met and fell in love with the New England born (in Providence, Rhode Island) Whitman at a Writers Conference on
Breadloaf Mountain, Vermont, in the summer of 1941.

"The smallest and the youngest," as she designated her status
in the three-part poem, "Breadloaf, 1941," Ruth found herself
in the presence of such luminaries as Robert Frost (a founder
of the Breadloaf Conferences), William Carlos Williams, Louis
Untermeyer, Theodore Roethke (then just entering the lime-
light), Richard Ellman, and the studious Cedric Whitman—
heady company for a budding poet who had just completed her
freshman year at Radcliffe. The first of the triptych, titled, "R.F."
describes the scene of her pleasantly delirious reaction. "R.F."
begins, "We drank beer, cheered/ Schwartzkopf, rolled/ in the
mown meadow/ and wondered/ which poet to marry." A number of the younger counsellors besides those named above were
eligible. Though Europe was seething, World War II brewing,
the second stanza continues, "We played/ on our plateau. heed-
less/ of Hitler. And the/ granddaddy/ of us all,/ shaggy as a bear/
wagged his white head./ His despair/ was so wittily said,/ we
didn't care."

The second poem, "On Theodore Roethke's Lap," gives a
graphic picture of "nine young geniuses, thirsty for beer," packed
in layers—Ruth on Ted's lap—in "a beatup Chevrolet," racing
down Breadloaf Mountain to quench their thirst by quaffing
beer in Middlebury: The motion, the momentary carefree surge
of youthful joy, sensual and sexual in expression are viewed in
retrospect, revitalized by the poet's touch. Obviously, however,
it did not take her long to decide "which poet to marry." Fascinated as she herself was by translations of poetry from ancient
and modern languages, she was drawn by Cedric Whitman and
his scholarly approach to the classics. One is reminded of "H.D."
and Richard Aldington thirty-seven years earlier, falling in love
as they pored over Greek poetry in pursuit of translation. Just

as they married within a few months, so Ruth Bashein and Cedric Whitman were married scarcely two months after the conference—on October 13, 1941, and scarcely more than a month before the devastating attack on Pearl Harbor, the fateful December 7, 1941.

That shocking event signaled a separation of the young couple soon afterward when Cedric was called to military service in the United States Army (1942), similar to Richard Aldington's departure for France to fight in World War I soon after H.D. and he were married. Unlike the earlier pair, however, Ruth and Cedric Whitman did not allow the separation to become permanent for seventeen years, during which time they pursued their careers, sometimes singly, sometimes together, both attaining a remarkable degree of success. Beginning with her first year at Radcliffe, Ruth was assistant editor and education editor at Houghton Mifflin Company from 1941 until 1945, a year after her graduation from Radcliffe, *summa cum laude*. And from the time she started school she wrote poetry of her own after hearing it read aloud, and reading her favorite selections for herself. She read avidly, living the lines, and then she began to write her own. As a teenager, she sat on the riverbank wall, "scribbling poems of longing and sudden rape"—living among the Green Mansions more exotic in their fantasy than W.H. Hudson's "jungle-bird." But as she grew out of adolescence, she outgrew child fancies and drew on the reality of personal experience in the light of her emotional reactions to life's events, trials, and triumphs. She commented in 1970 as a mature poet, "The point of writing poetry is to celebrate the human experience, and to communicate its value and intensity to other human beings."

After her marriage to Whitman, Ruth, who began sending her work to editors under her married name, celebrated the daily events of domestic life from the sublime (moments of sexual and maternal love) to the ridiculous (ballooning of bread dough). The latter poem, "The Act of Bread," for all its humor, reveals a faint bubble of trouble brewing beneath the yeast. Announcing this poem at a New York reading in 1980, the poet said, "This poem was written after I tried to bake bread from a recipe given to me by my first mother-in-law." Her remark brought a burst of laughter from the audience, in which she joined good-naturedly. She makes no secret of the fact that she has been married three times, and there are hints in certain lines of this poem that point to a cooling, or a repression, of the passion that caused her impetuous elopement. She and her first husband led a busy life: until the children came, Ruth continued at Houghton Mifflin as Education Editor (1941–45); after that she was a freelance editor for fifteen years, besides short-term teaching and writing poetry, mostly brief, lyric poems, which, as she said, "can be nurtured in short intervals between classes, dishes, children."

The Whitmans had two daughters, whose given names—the firstborn, Rachel, from the Old Testament, and the second, Leda, from Greek mythology—indicate the duo interests of their parents. For their middle names the same note is true in reverse: Rachel's is Claudia, and Leda's, Miriam. During the first ten years of marriage Ruth concentrated on personal, or "subjective" poetry, as she said, and was beginning to grow restive under the limitations of the short lyric, creating poems within the confines of her own life and times. Trips the Whitmans made to Greece in 1951 and 1953 transported her to the ancient art of living in the days of classical mythology and aroused her interest in the modern tongue, linking the past with the present. She had wanted to "move out of herself and into someone else's life," preferably in an earlier era, and she began to think of American women of the past whose stories had become legendary.

Her initial attempt was a long poem retelling the tale of Lizzie Borden, with whom she "felt a certain identity"; despite disparate backgrounds, the poet shared Lizzie's "sense of suppressed libido, living in a repressive society, enraged at being

held back from expressing herself as a woman, as a human being."
Ruth Whitman had thoroughly expressed herself in woman's
experience of motherhood and love for her children, but her
poems, the offspring of her other matrix, her brain, though they
made their appearance in top literary journals, from *The Atlantic Monthly* and the *Antioch Review* through *Poetry, The New
Yorker* and *New Republic* to *Yankee Magazine,* had not yet been
collected in a published volume. On the other hand, her husband had had his first book published—a volume of poetry,
Orpheus and the Moon Craters—by Middlebury College Press,
the year they were married (1941). He was a full professor at
Harvard (Department of Classics), and had held the Jones and
Eliot Chairs of Greek Literature there. In 1951 Cedric Whitman's *Sophocles—A Study in Heroic Humanism* received much
acclaim and won several awards. He immediately started on another long project concerning Homer and the Heroic Tradition. So it was natural for Ruth Whitman to feel an urgent need
to express herself as a whole person, a many-faceted poet, with
full recognition.

Much of the next ten years were spent in the study of the
famous "Fall River Legend," as it has been called in the ballet
form of Lizzie Borden's traumatic life, her drastic deed of double murder as a violent but viable solution to her unbearable
existence. The ordeal of her court trial and its outcome of acquittal held less fascination for Whitman than the motive for
Borden's murder of her father and stepmother. Rather, it was
"the anatomy of her emotions" that drew the poet's attention
to Lizzie's lurid legend. Like a literary sleuth, Ruth hunted
through the mounds of documentary material available until she
found the "essential metaphorical elements" she was after: the
hellish heat wave of August 4, 1892; the overripe fruit from
the backyard pear tree, and the egg Lizzie couldn't break. During the course of her research, Ruth visited Lizzie's house in
Fall River, wrote a long narrative poem, and a play based on
fact. But she threw most of her writing away and, after ten years

of fitful labor, "wound up with an eight-page poem published by the *Massachusetts Review* in its *Women* issue." In terse language using the present tense the poem reads like stage directions to a single tragic act, ending abruptly with four climactic words: "She raises the ax."

Eventually it appeared as the title poem in Ruth Whitman's fourth book, *The Passion of Lizzie Borden (New and Selected Poems)*. Long before then, however, three signal events occurred in the poet's personal life that altered the course and the pace of her literary productivity, with attendant recognition of her poetry. In 1958, the year that Cedric Whitman's work, *Homer and the Heroic Tradition,* was published and won the Gauss Award for the best book of literary scholarship in the United States, Ruth and he were divorced; and both were married again, within a month of each other, the following year. Ruth became the wife of Firman Houghton on July 23, 1959, and their son, David Houghton, evoked in his infancy one of her tender love poems—and there are many threaded through her work—this one celebrating both maternal and marital love. "David's Breath," beginning, "let's celebrate the/ breath and airs/ of love," appears to portend a long happy marriage, yet it lasted only five years: Ruth was divorced from Houghton in 1964.

Nevertheless, it was during this five-year period that her first volume, *Blood and Milk Poems,* (October House, 1963) was published, a definite milestone in her career. She was cited as "a poet of celebration and compassion, whose poetry springs from her background of Chassidic Judaism, her sense of identification with ancient and modern Greece, and her concern with American myth and tragedy." The triple source of her creative ability was evident in this initial volume and would become more so in those that followed. She had also been translating modern French poetry with some of her colleagues, and New Directions published *Selected Poems of Alain Bosquet* at the same time that *Blood and Milk* came out, 1963, broadening her reputation in the poetry world. She had been poetry editor of *Audience* magazine, but now gave it up to concentrate on her own poems and translations. She had begun work on translation of fourteen twentieth-century Yiddish poets, and her adviser for the project was no less an expert than Isaac Bashevis Singer. Impressed with the poet's ability to grasp the shadings within Yiddish words that altered their meaning in English, he asked her to be one of his assistants in translating his stories, always written originally in Yiddish.

Ruth agreed and found it a rare experience. Asked how she liked working with the master storyteller, she admitted, "I had a lot to learn about the nuances of Yiddish phrases and he taught me how to get them in translating; he was very exciting." She smiled. "Of course I got my share of pinches and ticklings," she said, referring to Singer's playful approaches to any attractive assistant. "But none of us minded; we knew it was harmless— his way of showing affection."

The two books—Whitman's *An Anthology of Modern Yiddish Poetry* and Singer's *Short Friday and Other Stories*—were published in 1966, the year that marked the poet's marriage to Morton Sacks, a painter she had known for some time, and to whom she is still married. In a later poem, "The Third Wedding," Ruth speaks of "the bridegroom long denied," and in the preceding stanzas, describes the speaker's terror on the way to her second wedding: where was "the minyan of ten good men? the cup under the bridegroom's heel and the floral canopy?" For her third try, "She gathered ten years for a minyan,/ plucked a canopy of planets," and "brought her body like a cup" to her final mate.

Whitman's next volume, published two years later (1968) by Harcourt Brace, indicates by its title, *The Marriage Wig,* that "the third wedding" brought greater concern with her religious heritage. Both the title poem and the one that precedes it, "Cutting the Jewish Bride's Hair," show an animosity if not a definite disapproval of the ancient custom, obsolete for generations, but part of Hebraic lore. The latter poem begins, "It's to possess more than the skin/ that those old world Jews/ exacted the hair of their brides." After addressing those old world Hebraic husbands sternly, the poem ends with the warning: "this little amputation/ will shift the balance of the universe."

In commenting on her work, Richard Damachek wrote: "*The Marriage Wig* is a much fuller exploration of being Jewish and Ruth Whitman: The poems ring with an authenticity lacking in her first volume. Although a few strain after too much identity with the past, most are effective." This was written at the time *The Passion of Lizzie Borden (New and Selected Poems)* appeared, and Damachek began his review by saying: "Ruth Whitman's three volumes have established her as a significant American woman poet." As if to substantiate his statement, Whitman chose—or was given by her poet's prescience—an American pioneer woman as the subject for her next volume: *Tamsen Donner.*

Coming out of the ether after a minor operation, Ruth found herself writing a passage of narrative poetry on the handy yellow pad she keeps nearby wherever she happens to be. Only half awake, she had written three stanzas before she realized that she was speaking in the person of a nineteenth century pioneer woman close to journey's end, wondering if she and her family would get across a last range of mountains safely. Mystified, the poet could not rest until she discovered the identity of the woman whose life she had subconsciously assumed. After months of research she finally came across the tragic story of the Donner party, and realized that she had read about it years before in high school when she studied George Stewart's account, *Ordeal by Hunger.* The brief portrayal of Tamsen Donner in that book obviously had impressed itself deeply in Whitman's psyche, though dormant for more than three decades. At last awakened, the figure of this ill-fated pioneer spirit would not fade into oblivion again, but kept demanding expression of the poet's empathy. So began another long siege of research in various libraries, followed by a grant from the National Endowment for the Arts in 1974, enabling Whitman to make the trek over the Oregon Trail by car that the Donner party had undertaken so bravely by covered wagon in 1846.

The result was a book-length poem, *Tamsen Donner: a woman's journey,* which proved to be a tour de force—a heroic, terrifying tale, told in the first person. The story of the educator who, with her second husband and their children, set out to establish a seminary in California but perished in the mountains above Sacramento is presented in tense, terse stanzas. Alternating prose passages with lines of free verse, Whitman recreated the lost journal that Donner evidently kept. The opening line of a poem depicting the trials of the desert when the Donners must discard excess weight in their wagon, "Go light go light I must walk lightly," is indicative of the emotional turmoil, torn between hope and despair to the point of near delirium in trying to keep sane that Whitman has captured in the narrative. The heroine asks: "what shall I let go? books:/ the least/ needed for survival: in the cold/ desert night/George lifts my heavy

> *crate of Shakespeare, Emerson, Gray's*
> *Botany, spellers and readers for my school*
> *and hides it in a hill of salt*
> *while the children sleep parched*
> *and the cows and oxen stand mourning:*
> *I put aside my desk with the inlaid pearl*
> *our great fourposter with the pineapple posts*
> *my love my study*
>
> *what else can I part with?*
> *I will keep one sketchbook one journal*
> *to see me to the end of the journey*

This poem ends as it began but in three fragmented lines instead of one, again evoking a sense of undefined delirium: "go light/ go light/ I must walk lightly"—like a chant challenging adversity. The final poem of the section is the one that is the

donnée Whitman received in the hospital before she had any
idea of the woman's identity. "We are facing/the last mountains" is the line that sets the scene of desolation; despite the
grandeur of the "unscalable" mountains, the weary travelers, the
weakened wagon, and lame oxen that pull it, there is a glimmer
of hope in the last stanza:

> *there is a surf I know*
> *on the other side of the pass:*
> *somewhere beyond this wall*
> *the end of land*
> *and a summer sea.*

As is well known to every tourist who hears the history of
the Donner Pass, Tamsen Donner was never to set eyes on the
"summer sea." The heartrending sequences describing the series of misfortunes that befell the family, including a gangren-
ous wound suffered by George Donner, are written with "dramatic concision," as poet-critic Edwin Honig put it; yet they
become so poignant that the reader can scarcely continue. The
blinding blizzards and dense snowfalls that buried their shelter
of pine boughs and made it an icy cave caused a six-month delay when they were only a hundred miles away from their goal.
A rescue party came, and Tamsen sent the children with those
who could carry them to safety, but she would not leave her
dying husband who could not be moved. A second rescue party
found his body, wrapped in a clean winding sheet amid filth
and decay, but there was no trace of Tamsen Donner herself;
presumably she was a victim of the cannibalism that had become a practice among the destitute, desperate travellers. In the
final poem of the volume, "Where is the West," she finds comfort in the fact that though her own boundary stops there, her
daughters will "draw new maps on the world"; she will wake
in the eyes of her children's children.

Tamsen Donner did much to advance Ruth Whitman's position in the poetry world. Before it appeared in book form, a

part of the "Desert" sequence won the John Masefield Award of the Poetry Society of America. The subject as a portrait of pioneer women in American history brought her the grant from the National Endowment for the Arts, and fellowships for three consecutive summers at the MacDowell Colony, where the poem was written. In 1977, the year it was published, she was one of the finalists in the Virginia Commonwealth University Manuscript Competition and she was invited to be resident poet at Mishkenot Sha'ananim, the cultural center in Jerusalem. In 1974 she had been visiting poet in Israel as a guest of the government along with other poets, but in 1977, she was the only and the first American woman to be invited as resident poet at the Cultural Center. She was asked to write and narrate a television documentary, "Sachuest Point," based on a poem she had written, the story of a "spit of land" jutting out of Rhode Island's shoreline, used as a "target base" during World War II. The documentary was produced under a grant from the Rhode Island Committee on the Humanities.

Besides writing her own poetry, Ruth Whitman has translated modern Greek and modern Yiddish poetry, compiling a bilingual anthology of the latter; she is represented in no less than ten anthologies herself. She has given innumerable readings all over the United States, several in England and Jerusalem, some on television and radio, many in libraries and poetry or cultural centers. Since 1970 she has been a lecturer at Radcliffe Seminars, along with her colleagues Adrienne Rich and Denise Levertov. Her energy is boundless. In 1976 she joined the writers' cooperative, Alice James Books in Cambridge, Massachusetts; originated and run by women, this rapidly developing firm places "an emphasis on publishing by women." *Tamsen Donner* came out under its imprint as did her next volume, *Permanent Address, (New Poems 1973–1980.)* Yet Whitman is no radical feminist, nor does she confine herself to women as her subjects. One of the poems in her 1980 volume is "Seven Variations for Robert Schumann," written in the first person, as if the composer himself were relating the story of his early life, insatiable appetite for music, his star-crossed romance and subsequent marital happiness with Clara Wieck, the brilliant young pianist who became his wife against her father's wishes; and finally his growing madness. While Whitman was writing this seven-part poem, she entered a competition offered in England, and purely on a whim, used the name "Robert Schumann" when she submitted another poem as her entry. She won the first prize, but the British were quite miffed when she revealed her true identity to learn that the prize-winning poet was a woman. She told the incident at a reading in 1980, making the point that the sex of an author is not always discernible, although some readers have remarked on the womanly quality of her work. The *Library Journal* called "Lizzie Borden" a "marvel of economy and feminine psychology."

Perhaps this poet has summed up her position best in the title poem of *Permanent Address*. The actual title of the poem is, "A Questionnaire," and the book's title is the second section. The third requests the applicant's sex: *"Male or Female."* And the poet's answer is: "Both. When I saw the Greek Hermaphrodite/ I recognized myself and you, each/ two in one." The entire poem is, in fact, a succinct delineation of Ruth Whitman's background, life, and outlook. Her reply to the first demand, *"Describe your early education,"* is to present a picture of herself at six, standing on a low stone wall beside her grandfather, making her taller than he and, with her hand on his shoulder "possessively," singing his lullaby, *"a moloch veynt,* an angel weeps." The second demand, *"What is your permanent address,"* evokes the sweet moments of youth along with lasting pleasures: "A flat rock in Central Park/ where an innocent policeman/ found me with my first sweetheart./ Under Cambridge clocks chiming each quarter hour./ Beside the sea./ Beneath Mount Zion./ On Boston's broad Victorian bosom . . ." The next, *"Are you married,"* receives, "Yes, many times./ I marry my first loves/ over and over. Like coming home." Most revealing is: *"List your awards and honors,"* the answer, "Three children./ One, a yellow tearose./ Two, a winedark peony./ Three, a young fox, heart's desire." The final one is a "brief statement" of love for her mate. This poem and the one on Robert Schumann were both cited by Stanley Kunitz in selecting the best pieces in the volume. The cover drawing on the book is a broad-lined sketch of the "rock in Central Park," done by Morton Sacks, her husband.

Permanent Address, like *Tamsen Donner* and *Lizzie Borden,* speaks for an American poet whose work has carved a permanent niche in American poetry.

Jean Burden

A mong the colleagues of Adrienne Rich who followed the course of the feminist movement in their poetry were any number of aspiring poets, some of whom have made an outstanding contribution to modern poetry, others who have won a reputation for poetry whose value is open to question. All have distinctive personalities and a determination to raise the status of women in the arts, particularly in the poetry world, as well as in the mainstream of society.

One of these is Jean Burden, who has led a double life for many years. Since 1955, she has been poetry editor of *Yankee* magazine, and at the same time developed a career in public relations to the point of becoming a columnist and author of four books (under the pseudonym of Felicia Ames) on pet care. Born in 1914 at her grandmother's house in Waukegan, Illinois, she grew up and attended private school in Evanston. An only child, frail, bookish, an overachiever in her studies, she began writing poetry at the age of ten and has never stopped. Fostered by her parents—her mother had been a Latin teacher in Waukegan before marrying—Jean's talent and studiousness cost her the friendship of her classmates; a shy girl, she was not inclined to "mix," and was too frail to take part in athletics, so, although she was not unhappy, hers was a lonely childhood.

One spring day, while she was sitting on the porch steps of her parents' home on Dempster Street in Evanston, half dreaming over the book she held on her knees, a stray kitten came along and jumped up the steps onto the page she had been reading. When she tried to pick him up and put him off, he started to purr and rubbed his head against her arm. His fur was so soft, his kitten-eyes so blue she could not resist petting him and his purr grew louder. He settled down on her book contentedly for a bit: then he jumped off and frisked around her on the porch, running to and fro playfully, but came back to take a little catnap on her book. Jean was enchanted; she begged her parents to let her keep him, and was given permission, provided she took entire care of him. She promised, and the kitten provided not only companionship but the inspiration for poems and books, since, from that day to this, Jean Burden has always had a cat or two—never more than two—that have figured in her work. One of the books, published first under her pen name, has been reissued under her real name—*The Classic Cat,* which is now in a New American Library edition. An anthology she compiled, entitled *A Celebration of Cats,* including poems on the subject by many of her colleagues, was published in 1974.

Graduating with the highest four-year scholastic average, Jean Burden received the one and only two-year scholarship offered by the University of Chicago to women (as opposed to many available to men). She lived in Foster Hall, the same dormitory her mother had roomed in twenty years before. College proved a great awakening to the poet, and brought a happiness she would not have believed possible from the restricted life she had led. The University of Chicago was in its golden era as a liberal institution of higher learning: Robert Hutchins, with his "new plan" emphasizing sociological subjects was only in his second year as president there. The faculty included among notables in other fields, Thornton Wilder, who taught Shakespeare and Dante, but in reality taught his students a sense of values: his enthusiasm for the great works of literature gave them a fresh outlook on the literary arts. He took genuine interest in those who displayed definite talent, and Jean was one he singled out for private interviews regarding her poetry. He was pleasant and spoke in a positive way, stressing dedication.

"You must be obsessed with your own calling," he told her early in their weekly talks. He gave her the "imprimatur" she said—confidence that her poetry was worth striving for: if she stayed with it to the point of obsession, he held, sooner or later some editor would accept and publish her efforts. He did not attempt to make any concrete suggestions, and their talks were more philosophical than practical, but Burden has always considered Thornton Wilder one of the early influences of her poetry-making career.

At the university she somehow lost her shyness, perhaps because of Wilder's attention, and "got off on the right foot" socially as well as intellectually. She discovered that she was a good dancer; much to her surprise, she suddenly became popular with boys, dating many boys during her first year, which did a great deal for her self-esteem, she admits frankly; it brought about an enormous change in her personality. She who had been so shy went out for all kinds of campus activities from journalism to dramatics and the women's committee. She made the campus newspaper with a by-line story in her freshman year, no small achievement at the University of Chicago. Fully committed to everything she did, she discovered a quality of leadership in herself that she never knew she possessed. A time of terror came when her two-year scholarship terminated, but luckily she had a generous godmother who stepped in and provided funds for her to continue. By her senior year, Jean was chairman of the board of the women's committee—the highest office a woman could hold at the time. During her four years of education in the progressive climate created by Hutchins's "new plan," Burden had changed from a conventional Republican to a liberal Democrat, a position from which she has never reverted.

Graduating with an A.B. degree in psychology in 1936, she could not find a job. She had chosen the social sciences rather than literature for her course of study because she thought she would have more chance of earning a living in that field; but the country was still too deep in the Depression. The only jobs open to women were in secretarial work, so she took a business course and became a secretary at a salary of twenty-two dollars a week. She had been writing poetry all along, but as a profession it was out of the question. It was said that unless you were Edna St. Vincent Millay you could not possibly earn a living from poetry. Although in a few years Millay's popularity would wane, it was then at its height. Jean, wanting to use her writing skill in some way, finally landed a job in the advertising office of Young and Rubicam, where she worked with Kenneth Laird, who had been an honors graduate in Latin and Greek from the University of Chicago. Like Jean he was an overachiever and compulsive worker. He was also a poetry lover, and the two once had a contest to see who could recite the most Millay sonnets; Ken won, she admitted cheerfully; and soon after that she met the man who was the subject of Millay's most celebrated sonnet series,* George Dillon.

Harriet Monroe had just died, and Dillon, whose volume, *The*

Fatal Interview

Flowering Stone, had won the Pulitzer Prize for poetry, was asked to step in as editor. Burden had read Dillon's poems and the translations of Baudelaire that he and Millay had made. Like most people, she was disappointed in the latter, but she had fallen in love with Dillon's poetry, his lyrical free verse lines in the mode of the "new poetry" Jean was trying to master. She had been wanting to meet him, and when she learned he had taken over as editor at *Poetry* she enlisted the help of a mutual friend, through whom a lunch date was arranged. It was one of the memorable events of her life, which got off to an amusing start. The moment Dillon walked out of his editor's cubicle in the cramped offices of *Poetry* and saw Jean Burden, who at twenty-four was attractive, slim, and long-limbed, a look of immense relief flooded his handsome face. "Thank God!" he said, extending his hand.

Jean was puzzled. She had dressed with extreme care and wore a wide-brimmed hat that made her look glamorous, she hoped. It was well known that Millay considered Dillon an Adonis, and had been unable to resist plunging into an affair with him despite the difference in their age. Jean did not expect to duplicate Millay's evanescent appeal, but at the same time she didn't want to appear like her old mousey self, a plain Jane. She laughed self-consciously as Dillon explained, "I was afraid you'd turn out to be a little old lavender-and-lace lady with a satchelful of jingles you expected me to publish, and here you are, an intelligent-looking young glamour-girl without so much as a manila envelope under your arm. Shall we go to lunch? I'm starved." Jean laughed more easily then; she had purposely left her poems at home. She told him she had wanted to meet him and talk about *The Flowering Stone,* about poetry in general, not hers.

Over their "Valhalla Lunch," as she later called it, they talked and talked. They went to an Italian restaurant in Chicago's near North Side, but Jean just sat and stirred her spaghetti, hardly eating a mouthful. She drank the red wine and talked, and listened as Dillon talked. When they finally decided to leave, he said, "You *will* send me some of your poems, won't you? I promise to send you a critique." Still feeling as if she had feasted in Odin's hall of heroes, she "floated" home, and sent him six poems that same night. Dillon not only sent the critique, but accepted one of the poems for the famous *Magazine of Verse*. And, after she had worked on them a little, he accepted three more: in May, 1939, her first poems appeared in *Poetry*. Her parents were astonished, and Burden herself could hardly believe it. Her father kept calling her "Amy Lowell, Amy Lowell," probably because she wrote in free verse; but Jean, not realizing that he meant it as a compliment since his generation had looked on Amy Lowell as the chief exponent of modern poetry, was put out, and asked him to stop. She wanted such lines as, "If I forgive you/ what pillar will bear my weight:/ what anger will thicken the skin into a wall/ to keep me separate and whole/ and straight?" to carry her own identity, and no one else's.

Once she felt well enough acquainted with the editor, she hung around the office and became a part-time reader at *Poetry*. She was one of the regulars who often went to lunch together; a "great group," she recalled, "congenial and scintillating," providing both stimulation and inspiration for a young poet. Among them were Peter deVries,* Marcia Masters, Edgar Lee Masters's daughter, Marge Peters, Seije Hayakawa, in those days a thoroughgoing liberal, whose book, *Language in Action,* was to revolutionize the study of speech and semantics; occasionally Inez Cunningham Stark would join the circle. (It was then that Burden learned of her experimental workshop with the black poets on Chicago's South Side, as she recalled long afterward in the 1970s when Gwendolyn Brooks read to a packed house in California; and Brooks, with her usual warmth, had burst into a paean of praise for the lady.) More often than not George Dillon was one of the select circle. He and Jean Burden were friends all through the years until Dillon's death in 1968. For almost

*deVries is still a close friend.

three decades they exchanged poems: she sent him every poem she wrote, and he sent her his translations. (Oddly, although he had won the Pulitzer Prize for *The Flowering Stone,* he never published another volume of his own poems, but concentrated on translations.) The relationship was purely platonic: without any involvement of sex, the two were close friends; the last time they saw each other was in 1967, when she visited him in the Dillon home in Virginia, the year before he died.

Not long after she made her first appearance in print as a poet, Burden met a British student of osteopathy, whom she married in 1940. Although happy at first, the marriage was never successful. Like Adrienne Rich, this poet wanted to experience a full life physically as well as mentally and artistically, but she was destined to be childless. The year her husband went overseas, 1943, their first baby was stillborn, a deep disappointment to both. Two further attempts resulted in miscarriages, and then a decision not to try again for fear of endangering the poet's life. In 1946 they had moved to California with the hope that the warm climate would improve her health and her husband's practice. Osteopathy was still frowned upon as a medical science in most states but not in California. Jean, in spite of her illnesses, had been paying the greater part of their expenses with various jobs in public relations and free-lance writing, all the while "making poems" whenever possible. Her husband could not understand her drive; their relationship deteriorated steadily, and in 1949 they were divorced. Prizing her freedom, she has never remarried.

Although she was now published in a number of little magazines, Burden had not yet collected her poems, and her first volume did not appear until 1963. She found that although she had more time for poetry writing, she still had to devote most of her days to earning a living through various public relations posts. Weekends and nights were devoted to poetry; and, through correspondence with the editor-in-chief at *Yankee,* with whom she later had a long, tempestuous love affair, she took on the task of reading literally hundreds of poems every week, from which she selects only a few she considers suitable for publication. When she had finally collected her own poems, the manuscript went the rounds of many publishing houses before it was accepted by October House. Her work was uniformly praised for its lyric quality, exact phrasing, and succinct, profound content. The only thing that bothered Burden was that she was linked to the Imagist poet H.D., or to the Imagist movement generally. The eminent poet and critic Howard Nemerov wrote: ". . . this is an immense, a rare, possibly unique, gift." He was speaking of her spareness, her "tact" in handling a line, but saw that "there is a great deal else: these poems really do move, the best of them. With deceptively simple means, they make big effects." James Dickey wrote, "Her voice is unforced and lovely . . . the gentle, reasonable urgency of a passionate woman."

The success of her book brought requests for readings, poems for anthologies, and poetry workshops, conducted by the poet in college adult education programs and privately in her home. The sessions were immensely popular. Jean Burden has a vivacious personality, a keen sense of humor, and a genuine appreciation of talent in others. Her appearances on platform, radio, and television in connection with her public relations work have given her a poise and confidence that carries authority. She conducted her workshops on the premise George Dillon once gave her—that young poets need to be encouraged more than criticized. As her reputation grew, she began to meditate on her own experience in becoming a bona fide poet; and the result was a book, *Journey Toward Poetry,* published by October House in 1966. She dedicated it to Dillon with a paraphrase of his statement: "For George Dillon," she wrote, "who encouraged when he could have criticized."

In a preface she made it clear that this was not a book of rules for writing poetry, but rather a "personal witness to the problems and possibilities of the creative imagination. A book to turn to for signs of what is genuine, difficult, and worth caring about in this art form." Her statement of purpose was followed by a prologue, "Woman as Artist," in which Burden, like Rich and others, analyzes the problems of the artist that are peculiar to women, but she comes up with a surprisingly different aspect of the situation. In her view, the overall problem is common to both sexes, but it is more acute: "How does a woman who is basically a creative artist live out her creativity while at the same time fulfilling her traditional roles as wife and mother?" she, like others, asks, and grants that the question is probably related to, but not the same as the "battle of the sexes" or the "emancipation of women from the kitchen." She herself, she says, feels "neither imprisoned nor embattled by the opposite sex." The problem she wishes to explore lies in another area. It involves a new kind of suffrage, not only for women as such but for the small and infinitely important minority of women artists—not the dabblers, but the truly gifted women who were born with talent of respectable size and have a responsibility to it. Inside such women "there breeds a far greater conflict than ever existed between man and woman, and few of either sex fully understand the *nature of the tension*"—these words are underscored—"let alone what to do about it."

The poet points out that women artists in any field of artistic endeavor have a difficult time discussing their problem with even each other, but they are "usually awkward and tongue-tied when trying to explain themselves to men." In her opinion the sense of alienation that the gifted woman feels springs, more than anything else, from the struggle between the masculine and feminine aspects of her own nature, and her total ignorance that these polarities even exist. She is propelled by both a masculine and a feminine drive, and must live out both sides of her nature. Burden cites Virginia Woolf and going further back, Coleridge as authority for her theory and says, stating it again simply, that the artist—of either sex—is essentially androgynous, psychologically. "It is from this polarity between her masculine and feminine natures that woman creates." If women recognize this fact, they will see that the "creative act in art is essentially an expression of a masculine drive. It is not passive; it is an aggressive action." She once discussed this idea with Thomas Sugrue, who said, "Whenever I write a poem I have to gather myself into the masculine side of me, and *thrust* into the feminine side. The result is a poem." She concludes that "the same analogy of course applies to the opposite sex. It occurs when a woman puts paint on a canvas, composes a sonata, conceives a ballet, writes a novel, or chips out a piece of sculpture. . . . This is one way she can live out her animus . . ." The concept is much the same as Adrienne Rich's "I am the androgyne" except that Jean Burden spells it out in clear prose as a viable solution, if the female artist will only recognize and accept her duo nature, allowing her drives to act in harmony, and so express her creativity without conflict.

The book went on to deal with the "stuff" of poetry—the "donnée," a given idea, phrase or line that comes to a poet unasked, unsought, eventually expanding and taking shape as a poem; and ensuing chapters discuss critics and criticism—which ends, "In the last analysis, neither the applause nor the boos are very important. One writes to keep alive a self that would wither away without it." Chapter Five, "Poetry as a Platform Art," draws upon Jean Burden's recollections of her afterclass meetings with Thornton Wilder, when he gave her pointers on diction and stage presence from his knowledge of the theatre, gained when he attended rehearsals of his plays.

Journey Toward Poetry, written originally as a personal record of the creative process, proved to be an unexpected success, a bestseller of its kind. It went into several printings right away, widely reviewed and praised by the critics, and was later issued in a paperback edition. Much to the astonishment of the author, the book was recommended for college poetry workshops all over the country, from the New School for Social Research in New York to the University of Chicago and Santa Barbara

College in California. Jean's own workshop increased in membership, and she was in demand for readings. Anthologists asked for poems, and in an odd situation she had nothing but a new one that had not yet been placed, so it was anthologized before being printed in a magazine or volume.

No matter what else she does, Jean Burden is constantly working on a new poem. Careful about craft, she sometimes has a single poem in the making for months after the "donnée" appears. Still poetry editor of *Yankee,* she is as conscientious in considering the piles of poems she receives as she is in writing her own; she will take the time and trouble to comment on the work of young hopefuls, or she will deal succinctly with those who complain about a rejection. A few years ago, the late Laura Benet, piqued by a returned poem, wrote on the rejection slip, "What kind of poetry do you want?" and mailed it back. And Jean, just as piqued, answered at once in two words below Benet's query, "Good poetry." In telling the incident, Burden commented, "I didn't know what else to say: It's obvious that I won't let a poem go through for publication in the magazine unless I think it's good, no matter who wrote it. Otherwise I wouldn't be poetry editor for all these years." She is also pet editor of *Woman's Day,* so her poetry writing is confined to off-hours, but she keeps it going. Although her output is small in quantity, it is distinguished in quality by apt imagery, spare phrasing, and rhythmic cadence. Too often used unthinkingly, the term "a poet's poet," appreciated by colleagues and critics, applies to her. It is a loss to the literary world that she has not been able to publish more volumes. Plagued by trouble with her back, Burden often writes in bed. She lives in a country house in California, where she has a garden with fruit trees, and a large, handsome white cat who appears in her poetry, in photographs on her book jackets, and on her Christmas cards.

Isabella Gardner

To those who knew her well, Isabella (Stewart) Gardner, like her great-aunt the famous "Mrs. Jack Gardner," whose namesake she was, the poet lived up to her heritage of a passionate, warm, generous nature, with a flair for the flamboyant and a dramatic disregard for convention. Her relative, notorious for the company she kept, had surrounded herself with artists, was the model for John Singer Sargent's painting, "Madame X." According to one apochryphal tale, she had a room in her Beacon Hill house draped in black velvet, where she posed "naked" for various visual artists, scandalizing Boston's high society. She eventually established the Isabella Stewart Gardner

Museum, which, with its distinguished collection, partially restored her respectability in the eyes of her contemporaries.

By the time her namesake was born in Newton, Massachusetts, the fashionable suburb of Boston in 1916, age as well as
respectability had taken over; and to the chubby redheaded child
who was to become a lyric poet of rare power, combining the
real with the dreamworld of her imagination, the relative whose
name she bore was an elderly, old-fashioned society lady to whose
home she was taken for obligatory visits, and who took her to
concerts, teas, and most often to plays because they were both
"Belles" of the family circle. And a highly distinguished familial
hierarchy it was: The future poet was not allowed to forget that
she was a descendent of the Peabody, Grosvenor, and Gardner
families of New England, who, like the Lowells and the Ca-
bots, contributed to the cultural life of the region, from Endi-
cott Peabody, the educator who founded schools of high standards for the elite, to great aunt Bella and her museum. Small
Bella, the youngest of four children in her particular family, was
fond if somewhat in awe of her patron aunt, who early instilled
a love of the theatre in her by taking her to matinees, though
the first time nearly proved a disaster.

"I'll never forget the first play we saw," she said in 1978, recalling her childhood. "I was only eight years old, and I was
scared to death: it was a murder mystery—something called *In
the Next Room*. It still gives me the shudders when I think of
all that shooting!" Her voice shook with emotion.

She did not know until then that the play had been written
by Mrs. August Belmont, the former Eleanor Robson, an English actress of great renown on both sides of the Atlantic for
her starring role in "Merely Mary Ann"; that Robson had formed
her own company, and had known poet Amy Lowell well
through her close friend Ada Russell, a character actress in her
company who, on retiring from the theater became Amy's
companion-lover. The play itself had been taken from a mystery novel written by Burton Stevenson, compiler of the widely

circulated *Home Book of Verse,* a copy of which was on the shelves of many American households, including the Gardner's, during the early part of the century.

Isabella, who had longed to be a great actress, and had trained for a career in the theater before she began to concentrate on poetry writing, listened intently as her biographer sketched the background of the play that had frightened her.

"I wasn't aware of all this," she said; "or if I ever knew it I'd forgotten the facts." Her green eyes twinkled. "I never was much of a student. And I had practically no formal education." She had been sent to the Foxcroft School for Girls, the fashionable boarding school attended by society girls, but she never went on to college or attained an academic degree. She continued, "I still feel that was a terrifying first play for a child to see, but I don't suppose my aunt thought twice about it. She had season tickets for the matinee on Saturday and she took me along. I liked almost everything else, loved Shakespeare right from the start. I expect the poetry of the lines appealed to me. But I never was a good student; lessons, homework bored me. I liked to play. I liked the summertime when there was no school."

Summers were spent in Easthampton near the ocean on the bay, as she recalled in her nostalgic poem, "Summer Remembered," with its evocative auditory figures: "Sounds sum and summon the remembering of summers./ The humming of the sun/ The mumbling in the honey-suckle vine/ The whirring in the clovered grass/ The pizzicato plinkle of ice in an auburn/ uncle's amber glass./" More specific words magically bring up "The whing of father's racquet and the whack/ of brother's bat on cousin's ball" but above all "calling voices call-/ ing voices spilling voices," for the Irish in her Gaelic clan did not hesitate to lift their lung power in the open air, especially at the end of day when one heard "voices calling calling calling/ 'Children! Children! Time's Up/ Time's Up' "—a phrase that has a double meaning in retrospect. Belle could still hear her mother, Rose Peabody Gardner, join other familial voices "Merrily, sturdily wantonly . . . cheerily chidingly call to the children Time's Up." The poem ends in a quasi-mournful couplet as "the mute children's unvoiced clamor sacks the summer air/ crying Mother Mother are you there?" One can read everyone's lost childhood in these two lines.

Except that she stammered in trying to make her own voice heard above her older sisters and brothers, the poet realized in recollection that hers was a happy childhood. As part of the busy, bubbling household in Newton, overflowing with children, Isabella was both innocent and intuitively wise. In another recollection of things long past, the inspired title poem of her third volume, *West of Childhood,* with its dedication, "for my brother, George Gardner," she revives the springtime of those early years, observing by way of introduction, "West of our childhood rote usurps the rites of spring, the wild sweet/ season is an act of year." We accept the "uniformed robins" and consult the seed catalogs. However, she continues (in the second stanza), "A child's fierce focused gaze can wholly enter/ and instantly become the bold gold center/ of a single crocus, a listening child is fused to the sole voice/ of that particular inimitable bird whose red choice/ breast is robiner than never. . . ." Further, she concludes, "the shout of spring out-rang the dinner bell." And, addressing him directly: "Brother do you remember the walled garden, our dallies in that ding dong dell/ where my fistful of violets mazed the air we moved through and upon/ and a swallow of brook skimmed your tabloid sloop to sea and gone?" Finally, the poet predicts that "North of tomorrow" their grandchildren will experience the same wild joys of spring: *"That bud will leaf again, that choice bird sing, and paper boats sail . . ."* The last lines were a rueful reference to the daughter and son of her second marriage, and the sorrows of her life through the sad, separate fates both her children were to suffer.

Other glimpses of the poet during her earliest years reveal her fanciful imagination, her Irish wit and clownish humor, the ability to laugh at herself. "When I was a clear-eyed child,/

reading about Artemis and Snow White," she confides in "A Word From the Piazza del Limbo," "I secretly got down on my knees when/ the light clicked out and my brother and I/ had said our I Lay Me's and been kissed./ We slept on a screened porch almost out of/ doors. In winter the bare floor was arctic/ and I made certain that my knees were bare./ Then (a confirmed believer in my own/ omnipotence) I prayed and prayed." She prayed for those in "every category of misery that she could, in innocence, imagine." She asserts: "Yes, I was magical then. I could fly./ When I climbed a tree I put my arms round/ the trunk and my ear to the bark and heard,/ faintly, the dryad speaking, and I had the evil eye;/ and the Unicorn's head once lay in my lap, and bareback / I galloped Pegasus. I moved Mt. Monadnock./ I walked across blue Mt. Hope Bay. I believed." In a few final lines she sums herself up: "I lived too long a time in innocence,/ but not quite long enough to wholly make break or addle/ me. A critic wrote 'the pilgrim for whom no chapel/ waits.' But still I wear the scallop shell/ and shall till I go down the well/ Ding Dong Belle."

Even more fanciful was the tale told in "Card Island or Cod Island?" She never knew which name was correct, but an island on the coast was her dream refuge almost every night during one extremely cold winter when she and George shared a room with a grate. After her little brother had gone to sleep she kept staring at the "quivering pictures" on the ceiling made by the "muttering embers" of the grate, and soon she was climbing the cobblestone streets of a hillside coastal village, where every little house was aglow with the light of whale-oil lamps, and every door was ready to open wide to her. Combining fairy tale with fishing lore, Belle created a loving community all her own, who welcomed her with shouts of joy and offered her bounties of cookies and milk, a bottomless pitcher of milk just for her. She belonged to them and they to her: how they hugged her! The poem of this nighttime daydream expresses everyone's secret wish to be universally and exclusively loved. Poor little

George, afraid of the dark, saw only wolves baring their teeth at him. When he heard Belle recount her "serial tales" only to their father at bedtime or to the Irish laundress who came several mornings a week, her younger brother would cry, "Take ME Take ME why can't I go too?" But how was she to answer him? However, the laundress, "crisp and tactful Celt," played the game of pretend seriously, asking about the islanders as if she knew them all, knew the place as well as Belle. The poem ends in a kind of conundrum, two-stanza ballad:

> *Cod Halibut Haddock Scrod*
> *In the afternoons my mother played Cards*
> *Scrod Haddock Halibut Cod*
> *At my bedtime my father played God*
> > *The King the Queen the Ace the Jack*
> > *I was the joker in the pack*
> > *Island Island Cod or Card*
> > *Once your coast was my backyard.*

After she had attended the Foxcroft School a few years, Isabella Gardner decided she had had enough academic schooling; she was enamored of the theatre by then—"stage-struck," her sisters called it, but her brother Bob, only two years older than she, understood. Belle admired her brother Bob, who was interested in photography from an early age; indeed, she felt closer to both her brothers than she did to either of her sisters, who were "older" and did everything they should according to 'Hoyle,' her father said, so why couldn't Belle be like them? Her mother said she was just like the aunt she was named after, but the young Isabella felt she was like nobody but herself, and she wanted to be an actress, not a debutante or a society matron. She also wanted to be a poet, had secretly started writing poetry, but that was an ambition she kept to herself. She finally convinced her parents that she should study for the stage at the Leighton Rollins Studio of Acting in Easthampton, an early theatre workshop performing experimental plays of literary value, whose productions the Gardners had seen occasionally during the summer. Rollins, himself a poet as well as actor, producer, and teacher, was a dynamic personality, full of enthusiasm for any project he undertook, any student whose work he thought showed promise. From the time Isabella enrolled, he felt she showed great promise, for, in spite of her stammer, Belle had a rich, resonant musical voice; full-throated, bubbling laughter came easily from her lips; she was best in comedic roles, but if her stutter were overcome, she could express deep emotions and succeed in dramatic roles as well. From the first, Rollins was her mentor, speech instructor, and friend; though they were to have many an argument when the hot words flashed between them, and though Leighton was sixteen years older than she, they remained friends till their lives ended, strangely, at almost the same moment. To Belle, Rollins represented man in the arts, and in her last volume, her poem, "Homo Gratia Artis" is dedicated *For Leighton Rollins;* ambivalent in its portrayal of the artist in general, the poem seems to apply specifically to Rollins in the lines: "You are Abel and his brother/ Eden Persepolis and Hell/ Raskolnikoff and Philomel/ The lamb the unicorn the goat/ The burning shirt and Joseph's coat." The juxtaposition of the contrasting elements adds up to the final definition of the artist: "You are the coffin and the cock."

Rollins helped Gardner to conquer her stutter to a certain extent, but he advised her to take further training, and suggested a year at the Embassy School of Acting in London; Belle persuaded her parents to send her there—when she wanted something badly enough she usually got it—but, though there was some improvement in her speech difficulty, she was cast in the same sort of role, comedy or character "bit" parts. The English director said she was the "perfect adorable silly ass" when he saw her in a part "in which I had to lisp and giggle," she wrote later in a long poem about her career in the theatre. For in England it was the same story: her snub-nosed round Irish face, topped by her red hair and mischievous green eyes, her tendency to clown and ability to laugh cast her at sight into comedic roles before she had a chance to read for any others. Few suspected the wild, rushing emotion deep within her, the eagerness for an all-consuming love that would sweep her off her feet. She returned to Rollins's studio much the same as she had left.

She returned in time to take part in the first production of Rollins's verse play, *Disasters of War,* in 1938, a crucial year leading to World War II. This experimental theatre piece was inspired by a book of Goya reproductions—the artist's record, in etchings and aquatints, depicting the horrors of war in his day. Rollins chose twelve of the eighty-three scenes, and in transposing Goya's realistic, fine-lined art to the drama, he wrote a coordinating verse for each selection, the lines delivered by a speaking chorus, while a group of nonspeaking actors posed in a series of tableaux, reproducing the Goyan scenes in living form. A small orchestra played appropriate theme music, and an intermittant singing chorus gave added richness to the production. When she was asked, in 1978, whether she had been in the speaking or the singing chorus, the poet said emphatically, "The speaking!" She had been only twenty-two in 1938, still innocent and impressionable, and had thrown herself into this production heart and soul. When the book of the play was reissued in 1980, it was dedicated to all those who helped to make the production an artistic success, and the first name on the list was Isabella Gardner.

She was inspired by Leighton's work to read him some of her own, and he encouraged her to start sending it around to literary magazines, but it would be years before she felt sure enough of herself as a poet to try for publication. She was still concentrating on the theatre, and she fell head over heels in love with the new director of the company, Charles Van Kirk, who became the first of the four husbands she was to have. Van Kirk, like Rollins, was much older than she; he had been married before and had a daughter by his first wife. Isabella felt flattered by the fact that the director of the company favored her during rehearsals, but both Leighton and his wife, Catherine, who felt protective of her, were uneasy about it, and they were dismayed when she announced she was going to marry Van Kirk. Her family was downright disapproving, but Belle was determined, and within a year after the marriage, which proved a dismal failure, she gave birth to her first child, a daughter she named Rose, after her mother, hoping her parents would be pleased and forgive her mistake. Her father, who had always made a pet of Isabella, was more than willing, but her mother was merely resigned to the madcap ways of the poet.

The baby, however, proved a heart's delight in her infancy and early childhood. One of Gardner's most successful lyrics, "At a Summer Hotel", later dedicated, "For My Daughter, Rose Van Kirk," which was accepted by *The New Yorker* on its first time out, to her surprise, reveals both tenderness and apprehension on the part of the poet: "I am here with my beautiful bountiful womanful child," she announces; "to be soothed by the sea not roused by these roses roving wild./ My girl is gold in the sun and bold in the dazzling water,/ she drowses on the blond sand and in the daisy fields my daughter/ dreams. Uneasy in the drafty shade I rock on the verandah/ reminded of Europa Persephone Miranda." Separated from Van Kirk and soon to get a divorce, she had decided to keep on with her stage career, if only to prove to herself that she could, or could not, succeed. As she says in her poem about life in the theatre, oddly titled, "Not At All What One Is Used To," she states at the outset: "There was never any worry about bread or even butter/ although that worried me almost as much as my stutter." She had her own income by now from a trust fund her aunt left, but she lived below her means, and reveled in her low rent room, complete with bedbugs. Whether in defiance of her affluent family, or because she actually preferred shabbiness, Belle Gardner always lived in second-rate, run-down hotels or raffish rooms.

As she relates in the poem, she dutifully made the rounds of producers' offices, praying half the time that she would be denied the interview she had begged for, and more than half the time her wish was granted. If rarely she did get the chance to read, she stammered and stalled so she would disqualify. She finally "became Equity" by joining a stock company "north of Boston," but again she was in character roles and comedy parts. At the height of her career, when she was getting laughs every night, the leads had her fired because, they said, she was stealing the show. But she persisted, playing one role or another with various companies, until 1943, when she decided she had had enough. She might not have made the decision to leave the theatre even then if she hadn't been writing poetry all through her trials and receiving acceptance instead of rejection slips. She was playing in Chicago when *Poetry: A Magazine of Verse,* whose office she visited after several of her poems had been accepted, asked if she would be interested in being associate editor. Poet Karl Shapiro, who was then editor of the magazine, needed someone, and thought she would be just the person for the job. Isabella Gardner jumped at the chance, and in that moment knew that she was more poet than actor.

She found the offices of *Poetry* a fascinating place to work; as Jean Burden had discovered, it served as a center for poets from all over the region, and people in the related arts often dropped in to "schmoose," as Seymour Shapiro, the photographer who sometimes worked for the magazine, would say. After Belle began her editing, he found reasons to stop by more frequently. He was charmed by her roguish wit and ready laugh, her warmth and willingness to listen to his pleas for more assignments, though *Poetry* never included photographs and rarely needed any for other purposes. As before, Belle was pleased to have someone make a fuss over her; she was amused by Seymour's conversation, liberally spiced with Yiddish phrases, and she was touched by his need for the encouragement she gave him. It is not surprising that he became her second husband

and, within a year, her second child, a son they named Daniel, was born. When she married again, Belle had sent for little Rose, who had been staying with the Gardners; though the poet was never much of a housekeeper—"sloth" was her ever-present sin, she admitted in a poem related to religion—she maintained a small household with Seymour in Chicago.

As before, the second marriage failed, though it lasted a little longer than the first, and for a few years all was well. The summer after Daniel was born, when he was just an infant, was a joyful time, as she recalled in a splendid poem of reminiscence, "That Was Then," written thirty years later, the title and last poem in her last volume. Though one senses a pervading note of mournful regret for a past that can never be relived, the narrative free verse gives a vivid, delightfully humorous picture of the poet's life in a summer community of Jewish people of Eastern European background. The sign said Union Pier, Michigan, but they called it "Shapiro Shangri La." Most were Slavic to some extent—Polish, Russian, Rumanian—and all spoke Yiddish with various accents when "they didn't want their children to understand." She needed a passport, they joked: She was the only "Shicksa" there. The term was spoken with affection, not resentment; as Jews they were political, not pious; the husbands, who came out on Fridays for the weekend—except Seymour, who came on Thursdays, bringing the white Chilean wine she liked—argued the merits and demerits of Marxian Socialism with the intensity of Talmudic scholars. The wives did not keep kosher kitchens, though they fixed all the traditional holiday dishes and showed "the shicksa" how to fix them. The small ethnic colony, so foreign to Isabella Gardner's Bostonian Episcopalian upbringing, took her into the fold without question. She and Seymour shared a cottage with Seymour's sister, Molly (the matriarch), and her husband, gentle Ben Blevitsky, who regarded Belle as much a daughter as their Riva, then a young girl. Molly was more mother to her than her own had ever been. The poet basked in the light of their affectionate love.

That first summer was like an idyll never duplicated in her bizarre history. Her children, too, were happy. "My daughter then five, now in/ Bedlam, chased butterflies and thirty years/ ago my infant son, now for some years/ lost, was happy too. I washed his diapers/ in a tub and hung them up in the sun./ . . . Seymour/ . . . made a paddock/ for him. Dan did not like to be cooped up/ (nor did Rose, my daughter Rosy; nor did she)/ . . . Simcha little Rosy littler Daniel/ and the Shicksa we were all of us joy-/ full then in Shapiro Shangri La when/ we were young and laughing." The picture the poet created from memory was no doubt idealized to some extent; but the poem, earthy, lusty, realistic in its detail, is a triumph of genuine deep feeling and dramatic effect in its final scene of high comedy, when "the Shicksa cooked a haser for the Shabbas!" and all fall to in high delight "while the infant Daniel slept," and, at the peak of its hilarity is cut off by a repetition of the title phrase, "That was then. That was then," like a mournful cry of sad remorse.

It was the very acceptance of his "Bellotchka," as they sometimes called her, that caused the poet's second marriage to sag and then to fail. For Seymour became jealous, first of the loving attention his "landsmen" showered upon his "shicksa," and then, as more of her poems were accepted, he was jealous of her success, of her gift for self-expression, of her every move. "I couldn't pick up a book without some snarling comment from him," she explained. "It was terrible. I couldn't *stand* it any longer!" Her voice shook. "He would hardly let me breathe!"

She finally got a divorce and began pouring out her recent experience in lines of poetry liberally peppered with Yiddish phrases she had picked up from Seymour and his people. She received complaints from some editors, and found it necessary to put an asterisk after certain phrases like, "Zei Gesund," the title of a memorial poem for a doctor whose untimely death at thirty-eight deprived her of an analyst of rare understanding. Or, for poems like the delightful "Saloon Suite," she used a lengthy footnote to explain a number of phrases, plus the fact that Part Two of the suite was written after hearing the "Third Man Theme," whose lines almost hum the tune itself. The piece is inventive, intriguing, an isolated instance of a poet setting music to words. It was first published in *The Chicago Review*, one of several Chicago journals that accepted her offerings.

Life for Isabella Gardner was not complete, however, without a mate; and her third husband, Robert McCormick, whom she married a year or two after her divorce, was the only one of whom her family approved. At the other end of the social spectrum from Seymour, and from a prominent family, he restored the poet's good graces with her parents; moreover, he was pleased with her growing success as a poet, which he regarded more as a hobby than a career—not the ideal attitude she longed for, but a relief after the paranoic jealousy she had to face day after day with Seymour. By 1954, Gardner had gathered together enough published poems for a manuscript, and her first volume was published by Houghton Mifflin in 1955. Entitled provocatively, *Birthdays From The Ocean*—the opening words of her philosophical poem, "That 'Craning of the Neck,'" based on a quotation from Martin Buber—the book was an immediate success. To her amazement, it was nominated for the National Book Award in poetry, a rare achievement for a first volume.

Critics were unanimous in their praise of Isabella Gardner's originality of expression, the lyric quality of her rhyme schemes, her penetrating conclusions. No less a poet than Wallace Stevens wrote, "I thought *(Birthdays From the Ocean)* the freshest, truest book of poetry that I had read in a long time." The title line, "Birthdays from the ocean one desert april noon," sets the tone for her entire stream of consciousness—the quest for identification with all creatures of one's desire. In this poem it is the "great blue heron" she has sighted in a strange stream while riding across the desert one day; wanting to come close to him, she directs her mare to the water's edge, but each time he senses her presence he "unlooses unwilling wings" and eludes her. "I followed him silently giving no quarter/ all that afternoon. He never flew far from me/ . . . but he always heaved doggedly out of touch. I/ only wanted to stare myself into him to try/ and thou him till we recognized and became each/ other. . . ./ But I could not reach/ his eye. He fled in puzzled ponderous pain/ and I at last rode home, conspicuous as Cain." The last lines concede the inevitable truth that "That fisher who heaved to dodge my eye/ has damned himself an It and I shall never fly."

First published in the *Partisan Review,* this early poem could be symbolic of the continual search for love that Isabella Gardner was to conduct throughout her days even though she failed to succeed—more than momentarily time after time. Just as her family was beginning to feel that the irrepressible child in her had settled down to a mature, well-ordered life, Belle met the poet who was her peer, whose work she revered and who reversed her life for the fourth time—Allen Tate. After the success of her first volume, Gardner found herself in demand for readings, and here her training in the theatre stood her in good stead. The stage diction she had learned in England, combined with her rich resonant voice and the subtle rhythms of her poetry, made her readings a theatrical experience. She had never stuttered when she sang, and now the cadence of her lines served to stay her stammer as the melody of song had done in the past. Her years in the theatre had given her stage presence. With the publication of her second volume, *The Looking Glass,* brought out by the University of Chicago Press, which proved a sellout edition in hardcover, the name of Isabella Gardner was well known in poetry circles.

Asked to read at the University of Minnesota, she accepted with pleasure, and met Allen Tate, who was teaching there. The attraction both felt was immediate, heady, and in Belle, overwhelming. Nothing short of marriage would satisfy her, though Tate was the husband of Carolyn Gordon, novelist, essayist, and teacher of creative writing at Columbia University, where her students adored her. As for Isabella, she simply told McCormick she had to get a divorce, and when asked in 1979 if there had been trouble between them, the poet shook her head. "Bob McCormick was a perfectly nice man," she said. "I suppose I could have gone on being married to him, but I wanted Allen Tate as my husband; and Bob understood." She sighed. "If we could only know how these things are going to turn out!"

She should have known that Allen Tate was scarcely more stable than she; that though they were married when her next volume came out—*West of Childhood* was copyrighted in 1965 by Isabella Gardner *Tate* instead of the surname McCormick used in her two previous books—Tate was already wavering in his devotion to her. Unknown to her, he had his eye on a younger woman; Isabella knew only too well that she had started showing signs of middle age some years earlier when she wrote "On Looking in the Looking Glass," the first stanza of which admits: "Your small embattled eyes dispute a face/ that middle-aging sags and creases./ Besieged, your eyes protest and plead,/ your wild little eyes are bright, and bleed." With "an instant's blink," she brings back the "total innocence" of childhood; and in another, the dazzling "flare of Youth"; "the kindling enkindled fire/ headless and sheer . . ." Of this image she says: "I see and fear the girl you were." In the next stanza she sees her Daemon, creativity, the "maker" she longs to be but is not. In the final stanza she closes her eyes and ends the poem, "with imagination's eye I see you dead." Reading this fantasy piece, it is not surprising to learn that Sylvia Plath, who admired Gardner's work, took her cue for repeated refrain in the "Mad Girl's Love Song," "I close my eyes and all the world drops dead," from the above.

For several years Bella Gardner lived happily with Allen Tate in Minneapolis, Minnesota. *West of Childhood* was dedicated "To Allen" followed by the quotation from Rilke: "Love consists in this: that two solitudes protect and touch, and greet each other." She tried to maintain a feeling of family life by having her children live with them, but Allen was barely tolerant of their presence; for some reason, he and Daniel took an instant dislike to each other: the boy was bright and brash; Allen could not abide his smart-alecky remarks. As for Daniel, he was wary of "strangers" from the time his mother and father were divorced. In a poem published originally in the *Minnesota Review* and included in *West of Childhood*, "A Loud Song, Mother" (For My Son, Daniel Seymour), Gardner gives a graphic picture of her five year old, who "chanted from his room enormously" a five-line rune, repeating the word "strangers" at the start of each line, which the poet calls "A deafening declaration this jubilant shout of grief/ that trumpets final fellowship and flutes a whole belief./ . . . He sings a world of strangers running on the burning stars/ a race on every-colored feet with freshly calloused scars." She speaks of her own fears of strangers in childhood, and ends by admonishing all "Sons, may you starve the maggot fears that ate our spirit's meat/ and stride with brother strangers in your seven-league bare feet." It is a peculiar poem, one that both recognizes and tries to minimize the problem of Daniel's maladjusted emotions.

This section of the book is dedicated: "For My Parents," followed by another part of the passage from Martin Buber that inspired "Birthdays from the Ocean," and exhorts them to "Believe in the simple magic of life, in service in the universe, and the meaning of that alertness, that 'craning of the neck' in creatures will dawn upon you." She still wanted understanding if not approval of her behavior from her parents. She hoped, too, that her children would love her and know that she loved them. She wanted to protect them from harm no matter how many "strangers" she brought into their lives. Several of the poems in *West of Childhood* speak directly or indirectly to her children. A lively fanciful lyric, "Summers Ago" (For Edith Sitwell), written in Sitwellian syllables and rhymes is addressed, "Children," in the opening and middle passages, but ends specifically, "Sister and brother, I your mother/ Once was a girl in skirling weather/ Though summer and swan must alter, falter,/ I waltzed on the water once, son and daughter." Though she felt that poets "should not write with cudgel or lance," there are lines in "Children are Game" that reveal her concern for the threat of nuclear war. The setting is the evergreen forest in winter, children skating on the pond: "What wings will whistle down this resined bark,/ what monstrous blooming blast belief?/ Children should not come to grief./ . . . I thawed my winters thinking spring/ and now am always cold, with reason,/ for bombs can blossom any season." A sonnet entitled, "Little Rock, Arkansas, 1957, Dedicated to the Nine Children," is indicative of social consciousness in the title alone, and the lines are definitely concerned with the plight of black school children—the fear for their safety in testing the newly passed integration law, as well as admiration for their courage.

For the most part, however, Gardner's poems "bear witness to her own particular joy and pain," as she stated on the jacket of *West of Childhood,* and in an afterward to her final volume, *That Was Then,* published the year before her untimely death. She was not prepared for the blow of Allen Tate's desertion of their household without warning, leaving her for love of a younger woman. It was a shock from which she never fully recovered, although she "played house" with a fifth man as she said in her narrative poem, "That was Then." She was almost frenetic in her search for a mate but she never found the lasting love she sought. She began going to the colonies for creative artists—to the MacDowell Colony, Yaddo, and other places—around 1967. She made many friends among people who knew what it meant to concentrate on one's creative ability; some of the men were her lovers, some her "seagreen lovers" as she called a friend who flirted with love; in a charming lighthearted lyric—"Lines to a Seagreen Lover," later ascribed, "For Maurice English," writer and editor, whom she met when she lived for a time in Pennsylvania. She became a patron of the arts; like her great aunt, she bought the paintings of her contemporaries—

Hyde Solomon, Larry Calcagno, Louis Tytell, three of the artists she came to know at various colonies—and she not only bought, but commissioned works from the noted sculptor, Blanche Dombek, with whom she became close friends. Whenever she came to Blanche's studio and saw a piece she especially liked, she would throw her arms around it, calling out, "I love this! I must have it!" She commissioned the sculptor to make twin statuettes of Capricorn, her zodiac sign and Allen's, one for the desk of each. She did not divorce him, nor drop the name Tate in copyrighting her poems. She found a strange satisfaction in holding onto his name, if nothing else. (Curiously, Carolyn Gordon did the same; indeed, Gordon never recognized that there had been a second Mrs. Tate.)

Many poets entered Belle's life and inspired some of her best work. Elizabeth Bishop, May Swenson, Marianne Moore, and James Wright, who wrote a glowing review of her first volume, and of her last, commented: "Isabella Gardner's *New and Selected Poems* is a rare moral and artistic achievement. It contains work of unmistakable serenity and wholeness, in which the trendy and the meretricious have no place. I am grateful for this triumphant book." He and his wife, Annie, were often guests in the suite of rooms at the Chelsea Hotel in New York City, which was as much permanent address as Belle Gardner could ever give. Like Virgil Thomson, Arthur Miller, and many other artists, she maintained rooms there year round, her headquarters when she was not travelling. One room, separate from the others, served as her office when she did not want to be disturbed. More than once she loaned this "cubby-hole" to some friend who needed a place to stay and work while in the city. Korean novelist Kim Yong Ik, whom she had met at the MacDowell Colony, had the use of it free of charge for several weeks while the poet was in Europe one summer.

She gave readings at least once a year in England and in Italy, where her lyrics found a warm response from listeners. The Italian poet Alfredo Rizzardi was moved to translate a group of her imaginative poems, published under the title, *Un Altra Infanzia*. Although she always claimed that her approach to poetry was not dialectical, Rizzardi said in a preface, "In Isabella Gardner, imagination has a clear dialectical function, and is essentially mythic." He felt that the new element in her use of it was consciousness, "with the bass note of mournful complaint, between reality and dreamland; and along with this, an elementary magical faith in the power of poetry." He also points to the "auroral, primitive feeling," the property of childhood one finds in her realistic scenes of the past. "Her world of feeling swings between the dominion of love and the terrible fact of death, the one linked to the other like light to shade." Such praise from abroad was a boon to her reputation as a poet of rare distinction in England and the United States.

Even as she made progress as a successful figure in the poetry world, tragedy struck her personal life when her son, Daniel, was "lost" at sea off the coast of Colombia, South America. Both he and Rose were victims of the drug addiction prevalent among the youth in the sixties. Daniel, who had written a bitter book about his mother's escapades, reporting her life as he saw it, in gross detail, had become involved with a ring of "pushers," and those who knew of his connection feared that he had been murdered rather than washed overboard during a storm while on a sailing party with friends. Rose, the "beautiful, bountiful daughter" of Belle's first marriage, like her half brother, became so deeply addicted that she had to be sent to a sanitarium.

If it had not been for her own immersion in her art, Gardner too might have lost her mind. In a poem later designated "for James Wright," she begins with an opening-line title, "Writing Poetry/ is one game that no-one quits while he or she's ahead. The/ stakes are steep. Among the chips are love fame life and sanity." Certain poems reveal that she had to struggle to win or hold onto her sanity. "Nightmare," for example, is packed with lurid images and actions that could only have been created by a tortured mind and soul. Both the dreamer and the fiendish, leering woman threatening her in the nightmare are "red-haired." "This Room is Full of Clocks" is a discursive poem dealing with the topic of time on different levels, linked to lon-gevity by a comparison of the life-spans of animals, birds, and fish with that of man, particularly "some of our poets" who died before they reached Biblical age. Citing Dylan Thomas, e.e. cummings, Theodore Roethke, and Louis MacNeice, she sug-gests "that there should be a Forest Preserve for poets/ each with his or her mate but I remind myself/ that the poet is rumoured to be less constant/ than the swan. No the bard must do his best with book/ and bed and booze and blunders of the heart and/ bearing witness burying friends banning bombs/ and us-ing onomatopoeia with restraint."

The items listed in these lines comprise Belle's own panacea for coping with, if not curing, the ills that befell her or her gifted fellow poets and treasured friends. Her paean of praise for Dy-lan Thomas, "When a Warlock Dies," done in fast-paced de-scriptive phrasing, an alliterative display of deviltry and love, has a Shakespearean flavor equal to the brewing speeches of the witches in "Macbeth." The closing lines of this beguiling eul-ogy reveal her deep grief and admiration for the wayward poet: "The roaring riming of this most mourned Merlin canticles his praise and His, and ours,/ and Jerichos the walls of heaven with a surfing shout of love, and blasts of flowers."

She relied on the love of her friends, young and old, for sur-cease from the pain of her emotional and physical troubles, for the latter grew as she relied more and more on "booze." She gave large parties in the Chelsea Hotel, some so large she did not know all the guests, to celebrate various occasions such as publication of her books or those of friends. When Leighton Rollins, who had moved to California for his health, came to New York for readings or some professional business, she al-ways entertained for him, as he and Catherine did for her when she went to California to give readings, usually in January. Through the years she kept in close touch with the Rollinses, and other members of that first theatre company in Easthampton. In her eyes, a friend once found remained a friend, a person once loved was not forgotten: Van Kirk's daughter by his first marriage, who had loved and admired Belle, was always remembered with gifts and cards. Even Seymour Shapiro, who had caused her the most aggravation, was still in touch with the poet.

Her reliance on liquor eventually affected her health to such a degree that she had to be hospitalized during the latter half of the 1970s. She confided to Blanche Dombek that the doctor had told her she had an "enlarged" heart and must lead a quiet life. Worried about Leighton Rollins, who was suffering from severe arthritis and a chronic asthmatic condition, Belle decided to spend a winter in California, perhaps settle there. She chose the Music and Arts Center of Ojai, south of Santa Barbara, where the Rollinses lived; she wanted to be sure of a warm climate, peace and quiet, and yet be close to her friends; Jean Burden, whom she had known since the days of her post on *Poetry* and who also was an old friend of Leighton and Catherine, lived in Alameda; Ann Stanford and other West Coast poets were not far away, so there was a prospect of readings if she felt up to them. But the tiny ingrown community of Ojai, intent on its main activity, the music festival held every year, did not take kindly to Belle's bohemian life-style. They did not approve of the man she was living with and generally turned a cold shoulder. She felt as if she was back in Boston, and after a few months she returned to the blessed anonymity of New York and the comfortable shabbiness, the interracial, international clientele of the Chelsea Hotel, where she resumed her former pattern of living.

The death of Allen Tate was an unexpected blow; though he had left her, she had continued to love him, to hope that they might come together again. She commissioned poet Ned O'Gorham to write a biography of Tate, an unprecedented gesture among poets. The more sudden, even less expected death of James Wright was another shock. "Jimmy was so young!" Isabella mourned. She helped Annie Wright arrange the memorial reading held at the Donnell Library, which was packed to the doors with devotees of the fifty-year-old Wright. It was then that Isabella, who was preparing the volume of new and selected poems, decided to designate "Writing Poetry," "for James Wright," as an appropriate memorial with its theme of the fateful game the poet plays in persisting with the gamble of this perilous art. Its closing lines are chillingly prophetic in the case of James Wright: "No-one has pocketed the moon since the game began . . ./ or . . . sooner than they did/ they died."

Though she may have surmised that she herself did not have long to live, and in fact implied as much in several poems, Isabella Gardner could not know that in another year she would be gone, too. She was fascinated with the idea that it was all a game, deeply serious like chess, or tense like high stakes poker; but the profession could have its lighter side: a new five stanza piece, evoked by the opening of the baseball season, was titled, "Are Poets Ball Players?" It begins "Marianne Moore loved baseball/ She was a winner/ I loved Marianne but that's a nothing/ answer to question marks in a title/ . . ." It is a clever poem, one that perhaps relies too much on puns for effect, but in answer to her question ultimately scores, making its point with a high mark. The last stanza reads:

> There are no free Walks for Poets to first
> base on balls. The Umpire counts and chooses
> So we Warm the Bench, jounce back to Left Field
> or, maybe, we touch all three bases and
> slide in peril to Home Plate
> That Home run at last

As a final equivocal note, she added in parenthesis: "(Allee Allee in free?)"

Belle Gardner almost made a home run, or, to use her other metaphor, pocketed a small segment of the moon before she died. She was able to complete the manuscript for a new volume in spite of all her sorrows and physical problems. In making her selections from previous publications, she included a poem that had appeared in *Kenyon Review* in 1955, but never in a book—a sestina, "The Music Room"—explaining that, for private reasons she had left it out of previous volumes. A well-structured poem, it is a strong, bitter brew of the poet's embroiled emotions, one that leaves the readers as devastated as she must have been at the time she wrote it. These six stanzas and customary three-line coda offer a startling clue to the suffering that lay behind the laughter and wit, the love of play on words that is found in the lines quoted above.

The book, published by BOA Editions, one of the distinguished American Poets Continuum Series, bore the revealing designation, "For Roland Flint"—the young poet who had been Allen Tate's protegé when Belle came to live in Minneapolis—and, directly below his name, "anchor to windward," for it was Flint who most helped to stabilize her life and work when the gale-force struggle with Tate began. And he continued to be supportive of her till the end. The stark jacket and frontispiece, designed by Aaron Siskind are indicative of the dark portent of death hanging over the poet despite the aura of sunny-tempered nostalgia surrounding her reminiscences of the past, particularly in the title poem, "That Was Then," the outstanding work in the collection, as already stated.

Again to Gardner's surprise, the volume was nominated for an American Book Award early in 1981. She was at the MacDowell Colony when word came, in low spirits over ill health, apprehension about the kind of attention her book would receive from the critics, and the ever-present problem of Rose; her errant daughter's future seemed bleaker than before since the birth of a baby boy whose male parent was not known. The poet wrote to this biographer, "News of the Nomination was heartening, but I doubt if the Award will follow." She did not spend much time speculating, but went on a short trip to Italy against doctor's orders in search of spiritual comfort from talks with William Congdon, a family connection of hers who had become a lay monk some years earlier. She had written a poem, "A Word From the Piazza Del Limbo," after a previous visit to him and had included it with his name in the new book. She returned from this visit feeling an inner calm, but her body was exhausted. Again the doctor ordered complete rest.

It was then that she received word that she had been awarded the Walt Whitman Citation of Merit, much to her astonishment, from the New York State Council on the Arts. The award carried with it a ten thousand dollar prize, and a stipulation that the recipient was to give two readings. Five poets, all her peers, including her friend May Swenson, served on the panel that chose Belle Gardner to be "poet laureate" of New York, as the prize came to be called because of readings. It was a signal honor. As gratified as she was amazed, Belle decided to give the ten thousand dollars to Yaddo, the creative artists' colony located in New York at Saratoga Springs. She was informed that the presentation would be made the following spring, but Fate decreed that the poet was not there to receive it. On the night of July 7, her heart gave out, and she died. She was found the next morning, sitting up in bed; she had evidently been reading. Her glasses had fallen down on the end of her nose and there was a smile on her lips, according to the account of those close to her; so she must have gone peacefully, without the pain and struggle she feared. When news of her death came out, the panelists voted to keep to their choice, and Isabella Gardner was designated the first posthumous as well as the first winner of the Walt Whitman Award. May Swenson offered to give the two readings required by the terms of the prize.

In its obituary on July 10, 1981, *The New York Times* quoted a statement the poet made in an afterword to her last volume: "If there is a theme with which I am particularly concerned, it is the contemporary failure of love . . . the love which is the specific and particular recognition of one human being by another." In the actual text she had added, "the response by eye and voice and touch of two solitudes. The democracy of universal vulnerability." She had demonstrated her own vulnerability throughout her life, to her joy and sorrow. The *Times* article reported that "Miss Gardner is survived by a daughter, Rose Van Kirk; her mother, Rose Peabody Gardner; two sisters, three brothers and a grandson."

Her friends were shocked and saddened; everyone knew that Belle had not been well, but few suspected that she was in imminent danger of dying. One friend who may have guessed, was gone: by an odd coincidence, Leighton Rollins, about whom she had been so concerned, died at nearly the same time as she; when her brother Bob called the Rollins's home in California to give them the sad news about his sister, he was told that Leighton's funeral had been held the day before. It was as if the person who had started her on her career had decreed that it should end with his. Both had received honors just before they died. Rollins had been given a gala celebration for his eightieth birthday, and Gardner, who was only sixty-six, the Walt Whitman Award. The ceremony for the latter took place as planned, on March 18, 1982, in Albany, New York, when Governor Carey, with Kitty Carlisle Hart, head of the state council, made the presentation and gave the ten thousand dollar check to Curtis Harnack, Director of Yaddo. It was learned that the poet also remembered the MacDowell Colony with a similar amount in her will. Her poetry was read by May Swenson then, and later at a cocktail party in New York City.

Two more memorial readings took place—one on April 4, in Great Neck, Long Island, arranged by avant-garde poet and teacher at Queens College, Harriet Zinnes, who read her own poem, a portrait of Gardner, "Dancing," written after she had observed the poet during an impromptu at the MacDowell Colony dancing by herself, without moving her body from one spot. Roland Flint, who came from Washington, D.C., where he was teaching at Georgetown, gave the principal reading.

Among the poems he chose was the lyric, "Lines to a Seagreen Lover," and in giving the title, he announced that the person for whom it was written, Maurice English, was present.* In between poems, Flint related anecdotes to illustrate Belle's outlook on life. In regard to friendships, he told about the time some man had made a nasty remark about Belle; when it was repeated to her, she laughed merrily, as if it were a huge joke; asked if she wasn't angry, she exclaimed, "Of course I'm not! I knew he didn't mean it: he's been a friend for over thirty years!" The "friend," it turned out, was Leighton Rollins.

The high point of this memorial came when Paul Kresh, editor of "The Spoken Arts" series, "A Treasury of 100 American Poets Reading Their Own Poems," played a tape he had made of Isabella Gardner's reading, and the poet's rich, musical voice spoke her lines as only she could—with dramatic emphasis and emotional shading. It was as if she had come into the room.

The other memorial took place on May 1 in New York City, at the West Side Y, and was arranged by Annie Wright, with some of Belle's intimate friends. Two of her brothers, George and Robert, came from Boston for the memorial, and George, the "little brother" with whom she had shared a room, read a prayer-poem he had written for his sister. Whether or not she would have been pleased, Isabella Gardner, whose pagan love of life had led her to excess, would have been touched by her brother's concern for her soul's salvation. Her poet's psyche might have cringed, but her warm heart would have responded with love.

* Maurice English, only a few years older than Gardner, died November 1983.

Audre Lorde

Unlike Gwendolyn Brooks, with whom she shared an office at City College, Audre Lorde, a native New Yorker, born on February 18, 1934, had a long, rough road to travel before she saw her poems published; and she feels that the delay was due in part to race prejudice. When asked during an interview in 1981 the same question that Brooks had been asked in 1967, namely if the fact that she was black was a handicap to her writing career, Lorde replied, "In my early days, definitely—directly and indirectly."

Asked what she meant by this enigmatic answer, she explained that there were few outlets for poetry of any sort when

she began sending her work around in the late 1940s and early
1950s. Poetry by a woman, let alone a black woman, stood little chance of getting into print, less chance than the period of
the 1930s, when Brooks was first published. World War II had
just ended when the McCarthy witch-hunts began, and anyone
with as strong a social consciousness as Audre Lorde's poetry
showed from the beginning was either ignored or declared sus-
pect as Communist. There was no black press—the term "black"
had not yet come into common use; and the women's press was
entirely a thing of the future.

An added obstacle was the difficulty blacks—especially black
women—had in finding jobs outside "domestic help" unless one
had a college education; and Audre Lorde, on her own by choice,
was determined to get her degree despite all odds. Her childhood had been constricted by the narrow confines of her mother's concept of rearing black children in a predominantly white
society: guided by her own bitter experience in coping with the
hazards of survival, Linda (Belmor) Lorde set up a strict regime, which she strictly enforced, out of anger and frustration
in her past. From thumbnail sketches scattered through Audre
Lorde's poems, one can easily piece together the picture of the
poet's childhood, particularly in "Black Mother Woman," which
opens, "I cannot recall you gentle"; yet in hindsight she can see
that her mother's "heavy love," hidden in the "the center of fu-
ries," was responsible for her ultimate success as a creative person: ". . . look mother/ I Am/ a dark temple/ where your true
spirit rises/ beautiful/ and tough as chestnut. . . . and if my eyes
conceal/ a squadron of conflicting rebellions/ I learned from you/
to define myself/ through your denials."

It would be many years before the poet could see the core of
love beneath her mother's thick layer of anger. In "Prologue"
she wrote: "Yet when I was a child/ whatever my mother thought
would mean survival/ made her try to beat me whiter every day/
and even now the colour of her bleached ambition/ still forks
throughout my words/ but I survived." Part of her mother's

"bleached ambition" was a good education for her daughter, who early showed an amazing aptitude for learning without having to study as hard as her sisters and brothers, all older than she. So young Audre was sent to a Catholic primary school where most of the children were white and the teaching staff reputedly better than in "Negro" schools. Audre had no trouble in graduating with honors, and was qualified to enter Hunter High School, where she breezed through her courses with ease, and spent more time writing poetry than studying. At eighteen she was full of vigor, ready to take on the world, but she was tired of her mother's goading ("hanging her with long-suffering eyes")—the eyes of a wife whose husband, weak and a failure as a real estate broker, had deserted her, leaving her with a brood of children to care for, a back-breaking burden she did not let them forget. Before Audre was a teenager, her sisters and brothers had all left home, and she had to bear the brunt of her mother's bitterness by herself. In a much later poem addressed to her own daughter she described her stealthy departure: ". . . you never tire of hearing/ how I crept out of my mother's house/ at dawn,/ with an olive suitcase/ crammed with books and fraudulent letters/ and an unplayed guitar." Those few lines of "Progress Report" reveal the daring and determination that mark Lorde's life and poetry from the time she left the shelter of her mother's roof.

Before she attained any kind of success, however, she had to overcome many obstacles, not the least of which was learning how to study under duress. She had to find a job, but those she applied for were not open to black women. She had moved into the tiny East Village apartment of a friend and enrolled at Hunter College night school. Hearing that black women were being hired by small textile firms in Stamford, Connecticut, she did get a job, but it turned out to be sweatshop labor. The embryo poet was so worn out she had practically no energy for study or poetry, but somehow she always managed to write and send out her poems, no matter how many times they were returned.

After about a year of this back-breaking schedule, she heard of an opening at the Sidney Hillman Health Center of the Amalgamated Clothing Workers for a clerical position in the nurses office. Recalling her joy on being hired, she said in 1981, "After the horror of the sweatshops, the Health Center seemed like sheer Heaven."

Now she was able to make some progress with her career, though she still had difficulty studying. To her surprise, college courses required much more preparation than any in her previous schooling, and she simply did not have the patience or the power to concentrate for the hours of research needed to write term papers. When, unexpectedly, her estranged father, who died in 1953, left her one thousand dollars, she decided on an impulse to go to Mexico City, where she attended the National University of Mexico for a year (1954). When the money ran low, she returned to New York and went back to Hunter, determined to get a degree somehow. She was able to get a part-time job as assistant to the librarian in the welfare department, and through her supervisor, who had a strong influence over her, she taught herself to concentrate, eventually receiving a degree from Hunter in 1959. A scholarship for library training school at Columbia University followed, and in 1961, she received a Master of Library Science degree from Columbia. Now she could support her poetry writing.

As her education broadened, the scope of her poetry had encompassed a wider landscape of experience, and she began to receive more acceptance slips than rejection. Her greatest encouragement and first real breakthrough coincided with completion of her Master's: In 1961, Langston Hughes accepted several of her poems for the anthology he was editing, *New Negro Poets, USA,* published by University of Indiana Press in 1962. The next year her work appeared in the British anthology published by Breman, Ltd. of London (1963) and was followed by a succession of appearances in foreign anthologies all during the 1960s: in Holland (*Beyond the Blues,* edited by R. Pool, Hand

& Flower Press, Amsterdam, 1964); Italy, (*I Negri—Poesie E Canti,* published in Rome by Edizione Academia); and finally an International Press anthology. Commenting on this, the poet said, "It was easier to get into anthologies abroad than in the United States." She was also a contributor to *Transatlantic Review.* As the black literary magazines came into being, she was frequently represented in *Black World, Journal of Black Poetry, Harlem Writers Quarterly,* etc.

Lorde lived with women most of the years she was building her career; some were her lovers, others were strictly friends. However, she had always wanted to have children, so when she met Edwin Ashley Rollins, an attorney whom she liked and who wanted to marry her, she decided the time had come (March 31, 1962). "I was married at twenty-nine and divorced at thirty-six," she said. "My husband and I parted amiably. My children were born a year after we were married, eighteen months apart. My daughter is eighteen now; my son sixteen and a half." In her forthright way, she continued, "I make no secret of being lesbian: my children know about it and they understand. I'm very proud of them. My daughter is entering Harvard this fall," she added by way of credential.

The significance she placed on having children is borne out by the number of times that children, her own (Elizabeth and Jonathan) and all children appear in her poetry, the object of her concern and sympathy. For example, at a "Writers for Peace" rally held at the Martin Luther King Labor Center in New York, sponsored by Mobilization for Survival and the War Resisters League on March 2, 1981, the first poem she read contained the line, "Our Wars are being fought/ by our children." Before beginning to read, she urged people in the audience to wear a green ribbon, as she did, to show sympathy for the black children who were being murdered in Atlanta, their bodies thrown into the river. Then she read strong lines written "For Emmet Till, Hacked to Death Whistling in the Street," retelling the story of the early young activist who was cruelly crushed in 1955, his mutilated body found floating downriver, by a poet whom she did not identify:

> *Images flow through my veins*
> *Despair weighs down my voice*
> *Like mud in Pearl River.*

The poem ends, "Emmet Till rises to the crest in Pearl River."

Children loom large in "Equinox," a poem evoked by the first day of spring marked by her daughter; yet it is not at all concerned with the change of season, but rather a recollection of the tragic events that took place the year her daughter was born, 1963, when Audre marched in Washington with thousands of others to protest the killing of six small girls in a church bombing in Birmingham. ". . . that year/ some of us still thought/ Vietnam was a suburb of Korea." Later that year saw Kennedy's assassination, and still later "Malcolm was shot dead/ and I ran to reread/ all that he had written," and as she read, "the dark mangled children/ came streaming out of the atlas/ Hanoi Angola Guinea–Bissau Mozambique Phnom-Penh/ merged into Bedford-Stuyvesant and Hazelhurst Mississippi/ haunting my New York tenement . . ." By then, she tells us, she was pregnant again and "afraid/ for whoever was growing in my belly." The last stanza contains the lines, "Today both children came home from school/ talking about spring and peace/ and I wonder if they will ever know it." When she wrote a description of the memorial service for folksinger Mahalia Jackson—"The Day They Eulogized Mahalia"—she could not resist turning it into a statement of irony, because at the moment Chicago was memorializing Mahalia, six black children burned to death in a South Side day care center, "kept in a condemned house/ for lack of funds." The poem ends, "Small and without song/ six black children found a voice in flame/ the day the city eulogized Mahalia."

The volume in which "Equinox" and the last-mentioned poem

appeared was a National Book Award nominee for poetry in 1974. Entitled, *From a Land Where Other People Live,* it was her third published book. Her first had come out in 1968, a year that marked a turning point in her career. From 1961, when she graduated from Columbia Library School, until 1968 she had held posts as librarian in various suburban and city libraries in New York; but with an award she received from the National Endowment for the Arts in 1968, she began to devote herself entirely to poetry, writing, lecturing (giving public readings), and teaching. That same year (1968) she was visiting professor at Atlanta University for a term, and then poet-in-residence at Tougaloo College in Mississippi. While at the latter, she was a contributor and editor of *Pound,* the literary journal. With the appearance of her initial volume, entitled *The First Cities,* which carried an introduction by Diana de Prima, well-known West Coast poet, and head of Poets' Press, publisher of the book, Lorde's career was definitely launched; but it had taken twenty years of perseverance from the time she sent out her trial poems in 1948.

However, once on her way, Audre Lorde moved rapidly to the forefront of her fellow poets. Dudley Randall, eminent poet, critic, founder and editor-in-chief of Broadside Press, praised *The First Cities* highly as a "quiet, introspective" work, whose "striking phrases" were those of a strong new voice among black poets. "She does not wave a black flag," he continued, "but her blackness is *there,* implicit in the bone." His enthusiasm prompted him to offer publication of a second volume, which led to *Cables to Rage,* published by Broadside in 1970, and was followed by the acclaimed volume mentioned above. As a nominee for the National Book Award, Lorde was sought after as lecturer, poetry reader, teacher (of English, creative writing, and literature). She has taught at Lehman College, John Jay College of Justice, City College of New York, and went back to her alma mater, Hunter College, a full professor. A year on the faculty at City College of New York brought added rewards of friendship with Gwendolyn Brooks, Adrienne Rich, and Muriel Rukeyser. "Adrienne was very helpful to me when I started," Audre recalled. "I met many colleagues through her. Muriel was one of my sponsors when I applied for a Guggenheim that year."

She discovered that she had the ability to hold an audience when she read her poems in her low-keyed yet resonant voice; her words carried authority because they came out of real experiences that evoked real, profoundly felt emotions. At the end of the chilling tale retold in her poem of Emmet Till there was always a moment of silence and then a wild burst of applause. She has become much in demand for appearances throughout the United States, especially popular with student audiences. At the University of Michigan she was one of the three "top drawing-cards" of the poetry series in 1979, with Gwendolyn Brooks and Marge Piercy; all three read to full houses at Rackham Hall, according to Maria Makris-Gouras, assistant librarian of the Avery Hopwood Room at the University, one of the sponsors of the poetry series.

When the Broadside Press was forced to cease publishing, Lorde's poems had little difficulty in finding a publisher. *Coal,* her first volume under the imprint of a general trade publisher, was brought out by W. W. Norton, who also published *Black,* in 1978, and her latest work, *Chosen Poems,* in 1982. A women's press, Spinsters, Inc., published *The Black Unicorn* in 1980, an indication of Lorde's loyalty to her sex as well as to her race. All during the 1960s and 1970s she was active in movements involving the connection between the writer (of poetry or prose) and social responsibility: first the protest marches to end the war in Vietnam, then the equal opportunity drives on behalf of women, blacks—and all minorities, for that matter—besides the continuing efforts to stop the proliferation of nuclear weapons and power plants that threaten to annihilate all people, even the earth itself. Asked in 1981 if these were her reasons for being a member of Mobilization for Survival, she replied, "I'm not a 'joiner,' per se,"—her only professional affiliations are the Harlem Writers Guild and the American Association of University Professors—"but I *know* what we all have to do to survive!" The emphasis on "know" is evidence of her strong convictions. She lists her politics as "Radical"; her religion, "Quaker." Her poem, "New Year's Day" concludes: "I am deliberate/ and afraid/ of nothing." Such is the essence of Audre Lorde's psyche and her poetry.

Marge Piercy

Among the younger poets who rival Adrienne Rich as a militant force in the new feminism, Marge Piercy is a strong and vibrant voice. Her name (which could be symbolic) calls up the image of the pen mightier than the sword, and has become almost synonymous with activism. Her poetry has the flash of steel tempered by the warmth of humanism. A native of Detroit, Michigan, she was born on March 31, 1936, to parents of Lithuanian background, and grew up in their house on Livernois near East Grand Boulevard. In her childhood the neighborhood was largely Jewish, middle class, and fairly stable; but shortly before World War II it began to change. In June, 1943, one of the worst race riots in the history of this century took place in Detroit near the auto factories, where most of the black labor force, imported from the South during the war, lived and worked. After things quieted down, workers and their families began leaving the factory district for other areas, some moving to the fringes of the Boulevard; but the future poet, learning to play a Liszt sonata at age seven, was hardly aware of socio- logical changes. She banged the keys of the upright piano hard to drown out the neighborhood noises.

The houses on their street were built so close together that if the Piercys kept their own mouths shut they could hear the families in the row houses on either side yelling. They could even smell the liver and onions frying in their neighbor's house on one side; and they could hear the hacking cough of the tu- bercular old man who lived six feet away on the other. The music helped soften the harsh sounds and took one's mind off the burning stench from close-by kitchens. When Marge was a very small girl, her mother sang the songs of the Lithuanian Jews to her. Sometimes her grandmother, with whom she slept in a tiny room of their boxlike row house, would join in, chanting the legends. Her grandmother, in an old country custom, drank tea holding a sugar cube between her teeth: "hot boiling/ strong black tea/ from a glass. A gleaming/ silver spoon stood up." So the poet described it long after her grandmother died.

Among other things she remembered from early childhood was the mirror of the twenties vintage that hung in a gilded frame over the secondhand buffet in the dining room, proving that they were "practically middle class," as did the table with claw legs draped in an ecru, crocheted cloth that formed a "cave of genteel lace" for small Marge, who crawled around un- derneath, running her toy car. The mirror was the redeeming feature of their pinched household; when the sun hit its be- velled edge, "rainbows would/ quiver out to stripe the walls/ as sugar candy, pure as/ her cry of hunger at that age." A Depres- sion-baby, she was often hungry during the first few years of her life. The carved frame of the mirror both fascinated and scared her; it seemed like an owl's head, with a predator's eye fixed on her. Her image in the glass, if she happened to glimpse it, was "the starving blue face of that unwanted brat" in her poem, "What the Owl Sees," written much later, when the mirror was the only furnishing that survived that household.

School brought a new life. An exceptionally bright child, Marge Piercy piled up a record of high marks from the time she entered the first grade. Neither of her parents was intellectually inclined; neither had had much formal education, so they were proud of their daughter's report cards, but they were not so pleased with her "gang brat" activity as she reached the upper grades; by then the neighborhood was "mixed," and in the gang wars typical of big city adolescents Marge was always on the side of the underdog. In high school she fought by means of words, on the debating team, in early poems published in the school paper, and in her leadership on committees, working for better conditions in the washrooms, and more female students in class offices. Yet her grades did not suffer because of all her activity, and in her senior year she won a scholarship to the University of Michigan.

Though her tuition was taken care of, the scholarship did not provide for board and room; money was still scarce in the Piercy family, so Marge worked her way through college by waiting on tables and winning awards. In her freshman year she won the Avery Hopwood Award for poetry and fiction; though categorized "minor," it was a major achievement on her part, since freshmen rarely won any Hopwood prizes. And she was fortunate enough to find followers among her classmates so that she could continue her political activity, organizing students to protest against the Korean war—or any war, for that matter. She was one of the first to organize student groups against proliferation of nuclear bombs and nuclear power plants. And she enlisted the girls in her dormitory to join both that and the women's movement, promoting women's rights on and off

Modern American Women Poets

campus. She wanted to live in an apartment so she would not
have to adhere to institutional regulations, but freshmen were
not allowed to live outside the dorm except in a sorority house,
and Marge Piercy scorned sororities and fraternities. She would
not have joined if she could have afforded it, and she had hardly
enough to live on, let alone spend on superficial nonsense and
the snobbishness of sororities. She was considered one of the
brilliant, gifted but dangerous radicals on campus. She was very
persuasive: a dynamic brunette, with a great shock of dark hair,
flashing dark eyes, and a generous mouth from which bursts a
robust laugh; she was—and is—a forceful personality. When
asked during an interview if she and her fellow organizers were
communist based, the laugh became almost a hoot. "The Com-
mies were way to the right of us!" she asserted. "We were the
extreme left—socialism closer to anarchism than communism.
But we were organized; we knew what our goal was, and what
we had to do." As she was to write in a later poem:

> War, long, long war
> How you have shaped me
> like a prevailing salt wind
>
> . . . .
>
> stunting and twisting the pines
> so they gnarl and stoop crooked
> yet stand tough as iron.
>
> War, you old bogey, for how
> many years I have lived in your
> burning entrails.

Farther on in the poem she speaks of "the streets of home/ where
in cameo we fought battles/ aimed at stopping battles/ there, in
the real place."

For all her extracurricular activity, the poet maintained her
high academic average, and her creativity did not lag. In her
sophomore year she won a second Hopwood Award, this time

for poetry alone, and a "Major Award." The following year saw the presentation of Piercy's third award from the Avery and Julia Hopwood Foundation—she was one of the few students to win three successive awards—this final one for literature, a Major Award. She also received a research grant from the Governor's Commission on the Status of Women. During her senior year, she was allowed to live in an apartment, which she shared with two friends working on the project. "I caused so much trouble in the dorm with my ideas I think they were more than glad to give me permission," she commented. She graduated from the University of Michigan in 1957, carrying off, besides her A.B. degree, a scholarship to Northwestern University, from which she received her Masters degree in 1958. Not wanting to return to Detroit and live under her parents' roof or be tied down to a regular job like teaching or copywriting or journalism, she rented a miserable hole of a place—"a rotting molar," she called it—on Wilson Avenue in Chicago, and tried to earn her living as a free-lance writer, concentrating on poetry.

It was a dreary existence, for the most part lonely and frustrating, except when she sold a few verses to the little magazines or worked at the headquarters of the feminist party for more love than money. She managed to squeak by, but it took grit and determination, and there were times when she wondered how long she could endure. As an outlet, she "used to write twenty-two-page-single-spaced letters to friends every week." She labelled them and herself in a poem ironically titled, "Women of Letters." She would type her heart out, "shipping off her dreams, her opinions, her terrors to people who did not bother to read them." Then, in a rhetorical query: "Who wants to get/ a twenty-two-page-single-spaced letter/ from a crazy ranting poetess housed/ in a rotting molar on Wilson Avenue, Chicago,/ with a stench of poverty like overripe cheese." The poem ends with a plea to the multitude of women who burden their friends with tedious letters of endless woe to "Stop writing letters! Stop! We will/ come together instead. . . . It is each other only/ who can save us with gentle attention/ and make us whole."

Eventually she herself grew tired of this fruitless self-applied therapy, tired of life on Wilson Avenue, and when the opportunity came to go to Paris with some of her colleagues in the women's movement, she spent a year or so in the City of Lights, living on the Left Bank, haunting the Cafe des Flores and the Cafe des deux Magots, where all the rest of the literary world, it seemed to Marge, hopefuls of all ages, lingered over a glass of pernod for hours, discussing and arguing the merits of the multiple schools of poetry and politics and painting, mixed in with the latest gossip of the famous figures in the world of art and politics. The situation in Southeast Asia was beginning to look like serious revolt against the French; neither Piercy nor her friends realized that in a few years they would be involved in open protest themselves against the conflict that became a bloody civil war in Vietnam.

After Paris, Piercy lived in Boston, then in San Francisco, where she met, among other sister poets active in the women's movement, the one called "Alda" (the only name that appears professionally on her volumes). These two discovered a kindred spirit between them at once, so they worked well together on any projects that came up in regard to publicity for the feminists. They read and criticized each other's poems. In a few years they began giving readings together, and they were booked as "Alda and Marge Piercy," without punctuation to separate the names. If anyone in the audience mistook them for actual sisters, they didn't mind. It did not happen often, however, for each was a distinct personality.

From San Francisco, Piercy returned East to live in Brooklyn, Manhattan, Boston again, and finally, Cape Cod. A successful career began with the publication of her first volume, *Breaking Camp*. Ostensibly these poems dealt with the physical activity of pulling up stakes, packing, picking up, and leaving a temporary campsite, but on a deeper level they depicted the emotional upheaval of pulling up stakes and breaking away from any place one has lived, whether the attendant memories be good or bad. The book was well received, paving the way for further volumes. Richard Ellman wrote: "Marge Piercy's are courageous poems. . . . *Breaking Camp* affirms poetry, and by extension, *life.*" He spoke of the wide range and varied means of her poems, using internal rhymes, unique images, and straightforward lines, without a feeling of contrivance. "Her work proves that modern poetry can be both compassionate and perceptive, well structured and inventive," he said. Jane Colville Betts added another positive note: "Marge Piercy's poems form a kind of definition of love. She has the eye of a poet."

With such approbation from critics, Piercy was definitely launched as a poet of definite force in contemporary literature. Her first novel was published shortly afterward, and her fiction has kept pace with her poetry. At about the same time, 1961, she met the people with whom she was to form a design for communal living. *Breaking Camp* was followed by *Hard Loving;* next came *4-Telling* (with three of the people close to her: R. Hershon, E. Jarret, and D. Lourie). Then her own, *To Be Of Use* and *Living in the Open.* The titles of her novels were no less graphic; they show the poet speaking in a different medium, as, for example, *Dance the Eagle to Sleep.* The young people of both sexes with whom she shared her life shared her literary, political, and sociological views. They set up a household in the country and began raising their own fruits and vegetables. But by 1964, the agrarian life had to take second place, for, as she said in a much later poem, "the war had begun/to inhabit me/ like a wandering cancer"; and inside of three years: "From 1967 through 1970/ I bought no wine,/ Ashamed of tastes unbecoming/ a guerrilla. I taught nothing/ to anyone but studied/ war in the streets and my garden grew moles and tracts./ Justice held me by the hair/ burning."

Not until the war was over did the poet return to cultivating the land as she had before, along with her political-sociological

activity. Nor did she uncork the bottle of 1961 Chateau Au-
sone, which sparked the poem, "The Rose and the Eagle," a
strong, symbolic poem linking the legend of the vintner Au-
sonius to her own, until the end of the war was in sight. The
last twenty-two lines give a credolike account of her life: "I am
the baby I was screaming/ into the dark, I am the child/ who
sucked her finger,/ I am the gang brat, I am/ the woman who
loved/ every woman and man/ I have loved, I am/ the body I
put on the line,/ the organizer,/ . . .

> I am the woman who fights,
> I am the woman who
> grows roses, I am the woman
> on whose tongue this one
> precious glass of Chateau
> Ausone glows like a velvet
> coal, I am the friend you turn from
> who cannot be used now.
> You want only half
> of me and I
> I want to be whole.

The doer and the dreamer, the activist and the artist equals
Marge Piercy, poet.

She voiced the same sentiments in no uncertain terms when
her fifth volume, *The Twelve-Spoked Wheel Flashing*, published
by Knopf, appeared in 1978: "As I cannot separate the personal and political in my life, as I will not separate emotional
and intellectual judgment and experience but try to weld them,
as I go back and forth from the vital dying city with its wars of
plunder to the vital dying country with its wars of plunder, I
have tried to shape this book as a growth ring, the record of a
year. . . . An issue is as real to me as the apples on my trees,
and that they sometimes have worms in them is political action,
as is loving, as is talking, as is shaping these poems from the
energy that comes through me from and for so many people,

whose lives cross and touch, as we struggle enmeshed, sometimes blind and sometimes seeing and sometimes seeing each
other."

After listing the various cities in which she has lived, Piercy
wrote of her personal life-style: "Now I live mostly in Wellfleet
on Cape Cod with one part-time and two full-time sharers of
land and house. Two days a week I spend in Boston in a house
I share with six adults and a little girl. . . . The house in town
is cohabited by two dogs. The house and land in the country
are inhabited by two cats and a wide variety of fiercely protected animal and vegetable life. We grow all our own vegetables and a fair amount of fruit. About a third of the time I am
on the road. I live off my writing and off traveling and giving
readings and workshops. I am active primarily in the women's
movement but, as the spirit seizes me, in other issues also. My
fifth novel, *The High Cost of Living,* will be out around the same
time as this, my fifth volume of poetry; and I just completed
my first play (with David Ira Wood), *The Last White Class."* By
1981 she and Wood were the only ones sharing the house in
the country. When asked how she felt about marriage, Piercy
said succinctly, "I don't believe in it." She is currently working
on a new book of poems. As usual, several of them have to do
with the revolt of women from the bonds of second-class status
and domesticity. When she and her friend Alda read at the
Manhattan Theatre Club in New York, a packed house cheered
her poem beginning, "All Over America housewives are burning the dinner"; and ending, after repeating the line: "This is
not ineptitude; this is Revolution!"

With the publication of *Circles on the Water, Selected Poems of
Marge Piercy,* in 1982, this sharp-eyed poet celebrated twenty
years of poetry writing, as *The American Poetry Review* pointed
out in review of her volume with Maxine Kumin's recent collection. This prolific poet-novelist is consistent in her creative
energy expressed in both poetry and realistic novels.

Freya Manfred

When Freya Manfred was no more than four years old she showed the unmistakable sign of a poet: a vivid imagination tempered with awareness of the world around her. By her own admission she began writing at that age "probably in imitation" of her father, Frederick Manfred, the noted novelist of the prairie lands. One incident in particular marked small Freya as a potential poet when she refused to finish the food on her plate, and announced to her mother and father that she was "saving it for 'Rall-da'." Her puzzled parents had no idea who "Rall-da" was, but Freya insisted that *she* knew: "He talks to me in the basement all the time."

Freya Manfred

It turned out, as she explained in a footnote to a poem written when she was a senior in college, that the creature was their pump, grinding away in the cellar darkness of their country home near Bloomington, Minnesota. "I thought 'Rall-da' was a good monster, come out of the earth to groan and call to me," she wrote. But her father found a different meaning, a word with a different spelling. An exceedingly tall man, he jumped up from the table, clapping his hands. "That's it! Freya's just named our new home," he said to her mother. "We'll call it *Wrâlda!*" And so it was that the Frisian word for world, or the age of man, became not only the name of her childhome, but in the poem, as in her life, served as a symbol of childhood to the future poet.

The firstborn of her parents, Maryanna (Shorba) and Frederick Manfred, her birth had taken place on November 28, 1944, in Minneapolis; but before she was two years old, they moved to the country because her father felt country living was healthier, a better place to bring up children than the city, besides being a better place for him to write. He himself had grown up on a farm, the son of farmers who had come from the Frisian Islands off the coast of the Netherlands in the 1880s to try their luck at farming in the great mid-West of the United States. It was said that Frisians were the distant but direct descendants of the Vikings, and indeed, Freya's father appeared to prove the claim: he stands six-foot-nine in his stocking feet. He is a lean, large-boned, sensitive, excitable, and exciting man who, as the oldest of five surviving sons, had worked hard with his father and brothers to wrest a meager living out of the land; but longing for learning had far outshone his devotion to the "green earth," the drudgery of farming. Through the church that his religious, God-fearing family attended, he secured a scholarship to Calvin College in Grand Rapids, Michigan, and while still an undergraduate had published poems and short stories. His first novel, *The Golden Bowl*, appeared to critical acclaim the year Freya was born, a good omen; for both brainchild and body-child should benefit each other.

And so they did. Freya was an exceptionally bright baby, long legged like her father, and round faced, like her mother, whose parents had come from Czechoslovakia. Although Freya's coloring, her red-blond hair and fair freckled skin, resembled her Frisian grandmother, Alice, who had died at the early age of thirty-eight after bearing six sons and wearing herself out as a farmer's wife, the planes of the future poet's face were Slavic, like her Grandma Shorba's. Her father claimed she was the image of Grandma Alice, who was six feet tall, strong-minded, but gentle as a saint. Her mother thought she showed more of the Shorba traits, but young Freya, looking up (almost to the ceiling) at her father when he stood beside her, did not care to be like either grandmother—certainly not like Grandma Alice, "too gentle for words, with an eaten-away heart." Rather, she said at ten, she would be the wild creature of some "stormy woodland," living like and with the wild, willful creatures of the forest; or better still, she would be a "fighter, like her Dad, who had licked T.B." after a two-year bout with the dread disease, lying flat on his back in a sanitarium. He had pushed away the "pap!" of hospital food and scared the day nurses into fetching farm fresh eggs for him, with crisp greens to give him strength. He cured himself, and he helped to cure another patient—Maryanna Shorba.

Freya's parents had met at the sanitarium, and when, pronounced "cured," they left, they decided to marry, their health providing a close bond between them. Maryanna Shorba had been a journalist before her illness; she had graduated from college in St. Paul and found a job on a newspaper. After her husband's first novel proved successful enough to warrant his career as a novelist and they moved out to the country, small Freya and later two other children took up most of her time, although she read a great deal and occasionally wrote book reviews. And she helped her husband read proof when the galleys of a new book arrived. By the time Freya was four, her father had had four books published and was well on the way to becoming "established." It was natural for Freya, who knew he "worked each morning on his novels in back of the house," to follow in her father's footsteps at a very early age. She wrote little two-line rhymes and her own tall tales to show her Dad when he came stomping out of his study hungry for lunch after finishing his daily stint.

Both her parents encouraged her; her mother read to her, her father told her stories of the "Siouxlands"—Iowa and the Dakotas—where he grew up; his novels were based on the legends and lore of the Sioux Indians. When they went for walks at sunset, he taught her the names of wildflowers that grew in the long prairie grasses; goldenrod was among the earliest to make a lasting impression. She learned, as if by osmosis, the names of both garden and fieldflowers, the names and habits of the animals, both domestic and wild, that inhabited the prairie lands and woods. Her first friends were animals: at six, a tiny kitten who was blown away by a gale-force wind because Freya had dressed her pet in doll clothes, a ruffled pink dress that served as umbrella to the wind, which scooped up the little bundle, hurling it over the cliff to be dashed to death on the rocks below. When her angry, terrified tears had subsided and she answered her mother's call to come into the shelter of the house and be soothed by "cocoa and a loving lap," Freya still felt a secret response to the rushing wind and pelting rain. She never saw the kitten again. In a poem written at age twenty, she observed, "sometimes I wish it had been me the wind carried/ out into the brawny rain./ I would rather fly wild with fear into thunder/ than wrinkle away my years."

Freya's first real friend, however, was "Eugene V. Debs," a golden retriever, who romped with her in fields of yellow mustard, and protected her from interloping (door-to-door) salesmen, and loved her with his loyal dog's heart, loved her with panting breath and long, slurping tongue on her lips, face, and arms. Though Freya fell in love with those salivary assaults, Debs had to be sold: "He sat on top of me too long, in his virile

way," the poet offered succinctly when she recounted her young
years. And her father explained to his small daughter, "He was
a hunter at heart."

Life was lonely without Debs. Even after her sister Marya was
born, followed in another year by Frederick, her brother, Freya
felt lonely. Her mother was occupied with the babies; her father with his writing. At night Freya cried with longing for "a
friend." It was her mother's mother, Grandma Shorba, who came
to the rescue by offering to pay for a pony, Chita Maria, a little
mare, who came with a silver-studded saddle so Freya could learn
to ride. Later she wrote in a long poem, "That horse was the
first dancing friend/ I loved so much I could have died./ I grew
up/ So I could ride her alone/ Across the Minnesota River."
These lines from "Grandma Shorba and the Pure in Heart," one
of the most personal of the poems dealing with Manfred's early
life, provide a close-up view of the poet's attachment to Chita
Maria, the horse she wouldn't have owned if it hadn't been for
Grandma Shorba. As much as she loved her mother's mother,
Freya suspected her of secret nightly mayhem because she was
so "NICE" to people all day long—and so sympathetic: because she couldn't stand to hear her granddaughter "cry young
honey tears all night" she provided the money for Freya's
"dancing friend."

Complete poems inspired by memories of the little horse
reinforce the feeling of affinity between animal and poet, as in
"Written To Chita, My Red Mare," especially the second stanza:

> She was my friend,
> More friend than any human face;
> Bigger than any pal
> She stood above me;
> Bitter soil stung me when I fell,
> A sheet of wind covered me as I rode;
> I sang off-tune to her,
> And told her jokes I could not tell another;
> Torn are the hairs of her neck that held me to her.
> Torn still is a startled place within me.

Freya Manfred

When Marya and Frederick were old enough to play with, the poet's siblings were also her friends. The three Manfred children played together or with children of the area they came to know at school. They "ran crazy" around the water tower near their house and, naked, through sprinklers on hot summer days. In games of pretend they were Indians, creeping silently "through asparagus trees and clover valleys." Like squirrels, they carried acorns in their cheeks to store in hideaways of their own. All the pastimes, events, and "child-named places" of note appear in "Visit to Wrâlda," a memory-piece in Manfred's first volume; but, with the disillusioned "adult" eyes of a twenty-year-old, the poet would warn her friends, now buying beef or sipping beer in town, not to attempt to return to the once enchanted "child-time land."

Although the volume itself was not published until 1971, most of the poems in *A Goldenrod Will Grow* were written when Freya Manfred was an upper-class student at Macalester College in St. Paul, Minnesota, for which she had received a full academic scholarship from 1962 till 1966 when she graduated *summa cum laude*. Such facts indicate an intellect, a seriousness of purpose often belied by the simplicity of language, the spirit of fun and fancy one finds in these early poems. During these years, she helped to pay her way by working in the college library, and in the summer took jobs as carhop and lifeguard, the latter since she was a class *A* swimmer from the start. She swims with the ease of a gliding swan, the long, smooth strokes of her long arms and legs scarcely disturbing the surface of fresh water lakes. Poems like "The Swim," and "Lake Nubanusit, New Hampshire," are evidence that she is as much at home in the water as on land. "I lie on my back/ in bright threads of moon and water." So the former poem begins. And the second stanza: "I look along the islands of my flesh./ My breasts swell like two jellyfish./ My toes are ten soft withered oysters. . . . I roll over and look down/ toward the warm roots of the lake./ I swim under water,/ nodding my round head/ over a round rock./ I am near sleep." The latter poem was based on an outing she had made to Lake Nubanusit while at the MacDowell Colony, where she had received a residence grant in the summer of 1972. She had driven to the lake with three fellow artists, all male admirers of hers. The three lounged on the sand, "sucking beer" before their swim, but she was eager to try the lake, and so "swam from shore alone," with only a brief backward glance at the men. Conscious that they are watching her she says in the fifth stanza: "I am a water animal/ on watch in the weeds of my hair./ I am a fish and they have poles./ I am a web foot./ They are tooth and nail./ I am the frog's throat bulge./ They are the prongs of stars./ I love them," the sixth stanza opens. They think she is beautiful; she heard them say so across the water. The poem ends with a sensuous imagery: "The salmon-colored flowers of my body open/ and tremble/ in the lake water." Symbol of the womb, water in all its forms comes into the scenario with varied significance in Freya's poems: besides lakes, streams, and ponds, rain is often seen (and heard) in Freya Manfred's poems.

The title of her first volume is taken from the last line of the first poem, "On a Night When Poetry on Paper Gets Us Nowhere," in which the poet throws her work to the four winds, hoping that the oncoming rain will soak it into the earth, and that a month later, from that poetry-fertilized spot, "a goldenrod will grow." The second poem, "The Last Time It Rained Like This," we can actually feel the rain "pummelling" down on the poet as she sits on the porch swing, huddled under a purple blanket, dreaming, until driven indoors; but, all-important to herself and her dreams, in the morning, she sees that the rain has brought "April *new*." Rain and mist prevail on "Memorial Day," when she discovers that her mare, Chita, has borne twin foals, one of which has died; but in the misty dusk, her father leads her back to the swamp, where, under a wild rosebush a brown-red colt, too small to stand, looks at her with shining silver eyes, his tiny bones rattling in proof of survival. This was a wishful-thinking poem, for in reality, told in a later poem, both foals died at birth. Even the bodily function of water is present among her similies: in the aforementioned "The Swim," as her blood "sucks back" she "thins like yellow pee." And in the more intimate "Grandma Shorba . . ." saga she was determined as a small girl to "pee facing the wall like Dad, . . . glancing amiably out the window at the pine trees." expressing not so much a feeling of penis-envy as penis-admiration.

When the attempt to "return to Wrâlda" results in disillusion, the dawn of sexual love replaces it, and in the section titled, "Love at Twenty," containing the poignant, "Moment of Spring," with its moving metaphor, "all my leaves/were still and perfect and lovely/ and then they began, gently,/ very murmurlike, to move." The reader finds awed emotion; and in "Love on the Lake," warmth and humor.

All the water areas of the earth may be found in Manfred's poems, from ponds, streams, rivers, and lakes to the mighty oceans in her latest volume, *American Roads,* which in the long title poem at the end of the book, contains this enigmatic passage: "Two giants sit in two oceans/ and grin at each other/ across the USA./ Knees up around their ears,/ toes in a New Jersey estuary,/ toes in San Francisco Bay,/ they lift a flap of Hwy/ in their fists/ and shake it up and down." And one of the most graphic poems in this volume deals with the giant mammal that has inhabited the oceans for millions of years, and is now an endangered species: "The Whale." It is also a poem of birth, the mystery and hazards of propagation, implying the dangers facing the birth of humans as well.

The poet James Wright, commenting on Manfred's first volume wrote: "There is a secret and proficient music in these poems that sings to itself, like the lake in Minnesota. . . . the Sioux Indians calling it 'the lake that whispers to itself.' This poet goes farther. She listens to herself. She hears the earth itself. Her approach to the earth is so patient and true that, I believe, her response to it, and to herself, will go on blossoming and blossoming. I can hear in her poems something that will outblossom hell itself and help us all to turn it back into earth again. I welcome these poems as I welcome spring."

The quality of being at one with the earth, its waters as well as its green-growing lands, and the creatures, both human and animal, that live within its boundaries, pervades all of Manfred's poetry. And, except for two years when she worked for her Masters degree at Stanford University and as applications analyst at Control Data Corporation in 1967–68, poetry writing has been her main creative concern. Her second volume, *Yellow Squash Woman*, reveals the maturing, emerging person within the poet, fully aware of her womanhood; feminine, but not feminist; positive in her independent outlook, but not political. She doesn't pound, but persuades, seemingly without trying. In a glowing review, Linda Hasselstrom observes that, unlike the Erica Jong—Diane Wakoski school of poets who keep championing women, Freya Manfred's poetic view, "rather than relying on simple stridency, gum-chewing sluttishness or political statements, encompasses the myriad possibilities of woman, including herself." In the title poem she is sensuous, dreamy, quixotic: "I wake this morning/ smoothing my full yellow squash breasts/ and thighs with my hands. If I love him,/ which I will decide any minute,/ I will follow him anywhere,/ even out of the wet ground/ where I grow in sweet gold fits and starts." In "The Dog in the Bar-Room Mirror" she sees herself "as I am, a country hick, pure ham/ and potato spuds and beer. Unabashed/ the toothy grin stands forth, and/ the large breasted body and the childish chin." In yet another mood, she speaks in graphic metaphor: "I unfurl/ like lettuce/ from inside out . . ." Describing "The Girl of My Dreams," she says of herself, "Her brain is amused and wrinkled."

Poet Peter Klappert cites the above line in his enthusiastic review of Freya's poetry. He says in part: "Freya Manfred has perfected a distinct, flesh-and-blood voice that puts her right there in the chair across from you—funny, exuberant, tender, curious, rebuffed, wounded, angry, and *always* disarmingly candid. I don't think I've ever felt the physical presence of a poet as clearly. . . ." He goes on to point out that "the poems have that air of spontaneity that comes only from long loving labor. The few little tics which might be taken for naïvete are nothing of the sort: they are an important part of the psychological music Freya Manfred makes. . . . The poet is immersed in the world *and* in herself. The poems are graceful and expansive." Here he quotes a short lyric cited by several reviewers for its exuberant delight in nature, "One Pine Cone." With utter simplicity she declares: "One pine cone/ can drive me crazy/ when I find it in the woods./ I have to wrap my arms/ around myself/ and hum/ and rock my body/ and watch/ one pine cone/ like a little brown swellfish/ who has thrust out his scales/ to breathe."

Many of Manfred's poems concern men, as a look at her titles alone reveals: "For a Young South Dakota Man"; "The Man Who's No Good"; "The Man I Never Met"; "For the Absent-minded Man"; "I Hate You, You Man"; "Ghost Man"; "The Too-Young All-Man"; and "To The Girl Who Got Her Man"; "To A Hostile Man"; and "Five Praise Poems For A Married Man." Finally, in a delicious spoof, she gives us her opinion—and her mother's—about "Male Poets" in short staccato lines: "My mother/ knows/ about poets./'Oh these poets,'/ she says./ 'Keep away from them.'" The poem continues with Freya's tongue-in-cheek opinion of male poets, and ends quizzically, poking fun at herself: "And what would one/ make of me/ in bed? padding/ my good lines,/ editing my best lines,/ fiercely counting/ my feet?"

The above poems appeared first in Part One of *Yellow Squash Woman,* published by Thorp Springs Press in Berkeley, California, 1976, a year that marked an equally important event—her marriage to writer Tom Pope, at that time becoming known in his present field, filmscript writing. They met through—not at—the MacDowell Colony in a unique manner. By then Freya had become well known in the poetry world as one of the most gifted and accessible young poets. She had taught at the University of South Dakota (1968–71) and had worked with the Upward Bound and Career Opportunities program there in Vermillion; the latter was conducted at the Rosebud Indian Reservation, and the Dakota Indians she came to know often had the same feelings about nature that she did, and, as she said in a jacket note on her first volume, some of her best feelings about "teaching" came from the response she received in her work at the Rosebud Reservation.

For two summers during her undergraduate years she had won the Tozer Foundation Award for independent study in poetry (summer, 1964–65). In the summer of 1965 she also had a residence fellowship at the Wurlitzer Foundation in Taos, New Mexico, where she wrote "Taos Mountain Stream," and poems influenced by the way of life of the pueblo Indians. She also held fellowships at Yaddo, Saratoga Springs, New York, and at the MacDowell Colony in Peterborough, New Hampshire, in 1972, 1973, and 1975. During her residence there in 1973, a documentary film of the Colony was made, and since Freya Manfred is both beautiful and photogenic, she appeared in a number of sequences. Among those at an early viewing was Tom Pope, who had been a Colony fellow earlier, and had not met Freya. But he was so taken with her from the photography that he determined to meet her. They were introduced through the mails by composer-musicologist Philip Ramey, who had been at the Colony when the film was made, and knew the poet well. After an exchange of very few letters, Freya and Tom arranged to meet, and before the year 1976 was out, on October 2, they were married in an outdoor ceremony at Blue Mound Park, near Luverne, Minnesota, where Freya's parents lived. The serene "Wedding Song" in her latest volume is a touching tribute to the marriage. With eloquent simplicity she voices her own vows:

> *I will*
>
> *live with you*
> *blessed*

Freya Manfred

with reason
and rhyme.

Say with you
worlds unsaid;
pray with you
for plain words.

   .   .   .   .

Wing over wing
wrap you
to my breast
at evening.

   .   .   .   .

Wish for wish
wake you,
want for want
take you.

The last but not the least promise is:

Old song after old song,
I'll sing for new weather—
sing of new shapes
for unchanging love.

The couple went to live in California, their first home an old "fisherman's hut" in Goleta, by the Pacific. It was here that the poet from the prairie began to learn the habits of deep sea creatures and formed the idea for the poem on whales, besides poems about the ocean itself. From Goleta they moved to Ojai, and here, in August of 1980, at the same time *American Roads* came out, twin boys were born to Freya and Tom; they were named Rowan and Bly—the latter after poet Robert Bly, a close friend of Freya's family. The boys bear the surnames of both parents, Manfred-Pope. As in the case of their mother's birth, body-children and brainchild have flourished.

American Roads reveals the maturing Manfred in greater measure than *Yellow Squash Woman*. Her poet's eye encompasses the whole country as she observed it on her trips back and forth by car in her capacity as Poet-in-the-Schools during the years from 1972 to 1979, in states ranging from Massachusetts to California. The poems in the third of this four-part book are the intensely personal stories of the Manfred family contained in her second volume. As in "My Basketball Brother Versus Windom," written with an objectivity that allows the reader to share the varying emotions of her parents, her own sibling loyalty and tenderness toward her brother, devoid of sentimentality, lightened by subtle laughter, so in *American Roads,* the poet gives a graphic account of her reactions to the regions, and, more importantly, to the people she meets as she speeds over the roads from one destination to another. Like the rapid reels of a movie camera, the poem presents a montage of America.

Although one critic complained that the views were too sketchy, fragmented glimpses of the poet's responses, most found it diverting and perceptive. *Publishers Weekly* wrote: "The long title poem is a free-wheeling, associative description of driving across America with scattered memories of sights, the poet herself feeling like a vast map." To quote her verbatim in lines near the end: "I am a map,/ snapped back into myself,/ filling with stadiums of people,/ lines, teams,/ choruses of people." The implication is that the poet identifies with the earth and its inhabitants.

She may become depressed at times, as she has through anxiety and worry over the incurable illness of her brother, who, at the age of thirty is dying of kidney disease. The poet's concern became so great that in June 1983, she and Tom, who had tired of writing for Hollywood, moved to Minnesota with the twins to be near the Manfred family. As might be expected, Freya's most recent poems are concerned with death: her lines are darker in tone than previously. Nevertheless, she maintains a philosophic attitude and is able to write both poetry and prose, working on her second novel.

Freya Manfred's lyrical affirmation of life is a definite contribution to contemporary poetry.

Carol Muske

Like Freya Manfred, Carol Muske comes from Minnesota, where she was born on December 17, 1945, in St. Paul; and she, too, is of Czech origin on her mother's side, and partially Germanic-Scandinavian on her father's. However, the similarity between the backgrounds of these two poets has no bearing on their respective work. Indeed, considering the fact that both their maternal and paternal ancestries are so much alike, the contrast in the poetry of Manfred and Muske is amazing, and points up the individuality of each poet.

Carol Muske, according to her first volume, *Camouflage,* claims to regard her poetry "as a kind of protective coloration," and it

Carol Muske

is true that the reader catches only brief glimpses of her personal life, often obliquely, as in the title poem: not until the last stanza does the poet reveal herself, troubled, transforming her outer self into "a new species" to conceal the suffering of her inner being. There is a sense of power, of passion held in check by strong emotional control, by restraint in revealing all, which in turn lends an aura of mystery to her poems, luring the reader to return a second and third time to discover the full meaning. As a result, one experiences a feeling of suspense and drama in her lines such as is never found in the outpourings of so-called "confessional" poetry.

For example, a poem entitled, "Coral Sea, 1945," concerns the advent of her emergence from her mother's womb, designated, "For my mother," and told in terms of the circumstances just prior to her actual birth a week later. After descriptive passages of her mother's walk to the beach during the final stage of pregnancy; of the tropical waters whose reef holds "a small fleet awaiting the end of the world"; and an imaginative passage of strange sights and events occurring in the Coral Sea, the poet draws a parallel between these unbelievable scenes and the equally unbelievable image of herself in the final stage of gestation, her body burning inside her mother's, "in the coral sea/ near the reef of her lungs." The poem concludes: "In the year the war ended/ the world opened,/ ending for me/ with each slow tremor/ cold/ invisible as snow/ falling/ inside the volcano." The last line is a reference to one of the unbelievable things cited in the above-mentioned passage, and is a striking evocation of the strange, stressful, mysterious, and awesome phenomenon of birth.

In her childhood, small Carol attended a primary parochial school of the Catholic church, called "School of the Holy Spirit." Designated, "For Sister Jeanne D'arc," a poem entitled, "Worry," depicts the little six-year-old girl carrying the first lilacs to the teacher she always was to call "John Dark," to her an ominous-sounding name. As a confirmed Catholic, she had been taught,

321

and believed that Christ would hold up the fallen; but at six, she lay awake worrying about the bough that breaks in the traditional lullaby. And carrying the lilacs wrapped in a cocoon of gauze, she worried for fear their necks would break before the bouquet was safely in the nun's hands. There were other classroom concerns to trouble a sensitive six-year-old, but Sister John Dark never knew; in a way it was heaven-on-earth to present the limp lilacs to her revered teacher, but somehow the posibility of danger lurked behind the "Dark."

At eight, in the company of twenty bored girls about her age, Carol took toe dancing from an elderly erstwhile Russian prima ballerina, who attempted to teach, through a vale of tears, in a Minneapolis basement studio, the art she had lost when a cab crushed her great toe eons before, in Dubrovnik. It is her story that the poet tells in a few tense stanzas, evoking the sympathy of the reader for the sad one who weeps as she sips brandy while instructing her pupils, sometimes "nodding when the needle stuck/ on a crack in *Romeo and Juliet*." The pathos of the poem entitled, "Swansong," is heightened by the neutral note at the end: "Those days we stood on ceremony:/ mute sisters of the dance, we froze/ holding second position till six/ when the mothers came."

There were many scenes that left a mark, but the one that made an indelible impression on Carol Muske as a child was the sight of a prison—Stillwater Prison in St. Paul. She was no more than eight or nine when, on a Sunday afternoon drive, her father pointed out to the children the huge fortresslike structure holding the state's criminal offenders behind bars. Formidable, gray, and dreary, it produced in Carol a feeling of horror mixed with sympathy for people locked up behind those walls. The picture of that grim place remained in her mind, and was to become an influence in one of the engrossing, rewarding interests of her adult creative life.

She began to feel the urge to write poetry when she entered Our Lady of Peace High School, which had a remarkably broad program in literature and the arts. Her first poems appeared in the high school publication, and by her junior year she was poetry editor, then editor of the paper. She read poetry avidly, from the classics to the romantics and the moderns, and tentatively tried her hand at her own verses, encouraged by the sisters in the English department. At graduation, they urged her to continue her studies of literature in higher education. Unfortunately, Creighton College in Nebraska, to which Carol was sent with one of her brothers who was studying engineering, placed more emphasis on science than the arts; and as a result, there was a hiatus in her poetry writing.

However, she did make an important alliance, one that influenced both her life and work. She fell in love and became engaged to Edward Healton, a pre-med student majoring in neurology, tendrils of which eventually found their way into the poet's lines. Through Edward's sisters, who lived in California, she learned that the State University of San Francisco had an excellent program in English and creative writing, and persuaded her parents to let her go there for a Masters degree. It was a fortuitous choice: her advisor for her Master's thesis was Kay Boyle, then teaching at Berkeley, but connected with San Francisco State. Still the rebel and champion of many causes as well as free verse in modern poetry, Kay Boyle was then involved with the protest movement against the Vietnam War; she was as outspoken as the vociferous Berkeley students and did not hesitate to join the marches. Besides critical advice on Muske's Master's thesis, she gave the young poet a strong sense of social consciousness, which in a few years was to bear fruit in a different area.

Following graduation, Carol had an opportunity to go to the University of Paris on a student visa, and her father, as a present, made it possible for her to accept. She was there a year, taking courses in French language and literature, and for a time was a member of the travelling company of "Hair," which toured Europe and Russia. On her return, she decided to stay in New

York, city of excitement and center of the publishing world. Edward was entering his internship in neurology at Columbia Presbyterian Hospital, and the thought of going back to Minnesota was inconceivable. New York was in the throes of the turmoil over Attica in 1970–1971, and the poet, remembering Stillwater, was immediately drawn into the struggle for rehabilitation of the unfortunate prisoners fighting for the right to regain some kind of a decent life, to express their feelings as human beings, and not to be treated as animals in an iron cage.

"*Attica* was more than a prison uprising," Muske said in 1982. "It was an organized movement—a metaphor signifying prison reform as a matter of principle." Joining the general surge of poets and writers who were sympathetic to the prisoners' cause, she conceived the idea of starting a poetry workshop at the Women's House of Detention on Riker's Island. She received permission from the court authorities to carry out her plan; but opposition unexpectedly came from the matrons, who seemed to resent the poet's presence as an intrusion of their territory, a threat to their authority. One of them tried to discourage Carol with hard-nosed prison warden logic. "Most of those girls can't even read or write," she said. "They're not going to turn out for some poetry class." But Carol argued, "I think they will. Let me put the notice up on the bulletin board and we'll see. . . ."

The matron agreed grudgingly, and the response was almost a complete turnout of the inmates. They came bringing diaries, notebooks, letters, filled with their attempts at self-expression, eager for instruction. The trial project was so successful it received support from the National Endowment for the Arts, New York Council for the Humanities, Poets and Writers, other organizations and foundations, and expanded to include all the arts. First called "Free Space," the title was changed to "Art Without Walls," extending to classes in poetry, fiction, graphic arts, dance, and videotape throughout the New York State prison system. Eighteen New York prisons formed an "inside circuit" for a lecture series on location to discuss prison reform from sentencing to cell conditions, the victimless crimes (drugs and gambling), and the overall subject of "Women and Violence." Among those who took part in the program were Adrienne Rich, Toni Morrison, and several other colleagues in the world of modern poets active in the feminist movement.

It was inevitable that the absorbing task of teaching poetry to prison inmates evoked poems of her own, some of which were published in Carol Muske's first volume, which did not appear until 1975. In the meantime, she was married to Edward Healton, and hired by Daniel Halpern, poet and editor of *Antaeus,* as his assistant after several of her poems appeared in the magazine. Her marriage to Edward did not work out, but they parted amiably, and are still friends. And the influence of his profession on her poetry is readily apparent in her imagery, not only in her first volume—which was dedicated, "For my mother and father For Daniel and . . . For Edward"—but in her second, *Skylight,* published by Doubleday; and even in her scheduled third, *Wyndmere,* one finds references to the basic structure of the body, with emphasis on the nervous system. In "War Crimes," dealing with the love-hate syndrome of war, she speaks of "the great nerve/ which runs from head to pelvis/ which makes us courteous/ shy/ scrupulous/ makes us touch one another with gentleness," turning the tortured victim of war toward pity for his torturers through the power of "the brain in the body." The "great nerve" then would tremble "till it was plucked," as if hot, held in pliers then in fire; in conclusion, "shriveling in that little violence/ of heat and light/ which in another form/ we often refer to/ as love." The striking metaphor of the poem, first published in *The New Yorker,* caused more than one reader to comment on its unique, strong character. The words "bone," "muscle," as well as "nerve" (or "nerves") appear often in Muske's lines.

"Fireflies," the poem that follows "War Crimes," is marked, "For Edward Healton," and was obviously written when they were separating. It speaks of the pain between them, and says, "Your hands that heal/ can't make us whole again." For an instant, the sky above them had "exploded in a shower of cold light from a nation of fireflies," like a brief, blatant reminder of "the old spark/ of nature's love." And then the sky over Vermont, where they had come on an emergency, was suddenly dark. On this dim note, presaging a dark future for further life together, the poem ends. There are other instances of references to this brief marital union and its dissolution, notably the title poem, "Skylight," which seems to symbolize the reach for happiness that never materialized. "Ex-friend, there's an elevator/ that never stops rising," a ladder that leads to the sky beyond "the scaffold of passion," are all figures indicating a rueful loss.

Skylight is offered "for Curtis Catherine Ingham and Thomas Lux," two people who were closest to her during the trying period of separation and divorce from Edward. Poet Lux, whose work bears the mark of muscular metaphor, directness of statement, and wry humor, was among the kindred spirits Carol met at the MacDowell Colony, where she received residencies in 1973 and 1974; she shared her life with him for a time. Both secured teaching posts to finance their poetry writing. Besides continuing as co-director of the Art Without Walls Program in New York State prisons, Carol Muske has taught or held the post of visiting lecturer at the New School for Social Research, New York University, YMHA Poetry Center, Columbia University, University of New Hampshire, George Washington University, and the University of California at Irvine, in the Graduate Creative Writing Program. She has received awards from the National Endowment for the Arts, the New York State Council on the Arts, The Poetry Society of America (the Alice Fay di Castagnola Award for a manuscript-in-progress), and has had her poetry published in anthologies as well as the leading literary magazines. She has given many readings at main universities.

Carol Muske

The daily life of two poets may have proved a strain, although there was no actual rivalry between Carol Muske and Tom Lux; each admired the other's work and was willing to accept criticism. For whatever reason, however, they separated after little more than a year together. And soon after her appointment as visiting poet at Irvine in California, she met and fell in love with actor David Dukes, who was equally drawn to the poet. With her large, expressive hazel eyes, the broad planes of her face, her slightly retroussé nose above a long lip of her well-formed mouth, Carol Muske is an extremely attractive young woman. She has the eloquence of a dramatic actress in her features, yet when she smiles it is the smile of a sunny-tempered, loving little girl. She can be vivacious yet meditative in the space of half an hour. She laughs easily, but when concerned about someone or some cause she is fighting for, she becomes formidably serious.

It was not long before she and David decided to cast their lot together; their professions complemented each other and were regarded with mutual admiration by both of them. One of the leading poems in Muske's third volume, *Wyndmere*, entitled, "White Key," first published in the 1982 summer issue of *The American Poetry Review*, is marked "for David," and contains several passages that reveal the core of their harmonious relationship, not the least of which stated in a few words: "You're sure/ of yourself, friend, and I like that." A poem of evaluation, of meditation during a plane flight—another frequent theme of this poet's work—it asks the question, "What do we deserve on this earth?" and answers (in italics) *"Not to be lied to by the mind:* the body bent/ by that conscious wind into habits of the cage." As the plane hovers above its landing site, she observes: "We wake up so few times in our lives./ The wheels touch—we lean up into love,/ *white on white,* a key unseen/ in a cylinder of entry. . . ."

In another poem, "Afterwards," the poet derives philosophic import from a comparison of two plane flights, the first short but rough, the second long but smooth, yet she did not fall asleep as she had during the first, because she was no longer in the arms of her beloved: each had to take a separate plane to "opposite ends of the country." It is only "afterwards" that the poet is able to analyze the cause and effect on her psyche of those two flights, and observes, "It has something to do with the power of loss,/ how it opposes itself at the last moment./ . . . how falling together/ our lives seemed the only constant objects in the sky, how impossible it seemed that thin air/ would ever begin to displace us."

Carol Muske and David Dukes were married on January 29, 1983, and the following fall a daughter was born, to whom they gave the first name Anne, and the surname of both parents, Muske-Dukes, thus preserving the identity of the poet as well as the actor.

In "Panus Angelicus" and "Coming Over Coldwater"—also published in *The American Poetry Review* prior to her third volume—Muske views with maturity some of the liturgical lessons learned by rote in primary school. By herself in Italy, the sight of a man selling *pani d'angeli*—bread of angels—recalls her childhood when they learned it in Latin: *Panis angelicus,* the host they "balanced on their tongues till it didn't seem like swallowing God." They would ask a blessing on their swallowing, but only now, as an adult, is the poet, as she admits, "learning patience, struggling each day/ to swallow what I'm given and, in that order, to bless it." "Coming Over Coldwater," a metaphysical poem, reveals the religious thought pattern of the poet while she is driving alone across Coldwater Canyon in California at night, again recalling the lessons and customs of school days, like swearing off sweets, then eating with extra delight at "Lent's end." And only then does she realize the significance of Christ's promise of Paradise to the good thief, and his murmuring, "Sitio"—I thirst—still desiring life, still drinking in the earth. She relates it to her own desire for "cold water/ and light, love preserved as Paradise." It serves as a signal to her to "hit the low beams" to preserve her life as she drives out of the canyon.

It is this blending of the physical with the transcendental that distinguishes Carol Muske's poetry. She can be pragmatic and mystical in her attitude toward life, and it is this ability to transform the small incidents of daily living into matters of consequence that infuses her lines with force and an element of surprise in her imagery. It is this distinctive quality that caused Carrolyn Kizer to write: "On a dark day, when I've read too much, and all the poets start turning into each other, I like to think about Carol Muske, who only turns into more wonderful versions of herself. Her dazzle and virtuosity are one of a kind: Mozartean. That's as high as I know how to go." Such enthusiasm from a fellow poet and critic who is well qualified to judge is obviously justified. And the applause of audiences whenever Carol Muske makes a public appearance at leading universities and libraries across the country accents the accolades of her peers. Here is a young poet whose bright future is undoubtedly assured.

Nikki Giovanni

O ne of the angry black poets who came to the fore in the late sixties, Nikki Giovanni, has also been called the "Princess" of black poetry because of her regal attitude toward her race in championing its right for real equality for every individual: she was a strong advocate of individualism during a period when the trend in the black community was away from individualism toward the mass. At the same time, she realizes the necessity for universal recognition of the talent that lies in her race for achievement in the artistic, scientific, and political worlds—for the wealth of love to be found in the individuals who comprise it. If there appears to be a dichotomy in her thinking it is because this poet is as realistic as she is idealistic: she understands that changes are won by both individual pragmatism and functional unity. To comprehend the apparent duality in her credo, one must examine her background and early years.

Nikki Giovanni was born in Knoxville, Tennessee in 1943, but soon after her birth her family moved to Lincoln Heights, Ohio, locally known as "Black City," just outside Cincinnati. It was here that the future "revolutionary" poet of the sixties grew up, surrounded by a family of college-educated social workers, whose loving care and belief in her genius is responsible for the emphasis of family in her work. As a child she was often ill, and her family sheltered her from the rigors of public school; she was especially attached to her grandmother, who took care of her a good deal of the time. A quick learner, young Nikki finished her schoolwork much faster at home than it was done in the classroom, and, as she said, her "poetry evolved out of a frustration with short stories," which she tried to write at an early age. Her grandmother, like her parents, encouraged her in all her attempts at writing, whatever the form. But as she said in 1976, "The poetry eventually worked much better than anything else I was doing."

With her facility for grasping elementary education, she was able to enter Fisk University at the age of sixteen, but like Edna Millay years before at Vassar, Nikki paid little attention to rules and regulations, and within a few months she was suspended for leaving campus without permission; the fact that she was going to visit her grandmother who was ill made no difference to the administration office: a rule must not be broken. Disgusted with such rigidity, she abruptly left college, and for the next three years, with her parents' consent, she travelled on her own, and became "sensitized," to use her word. When she finally decided to return to Fisk, with raised consciousness, she enrolled in John Oliver Killens's creative writing workshop, a study that changed the direction of her poetry and her life.

Up to that time she had taken her cue from her parents, who, though well educated, well read in current literature, were actually quite conservative. It was only natural for Nikki, growing up in an atmosphere of general acceptance toward the established system, to follow the lead of her parents, whom she loved and admired; as she put it with some exaggeration: "I went from Ayn Rand reading and Goldwater thinking to the Black Movement as practised in John Killens's workshop at Fisk." That workshop opened her eyes to aspects of her race and herself as a member of that race that she had never seen or fully comprehended before. She began to write poetry of a very different sort than she had been, edited the college magazine, and graduated with high honors, at the age of twenty-four, in 1967, the apex of the black revolution. The poems written during this early period of her involvement pound out the "black" concept with the rhythmic insistence of a religious chant: "Black Feeling, Black Talk/ Black Judgement," printed in italics, repeats the key word "black" used as both adjective and noun, over and over, as if to implant its new meaning in regard to her people in her own mind as well as the reader's. Besides chant-rhythm, she included the vernacular in lines following stanzas of academically correct English. The jargon of the street people certainly heightens the impact in a poem like "The Great Pax Whitie," which denounces the white system of segregation, of persecution, and death to all non-whites. The tone is mock-biblical: "In the beginning was the word/ and the word was/ Death/ And the word was nigger/ And the word was death to all niggers/ And the word was death to all life/ And the word was death to all/ peace be still . . ." After another stanza dealing with genesis—of life, death, and war—and a repetition of the be-still-peace refrain, and, "In the name of peace/ They waged the wars," the reader comes upon the line: "Ain't they got no shame?" Its variant in answer: "Nah, they ain't got no shame" after every instance of injustice, needless war, religious and racial persecution becomes a second refrain in street language; a third is; "Ain't we never gonna see the light?" And toward the finale of this epiclike poem, the three refrains are brought together—after a reference to the assassinations of both black and white leaders in the sixties—to end the poem with great impact: "and my lord ain't we never gonna see the light/ The rumblings of this peace must be stilled/ be still/ be still" An unexpected thrust comes with the closing lines:

> *Ahh, Black people*
> *ain't we got no shame?*

It is a call to revolution, to cry out against the death deeds of the centuries committed by whites against blacks.

Following her graduation from Fisk, the poet, who had edited college magazines, returned to Cincinnati and found a job as editor of *Elan,* a literary publication. A year later, when she was twenty-five years old, Nikki Giovanni decided it was time for her to have her own family, and so, whether by coincidence or family planning, her son Thomas was born in 1968, the same year her first brainchild, *Black Judgement,* appeared, published by Broadside Press, then newly established in Detroit by Dudley Randall. The poet once told an interviewer who questioned her about Tommy's birth, "I had a baby at twenty-five because I wanted to have a baby and I could afford to have a baby. I did not get married because I didn't want to get married and I could afford not to get married." A definitive, feminist answer that prevented further probing of her private life. Like Muriel Rukeyser's son, Thomas carries his mother's family name, which Giovanni always explains quite simply, "It just means that *our* slave masters were Italian instead of English or French." This, too, usually puts the quietus on any more inquiries.

Tommy became the focal point of the poet's busy life. She wanted her son to know the same sort of loving care that she had been given as a child. Like Gwendolyn Brooks, Nikki Giovanni has happy memories of her childhood. Her parents, like Brooks's, had a struggle to make ends meet, but they always managed to celebrate Christmas and the birthdays of their two children, Nikki and her sister Gary, with secret preparations and surprise presents, so that those days became events to look forward to, and happy memories. If her parents quarreled—again like Brooks's—it was over finances; but in the Giovanni household, the arguments were complicated by the fact that "Gus," Nikki's father, who held down three jobs at one point, was always trying to increase their income further by various investments that failed, or he would have to sell treasured stock to make the mortgage payments; then he would be depressed, and turn to drink. But it didn't matter so much because everybody was together; they were a family, and though there might be differences of opinion and disapproval, there was always love, a strong feeling that gave richness to the poorest home. A key phrase in "Nikki-Rosa" contains words that became famous in connection with Giovanni: "Black love is Black wealth," and from a number of poems in her early volumes, *Black Feeling, Black Talk,* (1968, Broadside Press); *Black Judgement* (1969, B. Press); and in 1970, her first hardcover by a major publisher, William Morrow & Co., under the triple title,* this poet is concerned with love, family love and relationships, as much as she is with the oncoming "Black Power through Revolution." Poems like "Nikki-Rosa" (above) and "Woman Poem," and "Knoxville, Tennessee," all contain recollections of happy moments in her childhood in contrast to polemic poems like "The Present Dialogue between Black vs. Negro," which begins, "Nigger/ can you kill/ can you kill/ can a nigger kill a honkie?" an idiomatic chant presenting a call to action, action against acceptance of white supremacy; or, "Our Detroit Conference—for Don Lee," another chantlike poem, employing a play on the words "bitter" and "black" to display the deep resentment felt by the people of her race in regard to the injustices of the past.

It was this combination of compassion and passionate rage

Black Feeling, Black Talk, Black Judgement

and militant protest that made Giovanni's poetry so appealing to her generation, inspiring them to write poetry of their own. They could identify with her "Black feeling, Black talk," spoken with bold, brave brash humor, as well as with her "Black Judgement," a stern indictment of "Whitey's" treatment of her race in the past. The two volumes published by Broadside Press brought her immediate recognition and led to countless invitations from colleges and universities for readings and lectures, besides publication in hardcover. As early as 1970, Orde Coombs wrote in his introduction to *We Speak as Liberators: Young Black Poets,* an anthology he collected and edited, published by Dodd, Mead & Company before Giovanni's first hardcover volume appeared: "It will be noticed that established names such as Don L. Lee, Mari Evans, Carolyn Rogers, and Nikki Giovanni appear. These poets are still young and modest and brilliant. They may oppose my calling them 'established,' but they will be hard put to deny the effect they have had on the other poets whose works appear in this collection. It was they, really, who forced many black poets to ask their colleges by what yardstick they were to be considered educated. And having forged their identities—painfully and at great cost—they compelled others to finely chisel theirs."

Nikki Giovanni forged her own identity painfully perhaps, but with great determination. She had left home with her infant son to set up her own household in New York City when she was offered a job as consultant and contributing editor to *Encore* magazine by publisher-editor Ida Lewis, who became her close friend. The poet's success, once she had been launched, was phenomenal. In ten years she produced thirteen books—a variety of writing that includes poetry, autobiography, "raps" with James Baldwin and Margaret Walker (released also on records), besides extensive travel for readings and lectures. In all she did she took into consideration her son.

She early established a regime for herself that would be backbreaking for a far more robust body than hers appeared to be.

When Tommy was small, she would be up in their three-bed-room apartment on the Upper West Side of Manhattan by six A.M., get him off to school nearby, do her household chores or shop until late morning, and then write most of the afternoon, at least until Tommy came home from school. After he went to bed she might work until dawn, depending on her deadlines. When she is on tour her son stays with a secretary, but from the time he was a small boy she took him with her to visit her parents, who had been aghast at the idea of their daughter, an "unwed mother," trying to bring up a child by herself, but they soon saw that she was entirely capable of parenthood as she had learned from them both the positive and negative aspects of it. One morning when she and Tommy were going toward the el-evator, he stopped halfway there and said, "Carry me." Switch-ing her constantly carried briefcase from her right arm to the left, Nikki picked him up. But she warned him, smiling, "If you aren't a good father, I'll brain you." Ida Lewis, who wrote the foreword to *My House,* Giovanni's second volume, noted that Nikki never said good husband or good provider, but "broke it down to a basic," as Ida wrote. Tommy had responded com-placently by putting his thumb in his mouth; he was used to his mother's hyperbole; from infancy he had been given the se-curity of her loving care. The two were partners in meeting life's challenge.

The poet did not spend time fretting about the way things looked to the outside world. The poem, "Categories," in the same volume, opens, "sometimes you hear a question like 'what is your responsibility as an unwed mother?' "—a question she does not even deign to answer in the lines that follow, except to say that she is "bored" with categories. Whenever possible, Tommy went with her: she had taken him to Africa when she and Ida suddenly decided to make a journey to the land where many "Afro-Americans" went in search of their "roots." Like her older colleague, Gwendolyn Brooks, and her contempo-rary, Alice Walker, Giovanni's poems reveal a feeling of ambiv-

alence about Africa because of the inequities she found in predominantly black Nigeria and Ghana, which, she had thought,
would mean a homecoming, as it had seemed when they landed.
However, she wanted Tommy, small as he was, to see the long-
ago home of his ancestors, just as she wanted him to know her
parents, and the story of her grandmother.

She had written a starkly realistic account of the death of her
grandmother, published by Bobbs-Merrill in 1971 with the
ponderously long title, *Gemini: An Extended Autobiographical
Statement*—a poetic prose piece written from the heart, containing tenderness and nostalgia as well as the outrage she felt
at the suffering her grandmother had been forced to bear. Ida
Lewis commented of this personal document: "In *Gemini* she
raked her emotions bare to write of the death of her grandmother. . . . knowing that neither she nor her mother would
ever be able to read that essay without crying, without wondering if more could have been done. In talking over the question with her friend, Nikki would always conclude, "But it's
important for Tommy to know."

It was even more important that he should know and love
her parents, should have the same strong sense of family feeling
that she did. "Mothers," a wise and witty poem in *My House*,
clearly illustrates how closely she associates family with love, at
the same time asserting her independence. The first stanza portrays her easy relationship with her mother: "the last time i was
home/ to see my mother we kissed/ exchanged pleasantries/ and
unpleasantries pulled a warm/ comforting silence around/ us and
read separate books . . ." The poem then narrates a childhood
scene: the first time the poet "consciously" saw her mother, when
that "beautiful lady" was sitting in the darkened kitchen of their
three-room apartment with the moonlight streaming in on her.
Noticing Nikki standing in the doorway, she bade her come near
and taught her an old religious rune about the moon. The last
stanza reads: "i taught it to my son/ who recited it for her/ just
to say we must learn/ to bear the pleasures/ as we have borne

the pains" (Giovanni rarely uses punctuation or capitals.)

Tommy became an integral part of the Giovanni family. He was literally as well as figuratively his mother's partner as early as 1970, when the poet formed a small firm, Niktom Ltd., obviously a merger of her first name with that of her two-year-old son, to publish her *Poem of Angela Davis*. Niktom Ltd. was also involved in the release of Atlantic Records discs, "Like a Ripple on a Pond," 1973, and, "The Way I Feel," 1975, but not in releasing Right On Records. The same year that *My House* appeared, 1972, Wilberforce University in Ohio, Black America's oldest institution of higher education, established in 1856, conferred an honorary doctorate of humanities on Nikki, to her vast and happy surprise. With wonder and delight she read the letter to Ida and a group of their close friends. The only hitch was that she had accepted a speaking date in a small Pennsylvania town the night before the ceremony, so getting to Wilberforce on time would be tricky. Her first thought was to make sure Tommy would be there: she sent him out to Ohio with his babysitter a day early, notified her parents, sent her friends out early, while she herself was on the road all night long; but she made it on the dot, falling into line minus cap-and-gown with the honor guard as they were marching into the hall.

Triumphant and happy, she stood behind the lectern moments later to give her acceptance speech, facing the overflow crowd of students with easy familiarity. "See what my motherfuckers got me," she began impishly, laughing. Her father, sitting in the front row, looked shocked, but the seniors gave her the first of four standing ovations—she spoke their language! And when she became serious, giving them straight from the shoulder advice, they were no less enthusiastic. She urged them to do what was important the *way* they felt was important, and not to be trapped by the past of their people or by their personal hopes for the future. And they listened and loved her.

It was this quality of being able to identify with her audiences and inspire them to acts of their own volition that has made Nikki Giovanni so popular and well loved by her people. Not that she is a fiery revolutionary; indeed, after her initial polemic volumes, her poetry is less controversial and more pragmatic, though no less compassionate, as her titles indicate: two slim paperbacks published just before *My House,* are *Re-Creation* and *Spin a Soft Black Song* (1970 and 1971).* Only a few controversial subjects are to be found in *My House;* one, "Homosexuality," nonracial, makes short shrift of that debatable matter: "homosexuality . . ./ is two people/ of similar sex/ DOING IT/ that's all" she concludes with finality. And for some reason this poem was omitted from the paperback edition issued by Morrow in 1972. In 1973, *Ego Tripping and Other Poems for Young Readers* appeared; of the title poem she says, "I love 'Ego Tripping' 'cause it's a happy poem, but if it's not useful I want my readers to feel free to reject that and choose something else." But her readers, especially the young ones, took it to their hearts. Her next book, *The Women and the Men,* in 1975, is obviously concerned with a universal problem, devoid of racial differences. One poem, "Mother's Habits," likens her own problems to her mother's, forging the link between generations. She felt the sexual generation was going to be crucial, she told Ida one day. "Why shouldn't a man learn to take care of children?" she demanded. The black activists, the big warriors, simply had to realize that the real war was over on the playground, and that they must relate to "black kids." At the same time, they must understand that women understand they are men. Yet Nikki has never married, nor revealed who Tommy's father is.

Her latest volume, *Cotton Candy on a Rainy Day,* is designated, "For Gus," her father, and the poem, "Gus (for my father)," is an affectionate portrait of her parent; he had always seemed a stranger to her when she was small—except for those

---

*The last of those published by Broadside.

times he cooked breakfast or hoed the neat rows of vegetables in summer and they had sweet corn and okra from "daddy's garden." As she grew to school age, and her quick, talented mind became apparent, he, like her mother, became aware of the unusual child and encouraged her early creative efforts. The poem evolves with wisdom to an understanding of the trials of responsibility that must have been troubling her father—problems the poet herself knows now that she has her own family household. One critic wrote of *The Women and the Men:* "her world contains implicit dimensions of race, suffering, solace and social sharing—and now and again her imagination catches fire." In *Cotton Candy on a Rainy Day* she is more introspective, searching to explain her inner loneliness despite her busy life, her phenomenal success.

Paula Giddings, herself a noted figure in the poetry world, friend and colleague of Nikki's, said in the Introduction to this volume that Giovanni is perhaps more mellow here, but like wine, her poems have a clarity that comes only with aging, though the word is figuratively applied. Nikki Giovanni has matured while still young. "I'll be terrific at forty," she told Paula. In the mid-seventies, during an interview for a feature story about her in *People* magazine, the once racial polemicist explained that she had already abandoned that role. "I'm talked out," she said at that time. "There is no longer the need, as there was in 1968, to explain. Everybody understands why kids want to go to decent schools. . . . My poems are less insistent. They're not so loud and abrasive. You gotta grow up. . . ."

Yet in 1981 she felt that there is still a great deal to be done, to aid the poor, and the hungry, and the young people of her race, of all races, who have suffered from the cutbacks in student loans. The world will always need its poets, its positive thinkers like Nikki Giovanni.

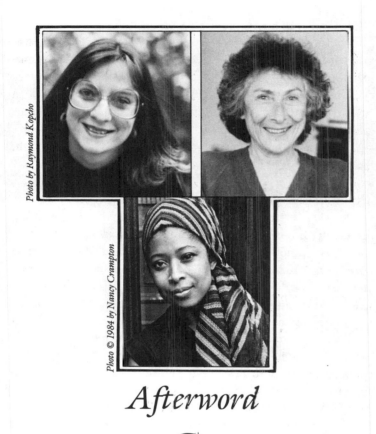

Photo by Raymond Kopcho

Photo © 1984 by Nancy Crampton

Afterword

A n "afterword" might be called the concrete expression of an author's inevitable afterthoughts on completing a work such as this. So much material has been collected, so many more figures have appeared on the scene than one expected. One cannot include them all, yet some mention must be made of those who merit attention.

One of the first whose outstanding career commands recognition here is Josephine Miles. As much scholar as poet, Miles has published twelve scholarly books on the subject of poetry in addition to thirteen volumes of her own poetry, most of them by university presses, notably Berkeley's University of California, where she has taught since 1940. She has received innumerable awards, grants, and fellowships besides an honorary doctorate from Mills College and membership in the American Academy and National Institute of Arts and Letters, the Linguistic Society of America, and the American Academy of Arts and Sciences. If all the above data reads like a staid, bookish, fusty poet's life, it is misleading as to both the poet and her work.

Born in Chicago, Illinois on June 11, 1911, Josephine Miles was stricken with a crippling arthritis in early childhood, and her family, hoping she would benefit by a warm climate when doctors could not help her, moved to California, where she grew up. Nature, making up for the mobility of body denied this poet, gave her an agility of mind that was evident from her primary school days, and she was a Phi Beta Kappa graduate from the University of California, Los Angeles, in 1932. Her record was so remarkable that she was urged by one of her professors to go on with higher education and try for a Masters degree. Despite her brilliance, Miles had grave doubts about her ability to succeed, to compete with students on the upper levels of education. "Do you think I can make it?" she asked her teacher. She was worried, she told Jean Burden in recalling the incident, not so much from a scholastic standpoint as from the physical and financial challenge such an attempt would mean.

However, her teacher persisted; though it was the depths of the Depression, he was able to secure financial aid for her by way of a scholarship at Berkeley, and arranged assistance for her in getting to and from class. Miles received her M.A. degree in 1934, and four years later received her Ph.D. from the same university. In between, and throughout her academic years, she had been writing poetry and winning awards successively: the Shelley Memorial Award in 1936; the Phelan Award in 1937; an AAUW Fellowship in 1939; and that same year her first volume, *Lines at Intersection,* was published by Macmillan. From then on, scarcely a year passed that did not see a volume of her own poetry or a scholarly work on the poetry and poets of the past come off the press. For example, in the latter category, one finds such titles as, *Wordsworth and the Vocabulary of Emotion* (her first, published by Berkeley Press, 1942); *Pathetic Fallacy in the 19th Century;* the *Continuity of Poetic Language,* a three-volume work dealing with the primary language of poetry in the 1640s, the 1740s and 1840s, and the 1940s to 1950s; by contrast, the titles of her volumes (of her poems) were indicative of the world around her: *Poems on Several Occasions; Local Measures; Civil Poems; Kinds of Affection; Saving the Bay.* There is no taint of the textbook in her lines or her subject matter, though it is rarely personal; her principal concern is humanity, or, in her words: "Main themes, human doubt and amazement. A strong beat of meaning playing against the beat of pattern. Some critics say 'western,' but I am not aware of this."

Literary critic David Ray interprets her poetry and her succinct statement in a different context: "Josephine Miles shares, with William Carlos Williams . . . credit for exalting 'the American idiom' into the standard language of poetry—a feat surrounded by risk, by the danger of being charged with flatness, or being forsaken by all but the most sensitive of critics. Her achievement is that she has successfully laid aside her academic powers (she is one of the land's best scholars) in order to paint with a great gentleness—and sense of this fragility and evanescence—the landscape of the American scene—its speech, jazz, billboards, comics and assassinations, and those dark streets of towns where three creeks meet. She has raised these to a high form of poetry and her insights provide an enlightened comment on American life. . . . Even when confessing her scholarship ('BAD quartos were my first love') she remains matter-of-fact. Her skill is in rendering the quotidian stillness of an American street. . . . She is most at home in rendering the sadness, the matter-of-fact, the every-evening miracle of the moon rising over the lumberyard, and perhaps a whiskey bottle; the rendition is pure, strikes life's tonic note of recognition. Her work is at once primitive and sophisticated, like that of Chekhov and Dr. Williams." And he adds significantly:

"It must be said, too, that an undercurrent of sharp physical pain runs through her poems. The fact that she must *be* helped, physically, as well as offer her help to the world, must partly account for the striking, beautifully developed theme of the acknowledgement of others—a sense of the connectedness of people, of obligation, of gratitude reciprocal and eternal. And her elegy on the death of John Kennedy is not only rhythmically enchanting and original, but it is a major statement on violence in America, on the resentment of real *qualitas* in American life, on the assertion of mediocrity, and the insistence on enshrining or turning power over to it: with the metaphor of Daniel Boone's shooting of the bear, Miles transforms history and myth as an explanation of Kennedy's assassination."

Though it was written twenty years ago, Ray's discerning discussion of Josephine Miles's contribution to modern American poetry is still valid. Her recent poetry has become more personal than any in her former volumes as she recalls incidents of early years. It is as if she is no longer reticent in speaking about herself. Yet the "undercurrent of physical pain" remains muted as always. According to her close friends, among them Muriel Rukeyser, with whom Miles had an instant rapport that ripened into a lifelong friendship from the time of the latter's first fellowship at Berkeley in the late 1930s, there is a gallantry and a gaiety in Miles's attitude toward life that makes one forget the magnitude of her physical trial. She has had to rely on wheelchair assistance in getting to and from her classroom at Berkeley for years. When she gives a public reading she is brought in and seated onstage well before the audience begins to arrive.

Her readings on the West Coast have always been well attended, and she usually receives a standing ovation from her listeners, many of whom are or have been her students. She has enjoyed a rare popularity as a teacher, not only because of her vast literary knowledge, but because of her understanding and support of student ventures. They came to her with personal problems, as well as those of prosody or the subject of a term paper. The young poet "Alda," who often gives readings with Marge Piercy, looked to Miles for support and advice when a small group of young poets (including Piercy) decided to start publishing their own work. With Miles's positive opinion that it was "worth a try," they went ahead, and the shameless hussy press was added to the growing list of small presses.

Besides Berkeley, the West Coast generally is a veritable bee-hive of activity in the poetry world. At Mills College, in Oak-land, under the able direction of poet Diane O'Hehir, whose own poetry reveals the wit of her Gaelic background, a full program of poetry readings is conducted annually. Poets from both coasts are invited to read or participate in workshops, among them Josephine Miles, Jean Burden, Ann Stanford, Di-ane Wakoski, Gwendolyn Brooks, May Swenson, Alice Walker, and, until her death in 1980, Muriel Rukeyser whenever she was in California. There are many others who have caused Mills College to become a literary mecca for poets of both sexes, with the emphasis on women, since it was founded as a women's college in 1852, and remained so for more than a century.

Ann Stanford, like Josephine Miles, is a noted scholar as well as poet. She edited the comprehensive anthology, *The Women Poets in English,* including both British and American women poets from the early seventeenth century to the present; pub-lished in 1972, the book has been widely used as source mate-rial in college courses. Stanford's own poetry is often anthol-ogized for its strong, intellectual quality, or, more accurately, its philosophic content.

From Whittier, California comes Diane Wakoski, poet of the NOW generation, feminist, extravagant in her use of words, wild in her images, and strident in voicing her opinion of society and the human condition. Born in 1937, Wakoski was an in-tellectually avid adolescent during the beat generation, received her B.A. degree from Berkeley in 1960, migrated to New York, mingled with the "deep image" poets of the city though not definitely associated with them, and soon began winning awards and grants. A prolific, compulsive writer of sprawling, on-rushing poetry, reeking with social consciousness, she published her first book, *Coins and Coffins,* in 1962 with Hawkskill Press in New York; and from then on, has produced one and sometimes two slim volumes a year with various small presses, plus several collections by major trade houses. In 1965 she married S. Shepherd Sherbell, a union that ended in divorce, and in 1973 she married again, this time to Michael Watterlond. She has given countless readings at colleges around the country, and is hailed with enthusiastic cheers from young listeners, who respond to her dramatic flair for inventive imagery and surrealistic humor. Titles indicating the latter are: *Inside the Blood Factory; The Moon has a Complicated Geography; The Lament of the Lady Bank Dick; Love, You Big Fat Snail; Seen in Dr. Generosa's Bar, Recruit for Hell's Angels & Black Mafia; The Motorcycle Betrayal Poems; The Pumpkin Pie, or, Reassurances are Always False, Though We Still Love Them; Sometimes a Poet Will Hijack the Moon; Dancing on the Grave of a Son of a Bitch.*

By contrast, the volumes that have received favorable attention from the critics bear simple, straightforward titles: *Discrepancies and Apparitions; The George Washington Poems;* and that endless, all-consuming series, *Greed,* extending to no less than eleven parts. There are those who dismiss Diane Wakoski as a poet suffering from verbal diarrhea, and it is true that her lines have a tendency to run on and on, long after the point of the poem has been made. In one of the discursive *Greed* poems, for example, she tells of first discovering "opulence" at a childhood birthday party, and admits that she, too, is a party to greed— but of a different kind: hers has been to "amass a fortune" ("greedily") in *words,* not possessions. She defines her wealth as "words which no one could spend, which could never be used up," and so on; the concept is both witty and wise, but it is overexpanded and repeated, beyond all reason, not only here, but in all of the related *Greed* poems. The series, which began in 1967 (with Parts I & II), continues for nearly ten years, and runs through other volumes besides those entitled *Greed;* the one referred to above is in *Magellanic Clouds* (1970), revealing an unexpected knowledge of astronomy; almost all of these are published by Black Sparrow Press.

Diane Wakoski is a poet who either attracts ardent admirers or repels poetry lovers who consider her work undisciplined. Yet so astute a critic as Hayden Carruth has deemed her "one of the two or three most important poets of her generation." He observed that although her early language was ordinary, prosy, talkative, rhythmless, a post-beat idiom and street jargon, she did reveal an individuality, an inventive imagination. He cites as the most notable of her early work, *The George Washington Poems* (first published as a chapbook in 1967, and later as part of a trilogy of her first three volumes in 1974, by Doubleday). This surrealistic sequence relates conversations of the poet with one "George Washington," who by turns takes on different identities: at times the traditional "Father of our country," he becomes a personal confidant, a Wakoski father-substitute, a willful lover, a watchful friend. As the diverse dialogs progress, the reader becomes aware that the poet is expressing a national social consciousness in terms of her personal experience, or, as Carruth says, "Her own body becomes a map of the states. It was a caprice, granted. But it was a caprice capable of serious extensions, and in any case, it was admirable preparation for her mature work." Of that mature work, it is to Wakoski's credit that she goes beyond anger and adverse criticism to show sympathy and even pity for both sexes, the masses who have helped to create a civilization that may well lead to their doom.

Vassar Miller, who hails from Houston, Texas, and received all her schooling there, is a poet whose strict adherence to the discipline of her particular art has made it possible for her to triumph over the severe handicap of cerebral palsy she suffered at birth, on July 19, 1924. Like Josephine Miles, she was a good student, though not a scholar of literary history. Following high school, she attended the University of Houston, received her A.B. degree in 1947, and went on to acquire an M.A. three years later. From then on, she not only dedicated herself to developing her gift for poetry, but, in sharp contrast to Wakoski and the poets of the beat-generation in which she, Miller, was actually writing, she chose to perfect her art in the mold of previous generations. As one critic wrote: "At a time when so much writing seemed a plunge into the welter of the inchoate, she devoted herself to the most delicately balanced concepts and the most orthodox rhymes." The method was more than an early exercise. For her most intricate statements in her collections, *Adam's Footprint,* (1956), and *Wage War on Silence,* (1960), she chose forms that are equally orthodox, and reveal a reverence for her religious upbringing. Like the English mystics, the spirit to which her lines conform is self-searching and secure. She was drawn to the works of George Herbert and Gerald Manley Hopkins, and her religious lyrics have been compared to those of both. Her sonnets stay within the bounds of formal tradition, yet they do not seem antiquated, but the present-day expression of a spirit that is both soul-searching and serene. Critics have attempted unsuccessfully to describe the compelling and convincing quality of her thought. Miller herself once said: "Poetry has a trinitarian function (like all art); it is creative, redemptive, and sanctifying. It is creative because it takes the raw material of fact and feeling and makes them into that which is neither fact nor feeling. It is redemptive because it can transform the pain and ugliness of life into joy and beauty. It is sanctifying because it purifies the soul." Anyone reading her statement would know that whatever mode she selected, Vassar Miller had to be a valid poet, both gifted and valiant.

It is not often that a person with creative ability possesses equal skill in two disciplines, but such is the case with Carolyn

Stoloff, who was an accomplished painter when she began to write poetry. From the time her first volume, *Stepping Out,* was published by Unicorn Press in 1971, she virtually stepped out into the mainstream of poetry and kept up the pace with her peers of many years' experience. After a successful reception of her initial work, she followed with two more volumes in 1973: one, *Dying to Survive,* by a major publisher (Doubleday) and the other, *In the Red Meadow,* by New Rivers Press. Midway in her newfound career, Stoloff applied for and received a residency at the Wurlitzer Foundation in Taos, New Mexico, a grant that proved uniquely productive for it brought out the qualities of both painter and poet in Stoloff. Anyone who has spent even a few days in that desert landscape under the shadow of the mysterious, "sacred" Sangre de Cristo mountain range with its changing lights and colors cannot help being inspired to give outward expression to inner feeling; and Stoloff, who experienced three residence periods at the Helene Wurlitzer Foundation, followed by a year in Taos, mingling with the pueblo Indians, and Spanish-speaking natives, recorded her impressions in poems as spare and sharply etched as the mountains against the clear blue skies over New Mexico. No lines could be more succinct than those of "Between Rock and Dream," as she describes "the sacred mountain/ as it thrusts up/ toward sun's many hands—." The volume that came from the months in Taos, entitled *Swiftly Now,* dedicated to Henry Sauerwein, director of the Wurlitzer Foundation, appeared in 1982 under the imprint of Ohio University's Swallow Press. The sustained high quality of the work caused no less a poet than May Swenson to comment: "The poems . . . begin crisp and vivid. The sequence gathers power as one reads, and the final climactic poems are stunning in their clarity and penetration. . . . The true colors of her feelings are deftly mixed. This show is her best yet." Rare praise from a sister poet.

Stoloff's latest, *A Spool of Blue,* (1983), a collection of new and selected poems is proof that she is a full-fledged poet as well as painter. However, the book does not have the cohesion of *Swiftly Now,* probably because no collection from accumulated volumes can have a central theme, and today the trend toward one central idea or experience is increasingly apparent in chapbooks or single "hardcovers" of contemporary poets. Whether this bent for personal expression started with the so-called "confessional" poetry of the sixties, or is simply a means of divesting oneself of the inner anxieties of our chaotic society, does not matter. The fact is that more and more contemporary poetry is fragmented autobiography in one form or another.

When the young poet Molly Peacock, whose first volume, *And Live Apart,* which takes its title from a poem by George Herbert, appeared in 1980, she was presented by her publishers as a "poet devoted to the language of emotion in conversation," and these poems adhere to the theme of communication—or lack of it—among all creatures, human and otherwise. Without it, we "live apart," as Herbert states in his poem written in the seventeenth century. Peacock uses this theme to delineate her relationship toward the people in her life, and, very subtly, the conditions that led to her divorce from the man she married at an early age. Her initial book was among the notable "Breakthrough Books" published by the University of Missouri Press and received critical praise for its warmth of feeling and freshness of expression. In 1976–1977 she was awarded the first postgraduate honorary fellowship from the writing seminars at Johns Hopkins University, as well as a Creative Artist Public Service grant, and was State Poet-in-Residence in Delaware.

Like Vassar Miller, and their earlier sister poet, Edna St. Vincent Millay, Molly Peacock is not afraid to write in traditional forms, and her second volume, *Raw Heaven,* is an entire book of modern sonnets. In the Millay manner, Peacock takes liberties with the form. Some are "fat sonnets," as she calls them, harking back to Milton's "coda" of extra lines following the standard fourteen. As in her first book, the poet here narrates her feelings and relationships toward the people in her life, particularly her Gaelic clan. "Girl at the Picnic Table," for example, describes a Peacock family reunion held every summer. As the sonnet progresses it depicts with some hilarity the Breugalian scene of eating and drinking; male relatives load up on beer to the point of saturation and the "girl at table" is so full of revulsion that she can't eat. There is both humor and hostility in many of the poems. The collection of sonnets has made its mark in that the manuscript won the competition held by the Virginia Commission on the Arts and the Virginia Center for the Creative Arts for a three-months' residency at the Center. The unanimous decision of the judges, including Maxine Kumin, now among the foremost of contemporary poets, speaks for itself. Directly after the award, *Raw Heaven* was accepted for publication by Random House and appeared in August 1984. Some of these poems first appeared in *The New Yorker, Antioch Review,* and similar literary journals.

Jane Kenyon, wife of the noted poet and critic, Donald Hall, in her first book, *From Room to Room,* published in 1980 by Alice James Books, builds on the single theme of exploring her husband's old family homestead in Maine, learning about his ancestry as she moves "from room to room." It is an interesting device, one that leads the reader on, and attained universally favorable notices for the volume and its author.

Carolyn Forché is a young poet who had come into prominence during the last few years through her political poetry. Like Marge Piercy, she was born in Detroit some years after the latter, and saw much of the same industrial social unrest that early gave her an awareness of the chaos of contemporary society. She managed to work her way through college as a journalism major, since poetry, her first love, was impractical; and she left home soon afterward to travel as a reporter. When she could afford the time and money, she joined poetry workshops to increase her knowledge of modern technique. At first she thought she could do anything she pleased, but she soon learned that syntax and cadence play as great a part in free verse as meter in blank verse and rhyme schemes in the sonnet or sestina. She began writing poems related to the news stories she had published, and soon earned a reputation as a social-consciousness commentator in poetry. Her subject matter knows no bounds; it runs from the revolutionary activity in San Salvador to lesbian sexual experience. Although she claimed that the former were based on scenes she had witnessed, rumor has it that she was never even in San Salvador, but wrote the poems from reports sent to her by a friendly newspaper colleague. Whether they were or not, her work has given her a place in the poetry world. She is now married and teaching in the English Department of the University of Virginia.

A number of women who possess a gift for poetry have concentrated on theater pieces and have earned a reputation as playwrights rather than poets. Elizabeth Swados, whose moving oratorio, *The Haggadah,* a pageantlike celebration of the Passover story with music composed by the author, enjoyed a long run in its first production and its revival in 1980 at the Public Theatre in New York, is a highly talented creative artist. She has written and presented numerous dramatic offerings in verse, as well as musical settings of poems, history, and works of others, at the Public and elsewhere, but she does not fall into the category of poets in these studies.

Eve Merriam, a brilliant satirist whose *Inner City Mother Goose* went into multiple printings, has both written and directed musicals and reviews. She is one of the few satirists in contemporary American poetry; *Inner City Mother Goose* is a bitter commentary on urban society. Some have called sacrilegious her lines, "Now I lay me down to sleep/ I pray the Lord my locks will keep/ the burglars from my door," and so on. But most readers enjoy her brazen versions of the time-honored nursery rhymes denouncing crime in our cities. However, she has gained more reputation from her work in the entertainment world and the women's movement than in poetry. Ntozake Shange, whose given name was Paulette Williams, comes from a well-educated black family; but when she became imbued with the spirit of fighting for equality with whites, she, like many others of her race, chose an African pen name. Another play, *For Colored Girls Who Have Considered Suicide When the Rainbow is Enuf,* made the name Ntozake Shange famous. The play, a series of vignettes, sung and danced by a capable cast, composed in swinging free verse, some of it humorous, but most of it starkly, savagely realistic tragedy, was an instant success off-Broadway and a long-run hit on Broadway. Like Swados, Shange is better known as a playwright than a poet, though most of her lines are in narrative verse. Another well-known figure, Maya Angelou, though she writes her own simple, poetic lyrics to the songs she sings on the air and recordings, might be called a balladier rather than a poet. Her lines have charm and speak warm truths, but they do not have the magnitude or power of a poet like Gwendolyn Brooks, Denise Levertov, or Alice Walker. The latter and Angelou are also known for their prose fiction. Angelou's book, *I Know Why the Caged Bird Sings,* is a fascinating account of her own story told as a novel. Walker's first volume of poetry, *Once,* received universal praise for its succinct, thumbnail descriptive poems regarding her trip to Africa—a journey that lengthened into a stay of months during which she came to know and be accepted as one of her ancestral race. This book, and a second volume, *The Purple Petunia,* both tell of her experiences in championing her people in America, participating in protest marches in Atlanta. Walker was a protegé of Muriel Rukeyser at the time of the latter's death. An attractive, distinguished-looking young woman, she was an editor on *MS* magazine for a few years, and began writing fiction in addition to poetry. She soon turned to the novel, and has published two successful books. Her third, *The Color Purple,* published in 1983, won the Pulitzer Prize for fiction, and has received wide acclaim.

Several women who have written poetry for years and are published frequently in top-flight magazines have become known for their activity in the world of poetry as program directors, editors, and officers in various literary organizations like the Poetry Society of America, the Authors Guild, and the International P.E.N. (American Center). Grace Schulman, program director of the Poetry Reading Series at the 92nd Street "Y" in New York, one of the most prestigious positions in the poetry world, has published only one volume, *Break Down the Idols,* though she is constantly working with the tools of the profession—the promotion of contemporary American poetry through public readings and competitions. As the daughter of parents who were in the graphic arts, Grace Schulman has known many writers, especially poets, from the time she was a child. Marianne Moore was an intimate friend of the family, and a delightful person to know, especially for a young girl with ambitions to become a poet. Moore encouraged the early efforts that Schulman made, criticized and argued with her as if she were an adult, never talking down to her. In college, Schulman began to have a few poems published, and when the *Nation* needed a new poetry editor, Moore suggested that she send samples of her work to the editor-in-chief. The girl, acting on her advice, sent in four poems, and got the job, to her vast surprise. She proved so astute in her judgment that her name soon became synonymous with efficiency in poetry circles; and when the post of program director at the 92nd Street "Y" was vacant, it was offered to Schulman. Since taking it, she has become a real force in promotion and public relations between poets and poetry-loving audiences. Her friendship with Marianne Moore continued to the end of the latter's life. Grace relates with relish the time she went to see the revered poet as Moore lay in bed during her last illness: Schulman had brought the old poet what she thought was a reproduction of a photograph of a tiger, and the venerable Moore, weak as she had appeared, sat bolt upright and admonished her protegé, "You're wrong; that's a cheetah, Grace!"

As might be expected, Schulman is now working on a book

dealing with the poetry of Marianne Moore. She has also done translating besides her multiple concerns with scheduling the poetry readings in Kaufmann Hall at the 92nd Street "Y." Small wonder that she has little time for her own work.

Jane Cooper is also caught up in various aspects of literary organizations besides teaching, which prevent her from writing more than a few poems during the school year. Born in Atlantic City while her parents were there on vacation, she spent her childhood in Florida, but when she was ten years old, her family moved to New York City, where she has lived most of her life on the Upper West Side. Her first volume *Six Mornings in March,* brought recognition to this quiet, gentle poet whose works have appeared in *The New Yorker,* the *New Republic,* and many other periodicals. She is often called upon to introduce important figures among her fellow poets at the readings held in the Donnell Library and the Guggenheim Museum auditorium, presented by the Academy of American Poets, an organization started at the suggestion of Robert Frost and headed by Marie Bullock, a woman dedicated to the fine arts.

Certain poets may be called experimentalists and foremost among them is Harriet Zinnes, who has been teaching poetry at Queens College in New York for many years, and is published in small presses like Gallimaufry, which features avant-garde prose as well as poetry. Zinnes, whose work recalls Gertrude Stein, and who is, in fact, a literary descendant of the brilliant eccentric of early twentieth century poetry, has gone one step farther in invention of phrase and form. Zinnes' recent collection of "entropisms"—also the title of her volume published in 1981—a term she explains at some length in a foreword, constitutes a series of conundrumlike poems in free verse, interspersed with a variant of Stein's "When this you see, remember me." Another of her inventions is the improvisational verse, in which the reader may fill in the blank denoting a missing word or phrase of a line, inserting whatever seems to be appropriate. This sort of poem is akin to the music of contemporary composers; it may be challenging to some, but is baffling and unsatisfactory as poetry to others. However, critics of the caliber of Anaïs Nin, and poet Tom Lux have praised Zinnes for her wit and quirky humor.

Finally, there are numerous workshops and poetry readings in colleges throughout the country that emphasize works by women. The University of New Mexico in Albuquerque, headed by writer-teacher Harvena Richter, daughter of the noted novelist Conrad Richter, holds an annual poetry conference to which students, amateurs, and professionals may contribute. Richter, who, like her father, writes novels and essays as well as poetry, has not found time to collect a volume for publication, though many of her individual poems have appeared in periodicals. Hers is a literary background; as a child, she listened to her father read aloud chapters of his novels to her mother; and as she grew up, he would ask her opinion as well as her mother's. His friends included people from the Bloomsbury circle in England, and since his death, his daughter has been continuing that friendship while preparing a book on her father's writings, papers, and letters. She has also written a book of criticism on Virginia Woolf. Her poetry reflects the intellectual quality of her prose, and at the same time shows the influence of the Indian culture of old Albuquerque that she felt from the time she was an adolescent, when the family spent most of each year in New Mexico because her mother's health required a warm climate.

At the University of Michigan there are poetry readings and discussions every Thursday afternoon in the Avery Hopwood Room, the library in Angell Hall, besides evening poetry readings by poets like Gwendolyn Brooks and Marge Piercy, who draw huge student audiences. In 1979, a large poster announced a reading in Pendleton Hall by eighteen sophomore coeds. At the University of Tulsa in Oklahoma, the Center for Women's Literature, headed by feminist Germaine Greer, features poetry as often as fiction and nonfiction in its publications and conferences. Hofstra University at Hempstead, New York,

holds an international conference dealing with women's literature each fall, and in 1982 featured twentieth century women
writers in every field, including poetry. The directors then selected the most interesting papers for publication in book form
as a collection of essays.*

   One could go on and on citing both trends and organizations in contemporary American Poetry—to say nothing of new
names among the women who write it. Some who come to mind
as having received recognition within the last few years are Amy
Clampitt, with her carefully structured lines; Katha Pollitt, whose
recent book won an accolade from more than one reviewer;
Linda Pastan, poet and editor of a small press; and any number
of young poets, among them Heather McHugh, Louise Glueck,
whose *House on the Marshlands* won her a permanent place on
the roster of professional poets; Catherine O'Neal, Laura Den-
nison, Mary Jo Salter, and so many more that it is impossible
to name them all. However, as stated in the Foreword, this book,
begun in 1975, is not a survey, but a selection of biographical
studies concerning the lives of women poets whose creative
powers have enabled them to contribute to the development of
contemporary American poetry.

*As a participant, this author delivered a paper at the conference on the sub-
ject, "Edna St. Vincent Millay, Saint of the Modern Sonnet," which was included in those selected.

Selected Bibliography

Muriel Rukeyser

1. Volumes of Poetry:
   Theory of Flight. New Haven: Yale University Press, 1935.
   U.S. 1 New York: Covici, Friede, 1938.
   A Turning Wind. New York: Viking Press, 1939.
   The Soul and Body of John Brown. New York: Doubleday, Doran 1941.
   Wake Island. New York: Doubleday, Doran, 1942.
   Beast in View. New York: Doubleday, Doran, 1944.
   The Green Wave. New York: The Centaur Press, 1945.
   Orpheus. New York: The Centaur Press, 1949.
   Elegies. New York: New Directions, 1949.
   Selected Poems. New York: New Directions, 1951.

Body of Waking. New York: Harper, 1958.
Waterlily Fire: Poems 1935–1962. New York: Macmillan, 1962.
The Speed of Darkness. New York: Random House, 1968.
Breaking Open. New York: Random House, 1973.
The Gates. New York: McGraw-Hill, 1976.
The Collected Poems. New York: McGraw-Hill, 1978.

2. Prose Works:
   Willard Gibbs (biography). New York: Doubleday Doran, 1942.
   The Life of Poetry. New York: Current Books, 1949.
   One Life. New York: Simon and Schuster, 1957.
   The Colors of the Day (play). Vassar Centennial, June 10, 1961.
   The Orgy (novel). New York: Coward, McCann, 1965.
   The Traces of Thomas Hariot. New York: Random House, 1971.

3. Translations:
   Selected Poems of Octavio Paz. Bloomington: Indiana University Press, 1963.
   Sun Stone (Octavio Paz). New York: New Directions, 1963.
   Selected Poems of Gunnar Ekelof (with Leif Sjoberg).

4. Children's Books:
   The Children's Orchard. San Francisco: Greenwood Press, 1947.
   Come Back, Paul. New York: Harper, 1955.
   Mazes. New York: Simon and Schuster, 1970.
   Bertolt Brecht, 1898–1956. New York: Simon and Schuster, 1974.
   The Outer Banks. New York: Unicorn Press, 1975.

5. Recordings and Films:
   Spoken Arts Series: "A Treasury of 100 American Poets Reading Their Own Poems." Edited by Paul Kresh. 1970.
   Spoken Arts Series: A Treasury of Twenty-Five American Jewish Poets Reading Their Own Poems." Edited by Paul Kresh. 1979.
   The Poetry and Voice of Muriel Rukeyser. Caedmon Records SWC no. 1536.
   Three Women: They Are Their Own Gifts. Film portraying the lives and works of Muriel Rukeyser, Alice Neel (painter), and Anna Sokolov (dancer and choreographer). New York Film Festival, 1979; on public television, 1979.

6. Radio Program:
   "Adventures in Judaism." Written and produced by Paul Kresh, over WEVD. 1968–1969

7. Biographical and Critical Material:
   Kunitz, Stanley, and Haycraft, Howard, eds. *Twentieth Century Authors*. New York: H. W. Wilson Company, 1942.
   Who's Who Among American Women. Who's Who in America. Contemporary Authors. Detroit: Gale Research Company, annually from 1963.
   Deutsch, Babette. *Poetry in Our Time* (1900–1950). New York: Holt, 1952. (Updated edition of *Poetry in Our Time* (1900–1960). New York, Doubleday, 1963.)
Following publication of her first volume, reviews and critical articles of Rukeyser's poetry appeared in all the leading literary·magazines, quarterlies, etc., from *Poetry, The Saturday Review, Partisan Review,* to *The American Poetry Review,* besides the major daily newspapers like *The New York Times,* the *Chicago Sun-Times* and *Tribune,* the *St. Louis Post Dispatch,* and *The San Francisco Chronicle* to name a few. The list is too long to itemize here, but it is important to cite the literary criticism of her last volume, *The Collected Poems,* published only a year and a half before she died:
Stevenson, Anne. "With Head and Heart: *The Collected Poems of Muriel Rukeyser.*" *The New York Times Book Review,* February 11, 1979.

A long unsigned obituary of Rukeyser appeared in *The New York Times* a year later, almost to the day—February 13, 1980.

Denise Levertov

1. Volumes of Poetry:
   Double Image. London: Cresset Press, 1946.
   Here and Now. San Francisco: Ferlinghetti, 1957.
   Overland to the Islands. San Francisco: Ferlinghetti, 1958.
   With Eyes at the Back of Our Heads. New York: New Directions, 1959.
   The Jacob's Ladder. New York: New Directions, 1961.
   O,Taste and See. New York: New Directions, 1964.
   The Sorrow Dance. New York: New Directions, 1967.
   Re-learning the Alphabet. New York: New Directions, 1970.

To Stay Alive. New York: New Directions, 1971.
Footprints. New York: New Directions, 1972.
The Freeing of the Dust. New York: New Directions, 1975.
Life in the Forest. New York: New Directions, 1978.
Light up the Cave. New York: New Directions, 1981.

2. Prose Works:
   The Poet in the World (essays and lectures). New York: New Directions, 1973.
   Rexroth, Kenneth, and Williams, William Carlos, eds. *Modern Poets* (anthology). New York and London: Penguin, 1967.

3. Biographical and Critical Materials:
   Mills, Ralph. *Poets in Progress.* Chicago: Northwestern University Press, 1967.
   Rexroth, Kenneth. *New British Poets.* New York: New Directions, 1948.
   ————. *American Poetry in the 20th Century.* New York: The Seabury Press, 1971.
   Wakeness, John, ed. *World Authors, 1950–1970.* New York: H. W. Wilson Company, 1975.
   Rosenthal, M. L. *The New Poets.* New York and London: Oxford University Press, 1967.

4. Articles and Reviews in Periodicals:
   Pritchard, William. "Denise Levertov." *The Hudson Review,* Summer, 1967.
   23, 1971.
   Baroff, Marie. Review of *To Stay Alive. Yale Review,* Autumn, 1972.
   Perloff, Marjorie. Review of *To Stay Alive. Poetry Chronicler,* 1970–1971. Also, study of Levertov's work in *Contemporary Literature.* Madison: University of Wisconsin Press, 1973.

5. Musical Settings and Phonotape:
   Rochberg, George. "Songs in Praise of Krishna." 1976.
   "A Discussion of poetry and its forms as an extension of life" (Charles Olson and Denise Levertov). New York: Center for Cassette Studies, 1973.

Elizabeth Bishop

1. Volumes of Poetry:
   North & South. Boston: Houghton Mifflin Company, 1946.
   Poems: North & South—A Cold Spring. Boston: Houghton Mifflin Company, 1955.
   (Paperback editions of the above two books; Boston: Houghton Mifflin 1965.)
   Questions of Travel. New York: Farrar, Straus & Giroux, 1965.
   The Complete Poems. New York: Farrar, Straus & Giroux, 1969.
   Geography III. New York: Farrar, Straus & Giroux, 1976.
   The Complete Poems: 1927–1979. New York: Farrar, Straus & Giroux, 1983.

2. Prose Works:
   Two autobiographical stories published in *The New Yorker,* 27 June and 19 December, 1953
   Brazil. New York: Life World Library, 1963.
   Collected Prose. Introduction by Robert Giroux. New York: Farrar, Straus & Giroux, 1984.

3. Translations and Editorships:
   Mindlin, Henrique. Modern Brazilian Architecture. (Edited and translated by Bishop.) New York: *Partisan Review,* 1956.
   Minha Vida de Menina (The Diary of Helena Morley). New York: Farrar, Straus & Cuda-huy, 1957.
   Anthology of Contemporary Brazilian Poetry. Bishop, co-editor with Emanuel Brasil. Conn.: Wesleyan University Press, 1972.

4. Biographical and Critical Material:
   From *World Literature Today,* Winter, 1977:
   Bertin, Celia. "A Novelist's Poet."
   Bidart, Frank. "On Elizabeth Bishop."
   Estess, Sybil. "Toward the Interior: Epiphany in 'Cape Breton' as Representative Poem."
   Mazzaro, Jerome. "Elizabeth Bishop's Particulars."
   Mortimer, Penelope. "Elizabeth Bishop's Prose."
   Moss, Howard. "The Canada-Brazil Connection."
   Newman Anne R. "Elizabeth Bishop's 'Songs for a Colored Singer'."
   Paz, Octavio. "Elizabeth Bishop, or the Power of Reticence."
   Schwartz, Lloyd. "The Mechanical Horse and The Indian Princess: Two Poems from *North & South.*"

Selected Bibliography

Slater, Candace. "Brazil in the Poetry of Elizabeth Bishop."

Taylor, Eleanor Ross. "Driving to the Interior: A Note on Elizabeth Bishop."

Vendler, Helen. "Domestication, Domesticity and the Otherworldly."*

Other source material in the following works:

Deutsch, Babette. *Poetry in Our Time* (updated, 1900–1960) New York: Doubleday, 1963

Kunitz, Stanley, and Haycraft, Howard, eds. *Twentieth Century Authors*. First Supplement. New York: H. W. Wilson Company, 1955.

5. Musical Settings:

Carter, Elliott. Song cycle: "A Mirror on Which to Dwell." (Five poems by Elizabeth Bishop.) Associated Music Publishers, Inc., 1976.

May Swenson

1. Volumes of Poetry:

Another Animal: Poems. New York: New Directions, 1949.

A Cage of Spines. New York: Holt and Rinehart, 1958.

To Mix With Time. New York: Scribners, 1963.

Poems to Solve. New York: Scribners, 1966.

Half-Sun, Half-Sleep (New Poems). New York: Scribners, 1967.

Iconographs. New York: Scribners, 1970.

More Poems to Solve. New York: Scribners, 1970.

New and Selected Things Taking Place. Boston: Atlantic/Little, Brown, 1978.

2. Drama:

The Floor: A Play in One Act. New York: American Place Theatre, 1965.

3. Translation:

The Poems of Tomas Transtomer (with Leif Sjoberg) Pittsburgh: University of Pittsburgh Press, 1964.

*Note: The articles in *World Literature Today* are indexed in *The Social Science and Humanities Index, Book Review Index,* and *International Bibliography of Book Reviews.*

4. Musical settings:
   Song series of four poems concerned with subjects of "Early Mornings," (series title) by Lester Trimble. Composed August, 1980; performed in New York, December, 1980. (Series includes "At Breakfast," "By Morning," "Early Morning: Cape Cod," and "The Exchange.")

5. Biographical and Critical Material:
   Pritchard, William. Review of Swenson's poetry in *The Hudson Review,* summer, 1967.
   Stanford, Ann. "May Swenson: The Art of Perceiving." *The Southern Review,* winter, 1969.
   Stevenson, Anne. Review of Swenson's *New and Selected Things Taking Place. The New York Times Book Review,* February 11, 1979.
   Stepanchev, Stephen. in "May Swenson." *American Poetry Since 1945.* New York: Harper & Row, 1965.

   Source material in earlier works:
   Deutsch, Babette. *Poetry in Our Time* (Updated, 1900–1960). New York: Doubleday, 1963.
   Kunitz, Stanley, and Haycraft, Howard, eds. *Twentieth Century Authors.* First Supplement. New York: H. W. Wilson Company, 1955.

Jean Garrigue

1. Volumes of Poetry:
   Five Young American Poets ("Jean Garrigue: Thirty-six Poems and a Few Songs"). New York: New Directions, 1944
   The Ego and the Centaur. New York: New Directions, 1947.
   The Monument Rose. New York: New Directions, 1953.
   A Water Walk by the Villa D'Este. New York: New Directions, 1959.
   Country Without Maps. New York: Macmillan, 1964.
   Chartres and Prose Poems. New York: Macmillan, 1965.
   New and Selected Poems. New York: Macmillan, 1967.
   Studies for An Actress. New York: Macmillan, 1972.

2. Prose Works:
   The Animal Hotel (a novella). New York: New Directions, 1966.
   Critical Study of Marianne Moore, or 75th birthday tribute to M.M., published 1965.

Selected Bibliography

Book reviews of fiction for *New Republic, Kenyon Review, Saturday Review, Tomorrow.*

3. Translations and Anthologies:
   Edited an anthology of translations of French poetry. New York, 1966.
   Compiled anthology, *Great Love Poems of the the World.* New York: Macmillan, 1975.

4. Biographical and Critical Material:
   Arrowsmith, William. Jean Garrgue in "Five Young American Poets." *Hudson Review,* Winter, 1953.
   Nomerov, Howard. On *The Monument Rose. Sewanee Review,* Spring, 1954.
   Fraser, G. S. "Poetry by Jean Garrigue." *Partisan Review,* 1968.
   Morris, Harry. On *Country Without Maps and New Poems. Sewanee Review,* 1969.
   Mayhall, Jane. "Jean Garrigue as Poet." The *Nation,* June 28, 1975.
   In Surveys: (also, Musical setting: "Rain" by Louise Talma; 1965)
   Deutsch, Babette. *Poetry in Our Time* (updated, 1900–1960). New York: Doubleday, 1963.
   Stepanchev, Stephen. *American Poetry Since 1945.* New York: Harper & Row, 1965.
   Kunitz, Stanley, and Haycraft, Howard, eds. *Twentieth Century Authors.* First Supplement. New York: H. W. Wilson Company, 1955.

Sylvia Plath

1. Volumes of Poetry:
   The Colossus. London: Heineman, 1960; New York: Alfred E. Knopf.
   Ariel. London: Faber and Faber, 1965; New York: Harper & Row, 1966.
   Three Women, Verse Monologue for Three Voices. London: Turret Books, 1968.
   Wreath for a Bridal. Frensham, Farnham, Surrey: The Sceptre Press, 1970.
   Million Dollar Month. Frensham: The Sceptre Press, 1971.
   Crystal Gazer and Other Poems. London: Rainbow Press, 1971.
   Lyonnesse: Poems. London: Rainbow Press, 1971.
   Winter Trees. London: Faber and Faber, 1971.

Crossing the Water: Transitional Poems. New York: Harper & Row, 1971.

Pursuit. London: Rainbow Press, 1973.

The Complete Poems. Edited by Ted Hughes. New York: Harper & Row, 1982.

2. Prose Works:

The Bell Jar. (Victoria Lucas, pseud.) London: Wm. Heineman, Ltd., 1963; London: Faber and Faber, 1966; New York: Harper & Row, 1966.

Letters Home: Correspondence, 1950–1963. New York: Harper & Row, 1975.

Johnny Panic and the Bible of Dreams and Other Prose Writings. London: Faber and Faber, 1977.

3. Biographical and Critical Material:

Butscher, Edward. *Sylvia Plath: Method and Madness*. New York: Seabury Press, 1977.

Butscher, Edward, ed. *Sylvia Plath: The Woman and the Work* (anthology of essays). New York: Dodd, Mead & Company, 1979.

Steiner, Nancy Hunter. *A Closer Look at Ariel: A Memoir of Sylvia Plath*. New York: Harper & Row, 1973.

Numerous articles and reviews in literary journals, British and American.

4. Dramatizations:

Monologue for Three Voices (verse play). London Radio, 1963.

The Bell Jar (film). Hollywood, 1969. Recent showing on television, July 2, 1983.

Note: All works by Plath published or produced after 1963 are posthumous.

Anne Sexton

1. Volumes of Poetry:

To Bedlam and Part Way Back. Boston: Houghton Mifflin 1960.

All My Pretty Ones. Boston: Houghton Mifflin, 1962.

Selected Poems. London: Oxford University Press, 1964.

Live or Die. Boston: Houghton Mifflin, 1966.

Love Poems. Boston: Houghton Mifflin, 1969.

Selected Bibliography

Transformations. Boston: Houghton Mifflin, 1971.

The Book of Folly. Boston: Houghton Mifflin, 1972.

The Death Notebooks. Boston: Houghton Mifflin, 1974.

The Awful Rowing Toward God. Boston: Houghton Mifflin, 1975.

45 Mercy Street. Edited by Linda Gray Sexton, post. Boston: Houghton Mifflin, 1976.

Words for Dr. Y: Uncollected Poems with Three Stories. Edited by Linda Gray Sexton, post. Boston: Houghton Mifflin, 1978.

2. Books for Children (with Maxine Kumin):
Eggs of Things. New York: Putnam, 1963.

More Eggs of Things. New York: Putnam, 1964.

Joey and the Birthday Present. New York: Putnam, 1971.

The Wizard's Tears. New York: Putnam, 1975.

3. Dramatization and Musical Setting:
Transformations (Eleven poems). Opera by Conrad Susa. Produced by Minneapolis Opera Center, 1973; the Manhattan Theatre Club, 1976. Score published E. C. Schirmer Music Company, 1974.

4. Biographical and Critical Material:
Hartman, Geoffrey. "Les Belles Dames Sans Merci." *Kenyon Review,* 1960.

Meyers, Neil. "The Hungry Sheep Looks Up." *Minnesota Review,* Fall, 1960.

Hemley, Cecil. "A Return to Reality." *Hudson Review,* 1962, 1963.

M.L. Rosenthal. "Seven Voices." New York *Reporter,* January 3, 1963.

Marx, Patricia. "Interview with Anne Sexton." Winter, 1965.

Mills, Ralph J., Jr. *Contemporary American Poetry.* New York: Random House, 1965.

Carruth, Hayden. "In Spite of Artifice." *Hudson Review,* Winter, 1966.

Boyers, Robert. "Achievement of Anne Sexton." *Salmagundi,* Spring, 1967.

Kevles, Barbara. "Interview with Anne Sexton." *Paris Review,* 1971.

Hughes, Allen. "Fascinating Opera of Fairy Tales." *The New York Times,* 1973.

Hughes, Allen. "Opera: Sexton's Grimm." *The New York Times,* May 28, 1976.

Porter, Andrew. "Household Tales." *The New Yorker,* June 14, 1976.

Obituary. *The New York Times,* Oct. 6, 1974 (unsigned).

Maxine Kumin

1. Volumes of Poetry:
   Halfway: Poems. New York: Holt, Rinehart & Winston, 1961.
   The Privilege: Poems. New York: Harper & Row, 1965.
   The Nightmare Factory. New York: Harper & Row, 1970.
   Up-Country, Poems of New England. New York: Harper & Row, 1972.
   House, Bridge, Fountain, Gate. New York: Viking Press, 1975.
   The Retrieval System. New York: Viking/Penguin, 1978.
   Collected Poems. New York: Viking Press, 1983.

2. Poems and Stories for Children:
   Spring Things; Summer Story; Follow the Fall; A Winter Friend (Four Seasons books). New York: Putnam, 1961.
   No one Writes a Letter to the Snail (Poems for Children). New York: Putnam, 1962.
   Collaborations with Anne Sexton: see Bibliography above.

3. Biographical and Critical Material:
   Booth, Philip. "Maxine Kumin's Survival." *The American Poetry Review*, November–December, 1978.
   Contemporary Authors. Detroit: Gale Research Company, 1962–1963.

Gwendolyn Brooks

1. Volumes of Poetry:
   A Street in Bronzeville. New York: Harper, 1944.
   Annie Allen, A Ballad of Chicago Negro Life. New York: Harper, 1949.
   Bronzeville Boys and Girls. (for children) New York: Harper, 1955.
   The Bean Eaters. New York: Harper, 1960.
   Selected Poems. New York: Harper & Row, 1963.
   In The Mecca. New York: Harper & Row, 1968.
   The World of Gwendolyn Brooks. New York: Harper & Row, 1971.
   Riot. Detroit: Broadside Press, 1969.
   Family Pictures. Detroit: Broadside Press, 1970.
   Aloneness (poems for children). Detroit: Broadside Press, 1971.
   Beckonings. Detroit: Broadside Press, 1975.
   Primer for Blacks. Chicago: Third World Press, 1980.
   To Disembark. Chicago: Third World Press, 1981.

Selected Bibliography

2. Prose Works:
   Book reviews and articles from 1943 to the present.
   Maud Martha (novel). New York: Harper & Row, 1969.
   Report From Part One (autobiography). Detroit: Broadside Press, 1972.

3. Anthologies:
   Jump Bad: A New Chicago Anthology. Edited by Brooks. Detroit: Broadside Press, 1970.
   A Broadside Treasury, 1965–1970. Edited by Brooks. Detroit: Broadside Press, 1970.

4. Biographical and Critical Material:
   "Gwendolyn Brooks: Beyond the Word Maker—The Making of an African Poet." Preface by Don L. Lee. *Report From Part One.* Broadside Press, 1972.
   "Gwen's Way." Preface by George E. Kent. *Report From Part One.* Detroit: Broadside Press, 1972.
   Angle, Paul M. "Interview with Gwendolyn Brooks." Chicago: Illinois Bell Telephone publication, 1967.
   Stavros, George. "Gwendolyn Brooks." Madison, Wisconsin: *Contemporary Literature*, Spring, 1969.
   Lewis, Ida. "Gwendolyn Brooks and the Black Revolution." Chicago: *Essence* magazine, 1971.
   Melhem, D. H. "Gwendolyn Brooks: The Social Act of Poetry." New York: *Time Capsule,* Summer/Fall issue, 1983.
   Randall, Dudley. "Reminiscence: Gwendolyn Brooks." New York: *Time Capsule* Summer/Fall issue, 1983.

Adrienne Rich

1. Volumes of Poetry:
   A Change of World. New Haven: Yale University Press, 1951.
   The Diamond Cutters and Other Poems. New York: Harper, 1955.
   Snapshots of a Daughter-in-Law. New York: Harper & Row, 1963. Reissued, New York: W.W. Norton, 1967; London: Chatto & Windus, 1970.
   Necessities of Life. New York: W.W. Norton, 1966.
   Selected Poems. London: Chatto & Windus, 1967.
   Leaflets. New York: W.W. Norton, 1969; London: Chatto & Windus, 1972.

The Will to Change. New York: W.W. Norton, 1971; London: Chatto & Windus, 1973.

Diving Into the Wreck. New York: W.W. Norton, 1973.

Poems: Selected and New. New York: W.W. Norton, 1975.

A Wild Patience Has Taken Me This Far. New York: W.W. Norton, 1982.

Sources (chapbook). Heyeck Press, 1983.

2. Prose Works:

Shaw, Robert B., ed. *American Poetry Since 1960.* Cheadle, Cheshire: Carcanet Press, Ltd., 1973. Also in *Adrienne Rich's Poetry.* Critical Edition. New York: W.W. Norton, 1975.

"When We Dead Awaken: Writing as Re-Vision." *College English* 34. National Council of Teachers of English, 1972. Also, *Adrienne Rich's Poetry.* Critical Edition. New York: W.W. Norton, 1975.

"The Anti-Feminist Woman." New York: *The New York Review of Books,* November 30, 1972. Also, *Adrienne Rich's Poetry.* Critical Edition. New York: W.W. Norton, 1975.

3. Tapes and Recordings:

Three Conversations. Tapes made with Barbara and Albert Gelpi. Stanford, California, May, 1974. Transcribed and published in Critical Edition. New York: W.W. Norton, 1975.

Spoken Arts Series: "One Hundred American Poets Reading Their Own Poems." Edited by Paul Kresh, 1970.

Adrienne Rich Reading at Stanford. The Stanford Program for Recordings in Sound, 1973.

4. Reviews, Essays, and Forewords:

Rich has written many book reviews published in literary magazines, the following among the most notable:

"Reflections on Lawrence: Review of *The Complete Poems of D. H. Lawrence.*" *Poetry,* CVI, 3 (June, 1965).

"On Karl Shapiro's *The Bourgeois Poet.*" In *The Contemporary Poet as Artist and Critic.* Edited by Anthony Ostroff. Boston: Little Brown, 1964.

"Foreword: Anne Bradstreet and Her Poetry." In *The Works of Anne Bradstreet.* Edited by Jeanine Hensley. Cambridge: Harvard University Press, 1967.

"Poetry, Personality, and Wholeness: A Response to Galway Kinell." *Field: Contemporary Poetry and Poetics,* 7 (Fall, 1972).

"Review of *Welcome Eumenides* by Eleanor Ross Taylor." *The New York Times Book Review,* July 2, 1972.

"Review of *The Women Poets in English: An Anthology* edited by Ann Stanford." *The New York Times Book Review,* April 15, 1973.

"Teaching Language in Open Admissions: A Look at the Context." Edited by Monroe Engel. Cambridge, Massachusetts: Harvard University Press, 1973.

"The Eye of the Outsider." Review of Elizabeth Bishop's *Complete Poems* in light of lesbianism. Boston: *The Boston Globe,* April 1983.

5. Biographical and Critical Material:

Auden, W. H. Foreword to *A Change of World.* (Rich's first volume) New Haven: Yale University Press, 1951.

Jarrell, Randall. Review of *The Diamond Cutters and Other Poems* from "New Books in Review." *The Yale Review,* Vol. 46, No. 1, September, 1956.

Gelpi, Albert. "Adrienne Rich: The Poetics of Change." *American Poetry Since 1960.* Edited by Robert B. Shaw. Cheadle, Cheshire: Carcanet Press, Ltd., 1973.

Boyers, Robert. "On Adrienne Rich: Intelligence and Will." *Salmagundi,* (Spring-Summer, 1973).

Vendler, Helen. "Ghostlier Demarcations, Keener Sounds." *Parnassus: Poetry in Review,* II, 1 (Fall-Winter, 1973).

Jong, Erica. "Visionary Anger." *Ms* magazine, July, 1973.

Martin, Wendy. "From Patriarchy to the Female Principle: A Chronological Reading of Adrienne Rich's Poems." *Adrienne Rich's Poetry.* Selected and Edited by Barbara Charlesworth Gelpi and Albert Gelpi. New York: W.W. Norton, 1975.

Milford, Nancy; "This Woman's Movement." *Adrienne Rich's Poetry.* New York: W.W. Norton, 1975.

Ruth Whitman

1. Volumes of Poetry:

Blood and Milk Poems. Boston: Clarke & Way, 1963.

The Marriage Wig and Other Poems. New York: Harcourt Brace, 1968.

The Passion of Lizzie Borden: New and Selected Poems. New York: October House, 1973.

Tamsen Donner: A Woman's Journey. Boston: Alice James Books, 1977.

Permanent Address, New Poems 1973–1980. Cambridge: Alice James Books, 1980.

2. Prose Works:
   Book reviews, and articles on the subject of poetry writing, some for specific poems such as the research and methods tried in her narrative poems, "Lizzie Borden" and "Tamsen Donner" the two outstanding figures in her poems on historical subjects.
   "Finding Tamsen Donner." Cambridge: *Radcliffe Quarterly,* Spring, 1978.
   Becoming a Poet: Source, Process and Practice. Boston: The Writer, Inc., 1982.
   "The Alice James Poetry Cooperative: Ten Years of Accomplishment." *Authors Guild Bulletin,* Summer, 1983.

3. Translations and Anthologies:
   Selected Poems of Alain Bosquet. New York: New Directions, 1963.
   An Anthology of Modern Yiddish Poetry. New York: October House, 1966. (Recently reissued by the Workmen's Circle Education Department 1979, with a note by Isaac Bashevis Singer.)
   Selected Poems of Jacob Galtstein. New York: October House, 1972.
   Poems of Cyprus. Modern Greek poetry. Europe Council, 1970.

4. Dramatizations and Musical Settings:
   Theatre-Dance Presentation of *Tamsen Donner: a woman's journey.* Composed by Evan Harlan; choreographed and performed by Julie Ince Thompson. Agassiz Theatre, Radcliffe College, Cambridge, October, 1982.

5. Critical Material:
   Dickey, James. Review of *The Passion of Lizzie Borden.* New York: *The New York Times Book Review,* 1973.
   Kennedy, X. J. Review of *The Marriage Wig.* Boston: *The Boston Globe,* 1968.
   Spector, Robert. "Ruth Whitman's Poetry." New York: *Saturday Review,* 1972.
   Falon, Janet. "Ruth Whitman's *Tamsen Donner.*" Boston: *The Boston Globe,* 1978.

6. Recordings and Film Tapes:
   Spoken Arts Series: "A Treasury of 100 Modern American Poets Reading Their Own Poems." Edited by Paul Kresh, 1970.

Selected Bibliography

Spoken Arts Series: "A Treasury of Twenty-five American Jewish Poets Reading Their Own Poems." Edited by Paul Kresh, 1979.

"Sachuest Point." Television documentary written and narrated by Ruth Whitman, filmed and directed by Peter O'Neill and Lee O. Gardner under a grant from the Rhode Island Committee on the Humanities.

7. Biography:
Who's Who In America.
Who's Who in the East.
Who's Who Among American Women.
Contemporary Authors. Detroit: Gale Research Company, annually from 1963.

Jean Burden

1. Volumes of Poetry:
Naked As the Glass. New York: October House, 1963.
Taking Light from Each Other. Manuscript.

2. Prose Works:
The Classic Cat. New York: New American Library Edition, 1974.
Journey Toward Poetry. New York: October House, 1966.

3. Anthologies:
A Celebration of Cats. Poems on the subject of cats, including several by Burden. Edited and compiled by Burden. New York: Paul S. Eriksson Company, 1974.
Borestone Mountain Anthologies (best poems of the year). Burden is included eleven times beginning in 1963.

4. Biographical and Critical Material:
Carruth, Hayden. "Jean Burden's Poetry." *Chicago Daily News,* 1963.
Scott, Winfield Townley. Review of *Naked as the Glass. Saturday Review,* November, 1963.

Isabella Gardner

1. Volumes of Poetry:
Birthdays From The Ocean. Boston: Houghton Mifflin, 1955.
The Looking Glass: New Poems. Chicago: University of Chicago Press, 1961.

West of Childhood: Poems 1950–1965. Boston: Houghton Mifflin, 1965.

That Was Then: New and Selected Poems. Brockport, New York: Boa Editions, 1979 (Soft-cover edition, 1980).

Un Altra Infanzia. Selected Gardner poems translated into Italian by Alfredo Rizzardi, 1959.

2. Translations:

Poems from the French *Jean Sans Terre* by Yvan Goll, 1958.

Poem from the Italian "Sentimento del Tempo" by Giuseppi Ungaretti.

In *Translations by American Poets.* Edited by Jean Garrigue. Athens, Ohio: Ohio University Press, 1970.

3. Biographical and Critical Material:

Contemporary Authors. Detroit: Gale Research Company, from 1963.

Who's Who in America.

Who's Who Among American Women.

Reviews by Richard Eberhart, Edith Sitwell, Delmore Schwartz, Wallace Stevens, and William Carlos Williams of *Birthdays From the Ocean,* 1955–1956 in leading literary journals.

Wright, James. "Isabella Gardner." *The Minnesota Review,* Spring, 1962.

———. Review of *That Was Then. The Minnesota Review,* 1979.

Audre Lorde

1. Volumes of Poetry:

The First Cities. New York: Poets Press, 1968.

From a Land Where Other People Live. Detroit: Broadside Press, 1973.

New York Head Shop and Museum. Detroit: Broadside Press, 1975.

Coal. New York: W.W. Norton, 1976.

The Black Unicorn. New York: W.W. Norton, 1978.

Chosen Poems, Old and New. New York: W.W. Norton, 1982.

2. Prose Works:

Zami: A New Spelling of My Name. Upstate New York: Crossing Press, 1983.

3. Biographical and Critical Material:

Who's Who in America.

Who's Who Among American Women.

Selected Bibliography

Who's Who in Black America.
Who's Who in International Poetry.
Contemporary Authors. Detroit: Gale Research Company.
Randall, Dudley. Review of *The First Cities. Negro Digest,* Fall, 1968.
Larkin, Joan. "Frontiers of Language: Three Poets." (Audre Lorde's *From A Land*) *Ms.* magazine, September, 1974.
Vendler, Helen. "Broadsides: Good Black Poems, One by One." (Review of Lorde's *From A Land*) *The New York Times Book Review,* March 29, 1974; later in *Modern American Poets,* Harvard University Press, 1980.
Vendler, Helen. "False Poets and Real Poets." Review of *The New York Head Shop and Museum. The New York Times Book Review,* September 7, 1975.
Gilbert, Sandra. "On the Edge of the Estate." *Poetry,* February, 1977.

Marge Piercy

1. Volumes of Poetry:

Breaking Camp. Middletown, Connecticut: Wesleyan University Press, 1968.
Hard Loving. Middletown: Wesleyan University Press, 1969.
To Be of Use. Garden City, New York: Doubleday, 1973.
Living In The Open. New York: Knopf, 1976.
The Twelve-Spoked Wheel Flashing. New York: Knopf, 1978.
The Moon is Always Female. New York: Knopf, 1980.
Circles on the Water: Selected Poems. New York: Knopf, 1982.
Stone, Paper, Knife. New York: Knopf, 1983.

2. Prose Works:

Going Down Fast. New York: Fawcett, 1969.
Dance the Eagle to Sleep. New York: Fawcett, 1970.
Small Changes. Garden City: Doubleday, 1973.
Woman on the Edge of Time. New York: Knopf, 1976.
Vida. New York: Fawcett, 1979.
Braided Lives. New York: Summit Books, 1982.
Parti-Colored Blocks For a Quilt: Poets on Poetry. Ann Arbor: University of Michigan Press, 1982.
The Last White Class: A Play About Neighborhood Terror (with Ira Wood). New York: Crossing Press, 1979.

3. Biographical and Critical Materials:
Who's Who Among American Women
Contemporary Authors. Detroit: Gale Research Company.

4. Reviews and Articles (Partial Listing):
Betts, Jane Colville. Critique of *Breaking Camp*. Wesleyan Review, 1968.
Elman, Richard. "Marge Piercy's Modern Poetry." 1968.
Mueller, Lisel. Review of *Breaking Camp, Hard Loving. Poetry,* February, 1971.
Donnely, Dorothy. Review of *Hard Loving. Michigan Quarterly,* Spring, 1971.
Blackburn, Sara. "Marge Piercy: Fiction and Poetry." *The New York Times Book Review,* 1973.
Jordan, June. "The Black Poet Speaks of Poetry: In Praise of Piercy and Her Work." *The American Poetry Review,* July, 1974.
Contoski, Victor. "The Poetry of Propaganda." *Margins,* January, 1975.
Atwood, Margaret. "An Unfashionable Sensibility." *The Nation,* December 4, 1976.

Freya Manfred

1. Volumes of Poetry:
A Goldenrod Will Grow. Minneapolis: James D. Thueson, 1971.
Yellow Squash Woman. Berkeley, California: Thorp Springs Press, 1976.
American Roads. New York: Overlook Viking Press, 1979.

2. Prose Works:
Two novels, 1980, 1981, as yet unpublished.

3. Biographical and Critical Material:
Who's Who Among American Women
Contemporary Authors. Detroit: Gale Research Company.
Hasselstrom, Linda. Review of *Yellow Squash Woman. Los Angeles Times,* 1976.
Klappert, Peter. Critical appraisal of Manfred's poetry. *Small Press Review,* Spring, 1972.
Rinard, Peggy. Feature story and interview with Manfred. Ojai, California: *The Ojai Valley News,* Feb. 4, 1981.

Whitman, Ruth. Review of *American Roads: Radcliffe Quarterly*, November–December 1982.

Wright, James. Commendatory notes on Manfred's poetry. Vols. 1971, 1979 *(A Goldenrod Will Grow, American Roads)*.

Unsigned review of *American Roads* in Publishers Weekly. January, 1980.

Carol Muske

1. Volumes of Poetry:

Camouflage. Pittsburgh: University of Pittsburgh Press, 1975.

Skylight. Garden City, New York: Doubleday, 1981.

Wyndmere. Pittsburgh: University of Pittsburgh Press, 1985.

2. Prose Works:

Reviews, essays, and editorials as assistant editor of *Antaeus*, 1972.

Wrote and edited, *Free Space*, later titled, *Art Without Walls*, publications of the poetry and creative arts programs in prisons; originally, Women's House of Detention, Rikers Island, 1971–1977.

Papers on "The Victimless Crime" (Drugs and Gambling) and "Women and Violence." *Art Without Walls* issued in eighteen New York State prisons.

3. Anthologies:

The American Poetry Anthology. Edited by Halpern. New York: Avon, 1975.

4. Biographical and Critical Materials:

Poets and Writers Directory

Who's Who Among American Women

Contemporary Authors. Detroit: Gale Research Company.

Kizer, Carolyn. "The Virtuosity of Carol Muske." *Poetry*.

Plumly, Stanley. "Carol Muske's Art." *The American Poetry Review*.

"Carol Muske: Four Poems." *American Poetry Review*, July–August, 1982/1983.

The Village Voice, *Ms. Parnassus*, others, besides the above.

Nikki Giovanni

1. Volumes of Poetry:

Black Feeling, Black Talk. Detroit: Broadside Press, 1968.

Black Judgement. Detroit: Broadside Press, 1969.

Black Feeling, Black Talk, Black Judgement. New York: Wm. Morrow & Sons, 1970.

Re:Creation. Detroit: Broadside Press, 1970.

Spin a Soft Black Song. Detroit: Broadside Press, 1971.

Poem of Angela Davis. New York: Niktom Ltd., 1970.

My House. New York: Wm. Morrow & Sons, 1972.

———. Paperback edition, Wm. Morrow & Sons, 1974.

Ego Tripping and Other Poems for Young Readers. New York: Wm. Morrow & Sons, 1973.

The Women and the Men. New York: Wm. Morrow & Sons, 1975.

Cotton Candy on a Rainy Day. New York: Wm. Morrow & Sons, 1980.

2. Prose Works:

Gemini: An Extended autobiographical Statement On My First Twenty-Five Years of Being A Black Poet. Indianapolis: Bobbs-Merrill, 1971.

Numerous reviews, articles, and editorials as consultant and contributing editor to *Encore* magazine.

"Raps" with James Baldwin and Margaret Walker.

3. Discographies:

"Raps" (see above) with Baldwin and Walker. Right On Records, 1972.

"Like a Ripple on a Pond." Atlantic Records discs, 1973.

"The Way I Feel." Atlantic Records, 1975.

"Poets Reading their Own Books (reels and cassettes). *Broadside Voices* series, 1973.

4. Biographical and Critical Materials:

Who's Who Among American Women.

Contemporary Authors. Detroit: Gale Research Company.

We Speak As Liberators: Young Black Poets. Edited by Orde Coombs. New York: Dodd, Mead & Company, 1970.

"Nikki Giovanni: Dynamite Voices." *Black Poets of the 1960s.* Edited by Don L. Lee. Detroit: Broadside Press, 1971.

5. Reviews and Feature Stories:

Llorens, David. Review of *Black Judgement. Negro Digest,* April, 1969.

Fabio, Sarah Webster. On *Black Feeling, Black Talk, Black Judgement.* Review in *Negro Digest* (now *Black World*), April, 1970.

Bryant, Jerry H. Review of *Gemini. The New York Times,* January 15, 1972.

Selected Bibliography

Giddings, Paula. Books noted: *Gemini. Black World*, August, 1972.

Duffy, Martha. "Hustler and Faubulist." *Time* magazine, January 17, 1972.

Bailey, Peter. "Nikki Giovanni: 'I Am Black, Female, Polite'." *Ebony*, February, 1972.

Jordan, June. "Nikki Giovanni." *The New York Times Book Review.*

Conner, John. Review of *My House. English Journal,* April, 1973.

Kalumu Ya Salaan. Review of *My House. Black World,* 1974.

Kent, George E. Review of *My House* and other Giovanni works. *Phylon: The Atlanta University Review of Race and Culture,* March, 1976.

Cotter, James Finn. "Book Reviews: *The Women and the Men.*" *America,* February 7, 1976.

INDEX

Index

Index

Index

Index

Index

Index

Index

"Said The Poet To The Analyst"
(Sexton), 156
Salmagundi (magazine), on An-
drienne Rich, 235
"Saloon Suite" (Gardner), 273–74
Salter, Mary Jo, 357
"Sandpiper" (Bishop), 72, 74
Sarah Lawrence College, 17, 18, 28
Saturday Review of Literature, May
Swenson in, 80; Jean Garrigue
and, 106; Anne Sexton in, 155;
Gwen Brooks in, 191
Sauerwein, Henry (Wurlitzer Foun-
dation), 349
Saving the Bay (Miles), 343
Schulman, Grace, 27, 354–55
Schwartz, Pearl, May Swenson and,
81–84, 88, 93
Scofield, Penrod, 26
Scribner's, 84, 85, 87, 90
"Seen in Dr. Generosa's Bar, Recruit
for Hell's Angels & Black Mafia"
(Wakoski), 346
Selected Poems (Gwendolyn Brooks),
199
Selected Poems of Alain Bosquet (Whit-
man, ed.), 243
Selected Poems (Rich), 226
Selected Poems (Sexton), 163
Selected Poems (Rukeyser), 17
"Sestina" (Bishop), 55
"Seven Variations for Robert Schu-
mann" (Whitman), 248
Seventeen magazine, Sylvia Plath in,
130, 131
Sexton, Alfred (husband of Anne
Sexton), 153, 173
Sexton, Anne, 151–75; early life of,
152–54; early career of, 153–
54; Sylvia Plath and, 141, 142;
Ann McMillan and, 158–62
Shange, Ntozake (Paulette Wil-
liams), 72, 352–53
Shapiro, Daniel (son of Isabella
Gardner), 272, 277, 280

Shapiro, Karl, 271
Shapiro, Seymour (husband of Isa-
bella Gardner), 271–73, 274,
282
Shelley Memorial Award (Poetry So-
ciety of America), to Muriel
Rukeyser, 23; Elizabeth Bishop
and, 66; to Anne Sexton, 165;
to Gwen Brooks, 208; to Ad-
rienne Rich, 230; to Josephine
Miles, 342
"Shooting Script (11/69–7/10)"
(Rich), 230
Short Friday and Other Stories
(Singer), 244
Sigmund, Elizabeth, Sylvia Plath and,
144–45, 148
Singer, Isaac Bashevis, Ruth Whit-
man and, 244
Siskind, Aaron, 284
Six Mornings in March (Cooper), 355
Skidmore College, 112, 119–20, 121,
122
"Skylight" (Muske), 326
Skylight (Muske), 325, 326
Smart Set, Jean Garrigue in, 113
Smith Bessie, 207
Smith College, Jean Garrigue at, 108;
Slyvia Plath at, 130–31, 135–
37, 140–41
Smith *Review,* 131
"Snapshots of a Daughter-in-Law"
(Rich), 220
Solataroff, Ted, 27
"Some Dreams They Forgot,
(Bishop), 60–61
"Sometimes a Poet Will Hijack the
Moon" (Wakoski), 346
"Song For a Lady" (Sexton), 165
"Song for 'Buvez Les Vins du Pos-
tillon'—Advt." (Garrigue), 116
"Song for the Rainy Season"
(Bishop), 69–70
"Songs for a Colored Singer"
(Bishop), 70–71, 72

Index

Theory of Flight (Rukeyser), 9, 22, 24

"Third Wedding, The" (Whitman), 244

Third World Press, 208

"Thirty-three" (Rich), 222

"This Day Is Not Like That Day" (Garrigue), 107

"This Room is Full of Clocks" (Gardner), 281

Thomas, Dylan, 131, 132, 212, 281

Thomson, Virgil, 279

"Three Women," 23

Three Women: A Monologue for Three Voices (Plath), 145

Tiger Who Wore White Gloves, The (Brooks), 202

"To a Hostile Man" (Manfred), 315

To Bedlam and Part Way Back (Sexton), 155, 159

To Be Of Use (Piercy), 303

To Disembark (Brooks), 205, 208

To Mix With Time (Swenson), 78, 87–88, 89

"To Stay Alive" (Levertov), 41

"To The Girl Who Got Her Man" (Manfred), 315

"To the Memory of My Brother (October 19, 1918–January 21, 1974) RAYMOND MELVIN BROOKS," 204

Tomorrow magazine, 16, 106

"Too-Young All-Man, The" (Manfred), 315

"Touch, The" (Sexton), 165

Tozer Foundation Award, to Freya Manfred, 316

Transatlantic Review, Audre Lorde in, 292

Transformations (Sexton), 166–70

Transtomer, Tomas, 93–94

"Treasury of American Jewish Poets Reading Their Poems, A" (Kresh, ed.), 23

"Treasury of 100 American Poets Reading Their Own Poems, A" (Kresh, ed.), 287

"Tree of Rivers" (Rukeyser), 24

"Trellis for R., A" (Swenson), 93

"Truro, January 1964" (Levertov), 47

"Truth the Dead Know, The" (Sexton), 157

Tubman, Harriet, 207

Turning Wind, A (Rukeyser), 13

Twelve-Spoked Wheel Flashing, The (Piercy), 304–5

Twentieth Century Authors, Jean Garrigue in, 98, 102

Tytell, Louis, 279

Un Altra Infanzia, (Gardner), 280

Unicorn Press, 349

"Universe, The" (Swenson), 78

University of Chicago, 100, 253, 254

"Unsounded" (Rich), 213–14

Untermeyer, Louis, 171, 239

Up Country: Poems of New England (Kumin), 166

U.S.1. (Rukeyser), 17

Ussachevsky, Vladimir, 85

"Vacant Lot, The" (Brooks), 195

Van Kirk, Charles, 269, 270

Variety, Sylvia Plath in, 137

Vassar College, Elizabeth Bishop at, 59

Vassar Review, 60

Vendler, Helen, 102, 119

Ventura, Edith, 114

"View of the Capital from the Library of Congress" (Bishop), 72

Virginia Center for the Creative Arts, 351

Virginia Quarterly, The, Jean Garrigue and, 112

"Visit to Wralda" (Manfred), 311

"Visits to St. Elizabeths" (Bishop), 65–66

Index

W. W. Norton, 220, 222, 295
Wylie, Elinor, 120, 131–32, 212
Wyndmere (Muske), 325, 327

Yaddo, 10, May Swenson at, 80, 81;
    Jean Garrigue at, 105, 112, 121;
    Sylvia Plath at, 142; Isabella
    Gardner at, 278, 285, 286; Freya
    Manfred at, 316
Yale Review, Jean Garrigue in, 116
Yale Younger Poets Award, 8, 9; to
    A. Rich, 212, 214

Yankee magazine, Ruth Whitman in,
    242; Jean Burden and, 251,
    257–58, 261
Yellow Squash Woman (Manfred),
    314, 315, 318
"You. Dr. Martin" (Sexton), 155
"Young" (Sexton), 152

"Zei Gesund" (Gardner), 273
Zinnes, Harriet, 286, 355–56
Zweig, Stefan, 13, 15